WHO'S BURIED
WHERE IN ENGLAND

WHO'S BURIED WHERE IN ENGLAND

Douglas Greenwood

Constable · London

Constable & Robinson Ltd
3 The Lanchesters
162 Fulham Palace Road
London W6 9ER
www.constablerobinson.com

This revised and updated edition published by
Constable, an imprint of Constable & Robinson
Ltd 2006

First published by Constable 1982

A copy of the British Library Cataloguing in
Publication Data is available from the British
Library.

ISBN 1-84529-305-3
ISBN 978-1-84529-305-5

Printed and bound in the EU

3 5 7 9 10 8 6 4 2

To those of the historically famous who
at one time proudly trod the soil of
England and now lie deep within.

Contents

Acknowledgements

The author and publishers wish to thank the following for their help and for permission to quote from material in which they held the copyright: *The Oxford Companion to English Literature*, fourth edition, in the section on writers; *Pears Cyclopaedia* (Pelham Books, London). And while biographical facts have also come from many other sources we would acknowledge in particular *The Dictionary of National Biography*; various Oxford and University Press histories; the authorized biographies of many lives; the National Portrait Gallery for the illustrations on pages 29, 35, 48, 50, 57, 60, 77, 79, 86, 106, 110, 130, 132, 140, 180, 193, 203, 213, 218, 231, 236, 282 and 303 and also Anna Williamson for the illustrations on pages xviii, 103, 183, 190, 198, 267, 277, 309 and 320.

Of the many readers throughout the world who have sent me their comments and suggestions, I must thank especially Mr George Frobisher, FRGS, and Dr R. J. Hetherington, whose specific and detailed suggestions I have been glad to incorporate.

Illustrations

All photographs are by the author except those illustrations from the National Portrait Gallery and Anna Williamson (see Acknowledgements).

Introduction

Among the peoples of the English-speaking world, especially those of us who live in England, there is an almost spiritual affinity to the past. Even those whose home may have been in another land for generations, the language they have been born to, or have acquired, seems to compel them to visit this country by the millions in search of historical roots and where it all began. Where better to find them than in a burial place?

It can be a strangely moving experience to stand beside a famous grave. One feels a closeness to our heritage that no other form of contact with the past ever brings; we recognise an unsuspected instinct for pilgrimage. 'We ought to quicken our memories of the great, and where they lie, by such a visit occasionally,' says Ethelberta in Hardy's *The Hand of Ethelberta*. We experience a strong feeling of reverence, frequently unbidden, for those men and women of the past whose final resting place is so close to us. We are reminded of the line from Gray's poem *Elegy in a Country Churchyard*: 'The paths of glory lead but to the grave' – true, but the fame lives on! Unless the grave is provided with a notice that gives us some biographical information, however, our knowledge is generally restricted to what is engraved on the tombstone, which gives us little information with which to conjure up the past. But if we can relive those remarkable lives through a knowledge of what they did, our pilgrimage becomes doubly worthwhile. Shakespeare's 'graves ... Have wake'd their sleepers – op'd and let them forth' (*The Tempest*, Act V scene 1) is perhaps an important cue for us to pick up. Thus, to reach back over the centuries to an understanding of our heritage and our roots, it is necessary to seek the resting places of the famous; those who have shaped our history.

A personal pilgrimage can have reasons other than a desire to commune with history. Painters, photographers, brass-rubbers, stone-masons and history scholars in search of their particular needs will also want to trace such graves.

This is not a guide to interesting graves as such, or even to those currently classified as national or historic monuments: it is a guide to the resting places of many of the most illustrious men and women of history who were buried in England. It is impossible to include in one volume every person of past renown – even some of the earlier kings have been omitted – but the graves listed here represent, I believe, those of the more famous figures mentioned in standard histories and encyclopaedias; and these persons have been categorized in a comprehensive index. Only the briefest biographical details have been given, to save space and thus provide a more exhaustive coverage. It has been a daunting and rather humbling task to presume an ability to arbitrate between illustrious lives; who to include, who to leave out. Space has indeed been an arbitrary and harsh censor, as well as fame. Where omissions do occur it is sometimes because a grave location has remained stubbornly untraceable. Also there are many illustrious churchmen whose tombs are to be found in the cathedrals and churches of England, but their inclusion would mean a list of almost book length in itself. If any reader does feel that a serious omission has occurred then his or her suggestion will be welcomed and considered for any further edition of the guide.

There will be instances when a person listed under one section could equally well be included in another. For example, Disraeli was both writer and statesman, as was Lord Macaulay. I have included them as statesmen rather than writers. General consensus would also surely place Shakespeare in the writers' section, although he was an accomplished actor. Such overlaps are inevitable. Should any reader disagree with my categorization I hope they will bear with me.

Where no actual grave exists to mark the resting place, as, for example, in the case of Queen Boadicea, whose grave is somewhere beneath platform 10 at King's Cross Railway Station, and Richard III, the reasons are given. Where English sovereigns have been buried on foreign soil, and therefore strictly outside the scope of this guide, they have nevertheless been included to avoid breaking the complete list of English monarchs in the guide. They are: William I, the Conqueror; Matilda; Henry II; Richard I, the Lionheart; James II; and George I. With the exception of George I, who was buried in Germany, all were buried in France. I should perhaps mention here that as the main royal line, from which the present queen claims descent, begins with the house of Wessex, I have begun my survey of English monarchs with them. In no other instance have I been able to include any figures, however famous, who were buried outside the borders of England, not even if those persons were buried within the British Isles. If, at some stage, a broadened guide is generally called for, Scotland, Wales and Ireland will then be included.

Many of the persons listed in the guide have close connections with the United States of America, either before or after its independence from Britain; some, even, are American born but lie buried in England.

For the interest of American readers, I have stressed the connection with the United States in the biographical information. Among such persons are Sir Ferdinando Gorges, the first Governor of Maine; William Penn, the founder of Pennsylvania; Sir Hiram Stevens Maxim, the American-born inventor of the machine gun; T. S. Eliot, the American-born poet, whose ashes lie buried at East Coker in Somerset, and Francis Bret Harte, the short-story writer born at Albany, N.Y.

Now a word about the pinpointing of the precise location of a grave. As a piece of sound advice, I recommend the purchase of a good road map, one listing the smallest villages and side-roads. Such a map is invaluable. Once there you will discover that most churches are sign-posted. But, where there is no signpost, or the map lets you down, all you need do is ask your way. Most persons in the locality will know where a famous grave is. Generally you will have little difficulty in finding it. Inside a church it is easy, whilst outside most historic graves tend to be either just by the east end of the church, near a path, or the east or south-east of the graveyard. Generally, of course, most churches are orientated east to west, with the tower at the west end. Some of the larger London cemeteries have plans to help you locate the grave you are looking for. Cemetery office staff are always obliging and will usually go out of their way in a large cemetery to direct you to a site.

One of the more frustrating facts about contemporary life is the locking of certain churches against vandals. Mostly this is done in large towns and cities, but even some remote country churches are now locked for large parts of the day, although the graveyards remain open at all times. Cemeteries with a gatehouse usually remain open during the morning and afternoon but it is as well to bear in mind the possibility of closure, for nothing is more exasperating than to arrive and find you cannot gain entry.

In a few cases burial places are privately owned, as in the case of Kirklees Abbey, which contains the grave of Robin Hood, or Shaftes-bury Abbey, where Edward the Martyr's remains were buried. That, however, is currently open as a museum for a small fee. With regard to photographs I had of necessity to be selective, and those reproduced here, I feel, are the most typical of the sites listed.

As an itinerary for a tour, such a pilgrim's path can show us parts of the country rarely seen on the usual tourist routes; parts of timeless England that otherwise might be seen merely as an accident of aimless peregrination. There is no question that this rich soil of England 'contains a richer dust concealed'. Rupert Brooke's words say it all with poetic economy.

DOUGLAS GREENWOOD, 1990

Preface to the Fourth Edition

This Fourth Edition of *Who's Buried Where in England* includes over eighty new entries. Unfortunately these revisions have had to be made without the valuable input of Douglas Greenwood, who sadly passed away in 2003. However, we have sought to preserve his vision for the book as a companion to pilgrimage and reflection on the men and women who have shaped our history.

To this end, we have added a number of historically significant figures buried in England since 1996. We have also taken the opportunity to look again at some of the earlier entries and have included some that were previously absent, for example Mary Seacole, L. S. Lowry and Herbert Spencer.

It has become evident that the more recent entries have reflected the changing nature of fame in our society – figures from the worlds of entertainment and sport are certainly more prevalent. We have changed the categories in the book to accommodate this.

Another modern trend has been the increased popularity of cremation, followed by the private removal of the ashes for alternative disposal. This leaves the public with no memorial or place of pilgrimage and we have decided not to include those people where there is no record of the location of the ashes.

THE PUBLISHER, 2006

Pinner Cemetery

Chapter 1
Sovereigns

EARLY RULERS

Arthur (c.496–d.539?)
Glastonbury Abbey (ruins), Glastonbury, Somerset.

Legend has it that he was the illegitimate son of Uther Pendragon, king of Britain. Arthur was a Romano-British general who controlled much of the south-west of England and his existence is a matter of controversy. Perhaps the securest document is the *Annales Cambriae* of Wales that records his leadership at the Battle of Badon, where he halted the advance of the West Saxons in 515, and his death at the Battle of Camlann in 539. Further details are given by the ninth-century monk Nennius and the twelfth-century Geoffrey of Monmouth. At that time monks are said to have found a tomb near Glastonbury which contained two caskets with male and female remains. The male had a skull wound, whilst the female had traces of yellow hair and was thought to be that of Arthur's wife Guinevere. The bodies were re-interred in Glastonbury Abbey on the order of Edward I, who was present at the ceremony.

Boadicea (d.c.60–61AD)
Under Platform 10, King's Cross Station, London.

Queen of the Iceni and widow of King Prasutagus. When the King died he left half his kingdom to the Emperor Nero and half to his daughters. The Queen was reputed to have been flogged by the Romans and her daughters raped; and when the Romans began to despoil the kingdom she led the Iceni in revolt, massacring large numbers of Romans at St Albans, Colchester and London. The Roman Governor, Caius Suetonius Paulinus, met Boadicea in battle on the present site of King's Cross Station, its former name being Battle Bridge. The Queen's forces were routed and she and her daughters took poison. By legend, Boadicea now lies buried somewhere beneath platform 10. Other places, however, do lay claim to be her burial ground: Parliament Hill, between Highgate Road and the Vale of Health, Hampstead, London; Soldier's Hill, Garboldisham Heath, Suffolk; and near St Andrew's Church, Quidenham, Suffolk.

Site of Arthur's grave, Glastonbury Abbey (ruins), Glastonbury, Somerset

Edmund, Saint (c.840–870)
Abbey of Bury St Edmunds (ruins), West Suffolk.

Became King of East Anglia in 855 whilst still a boy. In the year 870, the Danes, who had been wintering at York, marched through Mercia into East Anglia and the King engaged them in battle at Hoxne, some twenty miles south-east of Thetford. Edmund was slain, whether in battle or later as a martyr is not certain, but the widely current version of the story, which makes him fall a martyr to Danish arrows after refusing to renounce his faith or to hold his kingdom as a vassal of the Danes, may very probably be true. His shrine became one of the most famous in England and there are churches dedicated to his memory throughout the country. The date of his canonization is not known.

Ethelbald I (d.757)
The crypt of St Wystan's Church, Repton, Derbyshire (by repute).

King of Mercia, an Angle Kingdom, and not to be confused with King Ethelbald of Wessex who died in 860. In 731 Ethelbald was the acknowledged overlord of the southern kingdoms in England, having subdued the neighbouring rulers in battle. Despite his reputation as a liberal benefactor his treatment of his Saxon subjects was believed to have been oppressive. In 752 Ethelbald led his Mercian troops against the West Saxons, meeting them at Burford, near Oxford. After a hand-to-hand combat with the West Saxon Ealdorman, Ethelhun, Ethelbald's 'spirit weakened' and he fled the field leaving his troops still fighting. They were soon routed. From that victory stemmed the gradual ascendancy of Wessex. Later, Ethelbald was reputed to have been slain by his own bodyguards.

Oswy or **Oswio** (c.612–670)
Whitby Abbey (ruins), Whitby, Yorkshire.

King of Northumbria who succeeded in making the majority of the Britons, Picts and Scots tributary to him. He appears to have consolidated his power with the aid of the Church and by a series of judicious matrimonial alliances. In 655, he defeated Penda of Mercia at the Battle of the Winwaed, in thanksgiving for which he founded the Abbey of Whitby. In 664, at the Synod of Whitby, Oswy accepted the usages of the Roman as opposed to the Celtic Church, which led to the appointment of Wilfrid as Bishop of York.

Tomb of King Sebert and Queen Ethelgoda, South Ambulatory, Westminster Abbey, London

Sebert or Saba (d.c.616)
Westminster Abbey, London.

A tomb, said to be that of King Sebert and his Queen, Ethelgoda, now lies in the South Ambulatory of Westminster Abbey.

First Christian King of Essex who was converted and baptized by Mellitus, the first Bishop of London. Legend has it that Sebert was the founder of Westminster Abbey. In 1308 his tomb was reported to have been opened for relics, and his right hand and forearm were found to be perfectly preserved.

THE SAXONS OF WESSEX

Egbert (d.839)
Winchester Cathedral, Hampshire, in gilded mortuary chest, made to contain the bones of the pre-Norman rulers, which rests with other similar chests on top of the Presbytery screen.

Son of Ealhmund, an under-king of Kent. He was exiled in about 789 and spent his exile at the court of Charlemagne, returning to England possibly in the year 802 when he was accepted as King of the West Saxons. He waged constant war against neighbouring kingdoms and against the Welsh of Cornwall and Wales. Eventually he obtained the overlordship of the rest of the English kingdoms though he could never claim to be the actual first King of England. He repelled the incursions of the Scandinavians and at the Battle of Hengestdune in 837 routed the forces of the Danish pirates and the Cornwall Welsh.

Ethelwulf (d.858)
Winchester Cathedral, Winchester, Hampshire. His bones are contained in the mortuary chest on top of the Presbytery screen.

King of Wessex who succeeded his father, Egbert, in 839. During his reign he was under constant attack from Danish pirates, whom he finally defeated at the Battle of Aclea in 851. His attempts to subjugate the Welsh were unsuccessful. In 855, accompanied by his youngest son, Alfred, he made a pilgrimage to Rome, and on his return journey married Judith, daughter of Charles II (the Bald) of France. During his absence from the country, his second son, Ethelbald, had assumed power and when his father returned Ethelbald retained the crown of Wessex, Ethelwulf ruling only in Kent until his death.

Ethelbald (d.860)
Sherborne Abbey Church, Sherborne, Dorset.

King of Wessex who, during his father Ethelwulf's absence abroad on a pilgrimage to Rome, assumed power, refusing to relinquish it when his father returned. When his father died in 858 he married his widow, Judith, daughter of Charles II of France.

Ethelbert (d.866)
Sherborne Abbey Church, Sherborne, Dorset.

Third son of Ethelwulf, King of Wessex and Kent. On the death of his father in 858 he succeeded him as King of Kent and, in 860, on the death of his brother Ethelbald, King of Wessex, he united the two kingdoms under his rule. His reign was beset by Danish incursions, the invaders even sacking Winchester. A combined force of Hampshire and Wiltshire men defeated them but in the winter of 864–865 Danes landed in Thanet and were bought off by the men of Kent. An extant Anglo-Saxon document codifies Ethelbert's laws.

Ethelred I (d.871)
Wimborne Minster, Wimborne, Dorset, where a fifteenth-century brass bears his effigy.

Fourth son of Ethelwulf who succeeded his brother, Ethelbert, as King of Wessex in 866. His reign, like his brother's, was spent in constant war with the Danish invaders. The Battle of Ashdown in 871 in which the English were victorious was followed a fortnight later by a defeat at the Battle of Basing. Two months later at the Battle of Merton the English were again defeated and soon afterwards the King died on 23 April, possibly from a wound received in the battle.

Alfred the Great (b.849 r.871–901)
In Winchester in King Alfred Place off Hyde Street is St Bartholomew's Church, said to contain stone from Hyde Abbey. This was the parish church of Hyde, where Hyde Abbey used to stand. Alfred and his wife founded a nunnery near the site of the Old Minster, and he was first buried there. Later, in the ninth century, King Edgar combined the two minsters and the nunnery was moved to Hyde. Alfred's body was moved to the abbey, and some remains found where it stood are believed to be his. Their site is marked by a flat stone under which they were placed in the churchyard outside the east wall of St Bartholomew's Church. The old gatehouse of the abbey is virtually all that remains of the abbey; the 'Old' and 'New' minsters were close to the present Winchester Cathedral. Little Driffield Church, Humberside, also lays claim as a burial site of Alfred's body, claiming that it was brought to the Priory at Little Driffield where his sister was Prioress.

Youngest son of Ethelwulf, who succeeded his brother Ethelred I as King of Wessex in 871. Alfred realized, at his succession, that his forces were inadequate to repel the Danish advance, and therefore he offered them tribute, known as 'Danegeld', as a means of keeping the peace. During the next few years he gradually built up the strength of his army and navy, and then renewed his war against the invaders. Just after Christmas 877, the Danes invaded Wessex and found little resistance, overrunning Somerset without a fight. The king retreated to Athelney in the marshes and it was during this period that the legend of the burning of the cakes was born. Supporters rallied to Alfred's cause and, seven weeks after Easter 878, he marched out of the marshes at the head of a large force and defeated the Danes at the Battle of Ethandun (Edington). The Danes and their king, Guthrum, agreed to leave Wessex and to accept baptism. Following this peace, known as the Peace of Wedmore,

Part of Ethelred I's marble tomb lid in Sanctuary of Wimborne Minster, Dorset

Probable site of King Alfred the Great's remains, St Bartholomew's Church, Winchester, Hampshire

the Danes were restricted to the territory known as the Danelaw, north of the River Thames, leaving the south and west of England under the sole control of Alfred. In 893, Danes defeated by King Arnulf of Germany descended on Kent and Sussex and Alfred once again went to war, which continued almost constantly until 897 when the invaders withdrew.

Alfred was an ardent supporter of scholarship and it is to him that we owe the *Anglo-Saxon Chronicle*, for it was at his bidding that it grew from the older and local annals of the church of Winchester. It is a unique history and during Alfred's reign served as a contemporary narrative of the most stirring years of his life. As a ruler he introduced many important legal reforms and it is from his times that many of the precedents of the English Common Law stem. His writings include English translations from the Latin of Gregory the Great's *Pastoral Care*, Boethius' *Consolation of Philosophy* and St Augustine's *Soliloquies*. In Boethius' work Alfred put a lot of his own thoughts, while his translation of Orosius has Alfred's own account of voyages made by Norse explorers.

Edward the Elder (d.924)

'New' Minster, Winchester, Hampshire, on the site of which Hyde Abbey was built, the gatehouse of which is all that remains in Hyde Street.

Succeeded his father, Alfred the Great, as King of Wessex and overlord of the Angles and Saxons in 901. During his father's lifetime he played an active rôle in the fight against the Danes and may even have been co-ruler with Alfred. At his succession he had to contend with his cousin, Ethelwold's attempts to gain the throne with the help of the Danes. After Ethelwold's death at the Battle of Holme, Edward, with the help of his sister, Aethelflaed, the Lady of the Mercians, gradually subdued the Danes, forcing upon them the Peace known as 'the Laws of Edward and Guthrum'. Fighting off Viking attacks from overseas he fortified former Danish strongholds, extending his rule throughout England until he had established his sovereignty over the entire country including Northumbria and parts of Wales.

Athelstan (b.895 r.924–940)

Abbey Church, Malmesbury, Wiltshire. The tomb is now empty but it once contained the bones of the King.

Son of Edward the Elder, possibly illegitimate, whom he succeeded in

924. A favourite of his grandfather, Alfred, he had been brought up by his aunt, Aethelflaed, the Lady of the Mercians. Whilst his father succeeded in establishing his rule throughout the country, Athelstan was the first Saxon king to be acknowledged as King of England, receiving the homage of the other kings at the Congress of Emmet in 926; and after the Battle of Brunanburh in 937, where Athelstan defeated a coalition of princes, his supremacy and that of his house was unchallenged. William of Malmesbury wrote that Athelstan may have been in possession of the famous Spear of Longinus, or Destiny, with which the centurion pierced Christ's side on the Cross, at the Battle of Brunanburh. He is reputed to have given it later to Otto the Great as a wedding present and it is now in the Hofburg Museum, Vienna. Athelstan was an able ruler who introduced many new and just laws, reducing the previously severe penalties for young offenders. He pursued an imperial policy, allying himself dynastically with foreign rulers, marrying his sisters to French and German princes.

Edmund I, The Magnificent (b.921 r.940–946)
Glastonbury Abbey (ruins), Glastonbury, Somerset.

He succeeded his half-brother, Athelstan, in 940. His accession was marred by an invasion of Vikings and the King was forced to yield much of his territory in East Anglia and Northumbria. He reconquered northern Mercia and in the peace that followed the Viking Kings, Anlaf and Raegenald, were baptized. Towards the end of his reign, in 944 or 945, the peace was broken and Edmund expelled the two Viking Kings from Northumbria. Edmund was stabbed to death at the royal villa of Pucklechurch in Gloucestershire by an exiled robber called Liofa, and his body was taken to Glastonbury Abbey which, in 943, he had entrusted to Dunstan.

Edred (r.946–955)
'Old' Minster, Winchester, Hampshire; its site is no longer traceable with any accuracy.

Youngest son of Edward the Elder, he succeeded his brother Edmund as King of England in 946. At his accession he received the submission of Northumbria but in 947 the Northumbrians chose the Norwegian, Eric Bloodaxe, as their king. Edred ravaged the kingdom eventually receiving its submission. The King's public policy was largely influenced by St Dunstan and it was his statesmanship that brought peace between the King and the Danes by allowing the Danes to retain their own laws.

Edwy (b.940 r.955–959)
'Old' Minster, Winchester, Hampshire; its site is no longer traceable with any accuracy.

Eldest son of Edmund I, he succeeded his uncle, Edred, in 955, being crowned by Archbishop Odo at Kingston-upon-Thames. He offended his nobles at the coronation feast when he withdrew to pay court to a girl; he was persuaded to return by St Dunstan, which was one of the probable reasons for the King's resentment of the saint. Relations between the two deteriorated to such an extent that St Dunstan was forced into exile in Flanders. That same year the Mercians and the Northumbrians chose Edwy's younger brother, Edgar, as their king but the death of Edwy in 959 prevented civil war.

Edgar (b.c.943 r.959–975)
Glastonbury Abbey (ruins), Glastonbury, Somerset.

Younger son of Edmund I, he had been chosen during his brother, Edwy's, lifetime as king by the Mercians and the Northumbrians. His brother's early death in 959 seems to have prevented war and he succeeded peacefully as King of England. He recalled St Dunstan from his exile in Flanders and together they initiated major ecclesiastical reforms, as well as confirming legal autonomy to the Danes, thus keeping the peace so carefully negotiated by St Dunstan during the reign of King Edred.

Edward the Martyr (b.c.962 r.975–978)
Shaftesbury Abbey (ruins), Dorset. Bones, presumed to be those of the Martyr, were given a conditional resting-place in the Russian Orthodox sect's church at Brookwood cemetery in 1989 pending a legal decision about contested ownership. There is considerable doubt that these bones were his; they were unearthed from a place more than 50 feet away from where his sanctuary tomb was located. The bones, discovered 35 years ago, were in a small lead box, and since they were near the crypt steps in what was the north transept of Shaftesbury Abbey it is highly likely that they are merely the bones of some person of quality who had been buried there. I believe the martyr's bones still rest undisturbed somewhere in the ruins here. At Wareham, Dorset, there is a roundish stone receptacle in the Church of Lady St Mary that is said to have once held the king's body before it was translated to the Abbey by St Dunstan.

The eldest son of Edgar, he succeeded his father with St Dunstan's support in 975. His accession was contested by Edgar's second wife and widow, Queen Elfthrith, who was anxious to secure the throne for her son Ethelred. She was joined by some of the nobility and Edward's control of the kingdom was weak. His brief reign was marked by anti-monastic reaction. On 18 March 978 Edward was murdered at Corfe Castle, Dorset, probably at the instigation of his step-mother Queen Elfthrith. The king seems to have been personally popular and the poem on his death in the *Anglo-Saxon Chronicle* calls his death the worst deed in English history.

Ethelred II, The Unready (b.c.968 r.978–1016)
'Old' St Paul's Cathedral, London.

Son of King Edgar by his second wife, Elfthrith, he succeeded in 978 after the murder of his half-brother, Edward. A weak and vacillating king, Ethelred was unable to resist the renewed onslaught of the Danes, his situation being made worse by the treachery of his commanders. To keep the peace he was forced to pay tribute, Danegeld. On 2 December 1001, Ethelred, determined to be rid of his enemies, ordered the slaughter of 'all the Danish men who were in England'. The slaughter was great. It did not have the effect of ridding the King of his enemies but provoked fresh attacks from Sweyn, King of Denmark, and from then until 1013 Ethelred gradually lost control of his kingdom. In that year, Sweyn was acknowledged as King of England and Ethelred fled to Normandy, his wife Emma being the daughter of Richard I, the Fearless, Duke of Normandy. In February 1014 Sweyn died and the Witan recalled Ethelred on the condition that he ruled better in future. Sweyn's son, Canute, returned to claim the crown the following year and was advancing across the country to London when Ethelred died there on 23 April 1016. 'Unready', the epithet by which Ethelred is known in history, means 'without council'.

Edmund II, Ironside (b.c.980 r.April to November 1016)
Glastonbury Abbey (ruins), Glastonbury, Somerset.

Son of Ethelred II by his first wife, Aelfgifu. The death of his father on 23 April 1016 led to a double election to the English crown: London and some of the Witan choosing Edmund; the rest of the Witan meeting at Southampton electing Canute. Fierce fighting ensued and Edmund's courage earned him the appellation, Ironside. At the disastrous Battle of Assandun (now Ashingdon) in Essex, Edmund was defeated and, in a pact with Canute, they partitioned the realm. Edmund, however, died one month later and Canute was suspected of having poisoned him.

THE DANES

Canute (b.c.994 r. 1016–1035)
Winchester Cathedral, Winchester, Hampshire, in mortuary chest on top of the Presbytery screen.

Proclaimed King of all England in 1017 shortly after the death of Edmund II, he also became King of Denmark on the death of his brother Harald in 1018. Earlier, upon the death of his father in 1014, Canute had been forced to withdraw from England through a general uprising of the Anglo-Saxons. He returned a year later and ultimately partitioned the kingdom with Edmund before acceding to the whole. To avoid dynastic disputes he married Queen Emma, Ethelred the Unready's widow, who bore him a son, Hardicanute. His reign, after the initial conflict, was peaceful and brought stability to the realm.

Harold Harefoot (r.1035–1040)
Originally buried on the present site of Westminster Abbey, but his body was disinterred, beheaded, thrown into a fen before being rescued and finally buried 'with honour by the Danes' in St Clement Danes, Strand, London, though the precise location is not known.

The illegitimate son of Canute and Aelfgifu of Northampton, he claimed the throne on the death of his father. A compromise was reached whereby he would remain regent whilst the legal heir, Canute's legitimate son, Hardicanute, was in Denmark. Harold's mother, however, managed to persuade the Witan to accept her son and he was elected king in 1037. Whilst Hardicanute was preparing to invade England to claim his throne, Harold died at Oxford on 10 March 1040.

Hardicanute (b.c.1019 r.1040–1042)
'New' Minster, Winchester, Hampshire.

Legitimate son of Canute and his second wife, Emma. He became King of Denmark on his father's death in 1035 and was in Denmark when his half-brother, Harold Harefoot, claimed the throne. He was in the process of invading England when news of his brother's death reached him. He arrived with an invasion fleet of 62 ships but his succession was peaceful. His brief reign was oppressive but to avoid dynastic conflict he recalled his step-mother, Queen Emma, from exile in Normandy, together with Edward, her son by Ethelred II, the Unready, whom he named as his heir. In 1042 he died of convulsions at a marriage feast for Tostig the Proud.

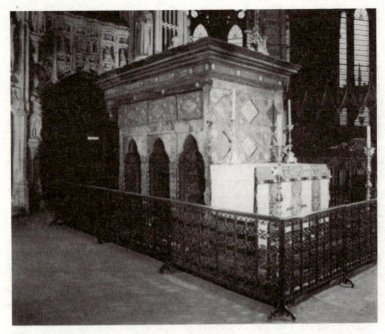

Shrine of St Edward the Confessor, Westminster Abbey, London

THE SAXONS OF WESSEX RESTORED

Edward the Confessor (b.c.1004 r.1042–1066)

Chapel of St Edward the Confessor, Westminster Abbey, London. The central shrine was constructed on the orders of Henry III.

Son of Ethelred the Unready and his second wife, Emma, daughter of Richard I Duke of Normandy, he was brought up at the court of Normandy whilst his mother remained in England as the Queen of Canute. Acknowledged by Canute's son, Hardicanute, as his heir, his accession was peaceful. An able but not a strong leader, Edward found himself in opposition to the more forceful nobles, chief of whom was Earl Godwin, whose daughter, Edith, the King married. The cause was the King's favouritism of the Normans. Godwin rose in rebellion but the King, with the help of the Earls Leofric of Mercia and Siward of Northumbria, subdued him and he was forced into exile, along with his family. During his absence, Edward is believed to have named William of Normandy as his successor. Godwin soon returned and asserted his influence over the King, forcing him to accept Stigand of Winchester as

Archbishop of Canterbury. Thereafter, Edward lost the effective control of the kingdom and turned his attention to religion, earning himself the appellation, Confessor. On his deathbed he is reputed to have named Godwin's son, Harold, as his heir.

Harold II (b.c.1022 r.January to October 1066)
Waltham Abbey, Essex. There is a stone marker in the abbey gardens.

Elected King of England on the death of Edward the Confessor who was married to his sister, Edith, although he had been the *de facto* ruler of the country since 1053. Having defeated an invasion led by King Harold Hardrada of Norway and Tostig, Harold II's brother, at the Battle of Stamford Bridge on 23 September 1066, he learned that William of Normandy, who claimed the English crown, had landed at Pevensey. Harold marched his troops southwards and engaged the Normans at the hill of Senlac, near Battle. There on 14 October 1066, in what has become known as the Battle of Hastings, Harold was said to

Stone marking the burial site of King Harold

have been killed by an arrow that pierced his eye. The high altar of Battle Abbey, now in ruins, stands over the exact spot where Harold was killed.

THE NORMANS

William I, The Conqueror (b.c.1027 r.1066–1087)
Buried in France at St Stephen's Church, Caen, Normandy. The tomb was desecrated in 1793 but a plain slab marks its original site.

Illegitimate son of Robert the Devil, Duke of Normandy, and Arletta, a tanner's daughter. When his father left on a pilgrimage to Jerusalem in 1034 he induced the baronage of Normandy to accept his bastard son as his heir, Robert having no legal son. The following year he died on his journey and William, although still a child, was accepted by the Normans as Duke. In 1051 William visited England and it is believed that during the visit his kinsman, Edward the Confessor, promised him the crown. In 1064, Harold, son of Earl Godwin and Edward's chief counsellor, accidentally found himself at William's court. There is strong belief that he too agreed to acknowledge William's claim to the English crown. This broken promise of support was one of the chief reasons for William's invasion of England after Harold's accession. The defeat and death of Harold at the Battle of Hastings on 14 October 1066 brought William to London where he was crowned at Westminster on Christmas Day 1066. However, five years were to elapse before he had the entire kingdom under his control, and a Norman aristocracy established. When he was firmly in control he ordered the compilation of the Domesday Book as a survey of the country. He died at Rouen in Normandy on 9 September 1087 after being thrown from his horse.

William II, Rufus (b.c.1056–1060 r.1087–1100)
Winchester Cathedral, Winchester, Hampshire, in front of the lectern. There is also a memorial marking the spot where he was killed in the New Forest: following a signpost at the turn-off on the Cadnam Road.

William, known as Rufus, was the third son of William I and Matilda of Flanders, and his father's favourite. On his deathbed England was bequeathed by the Conqueror to William, Normandy going to his eldest son, Robert. Rufus was crowned at Westminster on 26 September 1087, just fifteen days after his father's death. There were uprisings in favour of Robert and the hereditary principle which brought William into

Tomb of William II, Rufus, in Winchester Cathedral, Hampshire

conflict with his brother. In 1096 Robert, who wished to go on the Crusade, gave Normandy in pledge for money to William, and there can be little doubt that William determined to remain in lasting possession of the duchy. The *Anglo-Saxon Chronicle* says of the King that he was 'hateful to nearly all his people and odious to God'. He was killed by an arrow whilst hunting in the New Forest.

Henry I, Beauclerc (b.1068 r.1100–1135)
Reading Abbey (ruins), Reading, Berkshire.

The youngest son of William I and Matilda of Flanders. Hearing of his brother William Rufus's death he seized the treasury at Winchester. His elder brother, Robert Duke of Normandy, being at the Crusade, Henry was elected King. He married Edith of Scotland, daughter of Malcolm III and the Saxon princess, Margaret, granddaughter of Edmund II, Ironside, thus uniting the Norman and Saxon lines. At his

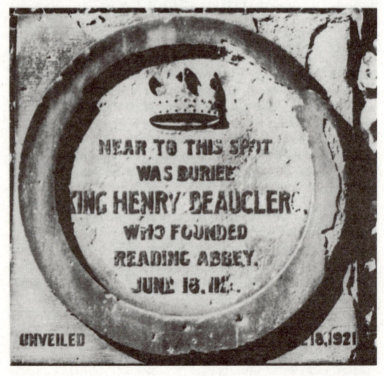

Stone marking the burial site of Henry I, Reading Abbey (ruins), Reading, Berkshire

coronation, he issued the famous charter which redressed grievances and rid the court of vice. His English government was severe and grasping, but he 'kept good peace'. After the death of his legitimate heir, William the Aethling, in the *White Ship* in 1120 he forced the baronage to recognize his daughter Matilda, widow of the Emperor Henry V, as his heiress by doing homage to her, first in 1126 and then in 1131 after her marriage to Geoffrey Plantagenet, Count of Anjou. Henry died at Gisors on 1 December 1135.

Matilda (b.1102 d.1164)
Buried originally at the Abbey Church at Bec; her tomb is now in the Cathedral Church of Rouen, Normandy, France.

Daughter of Henry I and his first wife, Edith of Scotland. She was married to the Emperor Henry V but at his death after eleven years of marriage she returned to England. In 1126, her brother William the Aethling having died earlier in the *White Ship* disaster, the Great Council of England did homage to her as her father's heiress. In 1129 she married Count Geoffrey of Anjou, and in 1133 gave birth to the future Henry II. On the death of Henry I in 1135, the nobles of England and Normandy accepted Stephen of Blois, a grandson of William I, as King; but, with the help of her half-brother, Robert of Gloucester, she invaded England and succeeded in capturing Stephen in 1141. Proclaimed Lady of Normandy and Queen of England at Winchester she entered London, but her arrogance alienated the nobles and the Papal Legate, Henry of Winchester. Routed at Winchester by forces loyal to Stephen, she was forced to exchange the King for Robert of Gloucester, and thereafter her cause steadily declined. She retired to Normandy in 1148, her husband having secured possession of the duchy, and lived to see her son crowned King, having renounced her claims in his favour. She died on 30 January 1164.

Stephen (b.c.1094–1097 r.1135–1154)
Faversham Abbey, Faversham, Kent. The base of the tomb was discovered in 1965.

Third son of Stephen, Count of Blois and Chartres, and Adela, daughter of William I. His nineteen-year rule was known as the reign of the 'nineteen long winters' owing to the continuous struggle with his cousin Matilda and, after 1149, with her young son, Henry, whom his parents had invested with the Duchy of Normandy in 1150. In 1141 Stephen was captured by Matilda and imprisoned, during which time she was proclaimed Lady of Normandy and Queen of England. After six months forces loyal to Stephen captured Matilda's half-brother, Robert of Gloucester, and she was forced to exchange him for Stephen. Owing to her unpopularity her cause declined and she retired to Normandy in 1148, assigning her rights to her son. In 1153, worn out by the conflict, Stephen agreed, after the death of his son Eustace, to acknowledge Matilda's son Henry as his heir. Thereafter until Stephen's death the two men acted together to counter the growing anarchy in the kingdom. Stephen died in October 1154, and was buried beside his Queen and his son.

Henry II (b.1133 r.1154–1189)
Fontevraud Abbey Church, Anjou, France.

The first of the long line of Plantagenet kings of England. On the death of Stephen in 1154 he succeeded peacefully to the English throne and immediately began to curb the lawlessness, a consequence of the previous reign. He introduced sweeping and lasting changes in the exercise of the laws of England. In 1171 he invaded Ireland. His controversy with the Church brought him into conflict with the Archbishop of Canterbury, Thomas à Becket, for whose murder on 29 December 1170 Henry was indirectly held responsible, through his impatient words, 'Will no one avenge me of this turbulent priest?' His marriage to Eleanor of Aquitaine, divorced wife of Louis VII of France, gave him, with his own inherited French domains, control of the larger part of what is now France and brought him into conflict with the French King. His sons, stirred up by their jealous mother, openly rebelled against Henry, and the latter part of his reign was spent in warring with them. He died on 6 July 1189 at Chinon.

Richard I, Coeur de Lion or Lionheart (b.1157 r.1189–1199)
Fontevraud Abbey Church, Anjou, France. His effigy may still be seen.

Third son of Henry II and Eleanor of Aquitaine. He succeeded peacefully at the death of his father but spent the majority of his reign out of the kingdom. In 1191 he went on the Crusade, winning a great victory over Saladin at Arsuf that same year. He left the Holy Land in 1192 after concluding a treaty with Saladin. During the return journey he was captured and imprisoned by Leopold of Austria in Durnstein Castle. There, rumour has it, he was found by a troubadour, Blondel de Nesle. Ransomed, he returned to England in 1194 but stayed in the realm only a few weeks before leaving for his French domains. He left the government of England in the care of Hubert Walter, whose skill as an administrator mitigated the effects of Richard's harsh tax demands. Whilst besieging the Castle of Chälus he was struck by an arrow and died on 6 April 1199.

John, Lackland (b.1167 r.1199–1216)
Worcester Cathedal, Worcester, in the Presbytery.
   The youngest son of Henry II and Eleanor of Aquitaine. During his elder brother's absence on the Crusade he tried to wrest the adminis-tration of England from the Chancellor, William Longchamp, and succeeded with the help of the nobles and the Londoners in expelling him. John, however, was prevented from heading the administration in Longchamp's place and, when it was known that Richard was impri-soned, he worked with his allies, including the French King, to prevent the release of the King. When Richard I returned to England in 1194 he forgave his brother though it was not until on his deathbed that the King reversed his previous decision to acknowledge Arthur of Brittany as his heir and made John his successor. On Richard's death his wishes were carried out and John was acknowledged King, despite the superior claims of the young Prince Arthur, who was captured in 1202 and imprisoned on John's orders, dying mysteriously a year later. John's misgovernment alienated all classes and he was forced by the baronage to sign the Magna Carta at Runnymede in June 1215. This did not bring peace and John's fight against the barons with the help of the French prince, Louis, is today seen as one of the most creditable episodes in an otherwise calamitous career in which the King lost all his continental domains. He died at Newark on 19 October 1216.

Henry III (b.1207 r.1216–1272)
Chapel of St Edward the Confessor, Westminster Abbey, London. His heart was sent to France and buried in the Abbey Church of Fontevraud, Anjou.
   Eldest son of King John and Isabella of Angoulême. He was nine when his father died and during his minority the country was governed by the aged William Marshal, Earl of Pembroke. At his accession his cause was in dire straits, the rebel barons and Prince Louis of France being in control of much of eastern England. As a consequence of this Henry was crowned at Gloucester, the western capital, his coronation at Westminster not taking place until 1220. During the ensuing year Henry's cause gradually triumphed, the French prince being defeated on

Tomb of Henry III, Chapel of St Edward the Confessor, Westminster Abbey, London

both land and sea until he finally renounced all his claims and retired to France. Henry's personal rule began in 1227, although he remained for some time under the influence of the Justiciar, Hubert de Burgh, who had succeeded William Marshal, who had died in 1219, as the chief administrator of the realm. In 1236 he married Eleanor of Provence and sought to regain the traditional Plantagenet lands in France which his father had lost. His continental ambitions meant harsh taxation which led to dissension with the English barons. The Provisions of Oxford in 1258 placed the government in the hands of a feudal oligarchy, and the King's defeat by Simon de Montfort at Lewes in 1264 meant that all effective power passed from the King to the barons. The following year, the King's cause triumphed when Prince Edward, later Edward I, defeated and killed de Montfort at the Battle of Evesham. Thereafter, the King remained under the influence of his eldest son who, by the Statute of Marlborough in 1267, brought peace to the land. Henry died at Westminster on 16 November 1272.

Edward I, Longshanks (b.1239 r.1272–1307)
Chapel of St Edward the Confessor, Westminster Abbey, London.

When his father, Henry III, died Edward was in Sicily, returning to England from the Crusade. Crowned at Westminster on 18 August 1274 he is chiefly remembered as the 'Hammer of the Scots' and for his defeat of the Welsh. He reorganized the laws of England by numerous statutes in an attempt to eliminate feudalism from political life. In 1295, he convoked a representative parliament of the three estates, which has since been called the Model Parliament, because it first illustrated the type which was to be perpetuated in all subsequent parliaments. The parliamentary constitution of England was established as the result of Edward's action. His continual wars against the Scottish nation did not effect long-term English rule and the only lasting result was the removal of the coronation stone from Scone to Westminster. His subjugation of the Welsh was in reality merely a subjugation of the territories of Llewellyn but he had established his hold on the principality by 1284 during which year he presented his son, Edward, to the Welsh as their prince and, in the Statute of Wales, provided the scheme for the future government of the country. On 7 July 1307, whilst on another Scottish campaign, Edward died at Burgh-on-Sands near Carlisle, and, despite his wishes that his heart be buried in the Holy Land and his bones carried by the army for inspiration, his body was taken to London on the orders of the new King for burial.

Tomb of Edward I, Chapel of St Edward the Confessor, Westminster Abbey, London

Edward II (b.1284 r.1307–1327)
Gloucester Cathedral, Gloucester: a beautiful tomb.

Fourth son of Edward I and his first wife, Eleanor of Castile. At his succession he immediately abandoned the Scottish campaign, leaving the way clear for Robert the Bruce to establish his rule and for his ultimate defeat of Edward and his English forces at the Battle of Bannockburn on 24 June 1314, thereby confirming the independence of Scotland. Edward was a weak king, 'destitute of any serious purpose', and under the influence of his favourites. Nevertheless, he was responsible for one of the most momentous stages in English constitutional history. His parliament held at York in 1322 revoked ordinances formerly granted by the baronage because 'they trenched on the rights of the crown and were drawn up by the barons only'. From this time on no statutes were technically valid unless the Commons had agreed to them. A rising against the Despensers, the royal favourites, inspired by the Queen, Isabella of France, and her lover, Roger Mortimer, in September 1326 brought about the death of the favourites and the capture of the King. On 20 January 1327 Edward was forced to abdicate in favour of his son,

Edward III, and he was murdered in Berkeley Castle on 21 September 1327 and his body interred in the Cathedral.

Edward III (b.1312 r.1327–1377)
Chapel of St Edward the Confessor, Westminster Abbey, London.

Succeeded to the throne after the deposition of his father in January 1327. He was fourteen and effective rule remained in the hands of his mother, Queen Isabella, and her lover, Roger Mortimer. In October 1330 he took Mortimer prisoner at Nottingham Castle, executing him at Tyburn the following month. Henceforth, the government was under his control. His long reign saw the outbreak of the Black Death, which intensified social and economic disturbances through its decimation of the population; the institution of the Order of the Garter; and the beginning of the Hundred Years War with France, in which Edward laid claim to the French crown. Sir Winston Churchill in his *History of the English Speaking Peoples* said that the Battle of Crécy in 1346 ranked with Blenheim, Waterloo and the final advance in the last summer of the Great War 'as one of the four supreme achievements of the British army', for the power and accuracy of the English longbow was infinitely superior to the crossbow used by the French and Genoese archers. During his reign the King fostered the woollen industry. Towards the end of his life his faculties were impaired and he fell under the influence of a greedy mistress, Alice Perrers, while his son, John of Gaunt, Duke of Lancaster, controlled the machinery of government. Edward died on 21 June 1377.

Richard II (b.1367 r.1377–1399)
Chapel of St Edward the Confessor, Westminster Abbey, London.

Son of Edward, the Black Prince, and Joan of Kent, he was the grandson of Edward III whom he succeeded whilst still a boy of ten years. In 1381, he showed courage in confronting the rebels during the Peasants' Revolt. Able and gifted, Richard's policies grew increasingly erratic during the later years of his reign. A rebellion led by his cousin Henry, Duke of Lancaster, son of John of Gaunt, brought his abdication and death in Pontefract Castle. After his death his body was brought to London and lay in state in Old St Paul's and was then taken to Langley in Hertfordshire for burial. It was transferred to Westminster in 1413 on the orders of Henry V and re-interred in the same tomb as that of Queen Anne, Richard's beloved first wife.

Tomb of Edward III, Chapel of St Edward the Confessor, Westminster Abbey, London

Tomb of Richard II and his Queen, Anne of Bohemia, Chapel of St Edward the Confessor, Westminster Abbey, London

THE LANCASTRIANS

Henry IV (b.1367 r.1399–1413)
Trinity Chapel, Canterbury Cathedral, Canterbury, Kent.

Eldest son of John of Gaunt, Duke of Lancaster, and Blanche, his first wife. He was first cousin to Richard II. He headed the rebellion which overthrew King Richard, forcing his abdication in September 1399. Henry then laid claim to the throne by 'right line of blood from Henry III' which was accepted by Parliament. He therefore became king, according to Capgrave, 'not so much by title of blood as by popular election', and was the first of the Lancastrian dynasty of Plantagenets to sit on the throne. His position was soon consolidated by the pursuit of sound practical policies.

Henry V (b.1387 r.1413–1422)
Chapel of St Edward the Confessor, Westminster Abbey, London. A casket, believed to contain the internal organs of the King, was discovered at Fosses, just outside Paris, in 1978.

Son of Henry IV and Mary de Bohun, he succeeded his father after an erratic youth. He renewed the Hundred Years War with France, started by his great-grandfather, Edward III, and showed brilliant generalship, defeating the French decisively at the Battle of Agincourt on 25 October 1415 with the loss of only 113 English soldiers as opposed to the loss of 5,000 French 'gentlemen of quality'. Following the Treaty of Troyes in 1420 he married Catherine de Valois, daughter of the French King Charles VI, who acknowledged his son-in-law as his heir to the French throne. But before he could succeed Henry died of dysentery at Vincennes on 31 August 1422.

Henry VI (b.1421 r. 1422–1461 restored 1470–1471)
St George's Chapel, Windsor Castle, Windsor, Berkshire, in the second bay of the choir, south side.

Succeeded his father, Henry V, as King of England when only nine months old, and, a few weeks later on the death of his grandfather Charles VI of France, he also became King of France. He was crowned King of England at Westminster on 6 November 1429 and King of France in Paris on 16 December 1431. A peaceful man, Henry supported pacific policies which gradually led to the loss of his French domains. Married to the warlike Margaret of Anjou who produced an heir, Edward Prince of Wales, in 1453, Henry increasingly withdrew from

King Henry V, by an unknown artist

politics leaving the reins of government in the hands of his wife and Edmund Beaufort, Duke of Somerset. When Henry's mind gave way in 1453, the realm was placed under the protectorship of Richard Duke of York, who was heir to the throne after the Prince of Wales. With the King's return to sanity the following year power once more reverted to the Queen and Somerset which shortly thereafter produced a conflict between the King's party and that of the Duke of York, thus initiating the wars which became known as the Wars of the Roses. York was killed at Wakefield on 29 December 1460 but his son, Edward Earl of March, reversed the defeat at the Battle of Towton on 29 March 1461, and forced Henry and his family into exile. Edward was proclaimed King and for the next three years Henry was a fugitive in Scotland. In 1465 he was captured in the north of England after an abortive attempt to regain the throne and was taken to the Tower of London as a prisoner. For six months, during 1470 and 1471, he emerged to hold a shadowy kingship as a puppet of Warwick, the Kingmaker, but the defeat of Warwick at Barnet, and his wife and son at Tewkesbury, in 1471, brought an end to his liberty and life.

THE YORKISTS

Edward IV (b.1442 r.1461–1470 restored 1471–1483)
St George's Chapel, Windsor Castle, Windsor, Berkshire, between the High Altar and the north choir aisle.

Son of Richard Duke of York and great-great-grandson of Edward III. After the death of his father at the Battle of Wakefield on 29 December 1460 Edward became the leader of the Yorkist faction. After his victory over the forces of Henry VI at Towton on 29 March 1461 he was proclaimed King as Edward IV. He antagonized his supporters by his marriage to Elizabeth Woodville and this led ultimately to a severance of his relations with the Earl of Warwick, the Kingmaker. During the years 1470 and 1471 he spent six months in exile in Burgundy following Warwick's successful campaign to restore Henry VI. He returned to England and with a force of loyal supporters defeated Warwick at Barnet and Queen Margaret at Tewkesbury in May 1471. Firmly established once more on the throne, the complete annihilation of the main Lancastrian claims brought peace and stability to the realm and with it increased foreign trade and the rise of the mercantile classes. Edward died in 1483.

Edward V (b.1470 r.briefly 1483)
Henry VII's Chapel, Westminster Abbey, London, 'Innocents' Corner'.

Elder son of Edward IV and Elizabeth Woodville, he was twelve when his father died. His uncle, Richard Duke of Gloucester, succeeded in ousting the young King's maternal relatives and gained possession of the boy's person. Declared illegitimate, he and his brother were kept in the Tower of London where they died, reputedly smothered, by whom or on whose responsibility is unclear, although legend has it that it was on the orders of their uncle, Richard III. Bones unearthed in the Tower in 1674 were believed to have been those of Edward and his brother, known as the Princes in the Tower, and the then King, Charles II, had them reinterred in Henry VII's Chapel at the eastern end of the aisle in what was described by Dean Stanley as 'The Innocents' Corner'.

Richard III (b.1452 r.1483–1485)
Leicester Abbey, Leicester; a tomb erected by Henry VII was destroyed at the Suppression. Plaque on Bow Bridge over River Soar in which his body was thrown at Suppression.

Younger brother of Edward IV. After the proclamation of the illegitimacy of his brother's children, Richard succeeded as the natural heir. 'An earnest and hardworking ruler', he introduced many new laws, including the bail law. He was defeated at the Battle of Bosworth Field in 1485, the last battle of the Wars of the Roses, by the Lancastrian pretender, Henry Tudor, Earl of Richmond. Richard III was the last of the direct Plantagenet line of English kings.

THE TUDORS

Henry VII (b.1457 r.1485–1509)
Henry VII's Chapel, Westminster Abbey, London, in the Nave.

Although known as the Lancastrian Pretender to the throne, Henry Tudor, Earl of Richmond, had no legitimate claim to the throne, for the Beauforts, through whom he was descended from John of Gaunt, fourth son of Edward III, were specifically barred from inheriting the crown. On his father's side he was descended from the Valois Kings of France through his grandmother, Catherine de Valois, widow of Henry V, who, after her husband's death, had secretly married the young and handsome Welsh squire, Owen Tudor. After the Battle of Bosworth Field Henry was careful to claim the throne by right of conquest although he

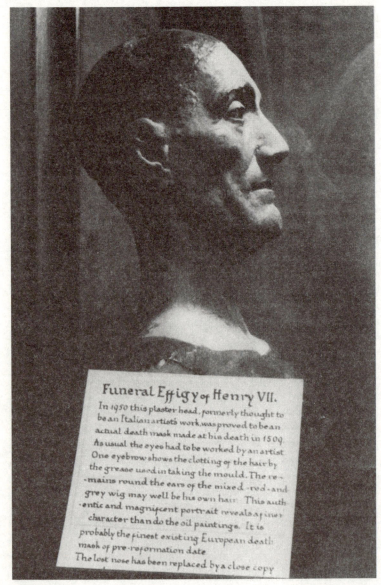

Funeral effigy of Henry VII, Henry VII's Chapel, Westminster Abbey, London

cemented his hold on it by marrying Elizabeth of York, eldest daughter of Edward IV, thus uniting the two houses of York and Lancaster. He successfully ended the baronial wars, curbed the power of the baronage, and, through his fiscal and economic policies, prepared the way for England's period of stability and expansion under the Tudors.

Henry VIII (b.1491 r.1509–1547)
St George's Chapel, Windsor Castle, Windsor, Berkshire, in the centre of the choir with his third wife, Jane Seymour.

Second son of Henry VII and Elizabeth of York, he became the first head of the Church of England after his break with the papacy over the question of his divorce from his first wife, Catherine of Aragon, the widow of his brother, Arthur Prince of Wales. The break began the ascendancy of the Protestant Church in England, although Henry never liked the reformed religion and remained a Catholic all his life. He was married six times: firstly to Catherine of Aragon, the mother of Mary I, whose inability to provide a male heir led to her divorce; secondly to Anne Boleyn, mother of Elizabeth I, whom he both divorced and beheaded; thirdly to Jane Seymour, the mother of Edward VI, who died in childbirth; fourthly to Anne of Cleves, 'the Flanders Mare', whom he speedily divorced; fifthly to the young Catherine Howard, who was beheaded for adultery; and lastly to Katharine Parr, who survived him. During Henry's reign the parliamentary system was developed, and the powers of Parliament were exercised more widely than hitherto. Royal supremacy over the Church, despite its harsh and violent enforcement, and although forced on Henry by private rather than public consideration, saved England from a serious civil war.

Edward VI (b.1537 r.1547–1553)
Henry VII's Chapel, Westminster Abbey, London, beneath the altar in the nave.

Son of Henry VIII and his third wife, Jane Seymour, he was only nine when he ascended the throne. His maternal uncle, Edward Seymour, Duke of Somerset, was appointed Regent. The issue of religion was of paramount importance during his reign, and the Catholic bishops, Gardiner and Bonner, maintained that the royal supremacy over the Church was, or should be, in abeyance owing to the King's minority. The execution of the Protector Somerset gave power to John Dudley, Duke of Northumberland, who, as the King's health declined throughout 1552 and early 1553, sought to maintain his own position and the Protestant ascendancy by ensuring the succession of a pliant Protestant sovereign. Edward was persuaded to leave the crown to his cousin, Lady Jane Grey, 'and her heirs male', effectively disbarring Edward's half-sisters, Mary and Elizabeth. Edward's last recorded words were vehement injunctions to Archbishop Cranmer to sign the will. He died at Greenwich on 6 July 1553.

Jane, Lady Jane Grey (b.1537 r.10–19 July 1553 d.1554)
St Peter ad Vincula, Tower of London, London.

Her cousin, Edward VI, had been persuaded by the all-powerful John Dudley, Duke of Northumberland, to break his father's will and to make a new settlement of the crown by deed, which was witnessed by members of the Council, many under duress. This left the crown to the Lady Jane Grey, an avowed Protestant, great-grand-daughter of Henry VII, who was also married to Northumberland's fourth son, Lord Guildford Dudley. Edward's death was kept secret for a few days, the Lady Jane being proclaimed Queen in the City on 10 July 1553; she was sixteen, and had only accepted the crown after much entreaty. Her reign lasted but nine days, Jane's own father, the Duke of Suffolk, proclaiming Mary, Henry VIII's eldest daughter, Queen on 19 July, informing his own daughter that she must return to private life, a request she told him she had no hesitation in accepting. Despite being found guilty of treason, Queen Mary allowed Jane and her husband a semblance of freedom and it was widely believed that she would have been pardoned had it not been for her father's involvement in the uprising led by Sir Thomas Wyat in January and February 1554. Jane and her husband were both executed on 12 February 1554 on Tower Hill.

Mary I (b.1516 r.1553–1558)
Henry VII's Chapel, Westminster Abbey, London, in the north aisle.

Eldest surviving daughter of Henry VIII and his first wife, Catherine of Aragon. Her accession was interrupted by the brief nine-days reign of her cousin, Lady Jane Grey. Her marriage to her cousin, Philip II of Spain, was unpopular and its announcement led to an immediate rebellion in January 1554 by Sir Thomas Wyat, in which he was joined by the Duke of Suffolk, Lady Jane Grey's father. Wyat's defeat led to the execution of Lady Jane Grey and to the imprisonment in the Tower of London of Mary's half-sister, the Princess Elizabeth. Mary restored the realm to the ecclesiastical control of the papacy, recalling her cousin, Cardinal Reginald Pole, whom she made Archbishop of Canterbury. Her

Queen Mary I, by Master John

persecution of the Protestants during her five-year reign earned her the epithet 'Bloody'. The loss of Calais, the last English possession in France, shortly before her death, was a severe blow to her.

Elizabeth I (b.1553 r.1558–1603)
Henry VII's Chapel, Westminster Abbey, London, in the north aisle.

Younger daughter of Henry VIII by his second wife, Anne Boleyn. No sovereign since Saxon times had been so purely English in blood; her nearest foreign ancestor being Catherine de Valois, widow of Henry V. No English king or queen was more insular in character or policy. Her reign has long been regarded as the Golden Age and one of the greatest periods in English history. Politically and intellectually able she was shrewd and lucky in the choice of her advisers among whom were Lord Burghley, Sir Francis Walsingham and the Earl of Leicester. She valued uniformity in religion and her reign saw the establishment of the Church of England. The reformation of the coinage and her fiscal policies gave the country a secure economic base whilst the defeat of the Spanish Armada in 1588 gave England the command of the seas and security from invasion. Her reign also saw the flowering of literature with such eminent figures as Sir Philip Sidney, Christopher Marlowe and William Shakespeare, much of whose work was written during Elizabeth's reign.

THE STUARTS

James I (b.1566 r.1603–1625)
Henry VII's Chapel, Westminster Abbey, London, in the nave.

Son of Mary, Queen of Scots, and Henry, Lord Darnley, he succeeded his mother to the Scottish throne after her abdication in 1566. In 1603, on the death of his remote cousin, Elizabeth I of England, he succeeded to the English throne, his claim stemming from his descent from Margaret of England, elder daughter of Henry VII, who married his great-grandfather, James IV of Scotland. During his reign he commissioned the Authorized Version of the Bible which was published in 1611; but his religious policies brought a growing confrontation between the Established Church and the Puritans. He continued the colonial adventures of Elizabeth, encouraging settlements in North America and Ireland. A scholar, not a practical man, he was commonly known as 'the wisest fool in Christendom'.

Tomb of Elizabeth I, Henry VII's Chapel, Westminster Abbey, London

Charles I (b.1600 r.1625–1649)
St George's Chapel, Windsor Castle, Windsor, Berkshire, in the centre of the choir.

The second son of James I and Anne of Denmark. A sincere but inept monarch, his autocratic policies soon led to a confrontation with the House of Commons and he attempted to rule without Parliament. He supported the strict Anglicanism of Archbishop Laud and this drove a number of moderate Protestants out of the Church into Presbyterianism, and created an intense feeling of hostility to the government throughout the realm. The resulting Civil War brought the King's final defeat and execution for treason at Whitehall on 30 January 1649, the only English sovereign to be so executed.

THE COMMONWEALTH

Cromwell, Oliver (1599–1658)
Henry VII's Chapel, Westminster Abbey, London, in the small east chapel, now known as the RAF Chapel, where a stone in the pavement records his burial there together with members of his family and some of the regicides. St Nicholas's Church, Chiswick Mall, London W also lays claim to his body.

Entered Parliament as Member for Huntingdon in 1628. When the Civil War broke out he served under the Earl of Essex. His own military ability proved itself when he reorganized the Parliamentary army, winning the battles of Marston Moor and Naseby. Following the execution of Charles I on 30 January 1649 Cromwell became the head of the government and in 1653 Lord Protector of the Commonwealth of England, Scotland and Ireland. He defeated a Scottish uprising at Dunbar and his harsh treatment of the Irish enchanced his government's difficulties there. He died in 1658 and was buried in Westminster Abbey. At the Restoration, however, his body together with those of other regicides was disinterred and hung on Tyburn gallows until 30 January 1661, the anniversary of Charles I's execution, his head being stuck on a pole on top of Westminster Hall. *The Times* of July 1969 reported that according to letters from Captain E. L. Dale, the son of the Reverend Lawford Dale, Vicar of St Nicholas's Church, Chiswick Mall in West London, in 1882, the Protector's remains had been switched at burial on the Protector's own orders and were later buried in the vaults of St Nicholas's Church. If this is true, they are now sealed under a thick cement floor. A letter to *The Times*, 31 August 1989, from Phillida Grantham, stated that she once held Cromwell's head, 'then in the possession of the Wilkinson family', and that it is now buried at his old Cambridge college, Sidney Sussex.

Cromwell, Richard (1626–1712)

Hursley Church, Hampshire, in the chancel; the original church being replaced by the present All Saints' Church built for John Keble during 1846–8.

Son of Oliver Cromwell, who succeeded his father as Lord Protector in 1658. He resigned on 25 May 1659 and went into exile on the continent using the name of John Clarke. He returned to England about 1680, living in the house of Sergeant Pengelly at Cheshunt, where he died on 12 July 1712.

THE STUARTS RESTORED

Charles II (b.1630 r.1660–1685)

Henry VII's Chapel, Westminster Abbey, London, in the Royal Vault below the south aisle.

Eldest son of Charles I and his French queen, Henrietta Maria, he returned to England and was restored to the throne in May 1660 after a long exile on the Continent during the Commonwealth under Oliver Cromwell and his son Richard. An able and astute politician, he was instrumental in re-establishing the monarchy as the pivot of the British constitution.

James II (b.1633 r.1685–1688)

Church of St Germains, France. Partial remains re-interred on orders of George IV after their re-discovery in 1824.

Second son of Charles I and Queen Henrietta Maria. He succeeded his brother, Charles II, peacefully despite earlier attempts to bar him from the throne because of his Catholicism. His religion played an important rôle during his brief reign but it was his lack of political insight rather than his religious bigotry which led to the Glorious Revolution of 1688, for, far from trying to impose Catholicism on the realm, he had merely tried to obtain concessions for his co-religionists. Allowed to escape to France by his daughter, Mary, and her Dutch husband, William of Orange, who had been offered the crowns of

England and Scotland to safeguard the Protestant succession, James lived the remainder of his life in exile at the Palace of St Germains in France, his one attempt to regain the throne by an invasion of Ireland being defeated by his son-in-law at the Battle of the Boyne in 1690.

Mary II (b.1662 r.1689–1694)
Henry VII's Chapel, Westminster Abbey, London, in the Royal Vault below the south aisle.

The eldest of James II's two daughters by Anne Hyde, she was proclaimed Queen jointly with her husband, William of Orange, after the flight of her father following the Glorious Revolution, in which not a shot was fired. She died of smallpox at Hampton Court in 1694.

William III, of Orange (b.1650 r. 1689–1702)
Henry VII's Chapel, Westminster Abbey, London, in the Royal Vault below the south aisle.

He accepted the crowns of England and Scotland jointly with his wife, Mary, eldest of James II's two daughters by the Protestant Anne Hyde, following the flight of his father-in-law in December 1688 during the Glorious Revolution. In 1689 the Bill of Rights defined the liberties established by the revolution of the previous year. William defeated James's attempts to regain his throne at the Battle of the Boyne in 1690. Much of the King's political concern was his war with Louis XIV of France which was finally brought to an end with the Peace of Ryswick in 1697. He died from the combined effects of a fall from his horse and a chill on 8 March 1702.

Anne (b.1665 r.1702–1714)
Henry VII's Chapel, Westminster Abbey, London, in the Royal Vault below the south aisle.

Sister of Mary II and younger daughter of James II and his Protestant wife, Anne Hyde. She was the first sovereign to reign over the united kingdom of England and Scotland, the two kingdoms having been united under the Act of Union of 1707. Guided by Tory and high church principles her reign was notable for the achievements of others: the Duke of Marlborough's victorious campaigns against the French; the scientific developments of Newton; the architecture of Christopher Wren and John Vanbrugh; and the literary works of Swift, Pope, Steele, Defoe and Addison. She established Queen Anne's bounty to improve the finances of the Church. By her consort, Prince George of Denmark,

she had seventeen children, all of whom died in infancy, only the young
Duke of Gloucester surviving to his eleventh year.

THE HANOVERIANS

George I (b.1660 r.1714–1727)
Hanover, Germany, in the vaults of the palace.
A great-grandson of James I through his daughter, Elizabeth of Bohemia, the Winter Queen. The Act of Settlement of 1701 settled the
succession on the Electress Sophia of Hanover, George's mother, to
guarantee the Protestant succession, debarring all closer claimants
including the exiled son of James II, the Old Pretender, who adhered to
the Catholic religion. Unable to speak English, George left the affairs of
the country in the hands of ministers and the system of Cabinet government under a Prime Minister evolved, the first such being Sir Robert
Walpole who was the chief minister of this and the succeeding reign of
twenty-one years. The first of the two Jacobite rebellions, led by James
the Old Pretender, known as James III, was defeated at Preston and
Sheriffmuir in 1715. George collapsed in his carriage during a journey to
Osnabruck and died there on Wednesday 12 June 1727, his remains
being taken to his palace at Hanover for interment.

George II (b.1683 r. 1727–1760)
Henry VII's Chapel, Westminster Abbey, London, in the nave. The son
of George I and his divorced wife, Sophia Dorothea of Celle, George II
continued the rôle of Sir Robert Walpole as his Prime Minister until Sir
Robert fell from power in 1742. George II was the last British monarch
to lead his troops personally, doing so at the Battle of Dettingen in 1743.
The second Jacobite uprising, this time under Bonnie Prince Charlie the
Young Pretender, was, after some initial success, defeated at Culloden in
1746 and put down with great severity by the King's son, William Duke
of Cumberland, thereafter known as Butcher Cumberland. In his will
the King left instructions that he be buried with his wife, Caroline of
Anspach, and that the sides of their coffins should be struck away in
order that their ashes might mingle.

George III (b.1738 r. 1760–1820)
St George's Chapel, Windsor Castle, Windsor, Berkshire, in the Royal
Vault below the Albert Memorial Chapel.

Eldest son of Frederick Prince of Wales, 'Poor Fred', he succeeded his grandfather, George II, his father having died in 1751. His reign was notable for the loss of the American colonies; but it also saw the expansion of British power in India. During his sixty years on the throne the country underwent the upheavals of the great agrarian and industrial revolutions. It was also an age of developments in other fields: science, exploration, chemistry, philosophy and invention under such great figures as Henry Cavendish who discovered hydrogen and the chemical composition of water, James Cook whose voyages of discovery took him to Australia and New Zealand, Joseph Priestley who shared with Carl Scheele the discovery of oxygen, Adam Smith the Scottish political economist who wrote the *Wealth of Nations* and Sir Humphry Davy who invented the miner's safety lamp which still bears his name. The King was a sufferer from intermittent porphyria which caused him to have two severe mental breakdowns and gave the royal power into the hands of his detested elder son, George, the Prince Regent; the first occurring in November 1788 and lasting until February 1789, the second in 1811 after the death of his favourite child, the Princess Amelia, and which lasted the remaining nine years of his life during which he also went blind.

George IV (b.1762 r.1820–1830)
St George's Chapel, Windsor Castle, Windsor, Berkshire, in the Royal Vault below the Albert Memorial Chapel.

Elder son of George III and Charlotte of Mecklenburg-Strelitz, he became Regent for the last nine years of his father's reign, from 1811 to 1820. Whilst Prince of Wales and without effective political power he had courted the Whig party in opposition, but when he gained power in 1811 he gave his support, after some hesitation, to the Tories, who remained in office during the Regency and throughout his reign. He was generally unpopular for his licentious and extravagant way of life, the general condemnation being inflamed by his treatment of his indiscreet wife, Caroline of Brunswick.

William IV (b.1765 r.1830–1837)
St George's Chapel, Windsor Castle, Windsor, Berkshire, in the Royal Vault below the Albert Memorial Chapel.

Third son of George III and Queen Charlotte, he succeeded his brother, George IV, in 1830. His reign saw a number of reforming statutes passed through Parliament, the most notable being the Reform

Bill of 1832 which extended the franchise and did away with many corrupt electoral practices.

Victoria (b.1819 r.1837–1901)
Royal Mausoleum, Frogmore, Windsor, Berkshire.

Grand-daughter of George III and daughter of Edward, Duke of Kent, and his wife Victoria of Saxe-Coburg, she succeeded her uncle, William IV, when she was but seventeen. Her accession meant the separation of the crowns of Great Britain and Hanover, for under Salic Law a woman could not succeed in Hanover. Her uncle, Ernest, Duke of Cumberland, therefore succeeded his brother William IV as King of Hanover. During the Queen's reign there was a general growth in many areas – industrial, humanitarian, the arts – as well as abroad; in 1877 Victoria was proclaimed Empress of India, a title her descendants held until the independence of India and Pakistan in 1947. Her devoted husband, Prince Albert of Saxe-Coburg-Gotha, the Prince Consort, and she set a high and strict moral standard for the age by their hard work and conscientiousness. After his death in 1861 of typhoid fever the Queen withdrew from public life for a number of years until she was persuaded back into public affairs by her friend and Prime Minister, Benjamin Disraeli, Earl of Beaconsfield, and in so doing firmly established the rôle of the constitutional monarch in British political life.

THE HOUSE OF SAXE-COBURG-GOTHA

Edward VII (b.1841 r.1901–1910)
St George's Chapel, Windsor Castle, Windsor, Berkshire, his tomb being on the south side of the High Altar.

Eldest son of Queen Victoria and Albert of Saxe-Coburg-Gotha, he was 59 when he came to the throne. His natural charm and political sagacity cleared the way for an end to the prolonged period of estrangement between Britain and France with the Entente Cordiale, as well as helping to establish harmonious relations with other European powers. It was left to him to consolidate the rôle of the constitutional monarch established by his mother.

THE WINDSORS

George V (b.1865 r.1910–1936)
St George's Chapel, Windsor Castle, Windsor, Berkshire, in a tomb designed by Sir Edwin Lutyens in the second bay of the north side of the nave.

Second son of Edward VII and Alexandra of Denmark, his accession was marred by the political controversy over the Parliament Act of 1911 which decisively reduced the powers of the House of Lords. His reign saw the duration of the first world war, 1914–1918; the formation of the Irish Free State on 6 December 1921; and the first Labour Government under Ramsay Macdonald in 1924.

Edward VIII, Duke of Windsor (b.1894 r.January–December 1936 d.1972)
Royal cemetery in Windsor Home Park, Berkshire. The gardens and mausoleum of Queen Victoria are open only on May 14, 15 and 21.

Eldest son of George V and Mary of Teck, he reigned for only 325 days before abdicating over the issue of his marriage to an American divorcee, Mrs Wallis Warfield Simpson. He took the title of Duke of Windsor and lived abroad. During the second world war he became Governor of the Bahamas.

George VI (b.1895 r.1936–1952)
St George's Chapel, Windsor Castle, Windsor, Berkshire, in a specially constructed side chapel adjoining the north choir aisle.

Brother of Edward VIII and second son of George V and Queen Mary, he succeeded after his brother's abdication on 12 December 1936. With the help of his wife, Elizabeth, the late Queen Mother, he overcame his natural shyness and nervous stammer. During the second world war he and his family led the way in maintaining a high morale in a beleaguered Britain. The Labour administration of Clement Attlee immediately after the war brought independence to many former colonies, including India.

Chapter 2
Nobles

Albert of Saxe-Coburg-Gotha, the Prince Consort (1819–1861)
Royal Mausoleum, Frogmore, Windsor, Berkshire.

Second son of the Duke of Saxe-Coburg-Gotha, he married his cousin, Queen Victoria, in 1840. He was a constant support to his wife in her political duties and in 1861 managed to avert war with the United States by advising a conciliatory course. He was responsible for the Great Exhibition of 1851. Ten years later he died of typhoid fever, and he is commemorated by the Albert Memorial in Kensington Gardens, London.

Anne Boleyn (1507–1536)
St Peter ad Vincula, Tower of London, London. She is also reputed to be buried in the Boleyn church at Salle, Norfolk; whilst two other churches claim to have her heart buried within their precincts: All Saints Church, East Horndon, near Billericay, Essex, in the altar tomb in the south transept wall; and SSs Andrew and Patrick Church, Elveden Park, near Thetford, Norfolk, which claims that the heart was discovered in the south wall in 1836 and reburied under the organ.

The second wife of Henry VIII and mother of Elizabeth I. It was her marriage to Henry VIII which brought about the break with Rome. In 1536 she was accused of adultery and incest with her brother, George Boleyn Viscount Rochford, found guilty and executed on Tower Green, the first English Queen to be so executed.

Anne of Cleves (1515–1557)
Westminster Abbey, London, on the south side of the Presbytery.

Fourth wife of Henry VIII. She was the daughter of John Duke of Cleves, the leader of the German Protestant princes. Sought in marriage for the King by Thomas Cromwell, when he saw her in December 1540 Henry was so abashed at her appearance that he forgot to present her with the gift he had brought her. The following day he openly expressed his dissatisfaction with her looks: 'she was no better than a Flanders mare'. Forced to continue with the marriage on 6 January 1540 he refused to consummate it and, with Anne's consent, the marriage was declared null and void by convocation and an act of Parliament on 9 July

1540. She agreed to live permanently in England and spent the rest of her life quietly at Richmond or Bletchingley, occasionally visiting the court. She died in Chelsea on 28 July 1557.

Caroline of Anspach (1683–1737)
Henry VII's Chapel, Westminster Abbey, London, in the nave.

Consort of George II. During her husband's reign she exercised her considerable influence in support of Sir Robert Walpole, maintaining him in power. She was also responsible for appointing many learned rather than orthodox bishops, being extremely tolerant by nature. She retained her good influence over her husband until her death, and when he died he instructed that the sides of their coffins be removed so that their ashes might mingle.

Catherine Howard (c.1521–1542)
St Peter ad Vincula, Tower of London, London.

Fifth wife of Henry VIII she was the daughter of Lord Edmund Howard, the son of the Duke of Norfolk. She caught the eye of the King and, supported by the Catholic party, his attentions were encouraged. They were married privately at Oatlands in July 1540 and soon afterwards she was publicly acknowledged as Queen. In November 1541 Archbishop Cranmer informed the King that his wife had not been chaste before her marriage. Imprisoned, she was later released on her confession and forgiven by the King. But not long afterwards fresh evidence was procured that she had committed adultery and she was beheaded on 13 February 1542.

Catherine of Aragon (1485–1536)
Peterborough Cathedral, Peterborough. The tomb was destroyed during the Civil War.

First wife of Henry VIII, she was the daughter of Ferdinand of Aragon and Isabella of Castile. First married to Henry's elder brother, Arthur Prince of Wales, who died in April 1502. She was betrothed a year later to the young Prince Henry but the marriage was not celebrated for six years, despite papal dispensation for it having been obtained. However, immediately after Henry's accession the marriage took place, on 11 June 1509, and fourteen days later they were both crowned. During Henry's invasion of France in 1513 Catherine was made Regent and she successfully organized the defence of the realm against the invading Scottish forces under James IV, and was riding north to put herself at the head of the English troops when news was received of the rout of King James and his army at Flodden Field, the King and much of the Scottish nobility being slain. Between January 1510 and November 1518 Catherine gave birth to six children, including two princes, all of whom were stillborn or died in infancy with the exception of the Princess Mary, and rumour did not fail to ascribe the Queen's failure to produce an heir to the curse pronounced in *Deuteronomy* on incestuous unions. By 1526 it was apparent the Queen would bear no more children, and, as no woman had yet held the throne in her own right, a male heir was vital if a civil war was to be avoided. The Queen refused to accept the annulment of her marriage which was pronounced after the King's break with Rome. She was treated harshly, her daughter being taken from her, but her spirit was not broken and she continued to enjoy great popularity with the people of England until her death.

Catherine Parr (1512–1548)
Sudeley Castle, near Winchcombe, Gloucestershire, where a nineteenth-century tomb has replaced the original destroyed in the Civil War.

Henry VIII's sixth and last wife, she surviving him. She later married the Lord High Admiral, Thomas Seymour, the brother of Protector Somerset and uncle to Edward VI. She died of puerperal fever after giving birth to a daughter in 1548.

Cavendish, Andrew Robert Buxton, 11th Duke of Devonshire (1920–2004)
Edensor Churchyard, in a village on the Chatsworth Estate.

11th Duke of Devonshire. Andrew Cavendish was educated at Eton and Trinity College, Cambridge. At the age of twenty he joined the Coldstream Guards and was awarded the Military Cross for his service during the Second World War. In 1945 he stood as the Conservative Party candidate for Chesterfield. He was unsuccessful again in the 1950 general election, the same year he succeeded to the dukedom. Harold Macmillan, his uncle through marriage, made him Under-Secretary of State for Commonwealth Relations in 1960 but by the early 1980s he had become a member of the new Social Democratic Party. In 1996 he was appointed one of the twenty-four Knights of the Garter.

Catherine Parr, attributed to W. Scrots

Cleveland, Barbara Villiers, Duchess of (1641–1709)
St Nicholas's Church, Chiswick Mall, Chiswick, London.

Mistress of Charles II, to whom she bore at least five children. She was the daughter of Viscount Grandison and married Roger Palmer, created Earl of Castlemaine in 1661, in April 1659. Shortly after her marriage her intimacy with Charles II began and she was made Lady of the Bedchamber to Charles's Queen, Catherine of Braganza, much to that lady's displeasure. She meddled in politics and was an opponent of Edward Hyde, Earl of Clarendon, at whose fall she was said to have 'exhibited a wild paroxysm of delight'. Her relations with the King declined because of her amorous exploits with others but by 1667 she was once again supreme at court. In 1670 she was made Countess of Southampton and Duchess of Cleveland with remainders to her first and third sons, the King denying he was the father of Henry, the second son. In 1670 her influence once again declined and by 1674 she was entirely supplanted in the King's affections by Louise de Kéroualle, Duchess of Portsmouth. She went to live in Paris but returned to London just before Charles's death in 1685. Samuel Pepys wrote of her in his diary that she was 'one of England's most high-placed whores'.

Diana, Princess of Wales, Lady Diana Frances Spencer (1961–1997)
In consecrated ground on an island in a small lake on the Althorp estate of Earl Spencer, near Great Brington*, Northamptonshire. The grave may be viewed at certain times of the year. Admission is by ticket only.

Princess Diana was the third daughter of the 8th Earl of Spencer, Edward John. Her mother was Frances Roche (now, after divorce, the Hon Mrs Peter Shand Kydd) the daughter of Lady Fermoy who had descended from a wealthy American family, one of whom had married the 3rd Baron Fermoy in New York. Born at Sandringham, Diana went to several private schools in England and a Swiss finishing school. Her stepmother Raine was Countess of Dartmouth and the daughter of novelist Barbara Cartland. Diana's marriage to Charles, Prince of Wales, heir to the British throne, brought world-wide approval. Although they had met in childhood, Diana as an eligible young woman met Prince Charles on the royal yacht *Britannia* during Cowes Week, I.O.W. in 1980. They were married in 1981 at St Paul's Cathedral in a 'fairy tale' royal wedding. Their two sons, Prince William Arthur Phillip Louis ('Wills') and Prince Harry (Henry Charles Albert David) were born in 1982 and 1984 respectively.

She was divorced in 1996 – the title Her Royal Highness was stripped

The Duchess of Cleveland, after Lely

from her by the Queen. Diana met Emad Fayed ('Dodi') in July 1997. He was the son of an Egyptian millionaire, owner of Harrods department store in London. They met first at Cannes then at St Tropez. She and her children were guests at Fayed senior's estate there. Photographers constantly followed them even at sea. They had been the bane of her life since before and after she was married to Prince Charles. It has been suggested that in an attempt to escape photographers in Paris, the car carrying Diana and Fayed was being driven too fast. It crashed while returning to his apartment from the Ritz hotel, killing Diana, Dodi and the chauffeur.

* George Washington's ancestors were buried in the church at Great Brington, on the edge of the Spencer estate. They moved in the 1600s from nearby Sulgrave where the Washington Museum was established earlier in the 20th century. It is on land where Laurence Washington's (7th ancestor in direct ascent from the first U.S. President) manor house stood.

Edward Prince of Wales, The Black Prince (1330–1376)
Trinity Chapel, Canterbury Cathedral, Canterbury, Kent, in a magnificent tomb on the south side.

Eldest son of Edward III and Philippa of Hainault he distinguished himself at the age of fifteen at the Battle of Crécy in 1346. Thereafter he gained a wide reputation as a general. He was the father of the illfated Richard II who succeeded Edward III whilst still a child. Edward was the first Prince of Wales to adopt the motto, *Ich Dien*, and the crest of three ostrich feathers, reputedly having taken them from the blind King of Bohemia who was slain at the Battle of Crécy.

Eleanor of Castile (1245–1290)
Chapel of St Edward the Confessor, Westminster Abbey, London.

Consort of Edward I. She accompanied her husband on his Crusade and is reputed to have sucked the poison from a wound inflicted by a poisoned dagger in an assassination attempt on her husband. When she died at Harby in Nottinghamshire the King had her body embalmed and taken to London. At each resting place a cross was erected in her memory, the most famous of which being the cross at Charing, now Charing Cross.

Elizabeth, Princess (1635–1650)
St Thomas's Church, Newport, Isle of Wight; small vault near the communion table.

Second daughter of Charles I, she was born at St James's Palace. She showed a remarkable talent for languages, being able to read and write Greek, Latin, Hebrew, French and Italian before she was eight years old. Confined at Carisbrooke Castle, she was horrified at being where her father had been imprisoned, pleading not to be sent there. Within a week of her arrival she caught pneumonia as a result of getting wet through one day. Parliament was on the point of allowing her to go to Holland when she died, with her cheek, it was said, on her Bible and a tear on her cheek. A white marble monument was placed near her grave by Queen Victoria. For two centuries all that commemorated this tragic princess in the church were the initials E.S. cut into the wall nearest to her burial vault.

Elizabeth, Queen Elizabeth the Queen Mother (1900–2002)
St George's Chapel, Windsor Castle, beside her husband, King George VI.

Affectionately known as the Queen Mum. Elizabeth Bowes-Lyon married the Duke of York, the king's second son, in 1923. They had two children, Elizabeth and Margaret, born in 1926 and 1930 respectively. When George V died in 1936 she did not expect to become Queen, but eleven months later King Edward VIII was to abdicate his throne and her husband became King George VI. During the Second World War, Queen Elizabeth earned the devotion of the people through her personal appearances and support of those suffering through the London Blitz. She was still one of the most popular royals when she died at the age of 101. She was given the title Her Majesty Queen Elizabeth the Queen Mother on the death of George VI and her eldest daughter became Queen Elizabeth II.

Fitzalan-Howard, Miles Francis Stapleton, 17th Duke of Norfolk (1915–2002)
Crypt of the Fitzalan Chapel, Arundel Castle. Access is through the Castle grounds, which are open to the public from Easter until the end of October.

17th Duke of Norfolk and premier peer of the realm. Miles Fitzalan-Howard held numerous titles, including Earl of Arundel and Surrey, and hereditary earl marshal of England. The Norfolk dynasty has a 500-year

Catholic history and, as the most senior Catholic layman in England, he was asked by the Queen to officially welcome Pope John-Paul II to Britain in 1982.

Before succeeding to the dukedom in 1975, Fitzalan-Howard served as an active soldier for thirty years. Joining the Grenadier Guards in 1937, he went on to win the Military Cross during the Second World War and served in Potsdam and Kenya. He commanded the first division of the Rhine army 1963–1965.

Gaveston, Piers, Earl of Cornwall (d.1312)
Dominican Friary (ruins), King's Langley, Hertfordshire.

The son of a Gascon knight favoured by Edward I, Piers Gaveston was brought up in the royal household where he became a close friend of the King's son, Edward Prince of Wales, later Edward II. Exiled by Edward I he was immediately recalled when his friend became King on his father's death and created Earl of Cornwall and given Edward's niece, Margaret, daughter of Gilbert de Clare, Earl of Gloucester. He was Regent of England during the King's absence in France in 1308 and played a prominent part at the King's coronation. His arrogance and haughty behaviour angered the nobles who called for his banishment, to which the King was forced to agree in 1311. At the end of that year he returned secretly to England and was publicly restored by Edward. The barons took up arms and Gaveston was captured, after being deserted by the King, and executed on Blacklow Hill near Warwick on 19 June 1312.

Godwin, Earl of the West Saxons (d.1053)
Old Minster, Winchester, Hampshire; some of his remains may be in the mortuary chests over the cathedral choir screen.

Father of King Harold, Godwin's origins are obscure. The Anglo-Saxon Canterbury Chronicle has him as the son of Wulfnoth, a South Saxon who plundered the south coast in 1009. Later writings make him the son of a wealthy farmer of Sherston, Wiltshire. After a battle there he sheltered Earl Ulf who took him to Canute, who made him an earl. Marrying Ulf's sister, Godwin gained vast wealth and power but never became overbearing, always displaying good temper. He became the most powerful man in the kingdom, after the king, representing Canute when he was in Denmark.

Guinevere (c.500)
Glastonbury Abbey (ruins), Glastonbury, Somerset.

Historically believed to be the wife of the Romano-British general known as 'King' Arthur. After his death she is reputed to have retired to a convent.

Gundrada de Warenne (d.1085)
St John's Church, Lewes, Sussex. The black marble tomb now inside the church was originally in Lewes Priory.

The daughter of Matilda of Flanders by either William the Conqueror or a previous husband. She was the wife of William de Warenne, the first Earl of Surrey, by whom she had several children. She and her husband founded the first Cluniac priory in England, that of St Pancras at Lewes. She died in childbirth on 27 May 1085 and was buried in the chapter house at Lewes. Her tombstone was found at Ifield Church at the end of the eighteenth century, presumably having been removed there at the Dissolution. Her remains, enclosed in a chest with her name on the lid, were found side by side with those of her husband on the site of Lewes Priory in October 1845.

Isabella of France (1292–1358)
Church of the Franciscan Greyfriars, Newgate, which was destroyed, being replaced by the Wren church, Christ Church, Newgate Street, London, which itself was destroyed by bombs in 1940. The burial ground is now a garden. An effigy of the Queen is among the figures which adorn the tomb of her son, John of Eltham, in Westminster Abbey.

Consort of Edward II whom she married in January 1308, she was the daughter of Philip IV, the Fair, of France. The Queen took her son, Edward of Windsor, later Edward III, to France to do homage to her brother, Charles IV, for Aquitaine in 1325, using the occasion to voice her antipathy to her husband's favourites, the Despensers. Whilst in France she met and became the mistress of one of the baronial exiles, Roger Mortimer, Lord of Wigmore. The scandal caused by their relationship soon reached England and, in September 1326, Isabella together with Mortimer and a force of mercenaries invaded England determined to rid the country of the despised favourites. Her husband fled but he was captured by Mortimer in November and forced to abdicate in favour of his son, Edward III. She and Mortimer ruled the kingdom until October 1330, when the young King overthrew his mother and her lover, forcing her retirement to Hertford and Mortimer's execution.

Jane Seymour (c.1509–1537)
St George's Chapel, Windsor Castle, Windsor, Berkshire, in the centre of the choir with Henry VIII.

Third wife of Henry VIII and mother of Edward VI after whose birth she died in 1537.

Joan of Navarre (c.1370–1437)
Trinity Chapel, Canterbury Cathedral, Canterbury, Kent.

The second wife of Henry IV whom she married on 7 February 1403. Her first husband had been John IV Duke of Brittany and after his death in 1399 she had become Regent of Brittany for her young son, John V. Relations with her stepson, Henry V, were strained over the war with France, one of her sons, Arthur, being captured at Agincourt and brought a prisoner to England. For a time she was kept under restraint but shortly before Henry's death in 1422 he relented and she spent the remainder of her life peacefully in England.

John of Gaunt, Duke of Lancaster (1340–1399)
'Old' St Paul's Cathedral, London.

Fourth son of Edward III and Philippa of Hainault. Through his second marriage to Constance, daughter of Pedro the Cruel King of Castile and Leon, he became titular King of Castile, but never succeeded in establishing his claim. Eventually, his daughter Catherine was granted her mother's rights in Castile and, on her marriage to Henry III of Castile, reigned in her parents' place. During the latter years of Edward III's life, owing to his growing weakness and the decline in the health of Edward, the Black Prince, John of Gaunt took over the reins of government. His ambitions on the succession were frustrated by the Good Parliament which confirmed the succession to the young son of the Black Prince, later Richard II. Unpopular with the public, John of Gaunt was a firm supporter of John Wycliffe, although politically he was forced to renounce Lollard opinions.

Margaret, Princess, Countess of Snowdon (1930–2002)
St George's Chapel, Windsor Castle.

Younger sister of Queen Elizabeth II and daughter to King George VI and Queen Elizabeth the Queen Mother. Margaret Rose was a controversial royal who loved the arts and nightlife. In the 1950s she fell in love with a divorced, older man but was not allowed to marry him without abandoning any claim to the throne. Instead she married the photographer Antony Armstrong-Jones in 1960 and he became Earl of Snowdon and Viscount Linley. They had two children, David, Viscount Linley and Lady Sarah Armstrong-Jones, but divorced acrimoniously in 1978. In later life the princess suffered from ill health and spent increasing amounts of time on the Caribbean island of Mustique, where she severely scalded her feet in the bath in 1998. She died in February 2001 at the age of seventy-one.

Mary Queen of Scots (1542–1587)
Henry VII's Chapel, Westminster Abbey, London, in the south aisle.

Grand-daughter of Margaret Tudor, elder daughter of Henry VII and Elizabeth of York, Mary had the strongest legitimate claim to the English throne after the children of Henry VIII. She acceded to the throne of Scotland whilst still a baby but was forced to abdicate in favour of her son James after her marriage to Lord Bothwell, the alleged murderer of her second husband Lord Darnley. She escaped from imprisonment and fled to England where she was kept in custody for nineteen years. Numerous plots, of which she may or may not have been aware, to place her on the English throne and to restore the Catholic religion, finally but reluctantly forced her cousin, Queen Elizabeth I, to sign her death warrant and she was beheaded at Fotheringay Castle in February 1587. She was first buried in Peterborough Cathedral but when her son, James, acceded to the English throne as James I, he had her body translated to Henry VII's Chapel in Westminster Abbey where he erected her monument beside that of her mother-in-law and his grandmother, the Countess of Lennox.

Monmouth, James, Duke of (1649–1685)
St Peter ad Vincula, Tower of London, London, under the Communion table.

An acknowledged illegitimate son of Charles II by his mistress, Lucy Walter. During his father's lifetime he had been exiled to the Netherlands for his implication in the Rye House Plot but on Charles's death in 1685 he claimed the throne and invaded the realm landing at Lyme Regis in Dorset. His ragged West Country troops were defeated at the Battle of Sedgemoor and the uprising was put down with great severity by Judge Jeffreys. The Duke was taken to London and beheaded, his uncle, James II, refusing to reprieve him.

The Duke of Monmouth, after Wissing

Montfort, Simon of, Earl of Leicester (1208?–1265)
Evesham Abbey ruins, Evesham, Worcestershire; stone in Abbey Gardens erected in 1965 where Montfort was buried at the site of the high altar.

Credited by some writers as being the creator of the House of Commons, but in fact he only summoned together a parliament of churchmen, peers and two citizens from all English boroughs in an effort to develop the cause of justice and righteousness; not a representative democracy per se. Born in Normandy, he came to England in 1229 expecting to gain the earldom of Leicester in exchange for his continental patrimony, but he was not formally invested as the earl until a year after his marriage in 1238 to Eleanor, Henry III's sister. He went on crusade in 1240 and, after returning to Gascony, was accused of oppression and violence as its governor, and became embroiled with Henry III. Parliament, however, denounced Henry and brought Montfort back to England. Montfort captured Henry at the Battle of Lewes, becoming virtually governor of the kingdom, but Montfort was later killed in the Battle of Evesham when his nephew Prince Edward (later Edward I) fought him to become real ruler of the country through his subservient father King Henry III. Henry of Montfort, Simon's elder son, was also killed at Evesham and buried in the Abbey.

Napoleon III, Emperor of the French (1808–1873)
Abbey Church of St Michael, Farnborough, Hampshire.

A nephew of Napoleon I, being the son of his brother, Louis King of Holland, and Hortense Beauharnais, daughter of the Empress Josephine. He assumed power in 1851 and proclaimed himself Emperor of the French on 1 December 1852, reigning until the overthrow of his Empire on 4 September 1870, two days after the Emperor's defeat and surrender at Sedan to the Prussian troops. He and his wife, the Empress Eugénie, and their son, the Prince Imperial, went into exile in England where the Emperor died two years later.

Pembroke. William Herbert, 3rd Earl of (1580–1630)
Salisbury Cathedral, Salisbury, Wiltshire; family vault in front of altar.

Courtier and literary patron, he was born at Wilton House, Wilton, Wiltshire and shared the literary taste of his mother and his uncle, Sir Philip Sidney. Herbert was handsome and accomplished, matriculating from Oxford when he was only thirteen years old. Often at Elizabeth I's court, he did not pander to her, displaying an independent spirit.

Although he got along well with men, he was also said to be 'immoderately given up to women', and indulged himself in 'pleasures of all kinds, almost in excess'. At one time he had a secret romance with Mary Fitton, a great favourite of Elizabeth's, and after his own father's death, he became the father of an illegitimate child by her. The child died in infancy, and Pembroke was imprisoned briefly for his part in the scandal.

When Sir Walter Raleigh was imprisoned in the Tower, Herbert tried to secure his pardon; there is some evidence that he actually instigated the attack on the Mexican fleet for which Raleigh was executed. He continued his mother's patronage of poets and writers, being friendly with John Donne, the dramatist, Philip Massinger (his father's steward's son), and Ben Jonson. He knew Shakespeare but was not a personal patron of his. Herbert became very friendly with James I, entertaining him several times at Wilton House and showing him Stonehenge. He took part in Parliamentary debates, siding at times with the Duke of Buckingham, at other times disagreeing with him. Herbert was at James I's deathbed and carried the crown at Charles I's coronation. He had been deeply interested in New England explorations, becoming a member of the King's council for Virginia and sending immigrants and cattle there, and he had incorporated the North West Passage Company in 1612. He died suddenly of apoplexy in London after a 'full and cheerful' dinner the night before. He had been Chancellor of Oxford University since 1617.

Robert II, Curthose, Duke of Normandy (c.1054–1134)
Gloucester Cathedral, Gloucester, before the High Altar.

Eldest son of William I, the Conqueror, and Matilda of Flanders, he succeeded his father as Duke of Normandy in 1087, his second brother, William II, ruling in England. Conflict with his brothers eventually lost him Normandy and after his capture by Henry I, his younger brother, at Tinchebrai on 28 September 1106 he was brought to England and imprisoned for twenty-eight years, first in the Tower of London and then in the castles of Devizes and Cardiff, dying at Cardiff in February 1134. Although a weak character he showed skill and ability as a warrior.

Rupert, Prince, Count Palatine of the Rhine and Duke of Cumberland (1619–1682)
Henry VII's Chapel, Westminster Abbey, London, in the south aisle.

Born at Prague, the son of Elizabeth the Winter Queen, daughter of James I, and Frederick the Elector Palatine and King of Bohemia, he was

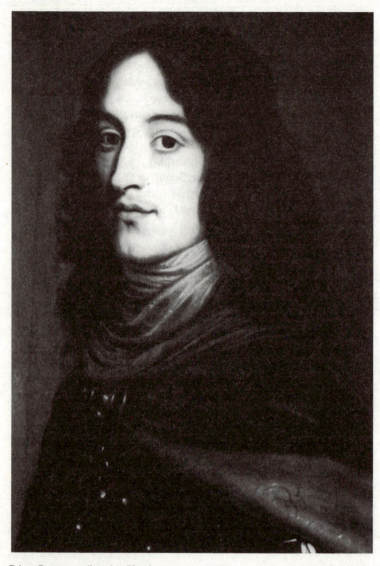

Prince Rupert, attributed to Honthorst

a nephew of Charles I. He actively supported his uncle during the Civil War and played a dominant rôle. A cavalry leader, his strategy was bold as well as skilful and in November 1644 he was appointed general of the King's army, an appointment which was obnoxious to the King's counsellors who resented the Prince's independent line. Following his surrender of Bristol to General Fairfax of the Parliamentary forces the King's counsellors prevailed upon him to dismiss the Prince, and he and his brother, Maurice, were told to seek their fortunes overseas. Convinced not only that the King's cause was lost but that it was bad, he tried to persuade the King to make peace with Parliament to no avail and reluctantly he and his brother went to France where he sought service in the French army, commanding a troop of English exiles. Later, his uncle relented and understood something of the Prince's feelings, giving him command of the royalist navy. The Prince however was still in conflict with the King's Council and once more relinquished his offices and for six years, from 1654–1660, was in Germany where little was known of his exploits. At the Restoration he returned to England where he was made a privy councillor by Charles II and, during the Dutch wars, bore a brilliant part as admiral. The Prince's scientific skill led to improved gunpowder and cannon-making, the invention of the alloy 'Prince's metal,' and a variety of scientific toys, including 'Prince Rupert's Drops', which are elongated glass drops that shatter when the tail is broken.

Southampton. Henry Wriothesley, 3rd Earl of (1573–1624)
St Peter's Church, Titchfield, Hampshire; in the crypt under the Southampton Monument. He is the kneeling figure on the west end of the monument, chancel side.

Famous as Shakespeare's only patron, he was a royal ward under Lord Burghley at five years of age, when he inherited his title. He was a brilliant student at St John's College, Cambridge and graduated at age sixteen. Southampton became a lover of literature and, it is said, of women. He was handsome, with blue eyes and dark auburn hair. He once hired Shakespeare's company to put on a performance of *Richard II* to incite the public to rise by presenting a royal abdication scene on stage. But the rising failed, and Southampton was imprisoned in the Tower of London for three years.

James I freed him as soon as he acceded, and under the new monarch he actively pioneered various colonies in America, including Virginia and those of New England, where he is commemorated in a town and river name; there was even an Indian tribe called 'Southampton' after him. He was a member of the East India Company, and in 1610 he helped to send Henry Hudson to seek the North-West Passage. In politics he strongly opposed George Villiers, Duke of Buckingham; once they nearly came to blows in the House of Lords. He had to devote much energy to championing the interests of the Virginia Company, in peril to hostile Spain. A treaty with the Netherlands against Spain allowed the Netherlands to raise 6,000 troops in England, and Southampton went with the English volunteers as their commander, taking his elder son James with him. They both caught a fever in the Low Countries and there died. Until the time of his death Southampton continued to be eulogized by poets and writers. He had been secretly married to his mistress Elizabeth Verdon, one of Elizabeth I's personal maids.

William Marshal, Earl of Pembroke (c.1146–1219)
The Temple Church, Temple, Fleet Street, London.
Served Henry II, Richard I who appointed him one of the council of regency during the King's absence on the Third Crusade, and King John, being one of the few barons who clung to the King's cause during the Barons' War. John appointed him his executor and after the King's death the barons elected him Regent for the young Henry III. In spite of his advanced age, he prosecuted the war against Prince Louis and the rebels, heading the King's army at the Battle of Lincoln in 1217. Self-restraint and compromise were the keynotes of his policy and he brought stability to the realm and confirmed Magna Carta. He died on 14 May 1219.

Windsor, Bessie Wallis Warfield, Duchess of (1896–1986)
Frogmore, royal cemetery in Windsor Home Park, Berkshire, beside Edward VIII's grave. The gardens and mausoleum of Queen Victoria are open only on 14, 15 and 21 May, each year; the Duke and Duchess of Windsor's graves can be seen from pathway.
American-born wife of the former Edward VIII, who abdicated the throne upon his marriage to her. She had previously been married, first to an American naval lieutenant, secondly to an American businessman, Ernest Aldrich Simpson.

Chapter 3
Statesmen (including politicians and the military)

Alexander, Sir Harold Rupert Leofric George, 1st Earl Alexander of Tunis (1891–1969)
St Margaret's Church, Ridge, Hertfordshire.

Field Marshal who served with distinction in both world wars, being born in Co. Tyrone, Ireland and educated at Harrow and Sandhurst. Winning the DSO and MC, among many other mentions and awards, he served for three years in the trenches in France, where he commanded a battalion at age twenty-four. He later held commands in north England and the North West Frontier of India. At Dunkirk in World War II he was the last officer to leave the beaches. After originating battle training schools in England he became General Officer Commanding in Burma in 1942 and then Commander-in-Chief, Middle East. By 1944 he was Supreme Commander in the Mediterranean theatre of war. The capture of Rome saw him promoted to Field Marshal. He became Governor General of Canada from 1946 to 1952, being recalled as Minister of Defence by Churchill. The Americans had earlier wanted him to command the British invasion forces of Normandy but Montgomery got the job because Alexander could not be spared from Italy. He received the Order of Merit in 1959 after a viscountcy in 1946 and an earldom in 1952. He is considered to have been the most outstanding British officer of the war.

Allenby, Edmund Henry Hynman, 1st Viscount Allenby of Megiddo (1861–1936)
St George's Chapel, known as The Warriors' Chapel, Westminster Abbey, London.

Field Marshal who on 9 December 1917 captured Jerusalem. Earlier he had commanded cavalry units on the Western front and, later, the new 3rd Army. His most notable achievement in Europe was the Battle of Arras in 1917 when his army advanced three and a half miles, believed to be the longest advance carried out by any belligerent on the Western front since trench warfare had set in. Created a viscount in 1919 he was appointed a special high commissioner for Egypt and the Sudan from

1919 to 1925 and during his period in office he persuaded the British government to abolish the protectorate and to recognize Egypt as a sovereign state. Strained relations between him and Austen Chamberlain, then Foreign Secretary, brought his resignation.

André, Major John (1751–1780)
Westminster Abbey, London, south aisle of the Nave.

English soldier who negotiated with Benedict Arnold for the betrayal of West Point, of which Arnold was commander, during the American War of Independence. Captured at Tarrytown by three militiamen he was tried by a court martial and condemned to death as a spy. He was hanged on 2 October 1780 at Tappan, despite Washington having admitted that he was 'more unfortunate than criminal'. His death excited much sympathy both in America and in Europe and in 1821 his remains were exhumed and brought to Westminster Abbey where a mural sculptured monument was erected to him. In America, a monument to his memory was also erected on the spot where he was taken.

Arnold, Benedict (1741–1801)
St Mary's Church, Battersea, London.

American soldier. A general in George Washington's army of independence he was appointed to command West Point, the key to the Hudson River Valley. He agreed to betray his post to the British forces and met with Major John André on 21 September 1780 to perfect the plan. Major André was captured whilst returning to the British lines and, unsuspecting, his captors informed Arnold, giving him time to escape. He then openly joined the British and led an expedition into Virginia and burned Richmond. In December 1781 he went to London and was consulted by the King and his ministers on American affairs. He spent some years in St John, New Brunswick, engaging in the West India trade, but, when the war broke out between Britain and France, he returned to London and was active in fitting out privateers.

Asquith, Herbert Henry, 1st Earl of Oxford and Asquith (1852–1928)
All Saints' Churchyard, Sutton Courtenay, Oxfordshire.

Statesman elected to Parliament as a Liberal in 1886; he became Home Secretary in Gladstone's last ministry. In 1908 he succeeded Sir Henry Campbell-Bannerman as Prime Minister and his government introduced an avalanche of social reforms including old-age pensions in 1908 and unemployment insurance in 1911. During the first world war

Grave of Henry Herbert Asquith, All Saints' Churchyard, Sutton Courtenay, Oxfordshire

he was forced to resign over criticism of his leadership and Lloyd George became Prime Minister in his stead. He resigned the leadership of the Liberal Party in 1926.

Attlee, Clement Richard, 1st Earl Attlee (1883–1967)
Westminster Abbey, London, in the north aisle of the Nave.

Statesman. A former Mayor of Stepney he became Prime Minister following the landslide victory of the Labour Party in 1945 at the end of the second world war. Previously he had been Churchill's deputy during the war having, since 1935, been the leader of the Labour opposition in the Commons. His government introduced legislation which created the welfare state and was also instrumental in granting independence to India and Pakistan.

Bacon, Sir Nicholas (1509–1579)
'Old' St Paul's Cathedral, London; his damaged effigy survived the Great Fire and is now in the crypt.

A Member of Parliament in 1545, he thereafter held a succession of appointments, the most important of which was Lord Keeper of the Great Seal in December 1558, shortly after becoming a Privy Councillor and receiving a knighthood. As a Protestant he distrusted Mary Queen of Scots and was alleged to be a supporter of the claims of the Lady Catherine Grey, sister of Lady Jane Grey, to the throne in the event of Elizabeth's death without direct heirs. He opposed the projected marriage between Elizabeth and the Duke of Anjou, his fear and distrust of the Catholics being increased by the massacre of the French Protestants, the Huguenots, on St Bartholomew's Day, 24 August 1572. He died in London on 20 February 1579. His son by his second marriage was Sir Francis Bacon.

Baldwin, Stanley, 1st Earl Baldwin of Bewdley (1867–1947)
Worcester Cathedral, Worcester, west entrance.

Statesman. Stanley Baldwin followed his father as Conservative Member of Parliament for Bewdley West when he was returned unopposed in 1908. In 1916 he became a member of Lloyd George's war cabinet and in 1923 became Prime Minister for the first time, resigning the following year to allow for the first Labour administration under Ramsay Macdonald, which lasted but a few months. He then became Prime Minister until 1929 during which term occurred the General Strike of 1926, his radio appeal at the time being credited with shortening the crisis. He became Prime Minister again from 1935 to 1937 and his handling of the issue of the King's marriage to Mrs Simpson brought about Edward VIII's abdication in December 1936. After the coronation of George VI he resigned the leadership of the party to Neville Chamberlain. His refusal to re-arm in the 1930s and his acceptance of Mussolini's annexation of Abyssinia has brought him much criticism.

Baring, Evelyn, 1st Earl of Cromer (1841–1917)
Wimborne Road Cemetery, Wimborne Road, Bournemouth, large marble cross about 50 yards from east side of chapel to the left of the path.

Statesman and diplomatist who 'rescued, refitted and piloted Egypt into modern civilization'. Baring, who was connected with the great financial family of that name, was born at Cromer Hall, Norfolk, and brought a life of already crowded achievement with him when, in 1877, he was chosen to represent British interests in Egypt, a country virtually bankrupt because of the criminal extravagance of Khedive Ismail. Baring had served first in the army and later as a diplomat in the Ionian Islands, where he 'picked up' Greek, as he put it, to add to the two languages he already knew; in Malta; in Jamaica, where he was able to spend some time with General Grant before Petersburg (1864) during the American Civil War; and in India during the Bengal famine, where he was private secretary to his cousin Lord Northbrook, Viceroy of India.

When Baring finally took the helm as consul-general in Egypt his rule

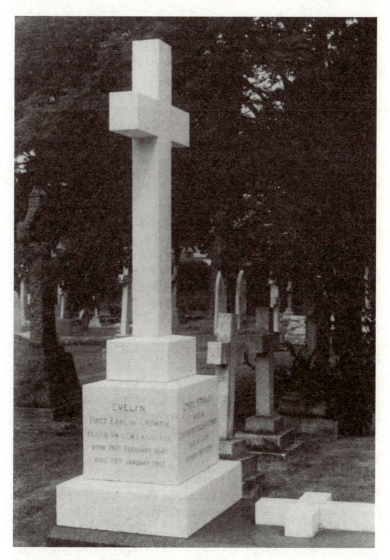

Evelyn Baring's Grave, Bournemouth Cemetery, Dorset

was virtually absolute, since British forces were in occupation. His first aim was to make Egypt financially sound by increasing the area of taxable land through irrigation rather than raising taxes. Through many dangers, including a cholera epidemic, nationalist insurrection and the personal crisis of his first wife's death, he eventually brought forth a modern Egypt.

He was a tall man, not inclined to small-talk, but possessing 'unusually powerful and versatile talents'. During his early career he had been known as 'Overbearing', and in Cairene society he was referred to as '*le Grand Ours*'. He could, however, recognize a lost cause and was willing to compromise instead of obstinately clinging to a position for the sake of pride. He wrote *Modern Egypt* (1908), *Ancient and Modern Imperialism* (1910) and three volumes of *Political and Literary Essays* (1912 onwards), based on books he reviewed for the *Spectator*. He was twice married.

Beatty, David, 1st Earl Beatty (1871–1936)
St Paul's Cathedral, London, in the crypt.

British admiral who succeeded Lord Jellicoe as commander of the grand fleet in 1916. Whilst in command of the British battle cruisers he fought the German fleet at Heligoland Bight in 1914 and the Dogger Bank in 1915. In May 1916 in a brilliant manoeuvre he lured the German navy into the uncertain Battle of Jutland after which the German fleet remained in harbour.

Beaufort, John, 1st Duke of Somerset (1403–1444)
Wimborne Minster (St Cuthburga's), Wimborne, Dorset; large tomb on the south side of the presbytery.

Long-time army campaigner, he was the grandson of Edward III's son, John of Gaunt. Beaufort's father, John, had been created Earl of Somerset, and in 1409 John the younger succeeded to the title on the death of his brother Henry. After fighting for Henry V in France when only seventeen years old, John was captured when attacking the Dauphin at Anjou. In the same battle Henry V's brother the Duke of Clarence was killed. Quickly released once a ransom was paid, Beaufort stayed in France fighting for Henry VI, his nearness to the crown giving him high command. He was created duke in 1443 and became a captain-general in Aquitania and Normandy. When passed over as Regent for France, the Duke of York being preferred, Somerset became disgusted and returned to England, dying within a year by his own hand, it was said. His quarrel with the government over his slight had brought him the disgrace of banishment from the court. It was too much for him to bear as a loyal and brave commander in all his years of fighting for his sovereign.

He had married Margaret, widow of Sir Oliver St John, and his daughter, Margaret Beaufort, had a son when she was only thirteen years of age. She had married Henry VI's half-brother, Edmund Tudor, Earl of Richmond, and the son became Henry VII. She it was who erected the monument to her parents in Wimborne Minster.

Bennet, Richard Bedford, 1st Viscount Bennet (1870–1947)
St Michael's Churchyard, Mickleham, Surrey.

Prime Minister of Canada 1930 to 1935, having been the Conservative leader from 1927. He was born in New Brunswick and brought about a system of trade preferences after an empire conference at Ottawa. He received his viscountcy in 1941.

Bevin, Ernest (1881–1951)
Westminster Abbey, London, in the north aisle of the Nave.

Ernest Bevin began life as a poor West Country boy. In 1911 he became assistant general secretary of the Dockers' Union which he eventually merged with others to form the powerful Transport and General Workers' Union of which he became general secretary. He was an influential member of the Trades Union Congress which called the General Strike of 1926. During the second world war he became the Minister of Labour in Churchill's war cabinet and, after the Labour victory at the polls in 1945, Foreign Secretary until his resignation in 1951, a few months before he died.

Bligh, William (1754–1817)
St Mary's Church, Lambeth, London.

His name is remembered as the captain of HMS *Bounty* whose crew, under the leadership of Fletcher Christian, mutinied on 28 April 1789. An excellent seaman, Bligh accompanied Cook during his second voyage around the world from 1772–1774, and it was on this voyage that the bread fruit was discovered. Thereafter Bligh was known as 'Bread Fruit Bligh'. In 1805 he was appointed Captain-General and Governor of New South Wales and during his term tried to suppress the illegal trafficking of spirits. Deposed by the military because of his harsh rule he was imprisoned for two years before obtaining his release and returning to England in 1811. He was made a vice-admiral of the Blue in June 1814.

Tomb of Admiral Bligh, St Mary's Churchyard, Lambeth, London

Bolingbroke, Henry St John, 1st Viscount (1678–1751)
St Mary's Church, Battersea, London, in the family vault which is no longer marked although there is a frontal bust on the north side gallery.

Politician. Entered Parliament in 1701 and held high office under Robert Harley Earl of Oxford during the reign of Queen Anne. He was created a viscount in 1712 and schemed for the return of James the Old Pretender but he was out-manoeuvred by the appointment of Lord Shrewsbury to the treasureship which ruined his plans. Dismissed by George I, he fled to France where he became secretary to the Old Pretender. He criticised the 1715 Jacobite uprising and severed his connections with James's court. Pardoned by George I, he returned to England, and although he tried to re-assert his influence any hopes he may have entertained were dashed by the death of George I, whose mistress, the Duchess of Kendal, was his chief support. In 1735 he went to live in France, his second wife being French, returning to England only occasionally. In 1744 he finally decided to settle once again in London and lived at Battersea, where he died.

Buckingham, George Villiers, 1st Duke of (1592–1628)
Henry VII's Chapel, Westminster Abbey, London, in the small chapel to the north that forms the apse.

A favourite of James I, to whom he was introduced by the anti-Spanish lobby led by the Archbishop of Canterbury, he rose rapidly to power after the eclipse of the former favourite, Robert Carr, Earl of Somerset. He played a prominent role in the government but veered erratically in his policies. He sided with the Spanish lobby and accompanied Prince Charles on a visit to Madrid to sue for the hand of the Spanish Infanta, but Buckingham's behaviour alienated the Spanish court and the match was called off. When Charles I came to the throne Buckingham became his principal adviser. He supported the Huguenots at La Rochelle but his intervention failed to relieve them. He was assassinated at Portsmouth before embarking for La Rochelle by John Felton, a disaffected seaman.

Buckingham, George Villiers, 2nd Duke of (1628–1687)
Henry VII's Chapel, Wesminster Abbey, London, in the small chapel to the north that forms the apse.

Son of James I's favourite. After the murder of his father he and his younger brother, Francis, born after Buckingham's assassination, were brought up with Charles I's children at court. Villiers was driven into exile with Charles II but he negotiated with Cromwell, estranging himself from the exiled Stuarts. He was imprisoned in the Tower of London by Cromwell in 1658 for suspected implication in a Presbyterian plot against the government, later being released on payment of a heavy fine. He met the returning Charles II at Dover and, despite an initial coolness in their relations, was soon back in favour. After some political setbacks he became a member of Charles II's Cabal of ministers. His affair with the Countess of Shrewsbury, whose husband he had killed in a duel, caused a public scandal, which together with his unpopular policies forced his political retirement. Later intrigue once again took him to the Tower of London as a prisoner but he was released. He died in April 1687 from a chill caught while hunting in Yorkshire.

Buckingham and Normanby, John Sheffield, 1st Duke of (1648–1721)
Henry VII's Chapel, Westminster Abbey, London, in the small chapel to the north-east that forms part of the apse.

English statesman and poet who became Lord Chamberlain under James II, whose natural daughter, Catherine, he married later. A keen supporter of James II he nonetheless acquiesced in the Glorious Revolution and was created Marquess of Normanby in 1694. During Queen Anne's reign he held many high offices of state and in 1703 was created Duke of Buckingham and Normanby. After the Queen's death in 1714 he held no further state appointments and died in February 1721. He is credited by Sir Winston Churchill with having said: 'Good God, how this poor nation has been governed in my time! During the reign of King Charles the Second we were governed by a parcel of French whores, in King James the Second's time by a parcel of Popish priests, in King William's time by a parcel of Dutch footmen, and now we are governed by a dirty chambermaid, a Welsh attorney and a profligate wretch that has neither honour nor honesty.' (*A History of the English-Speaking Peoples*, vol. III, Winston S. Churchill, Cassell, 1957, p.81.)

Burghley, William Cecil, 1st Baron Burghley or Burleigh, K.G. (1520–1598)
St Martin's Church, Stamford, Lincolnshire; large renaissance tomb along with other monuments to members of his family.

Statesman born at Bourne, Lincolnshire, who rose to be chief secretary of state under Elizabeth I, a position which he held for forty years. He is considered to have been the power behind England's greatness under the queen. After brilliant academic work at Cambridge he entered Gray's Inn, studying not only law but history, genealogy and theology. His first marriage while at Gray's Inn in 1541 was to a wineseller's daughter, but his second marriage to the daughter of Sir Anthony Cooke in 1545 brought him to the notice of Edward Seymour the Protector, Duke of Somerset. He appointed Burghley as his secretary. As such Burghley suffered two months' imprisonment in the Tower of London when Somerset fell from grace. Recognition of his talents soon brought about Burghley's release, however, and he served as Secretary of State with a knighthood in 1551 during the Duke of Northumberland's ascendancy.

Although conforming to Roman Catholicism under Mary I, he was not held in full favour by her but he did succeed in furthering his ideas of open trading and the abolition of some monopolies. Under Elizabeth I as her chief adviser he was responsible for the clever and bold diplomatic policies that helped England become a greatly respected power in Europe and the world. His spy network is reputed to have prevented many internecine schemes from harming England and the queen. He it was who bore the responsibility for Mary Queen of Scots' execution. In 1572, a year after awarding him a barony, Elizabeth made him a Garter Knight and Lord High Treasurer, which office he held at his death.

Chamberlain, Arthur Neville (1869–1940)
Westminster Abbey, London, south aisle of the Nave.

Prime Minister from 1937 to 1940, succeeding Stanley Baldwin as premier and leader of the Conservative Party. In September 1938 he flew to Munich to meet with Adolf Hitler, the German Führer, returning with 'a piece of paper' that promised 'peace in our time'. His appeasement policies failed with the outbreak of war on Sunday 3 September 1939 and he resigned the premiership to Winston Churchill in May 1940.

Chamberlain, Joseph (1836–1914)
Birmingham General Cemetery, Key Hill, Birmingham, in the Unitarian Section, under a large stone slab.

Statesman and industrialist (Nettlefold's screw factory at Birmingham) who quickly became influential as an MP for Birmingham, becoming president of the Board of Trade and a member of the cabinet under Gladstone (whom see). He resigned in a disagreement with Gladstone on Home Rule for Ireland and became the leader of the

Liberal Unionists. Secretary for the Colonies in 1895 in the Coalition government, he made his mark as a colonial administrator both during and after the Boer War. He advocated tariff reform and preferential treatment for colonial imports. He left public life in 1906 because of ill-health. His son Neville (whom see) was by a second marriage.

Churchill, Lord Randolph Henry Spencer (1849–1895)
St Martin's Churchyard, Bladon, Oxfordshire.

Conservative politician and younger son of the 7th Duke of Marlborough. He was elected to the Commons as Member for Woodstock in 1874 and soon made his mark as an exponent of independent conservatism, attacking the traditional Tory hierarchy with the vituperative invective that made him famous. An active promoter of the Primrose League he later became a controversial chairman of the National Union of Conservative Associations. He became Chancellor of the Exchequer briefly under Lord Salisbury in 1886 but resigned on 20 December 1886 over a dispute with the heads of the naval and military establishments. It was the end of his career as a leader of the Conservative Pary. In 1874 he married the American beauty, Jennie Jerome, by whom he became the father of Sir Winston Churchill.

Churchill, Sir Winston (c1620–1688)
St Martin-in-the-Fields, St Martin's Place, London.

Politician and historian who was elected to Parliament in 1661. He held influential positions at court during the reigns of both Charles II and James II. He was the father of John Churchill, 1st Duke of Marlborough, and of Arabella Churchill, the mistress of James II, to whom she bore four children, the most famous of which was James FitzJames, the Duke of Berwick.

Churchill, Sir Winston Leonard Spencer, K.G. (1874–1965)
St Martin's Churchyard, Bladon, Oxfordshire.

Son of Lord Randoph Churchill and his American wife Jennie Jerome. He entered Parliament in 1900 and held many of the high offices of state. During the Boer War he was a correspondent and was captured but escaped. He became Prime Minister and leader of the Conservative Party after the resignation of Neville Chamberlain in 1940 and his leadership symbolized the courage of the British peoples during the Second World War. Defeated at the General Election of 1945 he returned to 10 Downing Street as Prime Minister from 1951 to 1955, when he retired.

Graves of Sir Winston Churchill and his mother, Lady Randolph Churchill, St Martin's Churchyard, Bladon, Oxfordshire

He was a gifted amateur painter, exhibiting at the Royal Academy, as well as historian and writer.

Clive, Robert, 1st Baron Clive (1725–1774)
St Margaret's Church, Moreton Say, Shrewsbury.

General, whose military successes against the French helped to lay the foundations of British power in India. Originally a clerk in the East India Company, his dislike of his work nearly drove him to suicide. When the Seven Years War broke out in 1756 Clive soon proved his military genius and the following year he conquered Bengal with his victory at Plassey, becoming the first British governor, in which role he proved his administrative ability. He later returned to England and sat in the House of Commons as the member for Shrewsbury, for, being an Irish peer, he was able to do so. General John Burgoyne tried to get the House to impeach Clive for corruption but the motion was defeated by 155 votes to 55. Nonetheless it was a bitter blow to a man who had rendered his country 'great and meritorious services'. He committed suicide on 22 November 1774.

Cobden, Richard (1804–1865)
St Mary Magdelene Churchyard, West Lavington, West Sussex; large granite slab with only his surname cut in it. (He had not wished to be buried in Westminster Abbey 'among all those men of war'.)

An economist and politician, born at Heyshott, Sussex, he was sent to a poor boys' school in Yorkshire, 'Dotheboys Hall', because of his father's failure as a farmer. After becoming a clerk and extremely capable commercial traveller he went into business with two friends in London. Four years later they had a profitable calico–printing mill in Manchester, to where he then moved. After success had sent him to America and other places he started pamphleteering: *England, Ireland and America* (1835) and *Russia* (1836) both supported the causes he now favoured, namely free trade and non-intervention in Russian affairs.

Cobden became the foremost proponent of anti–corn-laws, his 1841 election as a Stockport MP now giving him the Commons as an influential platform. His speeches were considered by Peel to have helped greatly in the abolition of the Corn Laws in 1846. His cause had seen his financial downfall with its high costs, but private subscription let him purchase Durnford, the Sussex farmhouse in which he had been born. He was now able to travel in Europe and Russia again and threw his weight against the Crimean War, also strongly opposing Palmerston's

Robert Clive, by Dance

policy on China. Cobden also visited America again, supporting the North in the Civil War there. He was offered the Board of Trade presidency by Palmerston after failing in his bid for election as MP for Huddersfield but declined the offer. He still was, nevertheless, able to arrange a commercial treaty with France in 1859, though he was in ill health. He died in London.

Collingwood, Cuthbert, 1st Baron Collingwood (1750–1810)
St Paul's Cathedral, London, in the crypt near to Lord Nelson's tomb.

Admiral who assumed command of the British fleet at the Battle of Trafalgar after Nelson's death. His ship, the *Royal Sovereign*, led the fleet into battle and he is alleged to have replied to Nelson's famous signal, 'England expects ...', that all knew well enough what to do. He died at sea.

Cromwell, Henry (1628–1674)
St Laurence's Church, Wicken Fen, Cambridgeshire.

Fourth son of Oliver Cromwell. He spent most of his active political life in Ireland where he worked hard to ameliorate the poverty of the country. He became Lord Deputy in 1657. He urged his father not to accept the office of King and, when his brother fell from office in June 1659, he returned to England and resigned. After the Restoration he was unmolested by the government and died on 23 March 1674. Carlyle referred to him as 'the best of Cromwell's sons,' and this is inscribed on a brass plate in the church where he is buried.

Curzon, George Nathaniel, 1st Marquess Curzon of Kedleston (1859–1925)
All Saints' Church, Kedleston, Derbyshire; the north aisle was added from 1906 to 1913 as a memorial chapel for Lord Curzon.

Statesman. As Viceroy of India from 1898 to 1905 he initiated important currency, education and administrative reforms, though his partition of Bengal in 1905 angered the Hindus. After a quarrel with Lord Kitchener, then commanding the Indian Army, Curzon resigned. During the first world war he was a member of Lloyd George's war cabinet from 1916–1918. From 1919 to 1924 he was Foreign Secretary and at the European Conference in Lausanne he dominated the proceedings, disapproving of the French occupation of the Ruhr, whilst his consummate diplomatic skill restored British prestige in Turkey. He was deeply disappointed when the King finally chose Stanley Baldwin to

Lord Curzon, by Cooke after Sargent

succeed to the premiership after the resignation of Bonar Law in May 1923, having confidently believed he would be called. Following his death his coffin was taken to Westminster Abbey and after a funeral service there it was removed to lie beside that of his wife in Kedleston.

Disraeli, Benjamin, 1st Earl of Beaconsfield (1804–1881)
St Michael's Churchyard, Hughenden, Buckinghamshire, with a monument erected by Queen Victoria with a profile portrait by R. C. Belt in the church.

Statesman and novelist. He entered Parliament in 1837 and became Conservative Prime Minister in 1868 and from 1874 to 1880. He arranged the purchase of the Suez Canal shares and had Queen Victoria proclaimed Empress of India. He is regarded as the founder of the modern Conservative Party. He was a considerable novelist, his novels *Coningsby* and *Sybil* rousing the social consciences of his readership.

Dowding, Hugh Caswall Tremenheere, 1st Baron Dowding (1882–1970)
Henry VII's Chapel, Westminster Abbey, London, in the small east chapel, now known as the RAF Chapel, that forms part of the apse.

Air Chief Marshal. During the Second World War he was Air Officer Commanding-in-Chief of Fighter Command at the time of the Battle of Britain. His foresight in building up Fighter Command during the period between the two world wars together with his strategy and firmness during the battle was instrumental in the successful defence of Great Britain in 1940.

Eden, Sir Robert Anthony, 1st Earl of Avon (1897–1977)
St Mary's Church, Alvediston, Wiltshire, on edge of graveyard near car-parking area.

Statesman who, prior to succeeding Churchill as Prime Minister in 1955, had been Foreign Secretary for the third time in Conservative governments. After Eton and Christ Church, Oxford, he won the MC in the First World War, later becoming an MP for Leamington in 1923, holding the seat until he resigned in 1957. In the previous year he had involved Britain and France in a controversial occupation of the Suez Canal Zone. In failing health he resigned from politics in 1957, still a debonair but now somewhat crestfallen figure.

Fox, Charles James (1749–1806)
Westminster Abbey, London, in the North Transept; a monument stands in the Belfry Tower.

Whig statesman and orator. Entered Parliament at nineteen as Member for Midhurst; at twenty-one he became a junior Lord of the Admiralty under Lord North, a post he threw up to oppose the Royal Marriage Act which, along with his gambling habits, earned him the animosity of George III which was to last throughout his life. Edmund Burke drew Fox into association with the Whigs under Lord Rockingham and his great political career stems from the famous speech he made in the House on 2 February 1775 on the disputes with the colonies. However, he only held office for a few months in 1783, 1784 and shortly before his death in 1806. Nonetheless he was a major force in the politics of the time. He upheld the liberal causes of the day: American independence; the French Revolution; he pressed for the abolition of slavery and actually effected it during his brief term in office in 1806 although he died before the Act was passed through both Houses in 1807; the repeal of the Test Acts; and concessions to the Roman Catholics in Britain and Ireland. He planted the seed of the modern Liberal Party.

Fox, Sir Stephen (1627–1716)
All Saints' Church, Farley, Wiltshire; in vault in the north transept.

Statesman who served through the reigns of six rulers of England. From being an ordinary choirboy at Salisbury Cathedral he became not only respected and honoured for his dignity, ability and honesty, but, with the fortune he made, built or contributed to the improvement of churches and various public buildings. He fought in Charles II's ill-fated Battle of Worcester (1651) and assisted his escape to France. During the Commonwealth Fox was sent to England by Charles II as a trusted agent. After the Restoration Fox was given the post of Paymaster-General to the Forces, which brought him an immense fortune. With his riches he built a church at Farley, his birthplace, and also almshouses and a school there. In addition he built alms-houses, charity schools and churches in Suffolk and Northamptonshire and carried out improvements to Salisbury Cathedral. He also persuaded Charles II to found the Chelsea Hospital in 1681, the credit for which is generally ascribed to Nell Gwynne. Fox put £13,000 of his own money into its building. When James II became king he offered Fox a peerage if he would become a Roman Catholic, but Fox refused. He also refused to take an active part against James II when the Prince of Orange was brought to

England, and waited until James had left the country before paying his compliments to William III. Upon Anne's accession he wished to retire but the queen asked him to lead the Commons at her coronation procession. When he was 76 he married 26-year-old Christian, the co-heiress daughter of rector Francis Hopes. He wanted an heir and had four more children by her, one of them, Henry, becoming the first Lord Holland and father of the Whig statesman and orator Charles James Fox. Sir Stephen was knighted in 1665.

Fraser, Simon, 12th Baron Lovat (c.1667–1747)
St Peter ad Vincula, Tower of London, London.

Jacobite intriguer who reputedly acted as traitor to both sides. During the rebellion of 1745 he acted with characteristic duplicity. But, following the defeat of Bonnie Prince Charlie's army at Culloden in 1746, the Hanoverian army moved against Lord Lovat whose professions of loyalty to George II did not deceive them. Arrested on an island in Loch Morar he was brought to London and executed on 9 April 1747, the last peer to be executed for treason.

Freyberg, Bernard Cyril, 1st Baron Freyberg (1889–1963)
St Paul's Cathedral, London, in the crypt.

During the First World War he distinguished himself for bravery, particularly for his exploit in swimming ashore at Gallipoli ahead of the troops and lighting flares on the peninsula in the Gulf of Xeros to draw enemy tanks away from the true landing place. In the Second World War he commanded the New Zealand Expeditionary Force.

Gladstone, William Ewart (1809–1888)
Westminster Abbey, London, in the North Transept.

Liberal statesman. He entered Parliament in 1832 as a Conservative. He held office under Sir Robert Peel and was a convinced Free Trader. It was as a Peelite that he joined the coalition government of Whigs and Peelites under Lord Aberdeen, becoming Chancellor of the Exchequer and introducing his first budget on 18 April 1853. He became Liberal Prime Minister for the first time in 1868, his administration lasting until 1872 during which time it introduced the 1870 Education Act. He was Prime Minister again from 1880 to 1885, in 1886 and from 1892 to 1894, but he was never able to carry Home Rule for Ireland which he strongly advocated.

Gordon, General Charles George (1833–1885)
Recumbent effigy only in St Paul's Cathedral, London.

A Scotsman who, after distinguished service in the Crimea and in China, where he was instrumental in suppressing the Taiping rebellion, entered the service of the Khedive in Egypt. In 1877 he was made Governor of the Sudan but he resigned after three years owing to exhaustion. In 1884, following the rising of the Mahdi in the Sudan, he was asked by the British government to oversee the evacuation of the Egyptians from the Sudan, and he proceeded to Khartoum. Before he could complete the evacuation, the Mahdi's forces besieged the city and Gordon was murdered by the rebels on 26 January 1885 before the British relief force under Lord Wolseley could save him. His death was followed by an outburst of grief in Britain and in other countries. His body was not recovered.

Gorges, Sir Ferdinando (c. 1566–1647)
St Budiana Church, Victoria Road, St Budeaux, Plymouth, Devon.

English colonial pioneer and founder of Maine, receiving the Royal Charter in 1639. He was an advocate, especially in later life, of the feudal type of colony. He wrote the *Briefe Narration of the Originall Undertakings of the Advancement of Plantations into the Parts of America*.

Gorst, Sir John Eldon (1835–1916)
St Andrew's Churchyard, Castle Combe, Wiltshire.

Founder of the Primrose League, the Conservative Party's organization for supporters. Born in Preston, Lancashire, he went to St John's College, Cambridge. In New Zealand he became popular with the Maoris but he and his wife barely escaped death in a Maori rebellion. Back in England he was called to the bar at the Inner Temple and, as MP for Cambridge, he became friendly with Benjamin Disraeli the prime minister, whose favourite flower was believed to be the primrose. He became solicitor-general in 1875, afterwards holding several other ministerial offices. He wrote *Children of the Nation* (1906) and switched to the Liberal Party in 1909. Unsuccessful as its Preston candidate a year later, he retired from public office.

Grant, Bernard Alexander Montgomery, 'Bernie', MP (1944–2000)
Tottenham Cemetery, North London.

Labour MP and rights campaigner. Bernie Grant was born in British Guyana in 1944. He came to Britain in 1963, working as a British

Railways clerk before becoming a trade unionist. In 1975 he joined the Labour Party and was elected to Haringey borough council two years later. He worked on the council for ten years, until in 1987 he was elected MP for Tottenham. He remained MP for Totttenham until his death thirteen years later, seeing his constituents through the troubled times of the Broadwater Farm estate racial riots.

Throughout his political life Bernie Grant was an outspoken campaigner on behalf of Black people in his constituency, at home, and abroad. He famously campaigned for an inquiry into police conduct during the investigation into the murder of black teenager, Stephen Lawrence. He was also a longstanding friend of Nelson Mandela and organised the African Reparations Movement. His funeral was probably the largest funeral for a Black person that Britain has ever seen, and his coffin was carried through the streets of his constituency before the ceremony at Alexandra Palace.

Hardy, Sir Thomas Masterman (1769–1839)
In the mausoleum of the Greenwich Naval Hospital cemetery, between the present National Maritime Museum and Davenport Home for nurses. The cemetery is not at present accessible to visitors.

Vice-Admiral at the Battle of Trafalgar aboard HMS *Victory* with Nelson at the latter's death. Hardy had been born at Long Bredy, Dorset and was twelve years old when he joined the navy, leaving it shortly for school, then the merchant service. He returned to naval service in 1790 and first served with Nelson in 1796. He was on the *Victory*'s quarter-deck when Nelson received his mortal musket-shot wound in 1805 at Trafalgar. With his dying breath Nelson probably whispered to Hardy, 'Kismet (fate), Hardy', his words later being misinterpreted as 'Kiss me, Hardy'. Hardy served in the North and South American Stations after being created a baronet in 1806; he was later made KCB (1815) and GCB (1831). He was promoted to rear-admiral in 1825 and vice-admiral in 1837 while serving as Governor of Greenwich Naval Hospital, during which service he died. There is a large memorial to him on Black Down, near his Dorset birthplace.

Note: Also buried in the mausoleum were Admiral Sir Richard Goodwin **Keats** (1757–1834), Vice-Admiral Sir Thomas Boulden **Thompson** (1766?–1828), Admiral Sir John **Colpoys** (1724?–1821) and Admiral Samuel Hood, 1st Viscount **Hood** (1724–1816), who served under Admiral Lord Rodney (whom see); Keats and Thompson both served with or under Nelson.

Harvey, Sir Eliab (1758–1830)
St Andrew's Church, Hempstead, Essex.

English sailor who commanded the *Fighting Téméraire* at the Battle of Trafalgar where his skill and valour earned him promotion to rear-admiral. Later he was court-martialled and dismissed the service for the public manner in which he showed his disapproval of the promotion of Lord Cochrane to a special command; but in March 1810 he was reinstated with full rank and seniority 'in consideration of his long and meritorious services'. However, he was never employed again and in 1820 and 1826 he served as a Member of Parliament for Essex.

Hastings, Warren (1732–1818)
St Peter's Church, Daylesford, Gloucestershire.

Governor-General of British India for the East India Company. He reformed the finances and the administration and suppressed discontent. When he returned to England he was impeached before Parliament for corruption and though acquitted his defence impoverished him. However, the East India Company gave him an annuity and later he became a member of the Privy Council.

Jellicoe, John Rushworth, 1st Earl Jellicoe (1859–1935)
St Paul's Cathedral, London, in the crypt.

Commander-in-Chief of the Grand Fleet in World War I, who planned the strategy of the Battle of Jutland in 1916. As the victory was inconclusive he was censured by many and dismissed by the Prime Minister, David Lloyd George. From 1920 to 1924 he was Governor-General of New Zealand.

Heath, Sir Edward (1916–2005)
Salisbury Cathedral, Wiltshire.

Conservative Prime Minister (1970–1974). Heath had an early taste of Tory leadership when he was elected president of the Oxford Conservative Association in 1937 and president of the Oxford Union the following year. During the war he served in the Royal Artillery and he remained in Germany to attend the Nuremberg Trials in 1946. These experiences helped to form his lifelong commitment to a united Europe.

In the 1950 general election, Heath was elected as MP for Bexley. As Lord Privy Seal he tried to negotiate entry into the Common Market, but was vetoed by Charles De Gaulle. He became leader of the Conservative party in 1965 and in 1970 won the General Election with a

Warren Hastings by Lawrence

majority of thirty seats. He believed his greatest achievement was Britain's eventually successful application to join the European Economic Community. However, in domestic matters he was less successful and his term was beset with industrial disputes and unofficial strikes. In 1973, he was forced to call a general election, which he lost, and the following year Margaret Thatcher succeeded in her leadership challenge.

He remained for many years a disgruntled and critical backbencher and joined the House of Lords in 2001.

Hogg, Quintin McGarel, 2nd Viscount Hailsham and Baron Hailsham of St Marylebone (1907–2001)
All Saints Churchyard, Herstmonceux, East Sussex.

Politician and lawyer. Quintin Hogg was a successful lawyer and politician. He took silk in 1953 and at the age of forty-nine became MP for St Marylebone, like his father before him. He had many roles in Macmillan's cabinet and disclaimed his peerage in 1963 in order to stand for the leadership of the Conservative Party. He was granted a life peerage as Baron Hailsham of St Marylebone in 1970 when Edward Heath made him Lord Chancellor. In 1979 Margaret Thatcher also invited him to become Lord Chancellor. Lord Hailsham left office in 1987.

Jenkins, Roy, Lord Jenkins of Hillhead (1920–2003)
St Augustines, East Hendred, Oxfordshire.

Politician. Roy Jenkins was born in the mining valleys of South-East Wales and was immersed in Labour politics from an early age.

He gained a First at Balliol College, Oxford, before serving as a captain in the Royal Artillery during the Second World War. He also worked as a codebreaker and helped to crack the Enigma machine at Bletchley Park. After the war Jenkins entered Parliament as a Labour MP, like his father before him. He was a supporter of the right-wing leader, Hugh Gaitskell, although he was also a committed pro-European.

In 1965 he was made Home Secretary under the leadership of Harold Wilson. He oversaw radical social reforms, including the legalisation of abortion and homosexuality, and became known as 'the architect of the permissive society'. As Chancellor of the Exchequer, he was accused of losing the 1970 general election, due to his reluctance to make big tax cuts. Whilst in Opposition Jenkins found himself increasingly frustrated with the anti-European stance of the Labour Party. Against the views of his party, he led the successful 1975 referendum campaign to keep

Britain in Europe and was rewarded with the first British Presidency of the European Commission.

Back in Britain he formed the 'Gang of Four', with fellow ex-Cabinet Ministers Shirley Williams, David Owen and Bill Rodgers. Together they broke away from the Labour Party to create the Social Democratic Party (SDP) in 1981. Jenkins and Owen soon fell out but Jenkins went on to lead the new party for a year and fought the 1983 elections alongside the Liberals. The two parties were later to merge to become the SDLP. Jenkins entered the House of Lords in 1987 after losing his seat.

Kempthorne, Sir John (1621–1679)
St Thomas's Cathedral, Portsmouth, Hampshire.

Vice-Admiral and the son of a Devonshire attorney, he first went to sea in trading ships sailing from Exeter. He seems to have become rich, probably from booty, on Levant Company ships in the Mediterranean, and married a 'young person belonging to the Turkish ambassador's lady'. He was taken prisoner when his ship *Eastland Merchant* was captured by a notorious Spanish cruiser, but he was soon released and sent home. When the captain of the Spanish cruiser was captured by an English squadron and imprisoned in the Tower of London, Kempthorne is said to have arranged his release through an exchange of prisoners. In 1664 he joined the king's service as captain, was in battle the next year aboard the *Royal James* and, within another year, after a four-day action off the North Foreland aboard the *Royal Charles*, was promoted from flag-captain to Rear-Admiral of the Blue by Prince Rupert. After several more battles, during which a false report came that the French had burnt English ships in the Medway and entered the Channel, Kempthorne in 1669 hoisted his flag on the *Mary Rose* (IV). In this ship, after taking the English ambassador to Tangiers, he retook an English vessel from some Algerian pirates. Off Cadiz on his way back and after being driven north by a violent gale, he was attacked by six Algerian ships, but a lucky shot 'between the wind and the water' struck the Algerian admiral's ship. He hauled off, followed by the others. The *Mary Rose*, her rigging badly cut and with 11 men killed and 17 wounded, put into Cadiz the next day. On his return to England, Kempthorne was knighted for great valour 'against the pirates of Algiers'. After another fierce engagement in 1673 he was made Vice-Admiral.

Since the raising of the *Mary Rose* (I) of Henry VIII's reign from the Solent in 1982 generated great interest we should recapitulate the others:

Mary Rose (II) saw action against the Spanish Armada and carried Sir Walter Raleigh to the Azores; *Mary Rose* (III) was wrecked off the coast of Flanders in 1650; *Mary Rose* (IV) was Kempthorne's; *Mary Rose* (V) was sunk during action in 1917.

Law, Andrew Bonar (1858–1923)
Westminster Abbey, London, in the centre of the Nave.
 Conservative politician who was born in Canada. He held high office in Lloyd George's governments and succeeded him as Prime Minister from 23 October 1922 to 22 May 1923. He was a firm opponent of Irish Home Rule.

Macaulay, Thomas Babington, 1st Baron (1800–1859)
Westminster Abbey, London, in the South Transept now known as 'Poets' Corner', at the foot of Addison's statue.
 Historian and politician. Entered Parliament as Whig Member for Calne in 1830 and for Leeds in 1831. He held many offices including that of Secretary for War, 1839–1841, and Paymaster of the Forces, 1846–1847. His *History of England* appeared first in 1849, volumes one and two, the final two in 1855. He published a collection of his essays in 1843 and his 'Lays of Ancient Rome' in 1842, which was an attempt to reconstruct the lost ballad-poetry of Rome out of which its traditional history was thought to have grown.

Macmillan, Maurice Harold, 1st Earl of Stockton (1894–1986)
St Giles's Church, Horsted Keynes, East Sussex, in family plot with surrounding hedge.
 A Conservative Prime Minister who first became an MP in 1924 for Stockton-on-Tees, becoming successively Minister of Housing, Minister of Defence and Foreign Secretary in the 1951–55 period under Churchill, and succeeding Sir Anthony Eden (whom see) as Prime Minister in 1957. After the Vassal spy case and the 'Profumo scandal' he resigned in 1963 because of ill-health. A classical scholar at Balliol College, Oxford, he served in the Grenadier Guards during the First World War and was seriously wounded. After the war he became ADC to the Governor-General of Canada, the Duke of Devonshire, marrying his daughter Dorothy (d. 1966). During World War II he was Minister of Supply under Churchill and later Colonial Under-secretary. In his 'winds of change' speech at Cape Town in 1960 he accepted that African colonies would have to be given their independence. He wrote six autobiographical works.

Marlborough, John Churchill, 1st Duke of (1650–1722)
Chapel of Blenheim Palace, Woodstock, Oxfordshire. The coffins of the
Duke and his Duchess are in the vaults behind glass, those of their
descendants stacked on shelves nearby.

Brilliant general who won the famous battles of Blenheim (1704),
Ramillies (1706), Oudenarde (1708) and Malplaquet (1709), against the
French for which he was created a duke and granted a pension by a
grateful Parliament. His wife, Sarah Jennings, was a close friend and
favourite of Queen Anne. He was the ancestor of Sir Winston Churchill.

Methuen, Paul Sanford, 3rd Baron Methuen of Corsham (1845–1932)
St Bartholomew's Churchyard, Corsham, Wiltshire; by the east path,
large square grave.

Called the 'father of the British army' at a time when he was one of its
oldest living officers. During the Boer War he was widely criticized for
not pressing the enemy and following up some victories in his attempt to
relieve the besieged Mafeking. The truth was that the force of 10,000
under his command was far too small and suffered, through no fault of
their own, from lack of communications and supplies. Lord Roberts, the
Commander-in-Chief of British forces there, with Lord Kitchener,
Chief of Staff, retained Methuen, who later had considerable success in
the Western Transvaal when most officers of his seniority had gone
home. Towards the end of the war bad discipline and misconduct of
half-trained irregular troops caused him to be defeated in a critical battle,
wounded and taken prisoner at 57 years of age. After the war he became
Commander-in-Chief in South Africa, and after that, even though he
was in his seventieth year, Governor of Malta for another four years.
There, his foresight saw well-equipped hospitals available when needed
in the disastrous Dardanelles expedition. He had always shown three
great attributes: chivalry, great personal bravery in battle and dignified
endurance against baseless criticism. He was twice married, first in 1878,
secondly in 1884 to his cousin. In 1919 he was appointed GCMG,
having been promoted to the rank of Field-Marshal in 1911 while in
South Africa.

Milner. Lord Alfred Milner, K.G., 1st Viscount (1854–1925)
St Mary's Church, Salehurst, East Sussex, at far east edge of graveyard;
large, cambered, white-stone block designed by Sir Edwin Lutyens.

Statesman who became a powerful influence in British and South
African affairs after a brilliant scholastic career at New College, Oxford.

Memorial to John, 1st Duke of Marlborough, and his wife, Sarah, Duchess of Marlborough, in the chapel of Blenheim Palace, Woodstock, Oxfordshire

He was born at Geissen, West Germany, the only son of a Lancashire doctor. After a time as assistant editor for the *Pall Mall Gazette*, in 1889 he became under-secretary of finance in Egypt on the recommendation of Lord Goschen, whose private secretary he had been. In 1885 Milner had stood as Liberal candidate at Harrow but lost this first and only attempt to become an MP.

In Egypt, under Sir Evelyn Baring (later Earl of Cromer), he was to be praised by Baring as 'one of the most able Englishmen who had served the Egyptian government'. After three years he was recalled in 1892 by Lord Goschen to become chairman of the Board of Inland Revenue. Sent by Joseph Chamberlain to Egypt again, as governor of the Cape Colony and the Transvaal, and later high commissioner for South Africa, Milner was there from 1897 to 1905, receiving his barony in 1901 and viscountcy in 1902 for services prior to and during the Boer War.

During the First World War he had, at a critical stage, brought about harmony and co-operation between French and British forces at an Allied Conference in 1918; it marked the turning-point of the war. After his resignation owing to exhaustion, in 1921, he married and devoted himself to work in the City and to writing. His *Questions of the Hour* appeared in 1923, after which he paid a final visit to South Africa, where it is thought he caught the sleeping sickness from which he died after a brief illness at his home Sturry Court, near Canterbury.

Monck, George, 1st Duke of Albemarle (1608–1670)
Henry VII's Chapel, Westminster Abbey, London, in the south aisle; his funeral armour is now in the Undercroft Museum.

General and admiral who, following the resignation of Richard Cromwell in 1659, was largely responsible for the restoration of Charles II to the throne. Created a duke by a grateful sovereign, he was made Lord of the Admiralty in 1665, remained in charge of the government in London during the plague of 1665, and fought with the fleet in the Anglo–Dutch naval war of 1666. He died on 3 January 1670, standing, it is said, 'upright in his chair like a Roman soldier, his chamber like a tent, open with all the soldiers about him.'

Montgomery, Bernard Law, 1st Viscount of Alamein (1887–1976)
Holy Cross Churchyard, Binsted, Hampshire.

Field-Marshal Montgomery was best known for his North Africa campaigns during the second world war, when his 8th Army won the Battle of Alamein and drove the German Afrika Corps under Field-

Grave of Field-Marshal Viscount Montgomery of Alamein, Holy Cross Churchyard, Binsted, Hampshire

Marshal Rommel back to Tunisia. The 8th Army then went on to invade Sicily and Italy. After helping to plan the Normandy invasion he became Commander-in-Chief of the British Group of Armies and Allied Armies in Northern France in 1944. From 1951 to 1958 he served as Deputy Supreme Allied Commander Europe (NATO).

Mountbatten, Lord Francis Albert Victor Nicholas, 1st Earl Mountbatten of Burma (1900–1979)
Romsey Abbey Church, Romsey, Hampshire, in the south transept.

Great-grandson of Queen Victoria, he joined the British navy and fought at the Battle of Jutland in 1916. During the second world war he became chief of combined operations in 1942. As the last Viceroy of India he transferred power to the hands of the Indian government in 1947, becoming the first Governor-General of the Dominion of India. In 1955 he became the First Sea Lord and from 1959 to 1965 he was Chief of the Defence Staff. He was assassinated by the Irish Republican Army in 1979 whilst on holiday in County Sligo, Eire.

Napier, Sir Charles (1786–1860)
All Saints' Churchyard, Catherington, Hampshire; table-tomb hidden behind undergrowth on east side.

Admiral of the illustrious family that produced sailors, soldiers and a mathematician who invented logarithms – John Napier (1550–1617). Sir Charles was born at Merchiston Hall, Stirlingshire, and entered the navy in 1799. After service in the Miguelist Wars, for which he was made a count in the Portuguese peerage, he took Beirut from the Egyptians. He next took Acre and Sidon with his 84-gun ship *Powerful*. He received a KCB and in 1853 sailed to the Baltic in case of war with Russia. He had promised to be 'in Kronstadt or heaven within a month', a boast similar to one he had made before Portugal. But this time (after the Crimean War had begun), the land forts proved impregnable to warship bombardment. He became an MP for Southwark in 1855, and had bought an estate near Catherington in 1836, writing two books about his Portuguese and Syrian experiences.

Napier, Sir Charles James (1782–1853)
Royal Garrison Church, Portsmouth, Hampshire; tomb outside the west entrance.

Known as 'the conqueror of Sind', the vast area of south-east Pakistan north of the Indus river, he was cousin to Admiral Sir Charles. He joined the army when he was 13 years of age, the son of a colonel, and with two soldier brothers, both of whom he once met being carried away wounded from a battlefield in Spain. Charles himself, as a captain in an earlier battle during the Peninsular War, was five times wounded and listed as dead, but a French drummer-boy saved his life. Taken to the French Marshal Soult's headquarters he received medical help, being then 'paroled' by Marshal Ney not to serve until exchanged. A year later he was able to rejoin his regiment and, after two horses had been killed under him, was again wounded by a shot through the face that broke his jaw. He then took part in minor operations against the Americans in the War of 1812. In 1819 he went to Greece and had 'the happiest days of his life', helping them to build roads and attempting to protect the people from feudal oppression. Here he made a deep impression on Byron, who had also gone to Greece to help. In 1834 the colonists of South Australia asked him to become their governor, but his terms were not accepted.

The taking of Sind was to free its people from the Baluchis under Amir Shir Mohamed, who were oppressing the people 'who lived in a larder and yet starved' and were robbed by taxes and by hill-tribe brigands. In March 1843, after six months of incredible fighting, cholera, courage in desperate situations against hordes of stubborn enemy forces, not to mention the temperatures of 110°F. and sun-stroke, Napier finally achieved victory at Dubba. He still remained to fight in other campaigns, including the Sikh War of 1845, but finally retired to Oaklands near Portsmouth. Apart from his military ability he was also a prolific writer on military and social subjects, even writing a historical romance called *William the Conqueror*. He died of a liver disease he had caught during his many military privations.

Nelson, Horatio, 1st Viscount Nelson (and Duke of Bronte) (1758–1805)
St Paul's Cathedral, London, in the crypt directly below the dome.

Went to sea at twelve and was made a captain in 1793. He lost both his right eye (1794) and his right arm (1797) during active service. He was made a rear-admiral in 1797 and the following year gained his notable victory over the French at Aboukir Bay. In 1805 he defeated the combined French and Spanish fleets at the Battle of Trafalgar, where he was himself killed. His body was preserved in rum during its return to England, hence the expression 'Nelson's blood'. He had no legitimate children, his sole child, Horatia, being the daughter that his notorious mistress, the beautiful Emma Lady Hamilton, bore him.

North, Frederick, 2nd Earl of Guildford, 'Lord North' (1732–1792)
All Saints Church, Wroxton, Oxfordshire.

Generally known as Lord North, although he was Earl of Guildford, he was Prime Minister from 1770 to 1782 during the important years of the War of American Independence. A man of undoubted ability he nonetheless allowed himself to be influenced wholly by the King, George III, a circumstance which gave rise to speculation about their relationship, some claiming that North was an illegitimate half-brother of the King. Although not a successful politician he was unique in winning the esteem, and almost the love, of his most bitter opponents for, as a man, he was extremely good tempered and humorous.

Palmerston, Henry John Temple, 3rd Viscount (1784–1865)
Westminster Abbey, London, North Transept central aisle.

Whig statesman who entered Parliament originally as a Tory in 1807; his title, being Irish, did not bar him from the House of Commons. His vigorous foreign policy whilst Foreign Secretary offended many including Queen Victoria, but it made him popular with the people. He became Prime Minister on 5 February 1855, a position he held with one short interval in 1858 until his death in October 1865.

Peel, Sir Robert (1788–1850)
St Peter's Church, Drayton Bassett, Staffordshire; there is a monument with an inscription in black letter and a florid Gothic canopy over.

Conservative statesman who first entered Parliament in 1809, holding office the following year in Lord Liverpool's government. In 1812 he was made Secretary for Ireland, a post he held until 1818. In 1821 he became Home Secretary and during his term he reformed and humanized the criminal law and reorganized the London police along the lines he had introduced in Ireland. With the support of the Duke of Wellington he managed to obtain the King's consent to the bill for Catholic Emancipation and in 1834, on the dismissal of Lord Melbourne, reluctantly accepted the office of Prime Minister, but he dissolved Parliament the following year. The Bedchamber Crisis of 1840 led him to test his majority in Parliament and, in 1841, in the country when he was returned with a commanding majority. The repeal of the Corn Laws, of which he was an ardent supporter, though successful, nonetheless alienated a considerable and powerful section of his Parliamentary party and he resigned in 1846.

Pitt, William (the Elder), 1st Earl of Chatham (1708–1778)
Westminster Abbey, London, North Transept central aisle.

Statesman. He entered Parliament in 1735 as Member for Old Sarum. Though disliked by the King, George II, he was invited to join the Pelham administration, and in 1757 'The Great Commoner' as he was known, was *de facto* head of the government which was nominally led by the Duke of Newcastle in the Lords. His vigorous lead in the conduct of the Seven Years' War was instrumental in the British gains in Canada and India. Out of office in 1761 following his difference with the new King's favourite, Lord Bute, he was recalled in 1766 by George III and asked to form a government, but chose to become Lord Privy Seal and accept the earldom of Chatham, remaining in that office until October 1768. Dr Johnson said of Chatham that 'Walpole was a minister given by the King to the people, but Pitt was a minister given by the people to the King.'

Pitt, William, the Younger (1759–1806)
Westminster Abbey, London, North Transept central aisle in his father's tomb; his monument is at the west end of the Nave.

Statesman. Second son of William Pitt, the Elder, Earl of Chatham. He entered Parliament at twenty-one as Member for Appleby, becoming Chancellor of the Exchequer two years later in 1782. The following year he was Prime Minister at the age of twenty-four. His first administration lasted seventeen years, until March 1801. For three years he remained in opposition until May 1804 when he once again became Prime Minister, holding that office until his death from exhaustion on 23 January 1806. He was an able minister of considerable talents, 'honest intentions and liberal opinions'.

Powell, (John) Enoch, MBE (1912–1998)
Royal Warwick Regimental Cemetery, Warwick, in his wartime uniform, after funeral service in St Mary's Collegiate Church there.

Politician and classical scholar, he will be remembered for his perceived racism as a parliamentarian who pointed out that serious problems of national unity may be caused by excessive immigration of coloured, former Commonwealth and colonial persons.

Educated at King Edward's School, Birmingham (he was born at Stechford) and at Trinity College, Cambridge, he was a brilliant classical student and linguist. He became Professor of Greek at Sydney University, Australia from 1937 to 1939, when he enlisted as a private soldier in World War II, rising to the rank of brigadier, being the youngest of that rank in the British Army. Elected as Member of Parliament in 1950 for Wolverhampton, after serving as parliamentary secretary to the Ministry of Housing, then as financial secretary to the Treasury, he resigned that post, later to become Minister of Health and a Privy Councillor. In the 1974 election he decided not to stand as a Conservative, resigning from that Party in 1983, but was later returned as an Ulster Unionist member. Awarded the MBE in 1943, he married Pamela Wilson in 1952.

It has been said that it was not the public who condemned him for his racism but the 'opinion formers', and where Churchill pointed out that genius can spring from every class and from every part of the land and come to fame, Powell perhaps forgot that such a fact of human existence is dangerous to be perceived of as cutting down. He supported a truly free world market and exposed the true cause of inflation, where excess government spending is the reason, long before such became generally accepted by both government and most voters. He was concerned that without the union of the British Isles devolution would lead to a dissolution of the monarchy and the total absorption of sundered areas of Britain into a European mega-state.

Raffles, Sir Thomas Stamford (1781–1826)
St Mary's Church, Hendon, Greater London.

Governor in Sumatra and Java and founder by name of Raffles Hotel, Singapore. Born at sea off Jamaica, he was the son of a sea captain in the West India trade. At 14 he was a clerk in the East India Company and, showing great proficiency in languages with fluency in Malay dialects, he was appointed by Sir Hugh Inglis as assistant secretary in Penang in 1805, becoming a full secretary two years later. He stopped slave trading and did much to make Singapore a prosperous free-port. On his return home to retirement in Barnet he lost all his papers and valuable belongings when his ship caught fire because of a steward's carelessness. The survivors were in an open boat for many days before being rescued. His knighthood came in 1817. He also had two botanical species named after him that he had discovered in his East India travels.

Roberts, Frederick Sleigh, 1st Earl Roberts of Kandahar, Pretoria and Waterford (1832–1914)
St Paul's Cathedral, London, in the crypt.

Field-Marshal who first entered the service of the East India

Company and took part in the suppression of the Indian Mutiny in 1857 and in the war with Afghanistan where he relieved Kandahar. In 1858 he won the Victoria Cross for saving the life of an Indian. During the Boer War he commanded the British forces in South Africa, relieving Kimberley and advancing on Pretoria. At 82 he was in France with the British Expeditionary Force at the beginning of the first world war when he caught a chill and died three days later. He was the author of *Forty Years in India*.

Rodney, George Brydges Rodney, 1st Baron (1719–1792)
St Mary's Church, Old Alresford, Hampshire.

Admiral who in 1762, during the Seven Years' War, captured the island of Martinique from the French. In 1780 he defeated the Spanish fleet and relieved Gibraltar. During the American War of Independence he once again defeated the French fleet under de Grasse.

Scott, John, first Earl of Eldon (1751–1838)
Old Church graveyard, Kingston, Dorset; monument in new church of St James (old church became church hall).

Lord Chancellor for 26 years; longer than any other holder of this office. He was the third son of a Newcastle-upon-Tyne coal merchant, who owned several barges and a public house. A fair scholar, John was sent to Oxford. On the way there a Latin motto painted on the coach, *Sat cito si sat bene* (quickly enough if well enough), so impressed him that for the rest of his life he invariably cited it as a reason for his apparent procrastination. In 1796 he had been called to the bar as a member of the Middle Temple, and his maxim was that he should 'live like a hermit and work like a horse'. He became expert in common law and equity. As a Tory Member of Parliament, he supported many Acts said to be oppressive by some, including the suspension of Habeas Corpus. But those French revolutionary days were dangerously radical, even in England. He also supported a bill that would have prohibited the marriage of a divorced adultress and her lover. In 1793 he became Attorney-General and Lord Chief Justice in 1799. He was Lord Chancellor for five years (1801–6) under William Pitt the Younger until Pitt's death in 1806. A year later he resumed the Great Seal and held it for another twenty-one years. He was an implacable enemy of Napoleon and a great friend and influencer of George III, with whom he dealt even during the king's lunacy in 1804. Created Baron of Eldon in 1799, he received the titles of Viscount Encombe and Earl of Eldon in 1821 from

George IV, and lived to take the oath in 1837 to Queen Victoria. He died of old age, a man who was at once respected and, perhaps unfairly, reviled by many for his extreme conservatism. His wife had died in 1831 and he was laid to rest beside her remains in the Old Church graveyard at Kingston, near his seat at Encombe.

Seymour, Thomas 1st Baron Seymour of Sudeley (c.1508–1549)
St Peter ad Vincula, Tower of London, London.

Younger brother of Edward, Duke of Somerset and Jane Seymour, Henry VIII's third wife. After the death of Henry VIII he married his widow, Catherine Parr, who died of fever following the birth of their daughter. According to King Henry's will he was to be made a peer of the realm and Lord High Admiral, and both orders were carried out by his nephew, Edward VI. An intriguer, he plotted against his brother, the Protector, and was executed in 1549.

Shaftesbury. Anthony Ashley Cooper, 7th Earl of (1801–1885)
St Giles's Church, Wimborne St Giles, Dorset, in the chancel.

Known as the 'philanthropic' earl, he worked to bring about the amelioration of the grim conditions of factory workers. Schools, health and other reforms came under his aegis. Florence Nightingale said that as a Crimea health commissioner he 'saved the British army'. The statue in Piccadilly Circus, popularly known as Eros, is the Shaftesbury Memorial Fountain commemorating him.

Also buried here were his predecessors, the 1st 'Protestant' Earl (1621–83) and the 3rd 'Philosopher' Earl (1671–1713), who both had the same Christian and surnames. Their forebear Sir Anthony Ashley (1551–1628), who is credited with being the first to introduce the cabbage to England, has a stylized sculpture of the vegetable on his tomb here.

Sikorski, Wladyslaw (1881–1943)
Newark Cemetery, Newark-on-Trent, Nottinghamshire.

Polish general who was commander-in-chief in the second world war until 1943 of the Polish forces. He was born in Galicia and studied engineering. A Polish patriot, he was imprisoned by the Austrians after the Treaty of Brest-Litovsk. In 1920 as commander of a Polish Infantry Division he defended Warsaw during the Russian–Polish war, becoming Poland's Prime Minister in 1922. He became leader of the Free Polish forces during the second world war and led the government-in-exile from 1940 in London. He broke off relations with Russia in 1943 when graves of Polish officers were discovered in Katyn. He died in an air accident at Gibraltar.

Somerset, Edward Seymour, 1st Duke of (c.1506–1552)
St Peter ad Vincula, Tower of London, London.

Brother of Jane Seymour, Henry VIII's third wife, and uncle to the boy King Edward VI, he headed the Council of Regency after the death of Henry VIII and became Lord Protector of the Realm. He repealed the heresy laws and nearly all the treason laws passed since Edward III and introduced the first Book of Common Prayer in 1549 which was a studious compromise between the old and new learning. His ideas of liberty were in striking contrast with those of most Tudor statesmen and the main cause of his ruin was the divergence between him and the majority of the Council over the question of constitutional liberty and the enclosure of the Commons. The majority scouted his notions of liberty and deeply resented his championship of the poor against greedy landlords and others. He was executed on the strength of an allegedly forged warrant of his nephew, the young Edward VI, on 22 January 1552.

Suffolk, William de la Pole, 1st Duke of (1396–1450)
St Andrew's Church, Wingfield, Suffolk. There is also a fine tomb and monument to his parents, the Earl and Countess of Suffolk, as well as one to his son, John, 2nd Duke of Suffolk and his wife Elizabeth, a sister of Edward IV.

'The Englishman who surrendered to Joan of Arc' at Jargeau in 1431. Henry V made him Admiral of Normandy and he served in France for fourteen years without returning to England. After his surrender to Joan of Arc he returned to English politics and set himself in opposition to the young Henry VI's uncle, the Duke of Gloucester. He arranged for the King's marriage to Margaret of Anjou, accompanying the bride to England in 1445. His earldom of Suffolk was raised first to a marquessate and then to a dukedom in 1448. Virtually the ruler of England after the death of Gloucester and Cardinal Beaufort, his peace policy gradually lost England much of her French territory. In 1450 he was arrested and sent to the Tower of London and the King, to save him from his enemies, banished him for five years. He sailed from Ipswich on May Day, 1450 but before he could enter Calais his ship was intercepted and his head was hacked from his body with 'six strokes of a rusty sword'.

Sutch, David Edward, 'Screaming Lord Sutch' (1940–1999)
Pinner Cemetery, Middlesex. His grave is no. 27 and can be found in
section J2.

Politician and singer. David Sutch first stood for parliament as the
National Teenager's Candidate in Stratford-upon-Avon, following the
resignation of John Profumo in 1963. He went on to contest forty-four
elections in total and, although he never even retained his deposit, he is
mentioned in the Guinness Book of Records as the person who has stood
for parliament the most times. As a singer he recorded with Jeff Beck
and Keith Moon, amongst others, and 'Screaming Lord Sutch' was his
stage name. In 1983 he formed the Monster Raving Looney Party and
his greatest victory came in May 1990 when he stood against David
Owen, leader of the SDP. He received 481 votes to Owen's 156 and the
former Labour Foreign Secretary retired from politics. Sutch had a
history of depression and hanged himself on 16 June 1999.

Throckmorton, Sir Nicholas (1515–1571)
Laud Memorial Chapel, St Katharine Cree Church, Leadenhall Street,
City of London.

Diplomatist who, during the nine-days reign of Lady Jane Grey,
played the friend to both sides. He secured the favour of Queen Mary
but was suspected of being implicated in Sir Thomas Wyat's rebellion
and though acquitted was sent to the Tower of London. Restored to
favour by Mary shortly after, he rose rapidly when Elizabeth ascended
the throne, becoming first her Chamberlain of the Exchequer and, from
May 1559 to April 1564, her ambassador to France where he became
acquainted with Mary Queen of Scots whilst she was Queen of France.
In May 1565 he was sent as ambassador to Mary, who had returned to
Scotland, the first of many such missions he undertook for Elizabeth to
the Scottish Queen, whom he greatly admired. In 1569, during the Duke
of Norfolk's conspiracy to secure the release of Mary, who was by now
imprisoned in England, Throckmorton fell under suspicion but was not
proceeded against. He died on 12 February 1571. His daughter, Elizabeth, married Sir Walter Raleigh.

Trenchard, Hugh Montague, 1st Viscount Trenchard (1873–1956)
Henry VII's Chapel, Westminster Abbey, London, in the small east
chapel, now known as the RAF Chapel, that forms part of the apse.

Served in the Boer War and in the Royal Flying Corps during the first
world war. As Chief of Air Staff from 1919 to 1930 he shaped offensive

Lord Sutch

strategy. He became the first air marshal of the RAF and was largely responsible for the RAF College at Cranwell. When he became Commissioner of the Metropolitan Police in 1931 he was concerned in establishing the police college at Hendon.

Unknown Warrior
Westminster Abbey, London, at the west end of the Nave.

At the suggestion of an army chaplain, the body buried in a simple grave in an Armentières garden and marked with a wooden cross on which were the words, 'An Unknown British Soldier', was brought to England and re-interred with full honours in Westminster Abbey on Armistice Day, 11 November 1920, as a symbol of the thousands of British servicemen who died during the first world war. Soil was specially brought from France for the grave and it was covered by a slab of black Belgian marble bearing an inscription written by Dean Ryle. The Congressional Medal of Honour laid on the grave by General Pershing in 1921 is affixed to a nearby pillar.

Vane, Sir Henry, the Elder (1589–1655)
St Giles's Church, Shipbourne, Kent. The original church was rebuilt by James Gibbs in 1721 to 1722 and again in 1880 to 1881.

A courtier at the court of James I who knighted him on 3 March 1611. In 1630 he became chief adviser and a Privy Councillor to Charles I and thereafter held many high offices of state, ultimately, through the influence of the Queen, Henrietta Maria, becoming Secretary of State. He played an important part in Strafford's downfall. The King was suspicious of his loyalty during the early controversy with Parliament and dismissed him from his appointments in 1641. He joined the Parliamentary faction and remained with the Parliament after the King's execution in 1649.

Vane, Sir Henry, the Younger (1613–1662)
St Giles's Church, Shipbourne, Kent. The original church was rebuilt by James Gibbs in 1721 to 1722 and again in 1880 to 1881.

A strong Puritan, son of Sir Henry Vane, the Elder. In 1635 he emigrated to Massachusetts to obtain free exercise of his religion and was made Governor of that province in 1636. He returned to England the following year and supported Parliament in its struggle with the King, being a close associate of Oliver Cromwell, addressing each other as Brother Fountain (Cromwell) and Brother Heron (Vane). In 1650 he and

Cromwell quarrelled over the structure of Parliament, Cromwell seeking an entirely new Parliament with the supremacy of the army representation. It was a permanent breach. He was arrested in 1656 and for three months imprisoned in Carisbrooke Castle. He opposed Richard Cromwell and after his abdication Vane was restored to power. At the Restoration he was arrested but his life was at first spared. Subsequently he was accused of high treason and executed on Tower Hill on 14 June 1662, Pepys describing him at his execution as being 'rather a looker-on than the person concerned in the execution'.

Waller, Edmund (1606–1687)
St Mary and All Saints Church, Beaconsfield, Buckinghamshire.

As a poet and politician he was the leader of a plot to seize London for Charles I, but to save his life he revealed his conspirators. First imprisoned in the Tower of London, he was released and banished from the country. He went to Paris where he published his *Poems* in 1645. Pardoned by Cromwell, he returned to England where he published works that praised Cromwell, but upon his death wrote poems rejoicing in Charles II's Restoration. Waller returned to parliament until his death and in 1685 his *Divine Poems* appeared; a *Second Part* was published three years after his death.

Walpole, Sir Robert, 1st Earl of Orford (1676–1745)
St Martin's Church, Houghton Hall, near King's Lynn, Norfolk.

Whig statesman who from 1721 to 1742 was the chief minister of George I and George II. Considered to be Britain's first Prime Minister, he was known as a 'House of Commons man'. During his tenure of office he strove to keep England free from war and in so doing brought stability and prosperity to the realm.

Walsingham, Sir Francis (c.1530–1590)
'Old' St Paul's Cathedral, London, his body being placed in the same tomb as that of Sir Philip Sidney.

Elected Member of Parliament for Banbury in the first Parliament of Queen Elizabeth I, which sat from January to May 1559. He was largely responsible for the efficient secret service network during Elizabeth's reign which uncovered the plots aimed at unseating Elizabeth and placing Mary Queen of Scots on the throne and also gathered exact details of Spain's intended armada against England. He undertook many diplomatic missions where he was known for his devotion to Protestantism.

Robert Walpole, from the studio of Van Loo

Stone marking the burial site of Field-Marshal Earl Wavell, Chapel of Winchester College, Hampshire

Wavell, Archibald Percival, 1st Earl of Wavell (1883–1950)
Chapel of Winchester College, Winchester, Hampshire.

General who served initially in the Boer War in South Africa. During the first world war he served on Allenby's staff in Palestine, earlier having been blinded in one eye on the Western front. As Commander-in-Chief of the allied forces in the Middle East in the second world war from 1939–1941 he defeated the Italians in North Africa but was forced back by General Rommel. After being relieved by Sir Claude Auchinleck, Wavell became Commander-in-Chief in India from 1941 to 1943, when he became Viceroy, a post he held until 1947. A writer of history, biography and poetry, he published many books.

Wellington, Arthur Wellesley, 1st Duke of (1769–1852)
St Paul's Cathedral, London, in the crypt.

Field-Marshal who was born in Ireland, son of the Earl of Mornington. He gained his military experience in India and during the Napoleonic Wars was responsible for driving the French from the Iberian peninsula. His defeat of Napoleon at Waterloo in 1815 brought an end to the French emperor's career and his permanent exile.

Wellington entered politics as a Tory, holding the office of Prime Minister from 1828 to 1830, piloting the Catholic Emancipation Bill through Parliament in 1829. He fell from office over the issue of Parliamentary reform which he did not support. When Sir Robert Peel became Prime Minister Wellington supported the repeal of the Corn Laws.

Westmorland, Ralph Neville, 1st Earl of (1364–1425)
St Mary's Church, Staindrop, Durham, magnificent memorial in church.

A supporter of Henry IV against Richard II, he later helped the King put down the revolt of the Percies of Northumberland, the rivals to the Nevilles for supremacy in the northern counties. He later married the King's half-sister, Joan Beaufort, daughter of John of Gaunt and Katharine Swynford. In May 1405 the Percies were once again in revolt and Westmorland faced a superior force at Shipton Moor led by Archbishop Scrope of York and Thomas Mowbray. By a trick Scrope disbanded his forces and Westmorland arrested him, but he is not held responsible for the Archbishop's hasty execution.

Whitelaw, William, 1st Viscount (1918–1999)
Dacre Parish Churchyard, near Penrith, Cumbria.

Politician. William Whitelaw held many important posts in his long career as a Conservative politician. He served as Chief Whip, Secretary of State for Employment as well as Home Secretary under both Edward Heath and Margaret Thatcher. However, it was his role as the first Northern Ireland Secretary in 1972–1973 that had most impact on him personally.

After graduating from Trinity College, Cambridge, Whitelaw joined the Scots Guards. He served in the army 1939–1947 and was awarded the Military Cross in the Normandy campaign. In 1955 he was elected as MP for Penrith and the Border, a position he held until 1983 when he entered the House of Lords as Leader of the House.

Whittington, Sir Richard 'Dick' (c.1358–1423)
St Michael Paternoster Royal Church, Cannon Street, City of London.
Sir Richard's body was more than once disturbed after his burial and now cannot be found. Efforts in 1949 to locate his tomb only produced a mummified cat which, however, was unlikely to have been Whittington's.

Four times Lord Mayor of London, briefly in 1397, 1398, 1406 and

1419. Despite the legend Richard Whittington was the son of a knight of Gloucestershire or Herefordshire. He became a London mercer and was wealthy enough to make large loans to the King, Henry IV, and later his son, Henry V, in return for which he obtained valuable trading concessions. The famous legend of 'Dick Whittington' was not attached to his name until after 200 years later and seems to bear little relation to the reality of his career.

Wilberforce, William (1759–1833)
Westminster Abbey, London, buried in the North Transept. His monument is in the north choir aisle of the Nave.

Parliamentary leader of the campaign to abolish the slave trade. Elected to Parliament in 1780 he worked tirelessly against slavery and was known as 'the authorized interpreter of the national conscience'. He finally succeeded when slave trading was abolished in 1807. Thereafter he worked against slavery itself but that was not abolished until 1833, the year of his death.

Wilson, Sir Henry Hughes (1864–1922)
St Paul's Cathedral, London, in the crypt.

Field-marshal who in 1914 was responsible for the preparedness of the British Expeditionary Force at the outset of the Great War. He was elected to Parliament on a Conservative ticket for North Down in Northern Ireland in February 1921 but was assassinated by two Sinn Feiners on the doorstep of his London house the following year.

Wilson, Sir James Harold, K.G., 1st Baron of Rievaulx (1926–1995)
St Mary the Virgin churchyard, St Mary's, Isles of Scilly.

Labour prime minister of Britain, he was elected in 1964, 1966 and 1970 during the years of contentious Common Market negotiations, Rhodesian sanctions and balance-of-payments crises. Born at Huddersfield, he completed his education at Oxford, where he also became a lecturer in economics. After serving in the wartime Ministry of Fuel and Power he eventually became the youngest cabinet minister since Pitt. He was first elected in Ormskirk as a member of parliament.

Wolfe, James (1727–1759)
St Alfege's Church, Greenwich, London, in the crypt under 'Canadian Corner'; large statue on Observatory Hill.

British general who, defeating the French at the Plains of Abraham,

James Wolfe, by an unknown artist

Quebec, won Canada for the British but was mortally wounded on the battlefield. Born in Kent, he was the son of a general and served as an ensign at the age of 16 at the Battle of Dettingen – the last battle in which a British monarch (George II) personally led his troops. After further battle service in Scotland against the Jacobites, during which he was wounded, Wolfe commanded troops at Cape Breton as a colonel in 1758, capturing Louisburg. In 1759, after training 9000 men at

Hambledon Hill in Dorset, he sailed with them to Canada, where at dawn his force successfully scaled a poorly guarded part of the cliffs below Quebec city to defeat the French General Montcalm, who was killed in the action. Wolfe himself lived to know that his troops had been victorious before he died on the battlefield.

Wyat, Sir Thomas (1503–1542)
Abbey Church, Sherborne, Dorset; the stone in the north transept marks his grave.

Statesman and poet who was reputedly in love with Anne Boleyn before her marriage to Henry VIII. In 1509 he was made a Knight of the Bath on the accession of Henry VIII and he held various court offices. In 1536 he was arrested and imprisoned in the Tower of London, perhaps to incriminate Queen Anne Boleyn, but was released after a month. Knighted in 1537 he was sent as the King's ambassador to the Emperor Charles V. Subsequently he fell from Henry's favour but was later restored. He died of a fever at Sherborne on 11 October 1542 whilst escorting the Emperor's ambassadors from Falmouth to London. Henry Howard, Earl of Surrey, celebrated his death in these lines: 'Wyat resteth here, that quick could never rest.'

Chapter 4
Churchmen

Alban, Saint (d.c.303)
St Alban's Cathedral, St Albans, Hertfordshire, shrine reconstructed from fragments after original destroyed at the Reformation.

Usually styled the protomartyr of Britain, he is reputed to have been born at Verulamium (the modern St Albans) and to have served seven years in Rome as a soldier in the army of the Emperor Diocletian. On his return to Britain he settled in his native town and was put to death as a Christian during Diocletian's persecutions of the sect. About 793, King Offa of Mercia erected a church on the spot where he was alleged to have been killed, and later a monastery was added. He is commemorated in the Roman martyrology on 22 June.

Anselm, Saint (1033–1109)
St Anselm's Chapel, Canterbury Cathedral, Canterbury, Kent.

Archbishop of Canterbury who was born at Aosta in Piedmont into a noble family. At 27, after a disagreement with his father, he became a monk in the monastery of Bec, whose prior was the celebrated Lanfranc. When Lanfranc became Abbot of Caen in about 1063 Anselm was elected prior and, in 1078, Abbot of Bec. Under his rule Bec became the first seat of learning in Europe, due more to the great moral influence of his noble character and kindly discipline than to his intellectual powers. Anselm travelled often to England to supervize the monastery's possessions there and during these journeys he impressed the English greatly, so that on the death of Lanfranc he was regarded as his natural successor as Archbishop of Canterbury. But the King, William II, at Lanfranc's death seized the possessions and revenues of Canterbury and refused to appoint a new archbishop. After four years, in 1092, Anselm reluctantly agreed to travel to England to accept the see and was consecrated in 1093. The King's quarrel with Rome over who was responsible for investing the Archbishop caused friction between him and Anselm, and when in 1097 Anselm was finally allowed to travel to Rome he remained abroad until after William's death, being recalled by his successor, King Henry I. Again the question of the investiture was raised and once again Anselm travelled to Rome to seek papal guidance. The threat of excommunication against Henry finally brought about a resolution to the conflict, Henry renouncing his formal rights in 1107. Thereafter, Anselm spent his remaining years of life carrying out his pastoral duties. He died on 21 April 1109 and was canonized by Pope Alexander VI in 1494.

Ascham, Roger (c.1515–1568)
Church of the Holy Sepulchre without Newgate, Holborn, London.

Scholar and writer who was born in Yorkshire and educated in the household of Sir Humphrey Wingfield, Speaker of the House of Commons. At fifteen he went to St John's College, Cambridge, where he came under the influence of John Cheke. On the presentation of his book, *Toxophilus*, 'On the art of Shooting' (the long bow) to King Henry VIII he received an annual pension of £10. Shortly after the accession of Edward VI Ascham declared himself a supporter of the Reformed religion and in 1548 was appointed tutor to the young Princess Elizabeth. After two years he quarrelled with the steward and returned to Cambridge. During Queen Mary's reign he was her Latin Secretary and in 1555 he resumed his studies with the Princess Elizabeth. A humanist, he wrote a treatise, *The Schoolmaster*, on 'the right order of teaching', which was the first definite demonstration in favour of humanity in education.

Beaufort, Henry (d.1447)
Winchester Cathedral, Winchester, Hampshire, chantry in the south retro-choir.

Cardinal bishop of Winchester who completed the building of the cathedral itself, which had been largely rebuilt from Norman times by William of Wykeham (whom see) whose tomb and chantry are also in the south nave. Beaufort was the illegitimate son of John of Gaunt and Catherine Swyneford, and Henry V forbade him to accept the cardinalate, but in 1432 he defeated an attempt to deprive him of his see, because he was a cardinal, by the Duke of Gloucester. Beaufort crowned Henry VI king of France in 1431 in Paris and, in 1439–40, tried to arrange peace with France.

Becket, Thomas à, Saint (c.1118–1170)
Canterbury Cathedral, Kent. The original shrine was destroyed in 1538 during the Dissolution and Becket's bones were scattered. His skull, however, is reputed to have been preserved in or under the Corona, also known as 'Becket's Crown', at the extreme east end of the Cathedral.

A member of the household of Theobald Archbishop of Canterbury who, because of Becket's success in dissuading the Roman Curia from sanctioning the coronation of Stephen's son Eustace, recommended him for the appointment of Archdeacon of Canterbury which Becket accepted after becoming a deacon in 1154. The following year, the new King, Henry II, made him Chancellor. In 1162 Theobald died but before doing so he advised Henry II to appoint Becket in his place as Archbishop; Theobald seeing in Becket a champion of the Church's privileges and rights which the old Archbishop felt would soon be under attack from Henry II. Henry, however, sanctioned the appointment under the misapprehension that Becket would foremost be a king's man, and soon discovered his error, for the new Archbishop proved himself anything other than the King's tool, devoting himself uncompromisingly to the service of the Church. A dispute over the land tax at the Council of Woodstock in July 1163 brought Becket and Henry into open conflict and when Becket and his churchmen were required to approve the Constitutions of Clarendon, in which the King defined the relations between Church and State, Becket refused, supported by the Pope, although some of the bishops accepted the constitutions. He fled to France in November 1164 and succeeded in getting Pope Alexander III to condemn the constitutions formally. Pressure by the Pope effected a reconciliation at Fréteval on 22 July 1170 and Becket returned to England. However, he would not compromise his stand, taking steps to punish those bishops who had supported the King, and declared the Constitutions of Clarendon null and void. Within a month of his return to Canterbury, on 29 December 1170, he was murdered by four of Henry's knights at Canterbury. He was canonized two years later and his shrine became a place of pilgrimage.

Bede, The Venerable, Saint (c.673–735)
Durham Cathedral, Durham, County Durham, in the Galilee Porch.

Historian and theologian who, from the age of seven, spent his entire life in the monasteries of Wearmouth, founded by Benedict Biscop in 647, and Jarrow, founded about 681 or 682. He was ordained a deacon at nineteen, which was below the canonical age, and a priest at thirty. His *Ecclesiastical History of the English Nation* justly earned him the title Father of English History. There is a touching account of his death in a contemporary letter which tells us that his last hours were spent, like most of his life, in devotion and teaching, his latest work being to dictate a translation into the vernacular of the Gospel of St John.

Tomb of The Venerable Bede, Durham Cathedral, Durham

Bere, Richard (d.1524)
Glastonbury Abbey (ruins), Glastonbury, Somerset, near the Holy
Sepulchre on the south side.

Abbot of Glastonbury who was known equally for his scholarship, his
passion for building, and for his controversy with Archbishop Warham
of Canterbury over the siting of the relics of St Dunstan; the Archbishop
claiming they were at Canterbury, Abbot Bere claiming that as the shrine
was at Glastonbury, the popularity of which had caused jealousy at
Canterbury, the relics should be returned to Glastonbury. The quarrel
was resolved at the Dissolution with the general pillage of religious
houses, by which time Bere was dead.

Birinus, Saint (d.650)
Abbey Church, Dorchester, Oxfordshire. His body was later removed to
Winchester and there enshrined by Bishop Ethelwold (963–984).

Bishop of Dorchester. A Benedictine monk whom Pope Honorius sent
to Britain to convert the island. He landed in Wessex in 634 and the
following year baptized Cynegils King of Wessex. He founded the see of
Dorchester and became its first bishop. The *Anglo-Saxon Chronicle*
indicates that his influence was widespread and credits him with the
conversion of many princes.

Bodley, Sir Thomas (1545–1613)
Chapel of Merton College, Oxford, Oxfordshire.

Diplomat and scholar. During the reign of Queen Mary I he lived in
Geneva where his father, because of his Protestant sympathies, had been
obliged to move. On the accession of Elizabeth I the family returned to
England and Thomas entered Magdalen College, Oxford. After a tour of
Europe he returned to become Gentleman Usher to the Queen. In 1584
he entered Parliament as the Member for Portsmouth, and the following
year began his diplomatic career with a mission to the Protestant princes
of northern Europe to secure aid for Henry of Navarre. In 1588 he was
sent as minister to the Hague, but, because of intrigues at home, he
begged to be recalled, returning to England in 1604. His best remembered achievement was the endowment of the Bodleian Library at
Oxford for which he left the greater part of his fortune.

Bowett, Henry (d.1423)
The Lady Chapel, York Minster, York.

Diplomat and churchman. As Chaplain to Pope Urban VI he was the only Englishman at the papal court courageous enough to remain with the Pope after the riots at Lucia in 1385. During the reign of Richard II he was made Chief Justice of the Superior Court of Aquitaine, 1397, and in the following year Constable of Bordeaux. A supporter of Boling-broke, later Henry IV, he incurred Richard's disfavour and was banished, sentence of execution being commuted. On Henry's accession he became an influential adviser to the King, being appointed one of the regents for Henry's possessions in southern France. Appointed to the see of Bath and Wells in 1400, he was, shortly after returning from a Danish embassy, made Archbishop of York, the see having been vacant for two years following the execution of Archbishop Scrope. In 1417, despite his age and the fact that he had to be carried in a litter, he accompanied the army to fight the Scots, and his example was a contributory factor in the English victory.

Cantelupe, Thomas de, Saint (c.1218–1282)
Hereford Cathedral, Hereford, north transept.

English prelate and saint. Educated at Paris and Orléans, afterwards he taught Canon Law at Oxford and became Chancellor of the University in 1262. A supporter of Simon de Montfort in the Barons' War he represented the barons before St Louis of France at Amiens in 1264. He was made Chancellor of England but lost his position after the death of de Montfort at Evesham in the same year, 1265, and went to live abroad. Returning to England he once more became Chancellor of Oxford University and in 1275 was made Bishop of Hereford and became a trusted adviser to the new King Edward I. In 1279 he revisited Italy and died at Orvieto on 25 August 1282. He was canonized in 1330 by Pope John XXII after many miracles were reputed to have occurred at his shrine.

Coggan, Dr Frederick Donald, Lord Coggan of Canterbury and Sissinghurst (1909–2000)
St Albans Cathedral.

Archbishop of Canterbury. Donald Coggan was born in Highgate, London, on 17 May 1909. He was a distinguished Hebrew scholar and worked as a lecturer in Semitic languages at Manchester University from 1931 to 1934. The following year he was ordained as a priest but continued with his academic work, becoming professor of the New Testament at Wycliffe College, Toronto, in 1937. He returned to England in 1944 to take up a position as principal of the London College of Divinity.

In 1956 Dr Coggan was appointed Bishop of Bradford and he succeeded Michael Ramsey as Archbishop of York in 1965. He took over from Michael Ramsey again, this time as Archbishop of Canterbury, in 1974. Dr Coggan is remembered for his support for the ordination of women, which he first proposed at the Lambeth Conference in 1970 whilst still Archbishop of York. However, it was something that did not come to pass until 1994, fourteen years after his retirement.

Cranmer, Thomas (1489–1556)
Burned at the stake near Balliol College, Oxford; a cross on the surface of Broad Street, opposite Balliol College, Oxford, marks the spot where the burning took place.

Archbishop of Canterbury under Henry VIII and Edward VI and an ardent supporter of the Reformation. He was brought to the attention of Henry VIII when he suggested that the King's marriage to Catherine of Aragon could be declared null and void without recourse to Rome if the canonists and the universities should decide that the marriage with a deceased brother's widow was illegal. He pleaded the King's cause in Rome in 1530 and before the Emperor in Germany in 1531. Henry VIII appointed him to the see of Canterbury in 1532 and he was consecrated on 30 March 1533. He declared the King's marriage to Catherine null and void and pronounced the marriage of Henry to Anne Boleyn to be valid. On 1 June 1533 he crowned Anne as Queen and on 10 September that year stood as godfather to the baby Princess Elizabeth. At the death of Edward VI he supported the accession of Lady Jane Grey and he alone remained true to her cause. When Mary acceded Cranmer was first confined to Lambeth Palace and then in September 1553 removed to the Tower of London with the bishops Latimer and Ridley. In February 1556 he was degraded from his archbishopric and he recanted his allegiance to the Reformation. When he was asked to repeat his 'Recantations' publicly on 21 March 1556 he refused and affirmed his belief in Protestantism. He was then burned at the stake, extending his right hand to the flames as the instrument of his recantation.

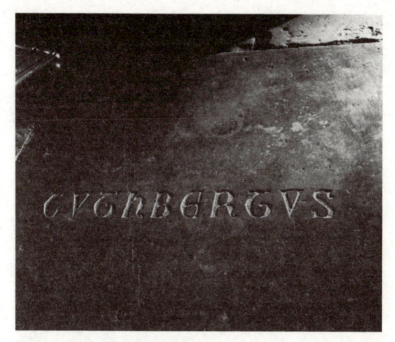

Shrine of St Cuthbert, Durham Cathedral, Durham

Cuthbert, Saint (d.687)
Durham Cathedral, Durham, County Durham; his shrine lies behind the High Altar.

Bishop of Lindisfarne. He was probably Northumbrian by birth and is reputed to have taken monastic vows after a vision at the death of Bishop Aidan and to have entered Melrose Abbey about 651. Bede, to whom we owe our knowledge of Cuthbert's life, informs us that he became Prior of Melrose in 661 and was transferred to Lindisfarne in 664 where he was also Prior. In 671 he became an anchorite on the island of Farne and is said to have performed miracles. At the instigation of King Ecgfrith of Northumbria he gave up his solitary life and became Bishop of Hexham in 685, afterwards exchanging the see for that of Lindisfarne. In 687 he retired to Farne, dying on the island on 20 March 687.

Darby, John Nelson (1800–1882)
Wimborne Road Cemetery, Bournemouth, Dorset; in the south-west section near the main path.

Founder of the Darbyites, a breakaway sect from the Plymouth

Brethren. The sect rejected all forms of distinction in denominational religion, and Darby wrote voluminously and travelled widely in the furtherance of his cause. In 1838 he worked in Switzerland for two years opposing Methodism, but Jesuit intrigue put his life in jeopardy when revolution broke out in the canton of Vaud. In 1854 he made a great impact in Germany when he translated the New Testament into German, and his travels took him to the United States, Canada, New Zealand and the West Indies, as well as to Germany. Pilgrims from Germany regularly visit his grave.

De La Mare, Thomas (1309–1396)
St Alban's Cathedral, St Albans, Hertfordshire.
   Abbot of St Albans and a member of Edward III's council. He resisted the attempts of Wat Tyler during the Peasants' Revolt of 1381 to 'shave the heads of the Abbot, Prior and monks' and to ransack St Albans.

Despenser, Henry le (c.1341–1406)
Norwich Cathedral, Norwich, Norfolk, before the high altar.
   Became Bishop of Norwich in 1370 and was known as the 'warlike bishop' for his military prowess. He put down a rising of Norfolk peasantry during the Peasants' Revolt of 1381 with great severity. In 1382 he led the forces of Pope Urban VI on a crusade against the supporters of the anti-Pope, Clement VII, in Flanders, but his army was defeated by the French and decimated by disease. A strong supporter of Richard II, he stood by the King after his deposition and was imprisoned. Released, he made his peace with Henry IV. A fierce opponent of the Lollards, whose leader, John Wycliffe, had denounced the Bishop's Crusade in Flanders.

Dunstan, Saint (924–988)
Canterbury Cathedral, Canterbury, Kent; the diaper on the south wall above the altar steps is considered to be part of his shrine.
   Archbishop of Canterbury. As a boy he entered the household of King Athelstan but was later banished. Recalled by King Edmund, he was made one of the King's counsellors. Again he was banished through the machinations of his enemies but shortly after Edmund revoked the order and made him Abbot of Glastonbury. Edmund's successor, Edred, showed him greater favour, but, at the succession of Edwy in 955, Dunstan's fortunes suffered a temporary eclipse, and he was compelled to flee to Flanders. In 957 Northumbria and Mercia chose Edgar,

Edwy's younger brother, as king and he recalled Dunstan, making him Bishop of Worcester in 958 and Bishop of London in 959. That year King Edway died and Edgar became sole king; Dunstan shared in his triumph, being made Archbishop of Canterbury. In 975 it was Dunstan's influence that secured the throne for Edgar's elder son, Edward, but with the accession of Ethelred II, the Unready, in 978, Dunstan's influence diminished and he returned to Canterbury, dying there on 19 May 988.

Etheldreda, Saint (c.630–679)
Ely Catherdral, Ely, Cambridgeshire.
    Queen of Northumbria and Abbess of Ely. The third of four sainted daughters of King Anna of East Anglia. In 652 she married, reluctantly, Tonbert, Prince of Southern Gyrvii, approximately southern Cambridgeshire. Her jointure was the whole of the Isle of Ely. Tonbert died in 655 and, after five years spent in seclusion at her home on the Isle of Ely, she was married to Ecgfrith of Northumbria who, ten years later, became its king. She refused to carry out her conjugal duties and despite an appeal by the King to Saint Wilfrith, who told the King that his wife had chosen the better life, that of sanctity, the King could not persuade Etheldreda to fulfil her rôle either as Queen or wife. She was allowed to enter the monastery of Coldingham in Berwickshire, founded by her aunt, St Ebba, receiving the veil from Saint Wilfrith. When her husband tried to force her to accept public life she fled south to the Isle of Ely and there founded her own monastic house in 673. She died there in 679.

Ferrar, Nicholas (1592–1637)
St John's Church, Little Gidding, Cambridgeshire; tomb outside west door.
    Theologian of high learning and influence who, after assisting as a member of parliament in the impeachment of the Earl of Middlesex, established an Anglican community at Little Gidding, Cambridgeshire. As a Fellow of Clare Hall, Cambridge, he had devoted himself to the affairs of the Virginia Company in 1619 and his community at Little Gidding later became a Royalist stronghold. A great friend of George Herbert, he was instrumental in publishing Herbert's poems.

Nicholas Ferrar and George Herbert window in St Andrew's Church, Bemerton, Wiltshire

Fisher, John, Saint (1469–1535)
St Peter ad Vincula, Tower of London, London, in the crypt of the
Tower Chapel (with Sir Thomas More).

Martyr, Bishop of Rochester who refused to swear the oath to the
1534 Act of Succession, whereby Henry VIII's marriage to Catherine of
Aragon was declared invalid and his secret marriage to the already
pregnant Anne Boleyn valid. Committed to the Tower after appearing
before Lambeth Palace commissioners, and attainted for treason, he was
imprisoned in the Bell Tower near the cell of Sir Thomas More (whom
see). Fourteen months later too weak to walk, he was carried in a chair to
Tower Hill and executed, two weeks before More. Previously, after
being educated at Cambridge and becoming Master of Michaelhouse,
Fisher had been made chaplain to Henry II's mother Margaret, Countess
of Richmond, in 1502 and two years later chancellor of the university.
Living a life of piety, he zealously resisted Martin Luther's schismatic
teachings. He was made a cardinal a month before his execution and was
canonized in 1935.

Gilpin, Bernard (1517–1583)
St Michael and All Angels' Church, Houghton-le-Spring, County
Durham, where he has an uncommonly large tomb chest whose sides are
decorated by large panels with squares and circles.

Known as the 'Apostle of the North' for his attacks on the clerical
vices of the times and for his high ideals. Towards the end of the reign of
Mary I he was installed as Archdeacon at Durham and, despite attacks
on him by those who felt his sermons on clerical vices were aimed at
them, given the rich living of Houghton-le-Spring in refutation of his
enemies' charges. Enraged at their defeat, his enemies appealed to
Bonner and a royal warrant was made out for Gilpin's arrest. During his
journey to London he broke his leg and, during the delay, Queen Mary
died. He returned to Houghton where he worked unceasingly for the
good of his parishioners: endowing a grammar school, remitting tithes at
times of bad harvests, and feeding the poor. He died at Houghton on 4
March 1583.

Grosseteste, Robert (c.1175–1253)
Lincoln Cathedral, Lincoln, south-east transept.

Bishop of Lincoln who was reputedly one of the most learned men of
his time. Of humble origin, he nontheless was educated at Oxford and,
possibly, briefly at Paris. Between 1214 and 1231 he held a succession of

archdeaconries but in 1232 resigned all offices but that of Lincoln owing to illness. In 1235, however, he accepted the bishopric of Lincoln and without delay he undertook the reformation of morals and clerical discipline through his diocese, incurring the wrath of his own chapter. The dispute over his rights was eventually settled in 1245 in his favour by the Pope. He supported the independence of the Church and when in 1244 Henry III tried to separate the clergy from the baronage, Grosseteste wrote 'It is written that united we stand and divided we fall'. When it became clear that Henry and Pope Innocent IV were in alliance to crush the independence of the English clergy, the Bishop openly criticized the Pope, even attacking the Curia whom he held responsible for the evils of the Church. The question of English benefices for foreigners arose when Grosseteste was commanded to provide in his own diocese for a papal nephew. His letter of expostulation and refusal was couched in strong terms. He died on 9 October 1253.

Gryn, Rabbi Hugo (1930–1996)
Golders Green Jewish Cemetery.

Rabbi. Hugo Gryn was a rabbi for thirty-two years in London and was president of the Reform Synagogues of Great Britain. He was well known outside the Jewish community as a regular and compassionate contributor to BBC Radio 4's *The Moral Maze*. Born in Czechoslovakia, the Gryn family were sent to the Auschwitz concentration camp when the German Army invaded the town of Berehovo in 1944. His brother and father did not survive the camp. Hugo Gryn came to Britain in 1946. He was a passionate campaigner against all forms of racism and helped to establish plans for a permanent Holocaust exhibition at the Imperial War Museum.

Herbert, George (1593–1633)
St Andrew's Church, Bemerton, Wiltshire; in the chancel. There is a beautiful stained-glass window in the church's west wall, showing Herbert holding a lute and his friend Nicholas Ferrar holding one of Herbert's manuscripts.

Churchman and poet who became famous as a poet only after his death. He was the younger brother of Lord Herbert of Cherbury and early showed great classical promise in his studies at Cambridge. He also became an accomplished singer and player of the lute and viol. Upon being appointed public orator at Cambridge University, he frequently attended James I at court. Eventually, however, he had doubts about the 'painted pleasures of court life' and revived an earlier desire to go into the Church. Among his friends were John Donne, Francis Bacon, Izaak Walton and Nicholas Ferrar. Persuaded by William Laud, then Bishop of London, he took the parsonage of Fuggleston and Bemerton, which had been offered him by Charles I. He wrote a series of sacred – but certainly not dull and sombre – poems, which were published after his death by Ferrar. They became famous. *The Temple, Sacred Poems and Private Ejaculations*, containing 169 of his poems, was read by Charles I while he was in prison. Most of Herbert's unpublished writings were burnt by Cromwell's forces.

Higden, Ranulf (c.1299–1364)
Chester Cathedral, Chester, Cheshire.

Chronicler who was a Benedictine monk in the monastery of St Werburg in Chester, in which he lived, it is said, for sixty-four years. He was the author of a popular work of general history, styled the *Polychronicon*. The work is divided into seven books in imitation of the seven days of *Genesis*, and, with the exception of the last book, is a summary of general history, revealing the scientific, geographical and historical knowledge of the time. A translation from the Latin by John of Trevisa was printed by Caxton in 1482.

Hugh of Avalon, Saint (1135–1200)
Lincoln Cathedral, Lincolnshire, shrine in cathedral.

Bishop who was born in Burgundy of a noble family and invited to England by Henry II (c.1175) to head a Carthusian house at Witlow, Somerset. He became the king's adviser and greatly helped the poor and the lepers. He excommunicated King John in 1194 as Bishop of Lincoln, which he became in 1186 until his death. Later John sought his goodwill and Hugh pacified Richard I in a personal interview. He was canonized in 1220. He had rebuilt a major part of Lincoln cathedral, where his shrine was much visited and venerated although he had always regarded miracles with dislike.

Hugh of Lincoln, Saint (c.1246–1255)
Lincoln Cathedral, Lincoln, in the south choir aisle.

A native of Lincoln. He was about ten years old when he was found dead on premises belonging to a Jew. It was said, and then generally believed, that the boy had been scourged and crucified in imitation of the death of Jesus Christ. A disclaimer is now exhibited in Lincoln

Cathedral. As a result a number of Jews were put to death. The incident is referred to by Chaucer in the *Prioress's Tale* and by Marlowe in *The Jew of Malta*.

Hume, Cardinal Basil (1923–1999)
The chapel of St Gregory and St Augustine, Westminster Cathedral.

Archbishop of Westminster. Cardinal Hume was Britain's spiritual leader for over twenty-three years. He was a liberal who campaigned against injustices such as homelessness and supported the Guildford Four in their bid to clear their names. He welcomed Anglican clergyman wanting to take full communion but was an orthodox catholic who believed that these would-be converts would have to accept the whole of Catholic teaching.

Keble, John (1792–1866)
All Saints' Churchyard, Hursley, Hampshire; the large marble tombstone lies near the church, that of his wife being next to his.

Poet and Divine. Obtained a scholarship to Corpus Christi College, Oxford, being elected a scholar in his fifteenth year and a fellow in his nineteenth. Ordained a deacon in 1815 and a priest in 1816. In 1831 he was elected Professor of Poetry at Oxford, a position he held for ten years. On Sunday 14 July 1833 he preached his famous sermon, 'National Apostasy', of which Cardinal Newman wrote: 'I have ever considered and kept the day as the start of the religious movement of 1833'. It was the beginning of the Tractarian Movement which asserted the claim of the Church to a heavenly origin and a divine prerogative, and led to action by some leading spirits in Oxford and elsewhere to revive High Church principles and the ancient patristic theology, by these means both to defend the Church against the assaults of its enemies and also to raise to a higher tone the standard of Christian life in England. The movement derived its name from the famous *Tracts for the Times*, to which Keble contributed four: numbers 4, 13, 40 and 89. After the end of his tenure as Professor of Poetry Keble saw little of Oxford, but the defection of Newman to the Roman Catholic Church, which affected him deeply, brought Keble into the forefront of the Tractarian Movement and with Pusey he strove to maintain the High Anglican principles with which he had always been identified.

Grave of John Keble, All Saints' Churchyard, Hursley, Hampshire

Knox, Ronald Arbuthnot (1888–1957)
St Andrew's Parish Church, Mells, Somerset, one of three low head-stones in a row which includes Sassoon and Hollis (whom see).

A Roman Catholic monsignor and writer, he was the son of an Anglican bishop. His retranslation (the 'Knox Bible') of the Vulgate occupied a major part of his energies from 1939 to its appearance in 1945, but in his life he also wrote many essays and novels and engaged in theological controversy. In 1924 the *Daily Mail* called him 'the wittiest young man in England' and in 1926 he broadcast a spoof eyewitness account of an uprising of the unemployed, who were supposedly attacking Westminster and hanging cabinet ministers from lamp-posts and so on; a forerunner by twelve years of Orson Welles's radio 'scare' in New York about Martian landings. One of Knox's brothers, Edmund George Valpy (1881–1971), was editor of *Punch*, and another, Alfred Dillwyn (1883–1943), was a code-breaker who helped break the Zimmerman telegram and the Enigma codings in the first and second world wars respectively.

Lanfranc (c.1005–1089)
St Martin's Chapel, Canterbury Cathedral, Canterbury, Kent.

Archbishop of Canterbury. Born about 1005 at Pavia, where his father was a magistrate, he studied law and, after his father's death, crossed the

Alps to found a school in France. Then he decided to move to Normandy where, in 1039, he became master of the cathedral school at Avranches. In 1042 he took monastic vows at Bec where he lived in absolute seclusion until 1045. He was then persuaded to open a school in the monastery and many prominent churchmen were pupils, including a man who later became Pope, Alexander II. While Prior of Bec he quarrelled with William I, then Duke of Normandy, over his marriage with Matilda of Flanders, but he and the Duke resolved their differences and Lanfranc successfully accomplished the difficult task of obtaining the Pope's approval for the marriage. In 1066 he became the first Abbot of St Stephen's, Caen, and thereafter he exercised a perceptible influence on William's politics. After the conquest of England he accepted the archbishopric of Canterbury after Stigand had been canonically deposed in 1070. In 1075 he detected and foiled a conspiracy against William by the earls of Hereford and Norfolk. In 1087 he secured the succession for William II (Rufus), and persuaded the English militia to resist the attempts by Robert of Normandy and Odo of Bayeux against Rufus. He died of fever on 24 May 1089.

Lang, (William) Cosmo Gordon, Baron Lang of Lambeth (1864–1945)
St Stephen's Chapel, Canterbury Cathedral, Canterbury, Kent.

Archbishop of Canterbury from 1928 to 1942. Earlier he had been Archbishop of York, and during the Great War he travelled extensively to encourage the troops and the fleet. During the abdication crisis of 1936 his advice was sought by both the King, Edward VIII, and the Prime Minister, Stanley Baldwin. He died of a heart attack while running to catch a train.

Latimer, Hugh (c.1485–1555)
Burned at the stake 'at the ditch over against Balliol College', Oxford, and ashes scattered; a cross on the surface of Broad Street, opposite Balliol College, marks the spot where his burning took place.

One of the chief promoters of the Reformation in England. Initially he was a punctilious observer of the minutest rites of the Roman Church, being described as 'as obstinate a Papist as any in England'. However, his sermons against the abuses of the Church earned him the wrath of his superiors but, following his two 'sermons on the cards', he was asked to preach before Henry VIII during Lent, 1530. The King was impressed and gave him the living of West Kineton in Wiltshire. Sentence of imprisonment and excommunication was passed on him by the

Convocation for his 'heretical' views on his refusal to subscribe certain articles, but Henry VIII secured his release. Disturbances in Bristol over his sermons brought a revocation from the Bishop of his right to preach but Cranmer, consecrated Archbishop of Canterbury in 1533, granted him a special licence. Following the formal break with Rome in 1534 Latimer, along with Cranmer and Cromwell, became one of Henry's chief advisers regarding the legislative powers necessary to implement the repudiation of Rome. In September 1535 he was made Bishop of Worcester but in 1539, being opposed to the 'act of six articles', he resigned. In 1546 he was arrested and sent to the Tower of London on account of his connection with the preacher Edward Crome. Henry died before he could be brought to trial and he was pardoned in the amnesty at the accession of Edward VI. He refused the offer to return to Worcester and began preaching. In May 1553, shortly after Mary I's accession, he was summoned to appear before the Council. He did so, and was removed to Oxford, where after a long and hard imprisonment he was burned with Ridley on 16 October 1555, having spoken the immortal words, 'Be of good comfort, Master Ridley, and play the man; we shall this day light such a candle by God's grace in England as shall never be put out.'

Laud, William (1573–1645)
Chapel of St John's College, Oxford.
Archbishop of Canterbury. Son of a Reading clothier, he won a scholarship to St John's College, Oxford, in 1589. In 1601 he took orders and became chaplain to Charles Blount, Earl of Devonshire. His High Church doctrines earned him the rebuke of the authorities in Oxford, but elsewhere they were welcomed and he made rapid advancement, becoming Bishop of St David's in 1621. He developed a close relationship with George Villiers, Duke of Buckingham, and, on the accession of Charles I, he provided a list of clergy, each name distinguished with an 'O' (Orthodox) or 'P' (Puritan) indicating that the orthodox should be advanced and the Puritans suppressed. By 1629 he was Bishop of London and Chancellor of Oxford University and, in August 1633, Archbishop of Canterbury. He tried to force his High Church methods on both England and Scotland and was instrumental in forcing the Scots to resort to arms to safeguard their national religion and national independence. A strong supporter of the arbitrary methods of Strafford and Charles I, he was himself impeached and imprisoned in the Tower of London. Convicted at his trial he was executed on Tower Hill on 10 January 1645.

William Laud, after Van Dyck

Leofric, (d.1072)
Exeter Cathedral, Exeter, Devon, in the crypt; the monument erected in 1568 is believed to stand on his burial place.

First Bishop of Exeter. A chaplain to Edward the Confessor, in 1046 he became Bishop of the united dioceses of Devonshire and Cornwall, the seat being at Crediton. He did much to reconstruct the diocese, repairing the ravages caused by plundering pirates. He sought the aid of Pope Leo IX to transfer the seat of the diocese to Exeter which occurred in 1050. He was confirmed in his see by William the Conqueror and died on 10 February 1072.

Merton, Walter de (d.1277)
Rochester Cathedral, Rochester, Kent, in the north choir transept.

Bishop of Rochester and founder of Merton College, Oxford. Ordained as a sub-deacon sometime after June 1235, he became a clerk in the royal chancery. In 1261 he was appointed Chancellor and continued in that office until 12 July 1263, when the supremacy of the baronial party forced his resignation in favour of Nicholas of Ely. After Evesham in 1265 he returned to the chancery but was known as Justiciar and on the death of Henry III in 1272 he was appointed Chancellor by the Council of Regency, holding office until the return to England of Edward I in August 1274. He was made Bishop of Rochester in July 1274 and died as a result of an accident while fording the River Medway on 27 October 1277.

More, Sir Thomas, Saint (1478–1535)
St Peter ad Vincula, Tower of London, London; his head was interred by his daughter Margaret Roper in St Dunstan's Church, Canterbury, Kent, in the Roper vault.

Writer and lawyer. In 1529 he succeeded Wolsey as Lord Chancellor but his refusal to swear the Oath of Supremacy, acknowledging the King, Henry VIII, as head of the Church in England brought about his dismissal, imprisonment, trial and execution for treason on 7 July 1535. As he mounted the scaffold he remarked to the lieutenant, 'I pray thee see me safely up, and for my coming down let me shift for myself.' His work, *Utopia*, describes an ideal state. He was canonized in 1935.

Sir Thomas More, after Holbein

Morton, John (c.1420–1500)
Chapel of our Lady, Canterbury Cathedral, Canterbury, Kent, in the crypt.

Cardinal Archbishop of Canterbury. Graduated in law at Balliol College, Oxford, and practised ecclesiastical law in London where he attracted the attention of Archbishop Bourchier. A supporter of the Lancastrians, he was exiled after the Yorkist victory at Towton in 1461. He returned with Warwick the Kingmaker but after the complete failure of the Lancastrian cause following their defeat at Tewkesbury in 1471 he made his peace with Edward IV. He became Master of the Rolls in March 1473, and undertook several diplomatic missions. In 1479 he was made Bishop of Ely and later was an executor of the will of Edward IV. He was arrested by Richard III and imprisoned in the Tower of London but later released into the custody of the Duke of Buckingham. He urged Buckingham in his designs against Richard III, put him in touch with the Queen-Dowager, Elizabeth Woodville, and Henry Tudor, Earl of Richmond, but, after Buckingham's defeat by Richard, Morton fled to Flanders where he devoted himself to the cause of Henry Tudor. Following Henry's defeat of Richard III at Bosworth Field and his accession as Henry VII Morton became his principal adviser and, in 1486, succeeded Bourchier as Archbishop of Canterbury, a year later becoming also the Chancellor. In 1493 he was made a cardinal and in 1495 was Chancellor of the University of Oxford. He died at Knole on 12 October 1500.

Osmund, Saint (d.1099)
Salisbury Cathedral, Salisbury, Wiltshire; the slab in the nave aisle is said to mark the exact spot where his remains were re-buried.

Bishop of Salisbury. Reputedly the son of Henry, Count of Séez, and Isabella, William the Conqueror's sister, he accompanied William to England as a chaplain and was made Chancellor, probably in 1072, a position he is presumed to have held until his consecration as Bishop of Salisbury by Lanfranc in 1078. He helped in the preparation of the Domesday Book. In 1095 he supported the new King, William II, against Anselm, but in May 1096 he sought and obtained absolution from the Archbishop. He died on 3 December 1099.

Penn, William (1644–1718)
Jordans, Quaker Meeting House, Chalfont St Giles, Buckinghamshire.
Quaker and founder of Pennsylvania, the grant to which he received

Grave of William Penn, Jordans, Quaker Meeting House, Chalfont St Giles, Buckinghamshire

from Charles II on 14 March 1681, in repayment of a debt of £16,000 lent by his father, Admiral Sir William Penn, to Charles II. Philadelphia was founded and the 'Great Law of Pennsylvania' passed in which Pennsylvania was to be a Christian state on a Quaker model. His ardent support of non-conformity led him to several clashes with the administration in Britain and he spent brief spells in prison, which did not deter him from preaching. He was the author of several works, the most important of which was *No Cross, No Crown*.

Poore, Richard (d.1237)
St Mary's Church, Tarrant Crawford, Dorset (his body): his heart is said to have been buried in Salisbury Cathedral at the west end of the north aisle of the nave next to William Longsword's supposed tomb. In the same aisle as Poore's heart are the tombs of Sir John de Montecute (d.1390), who fought at Creçy; Walter, Lord Hungerford (d.1449), an Agincourt hero; and Sir John Cheyney (d.1509), a giant who was bodyguard to Henry VII and fought at Bosworth.

As Bishop of Salisbury he was responsible for moving the see from Old Sarum to Salisbury, where the new cathedral was built. When he moved from Chichester to Salisbury there was general joy in Salisbury because he was much loved, and he lost no time in pressing forward with the plan for the new cathedral, which had been long contemplated. Sending special envoys to Rome, he got permission, in 1219, to choose a site, named Maryfield, and at once a wooden chapel and cemetery were provided. By Poore's efforts, including his own contributions of a manor and money (he had been an executor of King John), Henry III and many nobles supported the cathedral. On 28 April 1220 the cathedral's foundations were laid. The work went on steadily for five years, and in 1225 he consecrated a temporary high altar in the Lady Chapel. At the consecration of the entire site the next day there was an enormous audience. The first person to be buried there was William Longsword, Earl of Salisbury, in March 1226, and in June the remains of Osmund, bishop of Salisbury from 1078 to 1099, were removed to the new cathedral from the old one at Old Sarum, Poore pressing for Osmund to be made a saint. In 1220 Poore had obtained a royal charter for 'New Sarum' and laid out the town in rectangular areas, known as 'squares' or 'chequers'. In 1228 he was made Bishop of Durham, and in 1230 he refounded the Cistercian Abbey for nuns at Tarrant Crawford, which he handed over to Queen Joan of Scotland. He died and was buried there.

Ramsey, Arthur Michael, Baron Ramsey of Canterbury (1904–1988)
After a funeral at Canterbury Cathedral, his ashes were buried near Temple in the Cloisters.

Archbishop of Canterbury from 1961 to 1974. Michael Ramsey was president of the Cambridge Union Society whilst studying at Magdalene College. He became a well-respected academic theologian and a member of the High Church Group. In 1952 he succeeded Alwyn Williams as Bishop of Durham. Four years later he was promoted to Archbishop of York. Ramsey became the 100th Archbishop of Canterbury in 1961 and he was widely liked both within the church and beyond. After he retired he was created a life peer, which enabled him to retain his seat in the House of Lords.

Ridley, Nicholas (c.1500–1555)
Burned at the stake 'at the ditch over against Balliol College', Oxford, and ashes scattered; a cross on the surface of Broad Street, opposite Balliol College, marks the spot where his burning took place.

Bishop of London. Educated at Pembroke College, Cambridge, and the Sorbonne, Paris, he became Chaplain to the University of

Cambridge. In 1538 he was appointed Chaplain to Thomas Cranmer, Archbishop of Canterbury, and in 1541 Chaplain to Henry VIII and Canon of Canterbury. In 1543 he was accused of heresy but managed to allay the suspicions of the Commissioners. After Edward VI came to the throne he was one of the visitors appointed to establish Protestantism in the University of Cambridge and was made Bishop of Rochester. In 1548 he helped to compile the English Prayer Book and in the following year was created Bishop of London. A supporter of Lady Jane Grey, he declared the Princesses Mary and Elizabeth illegitimate. Arrested at Framlingham seeking the pardon of Queen Mary, after the failure of Lady Jane Grey's cause, he was sent to the Tower of London. Early in 1554 together with Cranmer and Latimer he was sent to Oxford to be examined where, on 16 October 1555, he and Latimer were burned at the stake.

Runcie, Robert Alexander Kennedy (1921–2000)
North Churchyard, St Albans Cathedral.

Archbishop of Canterbury. Robert Runcie's parents did not attend church and he first discovered god while following a girl he liked to confirmation classes. Runcie grew up in Crosby, now a suburb of Liverpool, and his father worked at the local Tate and Lyle sugar factory. He won a scholarship to read classics at Oxford, but left to volunteer for the Scots Guards at the outbreak of the Second World War. During the war he saw action in France, landing at Normandy soon after D-Day, and he won the Military Cross.

Runcie's career as a churchman took off in 1956 when he was elected Fellow and Dean of Trinity Hall, Cambridge. In 1970 he became Bishop of St Albans and, nine years later, was made Archbishop of Canterbury. His early years at Lambeth Palace were dramatic. In 1981 his 'special envoy', Terry Waite, was instrumental in the release of three missionaries held hostage in Iran. That same year he presided over the wedding of Prince Charles and Lady Diana Spencer. In May 1982 he welcomed Pope John Paul II to Canterbury Cathedral.

At the beginning of 1991, Robert Runcie retired to St Albans with his wife, Lindy. He was awarded a life peerage.

Scrope, Richard le (c.1350–1405)
The Lady Chapel, York Minster, York.

Archbishop of York. He was the fourth son of Henry Scrope, first Baron Scrope of Masham, and after graduating in arts at Oxford and law at Cambridge was ordained priest in March 1377. He is said to have held a canonry at York and in 1378 was made Chancellor of the University of Cambridge. By a Bull, dated 18 August 1386, Pope Urban VI appointed him Bishop of Coventry and Lichfield and in August 1387 he was installed in the presence of Richard II. He undertook missions for King Richard to Scotland and to Rome and, on 2 June 1398, against the wishes of the Chapter but at the King's request, Scrope was appointed by a Bull of the Pope to be Archbishop of York. He acquiesced in the revolution of 1399, being present when Richard II abdicated in favour of Henry IV. With the Archbishop of Canterbury he joined in the enthroning of the new King, Henry IV. He criticized Henry's government for 'its spoliation of the church proposed by the "unlearned parliament" '. He took up arms at York with Percy of Northumberland and Thomas Mowbray the Earl Marshal. At Shipton Moor in May 1405, despite his own superior forces, he agreed to treat with the Earl of Westmorland who had guaranteed favourable terms, a promise that was immediately broken. Removed to Pontefract, he was tried and executed at York where he begged the headsman to deal five blows at his neck in memory of the five sacred wounds.

Sudbury, Simon of (d.1381)
St Gregory's Church, Sudbury, Suffolk, in the vestry.

Archbishop of Canterbury. He studied at Paris and became Chaplain to Pope Innocent VI who sent him on a mission to Edward III in 1356. In October 1361 the Pope appointed him Bishop of London and he served Edward III on several diplomatic missions. In 1375 he succeeded William Wittlesey as Archbishop of Canterbury, and, for the remainder of his life, was a partisan of John of Gaunt, Duke of Lancaster. In 1377 he crowned Richard II. In 1378, very reluctantly, he agreed to proceed against John Wycliffe, the leader of the Lollards. In 1380 he became Chancellor and, during the Peasants' Revolt of 1381, he was one of their principal targets. The mob rushed the Tower of London, and, finding the Archbishop therein, captured and executed him on Tower Hill on 14 June 1381.

Swithun, Saint (d.862)
Winchester Cathedral, Winchester, Hampshire, where his golden shrine is near the Lady Chapel.

Bishop of Winchester and patron saint of Winchester Cathedral from the tenth to the sixteenth century, having been adopted by Dunstan and

Shrine of St Swithun, Winchester Cathedral, Hampshire

Ethelwold of Winchester when inaugurating their church reform. The body of St Swithun was transferred from his almost forgotten grave to the new basilica inside the restored church on 15 July 971. There many miracles are reputed to have occurred both before and after the translation of the body.

Temple, Frederick (1821–1902)
Canterbury Cathedral, Canterbury, Kent, in the cloister garth.
   Archbishop of Canterbury. Whilst at Oxford he leaned towards 'the Oxford Liberal Movement' and in 1846 entered the Church. In 1858 he became Headmaster of Rugby and, as a supporter of William Gladstone, was in 1869 offered the bishopric of Exeter. In 1885 he was translated to London and in 1896, although going blind, he became Archbishop of Canterbury. His radical views and his unfailing work amongst the poor made him a controversial figure.

Tenison, Thomas (1636–1715)
St Mary's Church, Lambeth, London.

Archbishop of Canterbury. He was educated at Cambridge, and after ordination became Vicar of St Andrew-the-Great, Cambridge. In 1680 Charles II gave him the important cure of St Martin-in-the-Fields. He opposed the religious policies of James II. The general liberality of his views brought him rapid advancement under William III and Mary II and in 1694 he was made Archbishop of Canterbury. A commissioner for the Union with Scotland in 1707, he supported the Hanoverian succession and was given power, with two others, to appoint a Regent until George I should arrive in England. He is also remembered for having preached the sermon at the funeral of Nell Gwyn in 1687.

Walter, Hubert (d.1205)
Canterbury Cathedral, Canterbury, Kent; his tomb, the oldest in the Cathedral, lies in the aisle just south of the entrance to Henry IV's Chantry.

Archbishop of Canterbury. He rose rapidly through the influence of his uncle, Ranulf de Glanville, Justiciar to Henry II. In 1186 he became Dean of York, and in October 1189 Bishop of Salisbury. He accompanied Richard I on the Third Crusade, organizing supplies and negotiating with Saladin. After Richard left the Holy Land in October 1192 he directed the return of the English army, returning to England himself in April 1193 where, on Richard's recommendation, he was elected Archbishop of Canterbury. In December of that same year he was made Justiciar. He organized the collection of Richard's ransom and suppressed the rebellion of Prince John. After the King's brief return to England in March 1194 Hubert Walter became the effective governor of the kingdom during Richard's absence. In March 1195 Pope Celestine III appointed him Papal Legate to England. He was instrumental in securing the throne for King John and was made Chancellor by the new King on 27 May 1199.

Watts, Isaac (1674–1748)
Bunhill Fields Burial Ground, City Road, Finsbury, London.

Nonconformist minister who is regarded as the father of English hymnody. His collection of hymns includes, 'O God, Our Help in Ages Past'; 'When I Survey the Wondrous Cross'; and 'Jesus Shall Reign'.

Isaac Watts, by an unknown artist

Wesley, John (1703–1791)
John Wesley Chapel, City Road, Finsbury, London.

Clergyman who became the founder of Methodism. Son of a former Nonconformist minister, he was educated at Oxford, where, on 9 September 1725, he was made deacon by the Bishop of Oxford. He joined with his brother Charles to form the Holy Club which carried out social and educational work among prisoners and the poor of Oxford. In 1736 he went to America as spiritual adviser to the new colony of Georgia, with a brief to convert the Red Indians. He did not. However, he did describe his experiences in Georgia as the 'second rise of Methodism', the first being the Holy Club. On 24 May 1738, having been strongly influenced by the Moravian, Peter Böhler, during a reading of Luther's *Preface to the Epistle to the Romans*, Wesley underwent a profound awakening. Thereafter he saw his aim as recalling the Church of England to its spiritual mission. In 1784, after trying to work within the jurisdiction of the Church of England, he declared that his societies and their work operated independently of the main Church, although to the end of his life Charles Wesley regarded himself as a loyal priest of the Church of England.

White, John (1575–1648)
Holy Trinity Church, St Peter's Chapel and All Saints Church, Dorchester, Dorset; in the porch.

Credited with being the founder of Massachusetts, White never actually went there himself. He was known as the Patriarch of Dorchester, being rector of Holy Trinity Church from 1606 until almost the end of his life. In 1624 he sent a colony of Dorset men to Massachusetts, and four years later he instigated the formation of the Massachusetts Company. Its capital cost was £1800 and Sir Richard Saltonstall was a chief shareholder, while John Endicott was sent out as the first governor of the colony. The first ministers, Francis Higginson and Samuel Skelton, sailed there on 4 May 1629 in the *George Bonaventura*, while John Winthrop, who became patriarch of the famous Winthrop family in America, landed at Salem in the *Arbella* in 1630 from Plymouth.

Wolsey, Thomas (c.1475–1530)
The Lady Chapel, Leicester Abbey, Leicester.

Cardinal and statesman. Son of an Ipswich grazier, he was educated at Magdalen College, Oxford. Ordained in 1498, he became a chaplain to Henry VII. By 1509 his obvious abilities had won him a place on the Royal Council. He attracted the notice of the young King, Henry VIII, and Wolsey's influence soon outstripped that of William Warham, Archbishop of Canterbury, whom he replaced, on 22 December 1515, as Lord Chancellor. His almost impregnable power, which lasted for fourteen years, suddenly disappeared in 1529 when he was stripped of office, the reason being his failure to secure for Henry VIII his divorce from Catherine of Aragon. The King did not proceed against Wolsey until his intention to have himself enthroned as Archbishop of York on 7 November 1530 alarmed Henry, who had him arrested. On his way to London he died at Leicester Abbey on 29 November 1530.

Worlock, Cardinal Derek (1920–1996)
Cathedral of Christ the King, Liverpool.

Roman Catholic Cardinal. Born in London, Derek Worlock was ordained a priest in 1944. He remained in the South, serving as secretary to three cardinals and as Bishop of Portsmouth, before moving north to Liverpool. He was Archbishop of Liverpool for twenty years – through the Hillsborough and Heysel stadium disasters – and he was proud to call himself an honorary 'scouser' when he was made a freeman of the city.

Wycliffe, John (c.1320–1384)
St Mary's Church, Lutterworth, Leicestershire; his body was later exhumed and his ashes scattered on the River Swift.

Ecclesiastical reformer and theologian. He inspired the Lollards and the Czech, John Huss; thus he was a major figure behind the Protestant Reformation. A protégé of John of Gaunt, Duke of Lancaster, who managed to protect Wycliffe against many of the charges brought against him for his heretical views, despite the Duke's own hostility to a number of those views. The clergy, Wycliffe argued, should be stripped of worldly offices and all surplus wealth. His Eucharistic teachings approximated closely to the later Lutheran doctrine of consubstantiation, although it is said that his views approached 'receptionism': the view that the nature of the consecrated elements depended on the spiritual state of the communicant. He died of a stroke, while saying Mass in his church at Lutterworth on 28 December 1384. In 1415 at the Council of Constance his teachings were condemned.

Wykeham, William of (1324–1404)
Chantry Chapel, Winchester Cathedral, Winchester, Hampshire. The three monkish figures at the feet of his effigy on the tomb are said to represent his master mason, master carpenter and clerk of the works.

Bishop of Winchester from 1367–1404, and twice Chancellor of England, from 1367–1372 under Edward III, and from 1389–1391 under Richard II. He was the founder of Winchester College and of New College, Oxford. He was dismissed from the Chancellorship in 1372 as a result of an anti-clerical movement among the barons. He had always

Tomb of William of Wykeham, Winchester Cathedral, Hampshire

opposed the designs of John of Gaunt, Duke of Lancaster, and as a result was tried for the conduct of affairs during his first term as Chancellor. He was convicted in November 1376 and sentenced to forfeit the temporalities of his see. But the following year saw the jubilee of Edward III and although he was exempted from the general pardon his property was returned. He was present at the coronation of Richard II in June 1377 and in July of that year Richard gave him a full pardon, restoring him to the chancellorship on 3 May 1389, a position he held for two and a half years.

Chapter 5
Thinkers (including philosophers, lawyers and scholars)

Ashmole, Elias (1617–1692)
St Mary's Church, Lambeth, London.

Antiquarian and writer. He was born in Lichfield. In 1638 he became a lawyer and in 1644 was appointed a commissioner in excise. Two years later he was initiated as a Freemason, the first gentleman, or amateur, to be accepted. He held various minor offices after the Restoration. He is chiefly remembered as the founder and benefactor of the Ashmolean Museum in Oxford. In 1672 he published his *Institutions, Laws and Ceremonies of the Order of the Garter*. He was a keen astrologer and alchemist.

Bacon, Francis, 1st Baron Verulam and Viscount St Albans (1561–1626)
St Michael's Church, St Albans, Hertfordshire, where his monument depicts a life-size marble figure seated comfortably and asleep.

Philosopher, essayist and statesman. Younger son of Sir Nicholas Bacon, Queen Elizabeth I's Lord Keeper, he held many high offices of state under James I, ultimately becoming Lord Chancellor in 1618. In 1621 he was impeached and sent to the Tower of London accused of 'corruption and neglect', to which he confessed. He lost all his offices and a heavy fine was imposed, though this was later remitted by the King. After his release from the Tower, he devoted himself to literary and philosophical works. His literary output can be divided into three classes: the philosophical, the most important of which are the *Advancement of Learning*, 1605; *Novum Organum*, 1620, and *De Augmentis*, 1623; the literary, which include the *Essays*, 1597 and 1625, *New Atlantis*, 1626, and the *History of Henry the Seventh*, 1622; and his professional works, of which *Maxims of the Law* and *Reading on the Statute of Uses* are the most famous.

Bentham, Jeremy (1748–1832)
University College, London, Gower Street, London, in the south cloister where his embalmed body is on display in a show case.

Utilitarian philosopher and writer on jurisprudence. His main works

Jeremy Bentham's 'Auto–Icon', his embalmed body on display in the south cloister of University College, London, Gower Street

were *Government* and *Principles of Morals and Legislation*. Determined to find a solid foundation for both law and morality, he taught 'the greatest happiness of the greatest number' in what he described in 1802 as 'utilitarian philosophy'.

Berlin, Sir Isaiah (1909–1997)
Jewish section of Wolvercote Cemetery.

Philosopher and historian of ideas. Sir Isaiah Berlin was one of the dominant scholars of his generation and his greatest works were on the history of ideas and on Russian thought. He was born into a Jewish family in Latvia but moved to England when he was ten years old. However, his early experiences of the Russian Revolution caused him to be intellectually opposed to absolutisms of any kind and he argued that the essential values for a liberal civilisation were pluralism and liberty.

Berlin won a scholarship to Oxford, became a lecturer there in 1932 and by 1966 was the first President of Wolfson College. He was a prolific writer and a popular lecturer and was said to have an encyclopaedic mind. He died on 5 November 1997 at the age of eighty-eight.

Burke, Edmund (1729–1797)
St Mary and All Saints Church, Beaconsfield, Buckinghamshire.

Whig statesman and political writer and one of the greatest names in the history of political literature. Born in Dublin in 1729 he moved to London in 1750 to study for the Bar after graduating from Trinity College Dublin. When the Whig Marquess of Rockingham accepted the premiership in 1765 Burke became his private secretary and in 1766 Member of Parliament for Wendover. After the fall of Rockingham in July 1766 he defended his chief in the Commons for his policies towards the colonies, advocating the emancipation of the American colonies though not their independence. He also advocated a better administration in India and whilst he had sympathy with some of the aims of the French Revolution he disapproved of it, seeing it as an attack on liberty despite the high sentiments of the revolutionaries and their English sympathisers. He did not believe that the French would be any better off under the new régime than under the old, considering that what basically required revision was the old system of government to make that work.

Coke, Sir Edward, commonly called Lord Coke (1552–1634)
St Mary's Church, Tittleshall, Norfolk, where there is a fine monument.

One of England's greatest lawyers, who was successively Chief Justice

Edmund Burke, from the studio of Reynolds

of the Common Pleas (1606), and Chief Justice of the Common Bench (1613). His challenge to James I over the King's supreme prerogative brought his dismissal from all his offices in 1616. In 1620 he entered Parliament as the Member for Liskeard and was an outspoken supporter of the freedom of Parliamentary discussion and the liberty of speech of its members. Together with Pym and Sir Robert Philips he was imprisoned for entering in the journal of the House the famous petition on 18 December 1621 embodying those principles. In 1628 he re-entered Parliament for Buckinghamshire and took an important part in drawing up the great Petition of Rights. At the end of his career in Parliament he bewailed 'with tears' the ruin he declared the Duke of Buckingham was bringing on the country.

Cowper, William, 1st Earl (c.1665–1723)
St Mary's Church, Hertingfordbury, Hertfordshire.

English jurist who, as Lord Keeper of the Great Seal, conducted the negotiations between the English and Scottish commissioners in 1706 to arrange for the union between England and Scotland. When Union between the two countries came into operation in May 1707 he became the first Lord High Chancellor of Great Britain. He resigned the office in 1710 but was reinstated by George I shortly after his accession. In April 1718, a month after he was elevated to the peerage as Viscount Fordwich and Earl Cowper, he resigned, having earned the King's disfavour by espousing the cause of George, Prince of Wales, later George II, in his quarrel with his father.

Denning, Lord Alfred Thompson (1899–1999)
Whitchurch Churchyard, Hampshire.

Judge. Master of the Rolls for twenty years and holding high judicial office for thirty-eight, Judge Denning was probably the most prominent member of the judiciary in recent history. He was called to the Bar in 1923, took silk in 1938 and was promoted to the High Court Bench when he was only forty-five.

Denning was committed to Justice and defending the individual. He was also a devout Christian and believer in traditional Christian morality. In his work he could be controversial: in 1957 he condemned homosexuality during the Lords debate on the Wolfenden Report and in 1965 he voted against the suspension of hanging. He was perhaps most famous for his investigation into the Profumo affair and the published report became a bestseller and made him a household name.

Judge Denning was born in the village of Whitchurch and died there a hundred years later. He is buried in the churchyard next to his second wife, Joan.

Gibbon, Edward (1737–1794)
St Mary and St Andrew's Church, Fletching, East Sussex.
   Historian. Educated at Westminster and Magdalen College, Oxford, he converted to Catholicism at the age of sixteen and was sent by his father to Lausanne. There he reconverted to Protestantism and read widely. Returning to England in 1758, he published his *Essai sur l'étude de la littérature* in 1761, the English version appearing in 1764. During a tour of Italy in 1764, while 'musing amid the ruins of the Capitol', he formulated the idea of writing a *History of the Decline and Fall of the Roman Empire*, the first volume of which appeared in 1776. In 1774 he entered Parliament and supported Lord North. The second and third volumes of *Decline and Fall* appeared in 1781 and the final three volumes, written whilst he was once again living in Lausanne, appeared in 1788. Thereafter he once again returned to England.

Godwin, William (1756–1836)
St Peter's Churchyard, Bournemouth, Dorset.
   Political philosopher. Originally a dissenting minister but abandoned his ministry after becoming an atheist and philosopher of anarchical views. He believed that men acted according to reason, that it was impossible to be rationally persuaded and not act accordingly, that reason taught benevolence, and that therefore rational creatures could live in harmony without laws and institutions. In 1793 he published his *Enquiry concerning Political Justice*, followed by two novels, *Adventures of Caleb Williams*, 1794, and *St Leon*, 1797, which contains a pen portrait of his wife, Mary. He also wrote a life of Chaucer and a biography of his first wife, Mary Wollstonecraft.

Hoare, Sir Richard Colt (1758–1838)
St Peter's Churchyard, Stourton, Wiltshire; large mausoleum to the east of the church.
   A Wiltshire historian and antiquary who, after being privately educated and joining his family's banking house in Fleet Street for a while, was given his financial independence by a large allowance from his grandfather. After travelling widely in Europe he devoted his zeal to the history and antiquities of Wiltshire, listing in his chronicles the position

Sir Richard Colt Hoare's mausoleum, Stourton, Wiltshire

and contents of hundreds of barrows. One of his main works is an 'everthing-you-want-to-know' *History of Modern Wiltshire* (1822–1844) in six volumes, besides travel books on Elba, Italy and Sicily. He also wrote a description of the house and gardens of Stourhead, which his grandfather had planned and built. They are a great tourist attraction.

Hobbes, Thomas (1588–1679)
St John the Baptist Church, Ault Hucknall, Derbyshire.

Philosopher who favoured strong government and supported the supremacy of the state, the absolute power of the sovereign stemming from the will of the people. His most famous work, *Leviathan*, was published in 1651.

Malthus, Reverend Thomas Robert (1766–1834)
Abbey Church, Bath, Avon, in the porch.

Economist. In his pessimistic essay 'The Principle of Population' he contended that population tends to increase faster than the means of subsistence and that its growth could only be checked by moral restraint or by disease and war.

Marx, Karl (1818–1883)
Highgate 'new' Cemetery, Highgate, London.

Political and economic philosopher. Born in Trier in Germany of Jewish parents he studied law, philosophy and history at both Bonn and Berlin. Later he took up the study of economics. With his friend Engels he wrote the *Communist Manifesto* in 1848, for the Communist League of which he was the leader. He was forced to leave the Continent because of his political agitation in 1849 and settled in London. It was in London that he wrote *Das Kapital*, which is an analysis of the economic laws that govern society. In 1864 he helped to found the first International, and he is generally regarded as the founder of modern international communism.

Mitford, William (1744–1827)
St Catherine's Churchyard, Exbury, Hampshire; remains translated from the Mitford vault in the eastern wall to the churchyard when church was lengthened c.1907.

A historian who knew the Utilitarian philosopher Jeremy Bentham at Oxford, and Edward Gibbon, who had been a brother officer in the South Hampshire Militia. It is said of Mitford that at Queen's College, Oxford he was distinguished by his good looks and physical strength. He did not study much, either at university or at the Middle Temple as a law student, never practising law, and when he was 17 years old he succeeded to the property at Exbury. Here it was that Gibbon, the historian of Rome, suggested that Mitford write a history of Greece. He could read Greek well and had made a hobby of studying that country's history. The Greek history he wrote became extremely popular, especially among those who favoured his attempts to show that the French Revolutionary visionary ideas of the time, based on Greek democracy, were impracticable. Other works included an *Essay on the Harmony of Language* (1774), an essay on the Corn Laws (1791), contending that England could be self-sufficient in wheat, and a *Review of the Early History of the Arabs* (1816). He is commemorated by a tablet in the church on the north wall of the nave. Nancy Mitford (1904–1973), the authoress, was descended from his younger brother, Lord Redesdale.

Moore, George Edward (1873–1958)
Parish of the Ascension Burial Ground, Cambridge.

Philosopher. Moore's most famous book, *Principia Ethica*, was published in 1903 and, along with Bertrand Russell, he is credited with opening the door to British analytical philosophy. Educated at Trinity College, Cambridge, he became Professor of Mental Philosophy and Logic there in 1925. He was succeeded in 1939 by Ludwig Wittgenstein, whom he had taught. Moore was editor of the journal *Mind* from 1921 to 1947 and received the Order of Merit in 1951.

Ricardo, David (1772–1823)
St Nicholas's Church, Hardenhuish, Wiltshire, large and intriguing monument near south-east corner of church exterior.

Economist and founder of the Geological Society (1807), he made his fortune by the time he was twenty-five, having been a member of the Stock Exchange only five years. He then turned to scientific interests, setting up a minerological laboratory. He wrote *Principles of Political Economy and Taxation* (1817), becoming an MP for Portarlington from 1819 to the year of his death. The classical school of political economy reflects his thinking as a principal founder. He derided Robert Owen's socialist theories, but contributed to nearly every London charity.

Roget, Peter Mark (1779–1869)
St James's Churchyard, West Malvern, Hereford and Worcester.

English physician and savant. He was for twenty-two years, from 1827 to 1849, the Secretary of the Royal Society. He played a role in the founding of London University but is principally remembered for his *Thesaurus of English Words and Phrases*, which was published in 1852 and has run into many editions.

David Ricardo's grave, Hardenhuish, Wiltshire

Ruskin, John (1819–1900)
St Andrew's Churchyard, Coniston, Cumbria. A bronze medallion portrait head commemorates Ruskin in Westminster Abbey, London, in the South Transept now known as 'Poets' Corner'.

Art critic and social theorist. As an art critic he was the greatest influence of his generation and was instrumental in promoting the Pre-Raphaelite school of painting. His *Stones of Venice*, 1851–1853, and *Modern Painters* which was begun as a defence of Turner, are masterpieces. During the 1860s his mind was concerned with economics and he began publishing essays on the subject which aroused strong opposition by their heterodoxy. He advocated a system of national education, the organization of labour, and other social reforms in these and other pamphlets. He attacked a politico-economic system based on the idea of 'economic man', actuated by no other motive than profit. Wealth, he insisted, is not the only thing worth having. His interest in social reform is reflected in his most popular work, *Sesame and Lilies*, 1865, and *The Crown of Wild Olive*, 1866. He inherited a large fortune which he distributed chiefly on philanthropic ventures and in 1871 he founded the Guild of St George on the principles that 'food can only be got out of the ground and happiness out of honesty', and that 'the highest wisdom and the highest treasure need not be costly or exclusive'. The members of the guild were to give a tithe of their fortunes to philanthropic purposes, and to these he contributed generously.

Saintsbury, George Edward Bateman (1845–1933)
Old Cemetery, Southampton, Hampshire.

Historian and literary critic. He was the author of a large number of works on English and European literature, including a *Short History of English Literature*, 1898, *Elizabethan Literature*, 1887, and *A History of Criticism*, 1900–1904. He also wrote interesting and entertaining *Notes on a Cellar Book*, 1920, *A Letter Book*, and *A Scrap Book*, 1922. He wrote several lives of, among others, Dryden, Sir Walter Scott and Matthew Arnold.

Selden, John (1584–1654)
Temple Church, Temple, Fleet Street, London, beneath a glass panel in the floor near the entrance.

Jurist and scholar. Studied at Oxford and the Middle Temple and was called to the Bar in 1612. Believed to be the instigator and perhaps the draftsman of the memorable protestation on the rights and privileges of the House of Commons, of which he was not a Member, and which was affirmed by the Commons on 18 December 1621. He, together with several of the Members of the House of Commons, was imprisoned first in the Tower of London and subsequently placed in the charge of the Sheriff of London, Sir Robert Ducie. In 1623 he entered Parliament as Member for Lancaster and allied himself with Pym. In the second Parliament of Charles I in 1626 he played a prominent part in the impeachment of George Villiers, first Duke of Buckingham. Thereafter he played an influential rôle in formulating Parliamentary policies in its quarrel with the King. As a scholar and writer he was pre-eminent among his contemporaries.

Spooner, Dr William Archibald (1844–1930)
Town Cemetery (near the entrance), Pye Lane, Grasmere, Cumbria.

Historian and philosopher, he rose from a New College, Oxford, scholarship in 1862 to become Warden of the college in 1903. He was author of *The History of Tacitus* (1891), *William of Wykeham* (1909) and other historical works. His endearing lapses of speech led to them being called 'Spoonerisms'. Attributed to him are such examples as: 'You have hissed my mystery lectures ... take the next town drain' and others that are no doubt apocryphal.

Stow, John (c.1525–1605)
St Andrew Undershaft, corner of St Mary Axe and Leadenhall Street, City of London. The monument of Derbyshire marble and alabaster in the north-east corner shows him bald-headed writing in a book at a table, flanked by square pillars richly decorated with ribbon-work, lions' heads, books and crosses. Each year, near the anniversary of his death on 5 April, the Lord Mayor of London, attended by Sheriffs, renews his quill pen and presents a copy of Stow's book to the writer of the best essay on London received that year.

Chronicler and antiquary. Formerly a tailor and a freeman of the Merchant Taylors' Company from 1547. He is chiefly remembered for *A Survey of London*, 1598 and 1603, a work invaluable for the detailed information it gives about the ancient city and its customs. He also wrote *The Woorkes of Geffrey Chaucer*, 1561, *Summarie of Englyshe Chronicles*, 1565, and *The Chronicles of England*, 1580. He occupied himself from 1560 onwards in transcribing and collecting manuscripts, spending all his money in their pursuit. He was suspected of favouring the Roman religion and was charged in 1568, 1569 and 1570 with being in possession of popish and dangerous writings, but, after examination before the ecclesiastical commission, escaped without punishment.

Wittgenstein, Luwig Josef Johann (1889–1951)
Parish of the Ascension Burial Ground, Cambridge.

Philosopher. Regarded by many as one of the most influential philosophers of the twentieth century, Wittgenstein was influenced by Schopenhauer, Frege and his Cambridge tutor Bertrand Russell. The *Tractatus Logico-Philosophicus* was published in 1922 and was the only book that Wittgenstein published during his lifetime. In the seven propositions of the *Tractatus*, he claims that all philosophical problems arise from the misunderstandings of the logic of language and it played a leading role in the 'linguistic turn' of modern philosophy. His much later work, *Philosophical Investigations*, published posthumously, was more complex and took the form of a dialogue.

Wittgenstein was born in Vienna, the youngest of eight children, three of whom were to commit suicide. He was a complex and enigmatic character with an ambiguous sexuality and his life was made into the 1993 film, *Wittgenstein*, directed by Derek Jarman. He died from cancer in 1951.

Wollstonecraft, Mary (1759–1797)
St Peter's Churchyard, Bournemouth, Dorset.

Educational writer famous for her *Vindications of the Rights of Women*, 1792, which was a courageous attack on the conventions of the day. She had originally founded a school in Newington Green with her sister, Eliza, and then went as governess to the children of Lord Kingsborough. During her sojourn in Paris from 1793 to 1795, she became the mistress of an American, Gilbert Imlay, by whom she had a daughter, Fanny, who, years later after the death of her mother, poisoned herself for no apparent reason. Subsequently, Mary Wollstonecraft married William Godwin, the political and philosophical writer, but died bearing him a daughter, Mary, who was to become Percy Bysshe Shelley's second wife.

Chapter 6
Scientists (including medical doctors, engineers and inventors)

Abel, Sir Frederick Augustus (1827–1902)
Nunhead Cemetery, Ivydale Road, London.

English military chemist who, in 1845, was one of the twenty-six original students of the Royal College of Chemistry. In March 1852 he succeeded Faraday as lecturer in chemistry at the Royal Military Academy at Woolwich and on 24 July 1854 became Ordnance Chemist, two years later being made chemist to the War Department. He developed a process for reducing gun cotton to a pulp, thus enabling it to be worked and stored in safety. Together with Sir Andrew Noble he developed new and important theories of explosives. In 1868 he developed the open-test for determining the flash point of petroleum, which, in 1879 was superseded by the Abel close-test with a flash point at 73°. Ten years later he and Sir James Dewar invented cordite. Sir Frederick Abel was also an accomplished musician.

Addison, Thomas (1793–1860)
Lanercost Priory, Lanercost, Cumbria.

Eminent physician whose contributions to the science of medicine were numerous and important. His researches into pneumonia revealed truths, novel at the time, but now generally accepted; he influenced the progress of knowledge of pulmonary phthisis; and, in 1853, produced his best-known work, his 'Essay of Disease of the Supre-renal Capsules', in which he announced that these organs, not previously known to be the seat of any definite disease, were in certain cases affected in such a way as to produce a fatal malady. It is commonly known as 'Addison's disease'. Its discovery was one of the most brilliant medical achievements of the nineteenth century.

Airy, Sir George Biddell (1801–1892)
St Mary's Churchyard, Playford, near Ipswich, Suffolk. There is a frontal bust of Sir George in an oval medallion.

Astronomer Royal who, for forty-six years, as Lucasian Professor of Mathematics at Cambridge, first drew attention to the visual defect known as astigmatism, from which he himself suffered. In 1838 he created a magnetic and metereological department at Greenwich Observatory. From 1826 to 1854 he conducted researches which led him to determine the mean density of the earth. He was consulted on a number of projects '... the launching of the *Great Eastern* steamship, Babbage's calculating machine, the layer of the transatlantic cable, the chimes of Westminster clock, and the smoky chimneys of Westminster Palace.'

Babbage, Charles (1792–1871)
Kensal Green Cemetery, Kensal Green, London.

Mathematician and engineer whose inventions and work on mechanical calculating machines laid the foundations for modern computers. He was instrumental in founding the Astronomical (1820) and Statistical (1834) Societies.

Baker, Sir Benjamin (1840–1907)
St Mary's Church, Idbury, Oxfordshire. Large memorial stone in the graveyard at the back of the church.

Civil engineer who built the Forth Bridge, completed in seven years in 1890, for which he was awarded the KCMG and Prix Poncelet of the Institute of France. Born near Frome, Somerset he served his apprenticeship at Neath Abbey ironworks before coming to London where his major works as a consultant were the building of Victoria Station, the Underground railways such as the Inner Circle Line, and the first 'tubes', including the Baker Street–Waterloo line. In 1902 he was awarded the KCB for his building of the Aswan dams (low and high) in Egypt. For devising the float to convey Cleopatra's Needle to England (1877) he was awarded the coveted Telford Medal of the Institute of Civil Engineers. At his death he was a Fellow of the Royal Society and one of the most respected engineers in the world.

Bessemer, Sir Henry (1813–1898)
Norwood Cemetery, Norwood, London.

Inventor of the process for converting cast-iron directly into steel, thus revolutionizing steel manufacture and extending its use.

Boyle, The Hon Robert (1627–1691)
St Martin-in-the-Fields, St Martin's Place, London.

Seventh son of the Earl of Cork. A member of the 'Invisible College', a group which devoted itself to the cultivation of the 'new philosophy' and which, in 1663, became the Royal Society, of which Boyle was a member of the council. His important work in physics – the discovery of the part taken by air in the propagation of sound, and investigations into the expansive force of freezing water – and in chemistry, which was his favourite study – he advanced towards the modern view of elements as the undecomposable constituents of material bodies – laid the foundations of the modern sciences of physics and chemistry.

Brunel, Isambard Kingdom (1806–1859)
Kensal Green Cemetery, Kensal Green, London.

Civil engineer, who was the engineer of the Great Western Railway, and who built several ocean steamships: the *Great Western*, the *Great Britain* and the *Great Eastern*. He also built the Clifton Suspension Bridge over the River Avon, and the Royal Albert Bridge over the River Tamar.

Brunel, Sir Marc Isambard (1769–1849)
Kensal Green Cemetery, Kensal Green, London.

Fled to New York from his native Normandy in September 1793, during the French Revolution, where he began to practise as a civil engineer and architect. He constructed the Bowery Theatre, but his highly ornamental designs for the National Capitol in Washington were not accepted. In 1799 he came to England to submit to the Government his plans for the mechanical production of ships' blocks in substitution for the manual process then employed; and these were eventually accepted. He designed swing bridges, and a floating landing stage at Liverpool in 1826; but he became famous for the use of his 'shield' in the construction of the Rotherhithe Tunnel which was finally completed and opened in 1843. He was knighted in 1841.

Cavendish, Henry (1731–1810)
Cathedral of All Saints, Derby.

Chemist and physicist who was the first scientist to recognize inflammable air, later called hydrogen. He conducted investigations which determined the specific gravity of hydrogen and carbon dioxide with reference to common air, showed the extent to which gases are absorbed by various liquids, and noted that 'common air containing one part in nine by volume of fixed air is no longer able to support combustion, and that air produced by fermentation and putrefaction has properties identical with those of fixed air obtained from marble.' He also carried out successful experiments into the chemical composition of water.

Comfort, Alexander (1920–2000)
Comforts Wood, Swattenden Lane, Cranbrook, Kent.

Biologist, writer, anarchist. Alexander Comfort had a dazzling academic career and published many political novels, but he is best known as the author of the 1972 sex manual *Joy of Sex*. The book was an international success and sold more than 12 million copies worldwide and Comfort is credited with bringing sexuality into the public domain.

Darwin, Charles Robert (1809–1892)
Westminster Abbey, London, in the north choir aisle of the Nave.

Naturalist who was one of the pioneers of experimental biology. His five years voyaging the world on the *Beagle*, 1831–1836, provided him with the material from which over the next twenty years he developed his controversial theory of evolution, which he published in *The Origin of Species* in 1859, arguing that the evolution of present-day morphology had been built up by the gradual and opportunistic mechanism of natural selection.

Dee, John (1527–1608)
St Mary's Church, Mortlake, Surrey.

Astrologer and mathematician. He was educated at St John's College, Cambridge, and was later elected a Fellow of Trinity College. In 1548 he was forced to leave England because of suspicions that he was a conjurer but returned in 1551 when he was awarded a pension by Edward VI. During the reign of Queen Mary I he was accused of issuing enchantments against the Queen's life and briefly imprisoned. He was released in 1555 by an order in council. When Elizabeth ascended the throne he was asked to name a propitious day for her coronation and he was introduced to the new Queen, who then took lessons from him in the mythical interpretations of his writings. Whilst he remained her favourite astrologer, she did not often carry out her promises to him, although in May 1595 he was made the Warden of Manchester College. He died in poverty and seclusion and is described by Aubrey as 'of a very fair, clear sanguine complexion, with a long beard as white as milk – a very handsome man – tall and slender. He wore a goune like an artist's goune with hanging sleeves.'

Eysenck, Hans (1916–1997)
His ashes were scattered in the grounds of Beckenham Crematorium.

Psychologist. Born in Germany on 4 March, 1916, Eysenck's family moved to England in the 1930s to escape the rise of the Nazis. He was professor of psychology at the Institute of Psychiatry from 1955 to 1983. Through his development of scales, e.g. the Maudsley Medical Questionnaire and the Eysenck Personality Inventory, he was a major contributor to the scientific theory of personality, although he was often controversial. He wrote over fifty books and was the founding editor of the journal *Personality and Individual Differences*.

Faraday, Michael (1791–1867)
Highgate 'old' Cemetery, Highgate, London.

Son of a Yorkshire blacksmith who had moved to Surrey, the young Michael Faraday was apprenticed to a bookbinder. He came to the attention of Sir Humphrey Davy who, in 1813, had him appointed as an assistant to the Royal Institution of Great Britain, becoming its director twelve years later, and then, in 1833, Fullerian Professor of Chemistry for life without the obligation to deliver lectures. He founded the science of electromagnetism which led to the modern developments in physics and electronics. Gladstone is reputed to have asked Faraday of what use electricity would be, to which Faraday replied, 'One day you will be able to tax it, sir.'

Ferranti, Sebastian Ziani de (1864–1930)
Hampstead Cemetery, Fortune Green Road, London.

Electrical engineer who was born in Liverpool of an Italian father and English mother. His first job was with Siemens Brothers, where in 1881 he assisted Sir William Siemens in his experiments with an electric furnace for making steel. At the same time he attended evening classes at University College, London. He made the first Ferranti dynamo with a cordless disc in 1882, patenting it as the Ferranti alternator; it had an electrical output far greater than its rivals. In 1887 he became chief electrician to the newly formed London Electric Supply Corporation, resigning in 1892 to devote his time to private business, founding Ferranti Ltd at Hollinwood in Lancashire. A pioneer in high-voltage systems, he may be considered the originator of long-distance transmission of high-tension electric current.

Flamsteed, John (1646–1719)
St Bartholomew's Church, Burstow, Surrey, in the chancel.

Son of a Derby maltster, he left the free school of Derby because of ill health. He interested himself in astronomy and read all he could buy or borrow on the subject. He observed a partial solar eclipse on 12 September 1662 and attempted the construction of measurement instruments. Became acquainted with Isaac Newton at Cambridge in about 1670, entered the university and took the degree of MA four years later by letters patent. He was appointed 'astronomical observator' by Charles II on 4 March 1675 at a salary of £100 per annum, during which year he was also ordained. In 1684 Lord North presented him with the living of Burstow in Surrey. During the latter part of his life Flamsteed was in disagreement with Newton over the results of their observations, Flamsteed not wishing to publish his results until they could be presented in complete form. But, being a public servant, he had to make known the progress of his observations and was forced to submit. The result, *Historica coelestis*, was nonetheless denounced by him as surreptitious, and he set about producing his own monumental work, the *Historica coelestis Britannica*, which was only partially published at his death.

Fleming, Sir Alexander (1881–1955)
St Paul's Cathedral, London, in the crypt.

Bacteriologist who in 1922 discovered the antibacterial enzyme, lysozyme, and in 1928, penicillin. In 1945 he shared the Nobel Prize for Medicine with Florey and Chain.

Freud, Sigmund (1856–1939)
Golders Green Crematorium, Hoop Lane, London NW11. Ashes in urn in East Columbarium; receptionist desk will provide key to allow viewing.

Physician, psychopathologist, founder of psychoanalysis, Freud was born at Freiberg, Moravia. After graduating in medicine he specialized in neurology. His interest in the Viennese Dr Breuer's work, whereby hysteria could be cured by hypnosis, led the young Freud to further study under Professor Charcot in Paris. Here Freud turned exclusively to psychopathology and gradually developed his famous methods of psychoanalysis. In this technique a person relaxes with the analyst and is guided in free thought-association. Previously such thoughts were brought out under hypnotism but Freud's method obviated such a procedure. Infantile sexuality and interpreted dreams were the basic work-blocks of his theories. Repressed sexual thoughts and desires manifested themselves, he believed in dreams, which were a subconscious way of repressing painful thoughts. If the person could be made to face these hidden thoughts, and replace them with rational judgement, mental illnesses could be cured.

Freud's work caused much controversy and still does. In 1938 he was forced to escape from Hitler's Austria and fled to England. Here he lived at Hampstead, London until he died of jaw cancer.

Friese-Green, William (1855–1921)
Highgate 'new' Cemetery, Highgate, London.

English inventor of the cinematograph through the production of continuous photographs on celluloid. He died virtually penniless.

Halley, Edmund (1656–1742)
St Margaret's Church, Lea Green, buried in the Old Churchyard in the southeastern corner near the road. A memorial stone can be seen at the Royal Observatory, Greenwich, London.

Astronomer. Edmund Halley was the son of a wealthy London businessman and was educated at St Paul's School, London, before moving up to Queen's College, Oxford. In 1675 he began working with the Astronomer Royal, Flamsteed, assisting him with observations in Oxford and Greensich. When the Royal Observatory opened at Greenwich later that year, Flamsteed began mapping the stars of the northern hemisphere. The following year, at the age of twenty, Halley sailed to St Helena to start mapping the stars of the southern hemisphere.

Halley's greatest contribution to astronomy is his study of comets and Halley's Comet was named after him. He also had a long standing friendship with Newton and is credited with financing the publication of the *Principia Mathematica*. In 1720 Halley succeeded Flamsteed as Astronomer Royal.

Harvey, Sir William (1578–1657)
St Andrew's Church, Hempstead, Essex.

Physician who first demonstrated the circulatory system of blood and the function of the heart. He has been called 'the grandfather of modern medicine'. He studied at Cambridge and Padua, and in 1607 became a fellow of the Royal College of Physicians and two years later physician to

St Bartholomew's Hospital. He was physician to both James I and Charles I, and carried out many reforms in the practice of medicine. His notes on the circulation of blood, the heart and other organs are still in the British Library. His treatise on circulation, *Exercitatio anatomica de motu cordis et sanguinis*, was published in 1628 in Latin.

Heaviside, Oliver (1850–1925)
Paignton Cemetery, Paignton, Devon.

A self-taught mathematical physicist and electrical engineer who discovered that when an electric current starts in a wire it begins on its boundary and works inwards. Thus, in the language of Heaviside, such a transient current is 'in layers, strong at the boundary, weak in the middle'. His work was responsible for the enrichment and clarification of the language of electro-dynamics. Also, in 1902, he remarked, with regard to 'wireless' waves, that there might possibly be a sufficiently conducting 'layer' in the atmosphere to aid their transmission. This useful conception became known as the 'Heaviside Layer'.

Herschel, Sir William (1738–1822)
St Laurence's Church, Upton, Slough, where there is a monument by J. Theakston in the form of a simple, heavy Grecian tablet. A commemorative stone lies in the north aisle of the Nave in Westminster Abbey.

German-born astronomer who joined the Hanoverian guards as an oboist and, about 1757, came to England, technically deserting his regiment for which, in 1782, he was granted a full pardon by George III. At first he made his living by training the band of the Durham Militia and, after incurring the notice of Dr Miller of Doncaster, going there to teach music. The study of harmony eventually led to an interest in astronomy and inspired his resolution 'to take nothing on trust'. He bought a small reflector with his brother's help, the better to study the heavens. On 13 March 1781 he discovered the planet Uranus and investigated the distribution of stars in the Milky Way, concluding that some of the nebulae he could see were separate star systems.

Herschel, Sir John Frederick William (1792–1871)
Westminster Abbey, London, in the north aisle of the Nave.

Astronomer. Son of Sir William, who continued with his father's researches, completing his own survey of the heavens in the southern hemisphere at the Cape of Good Hope in February 1834. His work at

Feldhausen near Cape Town marked the commencement in a wide sense of southern sidereal astronomy. He was also a highly accomplished chemist and in 1819 he discovered the solvent power of hyposulphate of soda on the otherwise insoluble salts of silver, which was a prelude to its use as a fixing agent in photography. In 1839, independent of Fox Talbot, he invented the process of photography on sensitized paper and was the first person to apply the terms 'positive' and 'negative' to photographic images and to imprint them on glass prepared by the deposit of a sensitive film.

Hooke, Robert (1635–1703)
St Helen's Church, Bishopsgate, City of London.
  Experimental philosopher whose inventions include the wheel barometer, the application of springs to the balance of watches, together with the explanation of their action by the principle *ut tensio sic vis*; he also originated the idea of using the pendulum as a measure of gravity. His scientific achievements would have been more striking if they had been less varied and while he originated much he perfected little. As an architect he constructed a model for the rebuilding of the City of London after the Great Fire of 1666, but Wren's was preferred though never realised. When rebuilding did commence Hooke was appointed Surveyor.

Hunter, John (1728–1793)
Westminster Abbey, London, in the north aisle of the Nave. His remains were removed here from their original burial site in St Martin-in-the-Fields in 1859.
  Physiologist and surgeon. In 1748 he moved to London from Scotland to attend dissections at Symonds' anatomical school where his brother, William, lectured. In 1754 he became a surgeon-pupil at St George's Hospital where, in 1756, he was appointed house surgeon. In 1761 he went with Keppel's expedition to Belleisle as staff surgeon and when he returned to London two years later he set up as a surgeon. He developed several new surgical techniques. His anatomical collection is now housed in the Royal College of Surgeons.

Hunter, William (1718–1783)
St James's Church, Piccadilly, London.
  Physiologist and elder brother of the more famous surgeon, John Hunter. He moved from Scotland to London about 1741 and entered St

George's Hospital as a pupil surgeon. He attained considerable fame as a lecturer. In 1747 he became a member of the Corporation of Surgeons, but, by degrees, he renounced surgery in favour of obstetrics, in which he excelled. In September 1756 he became a Licentiate of the Royal College of Physicians and in 1764 he was made Physician-Extraordinary to Queen Charlotte, wife of George III.

Huxley, Thomas Henry (1825–1895)
Finchley Cemetery, Finchley, London.

Biologist who began his career as an assistant surgeon on HMS *Rattlesnake*. During the voyage of 1846 to 1850 he studied marine organisms. In 1870 he gave the first recognizably modern lecture on the origin of life to the British Association, having become an ardent evolutionist after the publication of Darwin's *The Origin of Species*. He originated the term 'Agnostic'. His writings, which include *Man's Place in Nature*, attempted to interest the public in the importance of science.

Jenner, Edward (1749–1823)
St Mary's Church, Berkeley, Gloucestershire.

Physician. A pupil of John Hunter, in 1792 he obtained the degree of doctor of medicine from St Andrew's. He practised at Berkeley in Gloucestershire, where he was born, and pursued his earlier enquiries into the relations between cowpox and smallpox. He developed a vaccine against smallpox in 1798, the use of which, with the support of the King, George III and his wife, Charlotte, and their son, George, Prince of Wales, gradually spread throughout Britain and the world. His discovery helped lay the foundations of modern immunology.

Kelvin, William Thomson, 1st Baron Kelvin of Largs (1824–1907)
Westminster Abbey, London, in the central aisle of the Nave.

Mathematician and physicist who was born in Belfast. He is principally known for his work on heat and thermodynamics, and for his contributions to electrical science and submarine telegraphy. He introduced the Kelvin or Absolute scale of temperature. In 1902 he was awarded the Order of Merit on its institution, having been made President of the Royal Society in 1890 and created a baron in 1892.

Lister, Joseph, 1st Baron Lister of Lyme Regis (1827–1892)
Hampstead Cemetery, Fortune Green Road, London.

Surgeon. His early observation of gangrene and pyaemia at the University College Hospital, London, led him to suspect the parasitic nature of the disorders. He continued his researches as a young surgeon at Edinburgh and developed a fine spray of a watery solution of carbolic acid to destroy the germs in the atmosphere and on the surgeon's hands. The spray, which was but one of his antiseptic methods, and his arduous campaign for greater hygiene, especially in the sterilization of catgut used in suturing wounds, led to a dramatic improvement in patient recovery. While they met with ridicule and opposition in some quarters of the profession, his methods were eventually recognized as vital.

Lodge, Oliver Joseph (1851–1940)
St Michael's Church, Wilsford (Lake), Wiltshire, close to the south-east wall.

The virtual inventor of practical wireless telegraphy, he was born at Penkhull, Staffordshire, of a family of schoolmasters and clergymen. His paternal grandfather had twenty-five children, of whom Oliver's father was the twenty-third. Oliver left school when he was 14 years old and worked in his father's agency business until his aunt encouraged him to study science in London. He 'had his eyes opened' by a series of lectures on the physics of heat. He won prizes and studied under T. H. Huxley at the Royal College of Science. His discovery of the cohesion of metals under the influence of electro-magnetism earned him the Royal Society's Rumford Medal and made wireless telegraphy practical by taking away the 'disease which afflicted early transmitters' after he prescribed the remedy. Later he became interested in psychic phenomena, believing the mind lives on after death. He wrote several scientific works, but his psychical book *Raymond, or Life and Death* (1916), gained popular interest. His son Raymond had been killed in the war. Lodge was knighted in 1902, retiring in 1919 to Lake to devote his time to the 'ether of space', which he saw as a medium for the storage of mental energy.

Maudslay, Henry (1771–1831)
St Mary Magdalene's Church, Woolwich, London.

Engineer who first produced precision-cut nuts and bolts that were completely interchangeable by designing a precision thread-cutting lathe that produced the screw-thread within close tolerances to a uniform pitch. He also designed and invented many other engineering artefacts, including the first cup valve for high-pressure steam engines, the micrometer and steamboat engines. Brunel, with whom Maudslay had worked, specified a Maudslay slide-lever engine for his *Great Western*, the first successful transatlantic steamship.

St Michael's Church, Wilsford, Wiltshire; Sir Oliver Lodge's grave here

Newton, Sir Isaac (1642–1727)
Westminster Abbey, London, in the central aisle of the Nave.

Born in Lancashire he studied at Cambridge where in 1669 he became Lucasian Professor of Mathematics. He made three important discoveries: his theory of gravitation indicated that the universe was regulated by simple mathematical laws; that white light could be separated into a sequence of coloured components, forming the visible spectrum; and the use of the calculus, which he invented independent of Leibnitz, to investigate the forces of nature in a quantitative way. He propounded his views in his famous *Naturales Principia Mathematica* of 1687.

Rutherford, Ernest, 1st Baron Rutherford of Nelson (1871–1937)
Westminster Abbey, London, in the central aisle of the Nave.

Physicist. He was born in New Zealand. In 1911 he announced his theory on the structure of the atom, and in 1918 succeeded in splitting it, thus preparing the way for future nuclear research. In 1908 he received the Nobel Prize for Chemistry for his work on radioactivity and the discovery of alpha and beta radiation. He was the Cavendish Professor of Experimental Physics at Cambridge and Director of the Royal Society Mond Laboratory in Cambridge.

Siemens, Sir William (1823–1883)
Kensal Green Cemetery, Kensal Green, London.

Metallurgist and electrical engineer. Born in Hanover, he visited England in 1842 to set up his electro-plating service and equipment because the British patent laws afforded him better protection. He decided to settle there in 1844 and became a British citizen in 1859. He worked in two distinct fields: the application of heat, and the application of electricity. He was responsible for numerous inventions, and his improvements of the steel furnace which led to the 'open-hearth' process introduced Siemens' steel.

Snow, John (1813–1858)
Brompton Cemetery, West Brompton, London.

During his observations of cholera Snow discovered that this disease was communicated by contaminated water. He was the first doctor to use ether as an anaesthetic in England. He gave chloroform to Queen Victoria at the birth of her son, Prince Leopold, on 7 April 1853, and again in April 1857 at the birth of Princess Beatrice. The Queen was the first royal personage to receive an anaesthetic.

Sopwith, Sir Thomas Octave Murdoch (1888–1989)
Little Somborne Redundant churchyard, near King's Somborne, Hampshire.

Aircraft designer whose name will be ever associated with the fighter planes he built during the first world war. He flew across the English Channel in 1910, winning the Baron de Forest prize for so doing. His Kingston-on-Thames aeroplane manufacturing company designed and built the famous 'Camel' and 'Pup' fighters and others of World War I. Later he became chairman of Hawker-Siddeley's and also chaired the Society of British Aircraft Constructors. He was also a keen yachtsman, competing in the 1934 America Cup race. A CBE came to him in 1918 and a knighthood in 1953.

Spilsbury, Sir Bernard Henry (1877–1947)
Golders Green Crematorium, Golders Green, London; ashes dispersed on Garden of Rest lawn, Book of Remembrance in Chapel of Memory.

Pathologist who became famous at the trial (1910) of Dr Crippen, who had murdered his wife with hyoscyamine, which is difficult to detect after death. This was the first time this poison had been used in a murder – so far as is known! For thirty-five years after that Spilsbury was famous in England as a 'detective-pathologist' whose evidence as a Crown witness frequently helped to establish either the guilt or innocence of the accused person. Spilsbury, the son of a manufacturing chemist, was born in Leamington, Warwickshire. Depressed after the loss of a sister and two sons (one killed in an air raid) and suffering from increasing coronary thrombosis and arthritis, he took his own life by administering carbon monoxide to himself in his University College laboratory.

Stephenson, George (1781–1848)
Trinity Church, Chesterfield, Derbyshire, beneath the communion table.

Engineer and locomotive designer. In 1825 he and his son, Robert, built the *Locomotion* for the Stockton and Darlington Railway; and four years later his engine the *Rocket* won the £500 prize offered by the Liverpool and Manchester Railway when it reached speeds of 30 mph. He was also responsible for discovering the method on which the miners' safety lamp was based.

Talbot, William Henry Fox (1800–1877)
Lacock Cemetery, Lacock, Wiltshire, by the path on the right-hand side.

Often called 'the inventor of photography', but in the early days he really shared the honour with the Frenchman Louis Daguerre and in England with Thomas Wedgwood (1771–1805; buried at St Mary's church, Tarrant Gunville, Dorset) and Joseph Reade. Talbot's idea of getting permanent 'sun pictures' of the projected images of a camera obscura led him to the discovery that paper was made sensitive to light by coating it with iodide and nitrate of silver. Gallic acid was used to bring out the latent image so formed. This so-called Talbotype was the basis of modern photography. His photography, however, has tended to obscure his other skill in mathematics which he early displayed at Cambridge University. He won the Rumford Medal for his photographic discoveries. He was the first to decipher the cuneiform inscriptions on objects found in the 'Nineveh' excavations by Sir Austen Henry Layard (1817–1894).

Todd, Sir Alexander Robertus, Lord Todd of Trumpington (1907–1997)
His ashes were scattered in the master's garden of Christ's College, Cambridge.

Chemist. Born in Glasgow, Todd was an undergraduate student at Glasgow University before undertaking doctorates in Germany and at Oxford. He held academic posts in Edinburgh, London and Manchester universities before returning to Cambridge to accept a Chair in 1944. Todd was awarded the Nobel Prize for Chemistry in 1957 and his research led directly to the understanding of nucleic acids and to Watson and Crick's discovery of the helical structure of DNA. He was knighted in 1954 and raised to the Peerage as Baron Todd of Trumpington in 1962.

Tizard, Sir Henry Thomas (1885–1959)
Oriel College Ante-chapel, Oxford, Oxfordshire; ashes under stone bearing his initials.

Scientist and administrator who was responsible for much of the work behind the development of a series of radar stations that were ready in time to help give air victory in the Battle of Britain. A Magdalen College graduate in chemistry, he was in the Royal Flying Corps during the first world war when he worked on the early development of bomb sights. He was also among the founders of the aircraft and armament establishment

Fox Talbot's grave in Lacock Cemetery, Wiltshire

at Martlesham Heath in Suffolk, later moved to Boscombe Down, Wiltshire. He was a Controller of Aeronautical Research and later Chairman of the Aeronautical Research Committee between the world wars. He was valued by Churchill for his scientific advice but he also came into notorious disagreement with Churchill's official scientific adviser Professor F. A. Lindemann (later Lord Cherwell) over the mass bombing of Germany that Lindemann had championed – Tizard did not believe in wasting valuable pilots on blind bombing of population centres but in more wisely concentrating on destroying Germany's naval capabilities. He was a Fellow of the Royal Society and a Fellow of Oriel, whose Provost married him in 1915 to Kathleen Wilson, daughter of a mining engineer; there were two sons of the marriage.

Wallace, Alfred Russel (1823–1913)
Broadstone Cemetery, off Gravel Hill, Broadstone, Dorset; half-way down the main path on right with petrified tree-trunk on a plinth over his grave.

Naturalist, born at Usk in Wales, who shares with Darwin the honour of giving the theory of evolution to the world. Wallace, however, believed the soul of man came directly from God. One of eight children, whose father was a 'dabbler in many things but a master of none', he first worked as a surveyor with his brother in London. Alfred developed an interest in geology, astronomy and agriculture, and after meeting a famous naturalist, Henry Walter Bates, was introduced to entomology. This meeting became the pivot-point of Alfred's career. He proposed they join forces and go on a collecting expedition in 1848 to the Amazon in South America; they would finance the trip from the sale of specimens they brought back. Wallace became fascinated with the incredible variety of birds, butterflies and plants, and by the majestic equatorial forest. After four years, when Bates had parted company with him, he set sail back to England, but all his notes and specimens were lost in a fire at sea. He and the ship's company were rescued after eleven days at sea in open boats.

Undaunted, he went next to the Malay Archipelago, where he remained for eight years, visiting every island. In 1855 he published his work on the law governing the introduction of new species of life. In 1858, while recovering from yellow fever in Ternate, the idea of natural selection as the means of evolution 'flashed' through his mind. He wrote his views and sent them to Charles Darwin, who had also been working on the same theme. Their joint paper was read before the Linnaean Society in 1858. Wallace could have been the first, technically, to announce the theory but he generously shared the honour with Darwin. After achieving many honours and world-wide fame Wallace died at Broadstone, where he had lived since 1902.

Watt, James (1736–1819)
St Mary's Church, Handsworth, Birmingham.

Scottish engineer and inventor of the modern steam engine. This resulted from his important improvements to Thomas Newcomen's steam engine by inventing a separate condenser. He perfected a rotary engine and defined one horse power as the rate at which work is done when 33,000lbs are raised one foot in one minute. The electrical unit of power, the 'watt', was named after him.

Also buried at St Mary's Church were:

Matthew Boulton (1728–1809), an engineer who was a partner to Watt and in Boulton's workshops at Soho, near Birmingham, found the way to make Watt's steam engine work efficiently.

William Murdock (1754–1839), an engineer with Boulton and Watt whose experiment on the distillation of coal and wood first brought gas lighting to a practical stage, illuminating their factory with it in 1803. He advanced engineering by giant steps with his ability, being presented with the Rumford Medal by the Royal Society.

White, Gilbert (1720–1793)
St Mary's Churchyard, Selborne, Hampshire; small sign near path points to grave.

Naturalist and antiquary whose *The Natural History and Antiquities of Selborne*, based on letters to Daines Barrington and Thomas Pennant, was published in 1789 by White's brother Benjamin, a Fleet Street publisher. It is one of the few books on natural history to gain the rank of an English classic. Part of its secret was that White was a 'prince among observers', nearly always observing the right thing at the right time and writing of what he saw with a great economy of words. It has been said: 'open the book where you will, it takes you out of doors'.

White's father was a barrister, and his grandfather was vicar of St Mary's Church at Selborne. At Oxford White became a fellow of Oriel College in 1744, dean of the college in 1752, and was ordained as a priest between those two dates. He served as a curate at nearby parishes and at Selborne from 1751. He produced other works including *Of the House-Swallows, Swift, and Sand-Martin* but *The Natural History of Selborne* is his paramount claim to fame.

Chapter 7
Entrepreneurs (including businessmen and industrialists)

Arkwright, Sir Richard (1732–1792)
St Mary's Church, Cromford, Derbyshire.

Originally a Preston barber, he began experiments with cotton-spinning machines, and, in 1796, patented his water frame, so called because it was driven by water. His neighbours referred to it as the 'Devil's bagpipes' – a reference to the large number of pipes used in the experiments. Later, he adapted it for steam. Together with his partner, Jebediah Strutt, he established large cotton mills that began the movement known as the Industrial Revolution.

Baring, Sir Francis (1740–1810)
St Mary's Church, Micheldever, Hampshire; in the family vault.

Founder of the financial house of Baring Brothers and Company. He could be regarded as a British Rothschild, Rockefeller or Morgan, in the sense that all four gigantic financial houses were formed round about the same time. Sir Francis was the son of a clothmaker, who had settled near Exeter and who sent the young Baring to study commerce in London. Although he was deaf as a youth, his tremendous energy and ability overcame all obstacles and, after starting an import-export agency with his brother, he went on to found the merchant bank that helped Britain's financial needs during the Napoleonic wars. He became a friend of William Pitt the Younger and, as a director of the East India Company, Sir Francis was often asked for financial advice by the government. By the time of his death he is said to have earned £7 million. He was knighted in 1793, and his descendants included Evelyn Baring, first Earl of Cromer (1841–1917), 'maker of modern Egypt' (whom see). Sir Francis also wrote several works, largely to justify his belief that the issue of Bank of England notes should be limited.

Baskerville, John (1706–1775)
Originally buried in the brick windmill he had built as a papermill alongside his house, site of the present Baskerville House in Birmingham. It was destroyed in the Riots of 1791 and later the coffin was on

public display in a shop. It was secretly placed in one of the catacombs under Christ Church (Victoria Square) but, when that was closed in 1899, the coffin was moved to the vaults under the chapel in the Birmingham Church of England Cemetery, Warstone Lane. That chapel was demolished about 1955 but the vault remains. There is no visible monument.

Printer and typeface designer who about 1726 became a writing master at Birmingham where he showed an exceptional talent for calligraphy and for cutting inscriptions in stone. Whilst at Birmingham he made some important improvements in the process of japanning, and gained a considerable fortune. Around 1750 he began to make experiments in type-founding, producing types superior to any hitherto. He set up a printing house and in 1757 published his first book, a Virgil in a royal quarto, followed in 1758 by his famous edition of Milton. That same year he was appointed printer to the University of Cambridge. Baskerville's typefaces are still much used.

Cadbury, George (1893–1922)
In Friends Meeting House, Bourneville, Birmingham; ashes in urn.

Cocoa and chocolate manufacturer and philanthropist, son of a Quaker grocer, Cadbury worked for a time in Joseph Rowntree's grocery store. They both became world-wide competitors as chocolate manufacturers. Cadbury founded the town of Bourneville as a village trust in 1900 to ensure the new factory location he had selected would not become surrounded by slums as workers were attracted to the area. For a time he taught in the Adult School movement and, later, acquired several Birmingham newspapers to ensure that his liberal views were represented.

Caslon, William, 'The Elder' (1692–1766)
St Luke's, Old Street, Islington, London.

Born at Cradley in Worcestershire, he came to London and in 1716 started business as an engraver of gun locks and barrels, as well as a bookbinder's tool-cutter. He was induced, through his association with printers, to fit up a type foundry, and the distinction and legibility of his type secured him the patronage of the leading printers of the time in England and on the Continent. The use of Caslon type was discontinued at the beginning of the nineteenth century but revived about 1845 at the suggestion of Sir Henry Cole. Caslon's business was continued by his son William (1720–1798).

Cassell, John (1817–1865)
Kensal Green Cemetery, Kensal Green, London.

Publisher. The son of a Manchester publican, he was apprenticed to a joiner. Self-educated, he moved to London in 1836 where he became involved in the Temperance Movement. In 1847 he established himself as a tea and coffee merchant and soon afterwards started a publishing business with the aim of supplying good literature to the working classes. The firm, which in 1859 became Messrs Cassell, Petter, Galpin & Co., issued the *Popular Educator* (1852–1855), the *Technical Educator* (1870–1872), the *Magazine of Art* (1878–1903) and *Cassell's Magazine* (from 1852). A special feature of their popular books was the illustrations and, at the time of the Crimean War, he procured from Paris the cuts used by *L'Illustration*, and by printing them in his *Family Paper* (begun in 1853) secured a large circulation for it. The firm became Cassell & Co. in 1883.

Caxton, William (c. 1422–1491)
St Margaret's, Westminster, London.

Born in Kent, he was apprenticed to Robert Large, a rich silk mercer, who probably sent Caxton direct to Bruges, then the central market for the Anglo–Flemish trade. In 1463 Caxton was acting governor of the company, Merchant Adventurers, in the Low Countries, sometimes known as the 'English Nation', which was dominated by the Mercer's Company, and he undertook diplomatic missions to the Burgundian court. In about 1469 he entered the household of Margaret Duchess of Burgundy, sister to Edward IV, possibly in the role of commerical adviser, where he must have met her brother, the English King, during his brief exile at the Burgundian court in 1470. During Caxton's thirty-three years of residence in Bruges he would have had access to the rich libraries of the Duke of Burgundy and other Flemish nobles, and during the same time he learned the art of printing, possibly at Cologne, according to his disciple de Worde. He printed his first book, the *Recuyell*, in 1474 or 1475. In September 1476 he set up his press in the Almonry at Westminster at the sign of the Red Pale, from which many of his texts came.

Chippendale, Thomas (d.1779)
St Martin-in-the-Fields, St Martin's Place, London.

Son of a Worcester cabinet-maker, he moved to London in the reign of George I. In 1752 he describes himself as a 'cabinet-maker and upholsterer of St Martin's Lane'. His influence was so great that almost all mahogany furniture in the eighteenth century is erroneously referred to as 'Chippendale'. In 1754 he published the first edition of *The Gentleman and Cabinet Maker's Director*. Sheraton, writing of Chippendale and his work in 1793, said, 'As for the designs themselves, they are now wholly antiquated and laid aside, though possessed of great merit according to the times in which they were executed'.

Cohen, Jack (1898–1979)
Willesden Jewish Cemetery, London.

Grocer and businessman. Jack Cohen began selling groceries in London's East End markets in 1919. He had invested thirty pounds of his reward for military service to buy surplus food stock piles. Gradually the business grew and in 1924 he bought a large quantity of tea from T. E. Stockwell and sold it under the brand name 'Tesco', which was the amalgamation of T. E. Stockwell's initials and the first two letters from his own surname. In 1929 the first Tesco store was opened in Edgware, London, and the first self-service store was opened in 1948, one year after the firm was floated on the London Stock Exchange.

Darby, Abraham (1677–1717)
All Saints' Church, Broseley, Shropshire.

Quaker ironmaster of Coalbrookdale, Shropshire, who paved the way for the Industrial Revolution by developing iron metallurgy with his employee, John Thomas. His grandson, Abraham (1750–1791), built the first cast-iron bridge, over the Severn at Coalbrookdale, in 1779.

Fayed, ('Dodi') Emad (1956–1997)
Originally interred at the interfaith cemetery, Brookwood, Surrey but then moved to a new family burial spot on the country estate of his father Mohammed Al Fayed at Oxted, Surrey.

Born in Gamrok, Alexandria, Egypt. The wealth and influence his father achieved in adult life allowed Dodi to follow his early passion for the cinema. His uncle was Adnan Khashoggi, a Saudi financier who was said at the time to be the world's richest man. His father, Mohammed Al Fayed is the owner of London department store 'Harrods'. In England Dodi became 'adopted' by the Broccoli family after meeting Barbara, the youngest daughter of Albert 'Cubby' Broccoli, producer of James Bond movies. After taking a summer course in film making at Loyola University in New Orleans, Dodi displayed a remarkable talent for the art. His first major film was *Chariots of Fire*, for which he won a 1982

Academy Award for Best Motion Picture as executive producer. He became the epitome of a rich man-of-the-world with global residences, expensive cars and beautiful girls. In 1986 just after Christmas he married an international model Suzanne Gregard whom he had met in New York. The marriage lasted only ten months. On the day of a fatal car crash in Paris, in which he and Princess Diana were killed, he had bought an engagement ring, which he had presumably intended to offer Diana later that night.

Foyle, William Alfred (1885–1963)
Highgate Cemetery (East), London.

Businessman. William Foyle co-founded Foyles bookshop with his brother Gilbert, and went on to become its Managing Director. The brothers had started selling unwanted textbooks in 1903, after failing their Civil Service examinations, and moved the business to Charing Cross Road in 1906, where it has remained ever since. Foyles bookshop continues to be privately owned.

Getty, John Paul, Jr (1932–2003)
Mausoleum on the Getty Family Estate, Stokenchurch, near Oxford.

Businessman and philanthropist. John Paul Getty Snr was the richest man in the world in his day, due to the $6 billion fortune which was Getty Oil. John Paul Getty Jr was the third of five sons and he took charge of the Getty Oil business in Rome after studying at San Francisco University and serving a short time in the army. He lasted only six years in the family business and left to pursue an alternative party lifestyle, growing his hair and wearing the multi-coloured kaftans that were fashionable at the time. He was estranged from his father, who left him only a nominal amount in his will but the bulk of his fortune came from a family trust after the sale of Getty Oil to Texaco in 1984. In 1986 he was given an honorary knighthood by the British government for his services to charity. In 1998 he took British citizenship and was then invested with the full knighthood.

Gresham, Sir Thomas (1519–1579)
St Helen's Church, Bishopsgate, City of London, where there is a fine free-standing tomb-chest of Siena marble without effigy but large coats of arms.

Merchant and financier who gave his name to 'Gresham's Law', which states that 'Bad money drives good money out'. He advised and

Sir Thomas Gresham, by an unknown Flemish artist

served four successive sovereigns, including Elizabeth I, on money matters. He also founded The Royal Exchange.

Hansard, Luke (1752–1828)
St Giles-in-the-Fields, Holborn, London.
Printer. Born in Norwich, he went to London after the expiration of his apprenticeship to Stephen White, a Norwich printer. He joined the firm of John Hughs, printer to the House of Commons, who in 1774 made him a partner. In 1800 the business came entirely into Hansard's hands and was renamed later as Luke Hansard & Sons. From 1774 until his death he printed the *Journals of the House of Commons*. It was his son, Thomas Curson Hansard, who began printing the *Parliamentary Debates* in 1803 from his own press in Paternoster Row.

Lane, John (1854–1925)
St Nectan's Church, Hartland, North Devon.
Publisher. Born at West Putford in Devon, the only son of a miller and corn merchant. After working for eighteen years as a clerk in the Railway Clearing House he became an antiquarian bookseller in partnership with an Exeter friend, Elkin Mathews. He then founded the Bodley Head publishing house, whose imprint honoured Sir Thomas Bodley, an illustrious Devonian and founder of the Bodleian Library at Oxford. His list included many of the most famous literary figures of the day: Max Beerbohm, Baron Corvo, Anatole France and William John Locke. He started the celebrated illustrated quarterly, *The Yellow Review*; and opened a branch of his firm in New York.

Leverhulme, William Hesketh Lever, 1st Viscount (1851–1925)
Christ Church, Port Sunlight, Cheshire, in enclosure adjoining church, two tombs: he and his wife.
Soap-maker-philanthropist who, after expanding his father's grocery business, specialized in the making of soap for which he registered the name Sunlight, in partnership with his brother James. His first soap was purchased from a manufacturer but, changing the way it was made – from tallow to vegetable oils – he began to make it in his own factory, founding Port Sunlight as his headquarters. He housed his workers in new homes, providing schools and a pleasant environment for them in a forward-thinking social philanthropy that was to mark his future efforts and earn him a baronage in 1917 and viscountcy in 1922. The school of tropical medicine at Liverpool University was one of his many

endowments. He travelled widely and saw his firm grow into a world-wide enterprise after an early financial crisis.

Marks, Michael (1859–1907)
Old Jewish Cemetery, Manchester, Lancashire; small stone obelisk.

Co-founder of Marks and Spencer merchandising chain, Marks was born in Slonim, Russia and came as a penniless refugee from the anti-Semitic pogroms there to Stockton-on-Tees in 1881. Starting with a pedlar's tray he followed fairs and markets hawking his wares until 1884 when he was lent £5 by Isaac Dewhirst that enabled him to set up a trestle stall in an open market at Leeds. Within ten years he was operating eight penny bazaars. He still used the wording he had on his pedlar's tray: 'Don't Ask the Price – It's a Penny'; a marketing phrase that he kept for many years, originated to solve his language problem. He went into partnership in 1894 with Tom Spencer, who had been Dewhirst's cashier. With continued success he was living a happy family life in Manchester when he died suddenly of a heart attack on New Year's Eve. He had married Hannah Cohen in 1886 and his son Simon, later to become Lord Marks of Broughton, fought successfully to keep the business in the family.

Maxim, Sir Hiram Stevens (1840–1916)
Norwood Cemetery, Norwood, London.

An American engineer who was born in Maine, coming to England in 1884. He invented the machine gun, known as the Maxim gun, a delayed-action fuse, smokeless powder and an aeroplane. His Maxim Gun Company merged with Vickers in 1896. He became a British citizen in 1900 and was knighted a year later.

Murray, John (1778–1843)
Kensal Green Cemetery, Kensal Green, London.

Son of John McMurray who founded the London publishing house of John Murray in Fleet Street. His father died when he was fifteen and the firm was largely run by his father's partner, Samuel Highley. In 1803 John Murray dissolved that partnership and launched into literary speculation which earned him the name given him by Lord Byron, 'the Anak of publishers'. He was the publisher of Lord Byron, as well as of Sir Walter Scott, Jane Austen, Robert Southey and Francis Palgrave.

Hiram Maxim

Northcliffe, Alfred Charles William Harmsworth, 1st Viscount (1865–1922)

Finchley Cemetery, Finchley, London. There is a bust of Lord Northcliffe on the south front of St Dunstan in the West, facing Fleet Street.

Born in Dublin, the son of a barrister. He began *Answers* in 1888 with his brother, Harold (later Lord Rothermere). In 1894 he bought the *Evening News*, in 1896 the *Daily Mail*, and in 1908 he took over *The Times*. His real claim to fame is that he changed the whole face of English journalism, woke it up, made it come alive and also made it prosperous.

Nuffield, William Richard Morris, 1st Viscount (1877–1963)

Holy Trinity Church, Nuffield, Oxfordshire, where a plain, blue-slate slab at the south-east corner of the church marks his grave.

Motor-car manufacturer and philanthropist. He started his career in a bicycle shop but his genius for business led him to found Morris Motors which made him a multi-millionaire. He retired from the company's chairmanship in 1952. As a philanthropist he provided large sums for the advancement of medicine to Oxford University and for Nuffield College, Oxford, and, in 1943, established the Nuffield Foundation, endowing it with £10 million.

Rothschild, Nathan Mayer (1777–1836)

Jewish Burial Ground, Brady Street, Whitechapel, London.

Banker. German-born, he arrived in Manchester in 1800 to act as a purchaser of manufactured goods for his father. His boldness and skill in financial transactions, at first treated with reserve, excited the admiration and envy of the British bankers and merchants. By using carrier pigeons and fast-sailing boats for the transmission of news he was able to utilize to his greatest advantage his special information. In 1810 he staked his reputation on the downfall of Napoleon and the Allies negotiated loans through Rothschild to carry on the war against the Emperor. He effected immense profit by the purchase of stock which rose as soon as news of Napoleon's defeat at Waterloo, already transmitted to Rothschild several hours before by his own fast service, reached the public. He was the first to popularize foreign loans in Britain by fixing the rate in sterling and making dividends payable in London and not in foreign capitals.

Grave of Lord Nuffield, Holy Trinity Churchyard, Nuffield, Oxfordshire

Rowntree, Joseph (1836–1925)
Society of Friends burial ground, Skeldergate, York; alongside the River Ouse.

Cocoa and chocolate manufacturer and philanthropist, son of a Quaker. Rowntree first joined his father in the grocery business, then went into partnership with his brother Henry in a cocoa-making firm they had acquired. Joseph took care to avoid the expense of labour troubles and their wasteful disruptions of production by paying top wages for reasonable hours and providing employees with good working conditions. His social work marked him as a foremost philanthropist of the day, of 'gentle ways and strong convictions'. He strongly supported the League of Nations and the Society of Friends.

Selfridge, Harry Gordon (1857–1947)
St Mark's Church, Highcliffe, Hampshire; in south part of graveyard about half-way down beside the west fence.

An American-born businessman who completed the building of, and opened, his famous London department store in 1908. His father had owned a small dry-goods shop in Ripon, Wisconsin, but went away with the US cavalry in the Civil War of 1861–5, attaining the rank of major and never returning to his family. After getting a clerk's job and rising high in the Chicago mail-order firm of Marshall Field & Co., Selfridge left America with a small fortune he had accumulated. Despite contrary advice, he decided that a department store in Oxford Street, London, would do well. With a capital of £900,000 he opened 'Selfridge's' and included many innovations, such as a free information bureau for all kinds of difficult questions, a library and roof-garden, and a pioneer 'truth-in-advertising' guarantee.

The business prospered, especially during World War I and up to the mid-1930s, but, because of a series of expensive personal follies in the years before World War II, he drew too much capital from his company and was forced to resign in 1939 with the honorary title of president. The company was taken over in 1951 by Lewis's Ltd, of Liverpool. Thus did the fortunes of the 'merchant prince' rise and fall within 30 years, perhaps reflecting in some ways England's own fortunes during the same period. He rented Highcliffe Castle for a few years when it was a magnificent Gothic mansion, which had been built in the 1830s by Lord Stuart of Rothesay, some of the stones having come from a medieval castle near Rouen. Selfridge's wife and mother are buried near him.

Gordon Selfridge's grave, Highcliffe, Hampshire

Smith, Douglas Alexander, 1st Baron Strathcona and Mount Royal (1820-1914)
Highgate Cemetery, London.

Fur trader and governor of Hudson's Bay Company. Born in Scotland, Smith was transferred to Labrador by Hudson's Bay Company in 1847. He rose through the ranks of the company, becoming a chief trader and later head of the Montreal Department. He was a company leader when Canada purchased the company's territories in 1869 and became very wealthy. Within a year Smith had made a name for himself during the Riel rebellion, when he was sent to Red River by the Conservative government to negotiate with the resistance. This led to an appointment to the Executive Council of the Northwest Territories and in 1871 he was elected as a member of Parliament. Smith held office for seventeen years but continued with his business interests as a railroader and a financier. In 1896 he was appointed Canadian high commissioner to London and the following year he was made Baron Strathcona and Mount Royal. He remained high commissioner until his death in January 1914.

Smith, William Henry (1792–1865)
Kensal Green Cemetery, London.

Founder W. H. Smith, the high street chain of newsagents and bookshops. Smith was only twenty years old when he took over his father's newsagent in The Strand in 1812. At this time the business was valued at £1,280. He was a huge success and his son, who became a partner in 1846, helped him to make W. H. Smith & Son a household name. Nowadays the firm employs over 30,000 staff and has recorded profits of almost £3 billion, although recently it has encountered some difficulties due to increased competition.

Spencer, Thomas, 'Tom' (1842–1905)
St Giles's Churchyard, Whittingham, Lichfield, Staffordshire, well-maintained grave.

Co-founder of Marks and Spencer, he had been a cashier for Isaac Dewhirst whom Michael Marks had first sought as a partner when his 'penny bazaars' that he had started from a street vendor's basket grew to eight in number. In 1903 the two partners incorporated, dividing 30,000 shares equally. Spencer bought a chicken farm at Lichfield shortly after, leaving the running of the company to Michael Marks. Spencer's son Tom, who became a director, later had a falling-out with Simon Marks, the founder's son. Spencer was born in Skipton, North Yorkshire, but the house in which he was born is now the site of a Woolworth store. They magnanimously allowed an identification tablet of Spencer's birthplace to be put up there, where it was unveiled by directors from both companies.

Tate, Sir Henry (1819–1899)
Norwood Cemetery, Norwood, London.

Son of a cleric, he was born at Chorley, Lancashire. His father put him into business in Liverpool and he became a prosperous sugar broker. In 1874 he moved to London and there made Tate's Cube Sugar known all over the world. A collector of paintings which he left to the nation, paying for a new gallery to house them and others. This was the Tate Gallery which was opened on 21 July 1897. The following year he was made a baronet.

Tussaud, Madame Marie (1760–1850)
St Mary's Church, Cadogan Street, Chelsea, London. Her tomb is sealed in the vault and not visible, but there is a memorial tablet to her in the church.

Waxwork modeller. She learned her trade from her uncle in Paris and during the French Revolution she was forced to model many of the guillotined heads, and was, for a short time, herself imprisoned. She came to London in 1802 where, after touring for thirty-three years with her waxworks exhibition, she set up a permanent museum in Baker Street, where it still remains.

Verdon-Roe, Sir Edwin Alliot (1877–1958)
St Andrew's Church, Hamble, Hampshire, large white family grave just outside porch.

Pioneer aviator and aircraft manufacturer, born at Manchester, who after beating 200 competitors to win a model aeroplane competition, in 1908 designed, built and flew his own plane, the first Englishman to so do. In partnership with his brother Humphrey (1878–1949) he founded the Avro aircraft company (1910), where the Avro 504 was made in 1913. It became one of the most famous military aircraft of the 1914–1918 war, in 1914 bombing Zeppelin sheds in the first air raid in history. It was still in use twenty-five years later. In 1928 Roe sold his interest in Avro and formed Saunders-Roe, building flying boats. Knighted in 1929, he prefixed in 1933 the name Verdon to his surname in honour of his mother, Sofia Verdon.

Henry Tate

Chapter 8
Writers (including authors, playwrights and poets)

Addison, Joseph (1672–1719)
Henry VII's Chapel, Westminster Abbey, London, in the north aisle. His monument is in the South Transept, now known as 'Poets' Corner'.

Poet and writer. Son of a Dean of Lichfield. He was a distinguished classical scholar whose Latin verses attracted the attention of John Dryden. In 1704 he published his famous poem, 'The Campaign', in celebration of the Duke of Marlborough's victory at Blenheim. In 1706 he was appointed Under-secretary of State and from 1708 until his death he sat as a Member of Parliament. He later went to Ireland as Chief Secretary. The fall of the Whigs in 1711, however, meant that he too lost office. He was a close friend of Jonathan Swift and Richard Steele, to whose *Tatler* Addison contributed a number of papers between 1709 and 1711, and with whom during 1711 and 1712 he was associated in the production of the *Spectator*. Addison's tragedy, *Cato*, was produced successfully in 1713 but his prose comedy, *The Drummer*, failed. When the Whigs returned to office Addison once again went to Ireland as Chief Secretary. During 1715 and 1716 he started his political newspaper the *Freeholder*. He retired from office in 1718 and died the following year. His marriage to the Countess of Warwick was unhappy. Pope satirized Addison in the character of Atticus.

Amis, Sir Kingsley (1922–1995)
Cremated in Golders Green

Novelist, born in London, who was described around the time he wrote his first novel *Lucky Jim* (1953), as one of England's Angry Young Men. It had a satirical attitude to academic life but was well received. He graduated from St John's College, Oxford and was an officer in the Royal Corps of Signals during the war, after which he taught English literature at University College, Swansea. A variety of material came from his enthusiastic pen, from jazz essays to science fiction and poetry. *Lucky Jim* reflects an attitude of exasperation with the social life of the time. Later works, *That Uncertain Feeling* (1956) and *I Like It Here* (1958), have the same unruly and cynical character who appears respectively as a small-town librarian and as a small-town author away from England. His works included *One Fat Englishman* (1963), *The Anti-Death League* (1965), *Jake's Thing* (1978) and others. As 'Robert Markham' he wrote a James Bond novel *Colonel Sun* (1968) and *The James Bond Dossier* (1965). He had written of Bond's first novel *Casino Royale* that in an age of less literary snobbishness, it would have been 'hailed as one of the most remarkable to have been published in England in the previous thirty years.' He was knighted in 1990.

Arbuthnot, John (1667–1735)
St James's Church, Piccadilly, London.

Author, whose *History of John Bull*, a collection of pamphlets issued in 1712 advocating the termination of war with France, made him famous. This work was the origin of John Bull, the typical Englishman. Arbuthnot was also the principal author of the 'Memoirs of Martinus Scriblerus', which were published with Pope's *Works* in 1741. A doctor, who was Physician in Ordinary to Queen Anne, he published many medical writings which showed him to be in advance of his age in medical science. He was a close friend of Jonathan Swift and he was generally praised for his medical science, his wit and humour, and his kind heart. Dr Johnson referred to him as 'an unusual genius'.

Austen, Jane (1775–1817)
Winchester Cathedral, Winchester, Hampshire, in the north aisle of the Nave.

Novelist. Daughter of the Rector of Steventon in Hampshire, where she spent the first twenty-five years of her life. Her most famous novels were *Pride and Prejudice*, originally entitled 'First Impressions', which she began in 1796, but, when it was rejected by a publisher, she revised it before its publication in 1813; and *Sense and Sensibility* which, though it was started a year after *Pride and Prejudice* and not completed for many years, was the first to be published in 1811. In all she wrote six finished novels, the remaining four being *Mansfield Park*, 1814, *Emma*, 1816, *Northanger Abbey* and *Persuasion*, which were published posthumously in 1818. She also wrote three other unpublished works, *Lady Susan* and two fragments, *The Watsons* and *Sanditon*. She died at Winchester.

Jane Austen, by Cassandra Austen, c. 1810

Commemorative brass to Jane Austen in the wall beside her grave in Winchester Cathedral, Hampshire

Barnes, William (1801–1886)
St Peter's Churchyard, Winterborne Came, Dorset; tall Celtic cross
close to church's south-west window. Village is south side of the A352,
through white gate and left fork to sign to church.

  Poet who is generally known as the Dorset dialect poet. The son of a
tenant farmer, whose great-grandfather had been granted land by Henry
VIII, he went to Dorchester as a solicitor's clerk. He then became a
schoolmaster at Mere and a parson, contributing many articles to
magazines of the day. It is his dialect poetry that has claimed popular
memory of him, his best-known poem perhaps being *A Bit o' Sly
Coorten*, which first appeared in an 1883 issue of the *County Chronicle*.
One of his serious works on language was a study of fundamental roots
of Teutonic speech, entitled *Tiw*, after the god from whom the race
derives its name. He did not like the encroachment of Latin and Greek
words into the English language, preferring, for example, 'sunprint' to
'photograph' and 'wheelsaddle' to 'bicycle'. He became greatly loved,
and his appearance on Dorchester market days was much looked for.
There is a statue of him outside Holy Trinity Church there. At well over
80 years of age he worked as he had always done as rector of Came, the
benefice bestowed upon him by Captain Seymour Dawson Damer, who
sleeps almost beside the poet in the graveyard. A list of Barnes's works
numbers eighteen diverse and interesting titles.

Beaumont, Francis (1548–1616)
Westminster Abbey, Westminster, London, in the South Transept now
known as 'Poets' Corner'.

  Poet and dramatist whose name is inseparable from that of John
Fletcher with whom he collaborated closely in dramatic works from 1606
to 1616, their best-known joint productions perhaps being *The Maid's
Tragedy* and *The Knight of the Burning Pestle*. He also wrote commen-
datory verses for several of Ben Jonson's plays, as well as for Michael
Drayton. *The Woman-Hater*, a comedy which he published in 1607,
shows Jonson's strong influence.

Beckford, William (1759–1844)
Walcot Cemetery, Bath, Avon.

  Author and eccentric. He inherited a large fortune from his father
who was twice Lord Mayor of London. In 1783, after his marriage to
Lady Margaret Gordon, he travelled, having been involved in a
homosexual scandal, spending the majority of his brief married life in

William Barnes's statue, outside St Peter's Church, Dorchester, Dorset

Switzerland, his wife dying in 1786. He then moved to Spain and Porgual and wrote his *Portuguese Letters*, which rank among his best work. He returned to England and built a magnificent residence, Fonthill Abbey, on the site of his birthplace, which cost him about £273,000. He later sold it. His oriental romance, *The History of the Caliph Vathek*, is regarded as one of the finest productions of luxuriant imagination.

Beerbohm, Sir Max (1872–1956)
St Paul's Cathedral, London.

Critic, essayist and caricaturist. Known for his wit, irony and satire, and for his polished and incisive style which he directed at literary mannerisms and social pretences. He succeeded George Bernard Shaw as drama critic on the *Saturday Review*. His best-known critical work is possibly *A Christmas Garland*, 1912, which is a series of parodies of contemporary writers – Wells, Bennett, Chesterton, etc. His novel, *Zuleika Dobson*, 1911, is a humorous work about the impact of an adventuress on the youth of Oxford.

Beeton, Isabella Mary, 'Mrs Beeton' (1836–1865)
Norwood Cemetery, Norwood, London.

Author of *Mrs Beeton's Book of Household Management*, which was published in 1861 by her husband, the controversial publisher, Sam Beeton. It had originally been published in serial form in *The English-woman's Domestic Magazine*, and was a guide to 'cookery in all branches' as well as to the problems affecting 'mistress & servant, hostess & guest, menu making, sick nursing, the nursery, the home lawyer, the home doctor, marketing, trussing & carving' and the 'daily duties' of a Victorian household.

Belloc, Hilaire (Joseph Hilary Pierre) (1870–1953)
Church of Our Lady and St Francis (RC), West Grinstead, Sussex; a tablet by the church door gives the location of the grave.

Writer. Born in France but educated in England, becoming a British citizen in 1902. A versatile writer, his best-known works include *The Path to Rome*, 1902, describing his trek through France, Switzerland and northern Italy to Rome; a history of *Marie Antoinette; The Servile State*, a sociological work; his essays on *Nothing, Something*, and *Everything*. He and G. K. Chesterton founded a political weekly, *The New Witness*, which was devoted to their idea of 'distributism', a form of medieval communism. G. B. Shaw referred to the paper as 'Chesterbelloc'.

Mrs Beeton

Betjeman, Sir John (1906–1984)
St Enodoc's Church, Trebetherick, north Cornwall, near south side of church. The church is approached across the 10th fairway of the golf course.

Poet Laureate who also used his 'impish' but strong and popular voice against ill-conceived or excessive urban development, especially where it resulted in the destruction of Victorian architecture and our cultural heritage in general. After an unhappy school life at Marlborough he left Magdalen College, Oxford, in 1928 without a degree to find himself congenial work with the *Architectural Record*. His *Ghastly Good Taste* (1933) established him as an uncompromising critic of architecture. As a press attaché for the UK in Dublin during the war his poems first began to attract attention: *New Lights for New Chancels* (1940) and *New Bats in Old Belfries* (1945) brought him much popular acclaim. His total works make a long list. He was awarded the CBE in 1960 and made a Companion of Literature by the Royal Society in 1968, after which he succeeded Cecil Day Lewis (see entry) in 1972 as Poet Laureate.

Blackmore, Richard Doddridge (1825–1900)
Teddington Cemetery, Teddington, Greater London.

Author of *Lorna Doone*, 1869, which recreated his native Exmoor during the seventeenth century, as well as of other novels including *Springhaven*, 1887, a Napoleonic romance. Originally Blackmore was a barrister at the Middle Temple, but after a breakdown in his health he moved to Teddington where he pursued his literary work, supplementing his income by opening a market garden.

Blake, William (1757–1827)
Bunhill Fields Burial Ground, City Road, Finsbury, London.

Poet. He had no education but was apprenticed to the engraver, James Basire. His earliest poems, *Poetical Sketches*, were published in 1783, followed by *Songs of Innocence* in 1789, which first indicated his mystical leanings. His most important prose work, the *Marriage of Heaven and Hell*, 1790, took a revolutionary stance, denying the reality of matter, as well as denying eternal punishment and authority. In *The French Revolution*, 1791, *America*, 1793, and *The Visions of the Daughters of Albion*, 1793, Blake develops the theme of revolt against authority. The symbolic and imaginative qualities that pervade his literary works were also present in his illustrations and watercolours.

Blunden, Edmund (1896–1974)
Holy Trinity Church, Long Melford, Suffolk.

One of a number of poets associated with the First World War, Blunden saw action at both the Somme and Ypres and was awarded the military cross. Unlike many others, he survived the war, although the aftermath was to bring him close to despair. His first collection of poems, *The Waggoner*, was published in 1920 by Siegfried Sassoon, then literary editor of *The Daily Herald*. His most famous collection, *Undertones of War*, was published in 1928.

Blunden helped to promote the work of other war poets, alive and dead. He edited poems by John Clare, Wilfred Owen and Ivor Gurney. He won the Queen's medal for poetry in 1956 and was appointed Professor of Poetry at Oxford University in 1966.

He died at the age of seventy-seven and was buried with Flanders poppies on his coffin.

Bowles, Caroline Ann (1786–1854)
St Thomas the Apostle churchyard, High Street, Lymington, Hampshire.

Poet whose talents were 'rather those of a story teller' than a poet, it has been said. She was born at Lymington, Hampshire, and the parish register of St Thomas's Church records her baptism. Her father, Captain Charles Bowles, on retiring from the East India Company, had bought an old-fashioned house, surrounded by elms, called Buckland Cottage, and it was here that Caroline grew up. By all accounts she was happy enough, but she found herself virtually alone in the world when her mother died in 1816 and a dishonest guardian defrauded her out of the cottage.

When brought face-to-face with the necessity of supporting herself, she decided to see if her pen could provide for her. She had sent one of her poems to Southey, who praised it and recommended it to the publisher John Murray, who admired but did not publish it. Longman's eventually brought it out under the title *Ellen Fitzarthur: a Metrical Tale*. As with her other poems, its strength lay, it is said, in its pathos. *The Widow's Tale* (1822) 'marked an advance' in the art of poetry. She met her future husband in 1820 when he asked her if she would work with him on his new poem, *Robin Hood*. Little came of this because she was unable to master the rhymeless style in which the poem was to be written. She had gone to Southey's Keswick home, but he was busy reading his books so the poet Wordsworth undertook the job of showing her the countryside. After this she wrote the work for which she is most famous, *Chapters on Churchyards*. She followed with poems such as *Tales of Factories*, in which she protested about the ill-treatment of workmen, and *The Birthday*, for which she was called the Cowper of modern poetesses. She left 'my, our, dear New Forest' when she returned to Keswick to live as Southey's wife, after their marriage at the church in Boldre, Hampshire. The couple were congenial enough, but it was said that Southey's state of health should have forbidden the marriage, and his mental health deteriorated rapidly. After his death she said 'the last three years have done upon me the worth of twenty'. She had even forfeited her annuity upon marriage, and although Southey left her £2,000 it did not compensate for the loss of the annuity. In the last two years of her life a pension of £200 was given her by the government.

Bowles, William Lisle (1762–1850)
Salisbury Cathedral, monument east side of the south-west transept, near his grave.

Poet, who was prebendary of Salisbury cathedral and, in 1818, chaplain to the Prince Regent. His first volume, *Fourteen Sonnets* on 'picturesque spots during a journey' (1789), had an extraordinary success. His other poems and writing include *Combe Ellen* (1798), *The Battle of the Nile* (1799), *The Grave of the Last Saxon* (1822), *Ellen Gray* (1823), *Scenes and Shadows of Days Departed* (1837) and some histories, of which *Hermes Britannicus* (1828) was the most important. An eccentricity of his was a constant refusal to be measured by a tailor. He died at his home in the cathedral close.

Bradbury, Sir Malcolm (1932–2000)
St Mary's Church, Upper Tasburgh, Norfolk.

Writer and academic. The son of a railway worker, Malcolm Bradbury was born in Sheffield. Malcolm Bradbury was a prolific writer. He wrote many critical academic book as well as novels and TV scripts. His original television dramas included *The Gravy Train* and *Anything More Would Be Greed*, and he also adapted the works of Tom Sharpe and Kingsley Amis. His greatest love, however, was for the novel and his first book, *Eating People Is Wrong* was published in 1959. Like almost all his novels, it drew on his experiences of academic life to comic effect. His most famous work, *The History Man*, was published in 1975.

Bradbury joined the staff at the new University of East Anglia in 1965 and became professor of American studies in 1970. With Angus Wilson he founded the university's creative writing course, which boasts many famous alumni, including Ian McEwan and Kazuo Ishiguro. Bradbury remained at the university until his retirement in 1995. He was appointed CBE in 1991 for services to literature, and was knighted in 2000.

Brontë, Anne (1820–1849)

St Mary's Churchyard, Castle Road, Scarborough, Yorkshire. A memorial tablet to the three Brontë sisters is in Westminster Abbey, London, in the South Transept now known as 'Poet's Corner'.

Novelist. Daughter of Patrick Prunty, or Brontë, perpetual curate of Howarth in Yorkshire from 1820 till his death in 1861, and sister to Charlotte and Emily. She grew up in Haworth with her sisters and brother, Patrick Branwell. She was part author with Charlotte and Emily of *Poems* by Currer, Ellis and Acton Bell, published in 1846; and it was under the pseudonym of Acton Bell that she wrote *Agnes Grey*, 1847, and *The Tenant of Wildfell Hall*, 1848.

Brontë, Charlotte (1816–1855)

St Michael and All Angels' Church, Haworth, Yorkshire. A memorial tablet to the three Brontë sisters is in Westminster Abbey, London, in the South Transept now known as 'Poets' Corner'.

Novelist. Sister to Anne and Emily Brontë. She, together with three of her sisters, attended a boarding school for the daughters of clergy after the death of her mother in 1821. This school was the basis for Lowood in her novel *Jane Eyre*. During 1831 to 1832 she attended Miss Wooler's school at Roehead, to which she returned as a teacher from 1835 to 1838. Subsequently she became a governess, then, in 1842, she accompanied her sister Emily to Brussels to study languages, and there she also taught. Following the publication of *Poems* by Currer, Ellis and Acton Bell her novel *Jane Eyre* was published by Smith, Elder in 1847, her first novel *The Professor* having been rejected and not finally published until 1857, two years after her death. *Jane Eyre* was an immediate success and was followed by *Shirley*, 1849, and *Villette* in 1853 which recalled her memories of her time in Brussels. In 1854 she married her father's curate, but died a few months later.

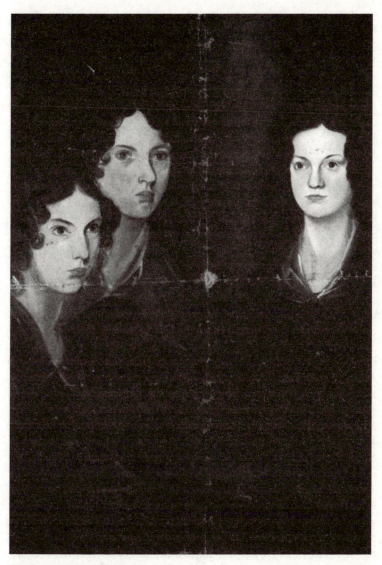

The Brontë sisters, by P. B. Brontë

Brontë, Emily Jane (1818–1848)
St Michael and All Angels' Church, Haworth, Yorkshire. A memorial tablet to the three Brontë sisters is in Westminster Abbey, London, in the South Transept, now known as 'Poets' Corner'.

Novelist. Sister to Charlotte and Anne Brontë. Also part author of *Poems* by Currer, Ellis and Acton Bell. Under the pseudonym of Ellis Bell she published *Wuthering Heights* in 1848. She was also an accomplished poet, her best-known poems being 'Last Lives' and 'Remembrance'.

Browning, Robert (1812–1889)
Westminster Abbey, London, in the South Transept now known as 'Poets' Corner'.

Poet. Son of a clerk in the Bank of England, he had little formal education. In 1835 his poem 'Paracelsus', attracted the encouraging attention of Carlyle and Wordsworth. He published numerous poems but perhaps his best known is 'The Ring and the Book' which he wrote during 1868 and 1869. He also wrote plays, his tragedy *Strafford* being produced at Covent Garden in 1837, and *The Blot on the 'Scutcheon* produced by Macready at the Drury Lane Theatre in February 1843. In 1846 Browning married Elizabeth Barrett and they spent the majority of their married life in Italy, at Pisa, Florence and Rome, where Mrs Browning died in 1861. Thereafter her husband returned to England and settled in London where he continued his writing. His last volume of poems, *Asolando*, was published on the day of his death.

Buchan, John, 1st Baron Tweedsmuir (1875–1940)
St Thomas of Canterbury Churchyard, Elsfield, Oxfordshire.

Author of the famous thriller, *The Thirty-Nine Steps*, 1915, as well as of *Greenmantle*, 1916, and other novels. He also wrote *Montrose*, *Oliver Cromwell*, 1934, and *Julius Caesar*, 1932. From 1901 to 1903 he was private secretary to the High Commissioner of South Africa, Lord Milner; from 1916 to 1917 he was director of information under the Prime Minister; and from 1935 until his death he was Governor-General of Canada.

Bulwer-Lytton, Edward George 1st Baron Lytton (1803–1873)
Westminster Abbey, Chapel of SS Edmund and Thomas The Martyr.

Perhaps most famous for his book *The Last Days of Pompeii*, which he wrote in 1834, he was a brilliant poet at an early age. At Cambridge from

1822–1825 he won a gold medal for a poem and had published *Ishmael And Other Poems* when he was only seventeen. Novelist, playwright, essayist and poet his prolific output of various works became extremely popular. It is said that his unhappy marriage to Rosina Wheeler, an Irish beauty, which ended in a separation, spurred his literary output to the good. He was a Member of Parliament for St Ives in 1831 for ten years, being made a baronet in 1838. He was the son of General Earl Bulwer and the former Elizabeth Barbara Lytton, who was heiress to the Knebworth estate in Hertfordshire to which he succeeded in 1843, when he assumed the name Lytton. As an MP again in 1852, for Hertford-shire, he was instrumental as Colonial Secretary in establishing British Columbia and Queensland. In 1866 he was raised to the peerage. His son Edward Robert Bulwer (1831–91) 1st Earl of Lytton wrote his father's life and Letters while his grandson the 2nd Earl of Lytton wrote his Memoirs in 1932.

Bunyan, John (1628–1688)
Bunhill Fields Burial Ground, City Road, Finsbury, London.
   Author of *The Pilgrim's Progress*. Son of a Bedfordshire tinsmith, he was educated at the local village school before working at his father's trade. When he was sixteen he was drafted into the Parliamentary army. In 1653 he joined a Nonconformist church in Bedford, where he preached. He came into conflict with the Quakers and his first writings, *Some Gospel Truths opened*, 1656, and *A Vindication*, 1657, were antag-onistic to them. His first wife died in 1656 leaving four small children and three years later he married his second, Elizabeth. The following year he was arrested for preaching without a licence and was imprisoned for twelve years for refusing to comply with the law. During his first six years in prison he wrote nine of his books including *Grace Abounding to the Chief of Sinners*, 1666, and *The Holy City, or the New Jerusalem*, which also appeared in 1666. There was a gap of five years before the publication of *A confession of my Faith, and a Reason of my Practice* in 1671. The next year he was released and appointed pastor to the same church in Bedford. Shortly afterwards he was again imprisoned briefly, and it was during this short spell that he wrote the first part of *The Pilgrim's Progress from this World to that which is to come*. The second part, with the whole work, was published in 1678. Thereafter he preached in many places but was not molested.

Burney, Fanny, Madame d'Arblay (1752–1840)
Walcot Cemetery, Bath, Avon; but her gravesite is no longer identifiable.

Novelist. The daughter of Dr Burney, she grew up in a literary society which included Dr Johnson and Edmund Burke. Her first novel, *Evelina*, was published anonymously. When her authorship was revealed she received much acclaim and was invited by Queen Charlotte to become the Queen's second keeper of the robes, a role which she accepted in 1786 although her health was not good. Her *Diary and Letters 1778–1840* gives an interesting account of her period at court. However, her health was not up to the rigours of the position and, after some difficulty, she was given permission to retire. In 1793 she married General d'Arblay, a French refugee in England, whom she later accompanied to France where, from 1802 to 1812, she was interned by Napoleon. In 1782 she had published her second novel, *Cecilia*, which was followed in 1796 by *Camilla* and *The Wanderer* in 1814. Her *Early Diary 1768–1778* with its pleasant sketches of Dr Johnson and David Garrick was published in 1889. She is known as the originator of the simple novel of home life.

Byron, George Gordon, 6th Baron Byron (1788–1824)
St Mary Magdalen Church, Hucknall Torkard, Nottinghamshire, in the family vault. A white marble memorial was placed in the floor of Westminster Abbey, London, in the South Transept, now known as 'Poets' Corner', by the Poetry Society and dedicated on 8 May 1969.

Poet. Educated at Harrow and Cambridge, and it was while he was at the university that he published his much criticized 'Hours of Idleness' in 1807. Two years later he went abroad, travelling in Portugal, Spain, Greece and the Levant, returning to London in 1811. The following year he published the first two cantos of 'Childe Harold', which brought him much critical acclaim. This was followed by 'The Giaour', 'The Bride of Abydos' and the beautiful visionary poem in blank verse, 'The Dream', among others. In 1815 he married Anne Isabella Milbanke from whom he was separated the following year. His personal life was the subject of much controversy and after his separation he left England for good, embittered by what he described as a hypocritical society. He lived most of the time in Italy. In 1816 he published canto iii of 'Childe Harold', canto iv in 1818. He wrote the first five cantos of 'Don Juan' during 1818 to 1820, the later cantos of the unfinished poem appearing whilst he was living at Pisa. In Italy he began his connection with Teresa, Countess Guiccioli, who lived with him for a time at Venice and whom he followed to Ravenna. He also wrote several dramas including

Grave of Lord Byron, St Mary Magdalen's Church, Hucknall Torkard, Nottinghamshire

The Two Foscari, Mazeppa and *Sardanapalus*. In 1822 he joined with Leigh Hunt in the production of the short-lived magazine, *The Liberal*. The following year, 1823, he set out to join the Greeks in their war of independence from the Turks and died of fever at Missolonghi in April 1824.

Caedmon (c.670)
St Mary's Churchyard, Whitby, Yorkshire, where there is a memorial cross. A stone in the floor of Westminster Abbey, London, in the South Transept, now known as 'Poets' Corner', commemorates Caedmon 'who first among the English made verses'.

Entered the monastery of Whitby when already an old man. Bede tells us that he was an unlearned herdsman who suddenly, in a vision, was granted the gift of song, and that he later rendered into English verse passages translated to him from the Scriptures. The only authentic fragment of his work that survives is his first Hymn, which Bede quotes.

Carroll, Lewis (Charles Lutwidge Dodgson) (1832–1898)
Guildford Cemetery, Guildford, Surrey.

A mathematics don at Christ Church, Oxford, who wrote several books for children, the most notable of which were *Alice's Adventures in Wonderland*, 1865, and *Through the Looking-glass*, 1872. He also published *The Hunting of the Snark*, 1876, as well as various mathematical treatises including *Euclid and his Modern Rivals*, 1879.

Cartland, Dame Barbara (1901–2000)
Camfield Place (her private residence), Hatfield, Hertfordshire. She was laid to rest in a cardboard coffin, which she believed was more environmentally friendly, beneath a tree planted by Elizabeth I.

Author and holder of the Guinness Book of World Records title for Most Published Author. Barbara Cartland was born on 9 July 1901 and published her first novel, *Jig-Saw* in 1923. She went on to publish five autobiographies and several books on cooking and health, but is best remembered as the 'Queen of the Romance Novel'. Able to dictate and write on average one book a month, Barbara Cartland published over 700 romance novels, which were translated into thirty-six languages worldwide and sold over 1 billion copies.

Easily recognisable by her pink chiffon outfits and lap dog, Barbara Cartland, married name McCorquendale, was also known as the stepgrandmother to Princess Diana.

Grave of Lewis Carroll (Charles Lutwidge Dodgson) in Guildford Cemetery, Guildford, Surrey

Tomb of Geoffrey Chaucer, Westminster Abbey, London, in 'Poets' Corner'

Chaucer, Geoffrey (c.1343–1400)

Westminster Abbey, London, in the South Transept now known as 'Poets' Corner'; it was Chaucer's tomb which originated 'Poets' Corner'.

Poet and civil servant. As the author of the *Canterbury Tales* he ranks next to Shakespeare as perhaps England's most famous poet. He entered the service of Lionel, Duke of Clarence, third son of Edward III and subsequently held various offices in the King's household. He made various diplomatic trips abroad: to Flanders in 1376 and 1377, to France and Lombardy in 1378. At home he was appointed controller of customs in the port of London, was knight of the shire for Kent in 1386, and Clerk of the King's Works in 1388, at the time when he made the pilgrimage to Canterbury. His wife Philippa was the sister of Katharine Swynford, John of Gaunt's third wife and ancestress of Henry VII and the Tudor dynasty. Chaucer's writings fall into three periods: that of French influence, 1359–1372, which produced, amongst others, the 'Romaunt of the Rose' and 'The Boke of the Duchesse', written, it is believed, for the death of John of Gaunt's first wife, Blanche of Lancaster; the period of Italian influence, 1372–1386, which produced

'Troylus and Crysede', 'The Parlement of Foules' and 'The Legende of Good Women'; and the period of his maturity, 1386–1400, which saw the publication of the *Canterbury Tales*.

Chesterton, Gilbert Keith (1874–1936)
Roman Catholic Cemetery, Beaconsfield, Buckinghamshire (down a lane off Aylesbury End near the old town centre). Headstone sculpted by Eric Gill.

Author and essayist who, born in London, first studied art at Slade School but never painted professionally. It is said that his best work was in the essays he wrote for various periodicals such as *The Speaker, The Bookman* and the one that had been his brother's (Cecil Edward: 1879–1918) *New Witness*, changed by Gilbert to *G.K.'s Weekly*. His famous detective-priest Father Brown won Chesterton popular acclaim with *The Innocence of Father Brown* (1911). Of his religion, Catholicism, to which he was a convert, he said, 'It is quite possible that everything is wrong about it, except that it is right.' He was a large man of vast girth but possessed of great zest, vigour and humour. His short novel *The Man Who Was Thursday* (1908) reveals his political humour and satire probably better than anything else he wrote.

Christie, Dame Agatha Mary Clarissa (1891–1976)
St Mary's Church, Cholsey, Oxfordshire, large grey stone in west part of graveyard.

An author famous for her mainly detective novels and stage plays, she was born in Torquay. Her first marriage, after a courtship of two days, was to a young subaltern, later Colonel Christie. Divorced in 1928, she married a distinguished archaeologist, Sir Max Mallowan. Her works include more than 70 mystery novels, plus some romances and children's stories, in which her most famous characters, the Belgian Hercule Poirot and the elderly village lady Miss Marple, appeared as remarkably astute detectives. She disappeared mysteriously for some time in 1926 after registering at a Harrogate hotel in the name of Miss Steele, her first husband's mistress. *The Mysterious Affair of Styles* and *The Murder of Roger Ackroyd* were among her earlier novels in the twenties, while her plays *The Mousetrap* and *Witness for the Prosecution* appeared in 1952 and 1954 respectively. The former is still running in London. She was awarded a CBE in 1956 and created a Dame in 1971 for her important contributions to literature.

Cobbett, William (1763–1835)
St Andrew's Church, Farnham, Surrey; in the tower there is a medallion bust under a simple pointed canopy.

Journalist. Self-educated son of a Farnham labourer, he served as a soldier in Florida from 1784 to 1791. Then he bought his discharge, accused some of his former officers of peculation and fled to America to avoid prosecution in 1792. There he published pro-British pamphlets under the pseudonym of Peter Porcupine. In 1800 he returned to England and edited *Cobbett's Political Register* in 1802, which established him as a Tory journalist. He published *Parliamentary Debates*, which Hansard later took over, an *English Grammar*, 1817, and a number of other works on economics. He spent some time in America during 1817 to 1819, and in 1832 became a Member of Parliament for Oldham. Perhaps the most interesting of his writings to survive are his *Rural Rides* which were collected in 1830.

Coleridge, Samuel Taylor (1772–1834)
St Michael's Church, Highgate, London, in the aisle.

Poet. Son of the Vicar of Ottery St Mary in Devon, he was educated at Christ's Hospital and Jesus College, Cambridge. Whilst only twenty-one he was contributing verses to the *Morning Chronicle* and in 1794, together with his friend and brother-in-law, Robert Southey, he published a play, *The Fall of Robespierre*. In 1796 he briefly launched a newspaper, *The Watchman*, which lasted for only ten numbers. He had met and formed a close association with Wordsworth, and they lived together for about a year at Nether Stowey and Alfoxden in Somerset. Their *Lyrical Ballads*, 1798, contained one of Coleridge's most famous and finest poems, 'The Rime of the Ancient Mariner', which together with the later poems 'Kubla Khan' and 'Christabel', is characterized by a sense of mystery. In 1809 he launched his second periodical, *The Friend*, a literary, moral and political weekly paper, which was subsequently re-written and published as a book in 1818. After his return from Malta and Italy during the years 1804 to 1806, his health broke down and he became addicted to opium. In 1825 he published his *Aids to Reflection*, which did much to introduce German philosophy to the English, and tried to influence English thinkers away from their current doctrines, advocating a more spiritual and religious interpretation of life, based on what he had learned from Kant and Schelling.

William Cobbett, by an unknown artist

Collins, William Wilkie (1824–1889)
Kensal Green Cemetery, Kensal Green, London.

Author. Originally trained as a barrister, he forsook that profession for literature, contributing to *Household Words* from 1855. It was in this periodical that he published the work which was to establish him in the literary world, *The Woman in White*, for he was practically the first novelist to deal with the detection of crime. His contributions to the periodical brought him into collaboration with its proprietor, Charles Dickens, and they became close friends. Collins wrote numerous other novels, perhaps the best known being *The Moonstone*, 1868.

Congreve, William (1670–1729)
Westminster Abbey, London, in the south aisle of the Nave.

Dramatist. Educated at the Kilkenny School and Trinity College, Dublin, at both of which he was a fellow student of Swift, he entered London's Middle Temple, which he quickly forsook for literature. An unsuccessful attempt at a novel, *Incognita*, 1692, was followed by the success of *The Old Bachelor*, a comedy, which appeared in 1693. He subsequently published *The Double Dealer*, 1694, *Love for Love*, 1695, and *The Way of the World*, 1700, all comedies of manners, displaying the narrow world of fashion and gallantry. A friend of Swift, Pope and Steele, as well as of the enchanting actress, Anne Bracegirdle, whose role in his comedies contributed largely to their success. After his death, his body lay in state in the Jerusalem Chamber, and Sir Robert Walpole was one of his pall-bearers. The monument was erected by Henrietta, Duchess of Marlborough, to whom he left the bulk of his fortune, and she wrote the epitaph. She also had a statue of Congreve made in ivory, which moved by clockwork, setting it daily on her table where she talked to it as if it were alive.

Conrad, Joseph (1857–1924)
The Roman Catholic Cemetery, Canterbury, Kent.

Born of Polish parents in the Ukraine, his full names were Teodor Josef Konrad Korzeniowski. His parents were exiled to Vologda in northern Russia for revolutionary activities and his mother died there. Later he attended a school in Cracow, but in 1874 he fulfilled his ambition to go to sea, signing up as a crew member on a French ship. Four years later he joined an English merchant ship and in 1884 gained a Board of Trade certificate as a Master. He became a British citizen. In 1894 he left the sea to devote himself to writing, though his sea-faring life provided the setting for many of his subsequent novels. His best-known works are *Lord Jim*, 1900, *Nostromo*, 1904, and *The Nigger of the 'Narcissus'*, 1898, and his short stories amongst which is 'Typhoon', 1902.

Corelli, Marie, pen-name of Mary Mackay (1855–1924)
St Stratford-upon-Avon Cemetery, Stratford-upon-Avon, Warwickshire.
    Novelist. As a child she showed a precocious talent for the piano, in which she was encouraged by George Meredith, a near neighbour at her parents' home at Box Hill, Surrey. She pursued a musical career, being proficient as a singer as well as a player of the harp and the mandolin, before turning to writing. She first caught the public's attention with *Barabbas*, 1893, but it was her next novel, *The Sorrows of Satan*, 1895, which brought her great fame, being described as an 'hysterical triumph'. A deeply emotional woman, she often found herself at odds with those opposed to her thinking, especially at Stratford-on-Avon where she settled in 1901. During the Great War she was arrested for food-hoarding at the instigation of her local enemies, but she protested that the large sugar purchases were for jam-making, the jam to be distributed to the public; nonetheless she was convicted.

Cowper, William (1731–1800)
St Nicholas's Church, East Dereham, Norfolk.
    Educated at Westminster School and thereafter, during the years 1750 to 1752, was articled to a solicitor. In 1754 he was called to the bar and nine years later was offered a Clerkship in the House of Commons. However, his fits of depression developed into insanity at the time and he tried to commit suicide. Though he recovered he lived in retirement and became a boarder in the house of Morley Unwin at Huntingdon, after whose death he removed with Unwin's widow, Mary, to Olney. There he came under the influence of John Newton, the evangelical curate, and contributed to the collection of *Olney Hymns* with such famous hymns as 'God moves in a mysterious way' and 'Hark, my soul! it is the Lord'. From 1779 onwards he wrote numerous poems, including 'John Gilpin', 1782, 'The Task', 1784, the sonnet 'To Mrs Unwin', 'To Mary', 'Yardley Oak', 1791, and 'On the loss of the Royal George'. In 1785 he undertook the translation of Homer, which was unsuccessfully published in 1791. The death of Mrs Unwin in 1796 left him bereft. His poetry is notable for its simple and more natural style than that of the classical Pope.

Dahl, Roald (1916–1990)
Church of St Peter and St Paul, Great Missenden, Buckinghamshire.
His plot is in the lower half of the cemetery and is often covered with
chocolate bars.

Author of adult and children's books. Roald Dahl was born in Wales
to Norwegian parents. He was unhappy at boarding school and, rather
than go to university, he took a job at the Shell company in order to
travel and have adventures. Dahl was sent to East Africa, where he lived
in the jungle and learned to speak Swahili, until joining the Royal Air
Force during the Second World War. After the war he went to
Washington, where his first children's book, *The Gremlins* was published
with Walt Disney in 1942. His first book of adult short stories followed
two years later.

Roald Dahl went on to become one of the most influential and widely
read authors of his generation, both among children and adults. His
books are noted for his macabre imagination and cruel humour and Dahl
has created some of the most memorable and, often grotesque, characters
in literature, such as Willie Wonka, My Uncle Oswald and the two aunts
in *James and the Giant Peach*. Many of his books have been made into
films, the latest, *Charlie and the Chocolate Factory*, starring Johnny
Depp.

Defoe, Daniel (c.1661–1731)
Bunhill Fields Burial Ground, City Road, Finsbury, London.

Novelist. The son of a London butcher by the name of John Foe; the
change of name to Defoe occurring about 1703. In early life he became a
hosiery merchant, but his business was unsuccessful. He took part in
Monmouth's rebellion and, in 1688, joined the army of William of
Orange, later William III. It was his poem, 'The True-born Englishman', a satire combating the prejudice against a king of foreign birth,
that first brought him to the public's notice. The following year he
published a pamphlet, 'The Shortest Way with the Dissenters,' portraying the absurdity of ecclesiastical intolerance for which he was fined,
imprisoned from May to November 1703, and pilloried. During the
ensuing years he published odes and pamphlets and was for a time
employed as a secret agent in Scotland on behalf of the government,
seeking support for the Union. During 1712 and 1713 he was briefly
imprisoned for his ironical anti-Jacobite pamphlets; and in 1715 he
escaped further punishment, when he libelled Lord Annesley, because of
the favour of Lord Townshend for whom he worked as a secret agent

and journalist. It was not until his late fifties that he published the first volume of his most famous work, *Robinson Crusoe*, 1719, the second volume, *Further Adventures*, following a few months later. The next five years saw the emergence of many of his most important novels: *Moll Flanders*, 1722, and *Roxana*, 1724, and *The Four Voyages of Captain George Roberts* in 1726. His guide book, *Tour Through the Whole Island of Great Britain*, in three volumes, appeared between 1724 and 1727. Despite his political manoeuvrings, he was a liberal, humane and moral writer.

Dickens, Charles (1812–1870)
Westminster Abbey, London, in the South Transept now known as 'Poets' Corner'.

Son of a government clerk who was imprisoned in the Marshalsea for debt. His early experiences as a labourer were similar to those depicted in his favourite novel, *David Copperfield*, 1849–1850. He received a scanty education but enough to enable him to obtain employment as a reporter of debates in the Commons for the *Morning Chronicle*. He contributed to various periodicals articles which were later published as *Sketches by Boz, Illustrative of Every-Day People*. His novels have had perhaps the largest circulation of any English works of fiction and include *Nicholas Nickleby*, 1838–1839, *Great Expectations*, 1860–1861, *A Christmas Carol*, 1843, *Dombey and Son*, 1848, *Bleak House*, 1852–1853, *Our Mutual Friend*, 1864–1865, *Martin Chuzzlewit*, 1843–1844, *Little Dorrit*, *A Tale of Two Cities*, 1859, *The Old Curiosity Shop*, 1840–1841, *Oliver Twist*, 1837–1838 and *The Pickwick Papers*, 1836. He also edited two journals, *Household Words* and *All the Year Round*, and took part in the movement for the abolition of the slave trade as well as carrying out other philanthropic works.

Donne, John (1572–1631)
St Paul's Cathedral, London. His monument by Nicholas Stone was one of two to survive the Great Fire of 1666 (see Bacon, Sir Nicholas).

Poet. Son of a London ironmonger, he was educated at both Oxford and Cambridge before entering Lincoln's Inn. He accompanied the Earl of Essex on two expeditions, to Cadiz and to the Islands, in 1596 and 1597, which he mentioned in his early poems 'The Storm' and 'The Calm'. Originally a Roman Catholic, he took Anglican orders in 1615 and for the last ten years of his life was Dean of St Paul's, frequently preaching before the King, Charles I. His best known poems are 'The

Charles Dickens, by A. Scheffer, 1855–6

Ecstasie', 'Hymn to God the Father', the sonnet to Death ('Death, be not proud') and 'Go and catch a falling star'.

Doyle, Sir Arthur Conan (1859–1930)
All Saints' Churchyard, Minstead, Hampshire, at the east end of the churchyard beside a large oak tree.

Educated at Stonyhurst and Edinburgh where he trained as a doctor and practised at Southsea from 1882 to 1890. He is chiefly remembered for his creation of the amateur detective, Sherlock Holmes, who appeared in a cycle of stories, *The Adventures of Sherlock Holmes*, 1891, *The Memoirs of Sherlock Holmes*, 1894, *The Hound of the Baskervilles*, 1902, and others. He also wrote a number of historical works, *Micah Clarke*, 1889, *The White Company*, 1891, *The Exploits of Brigadier Gerard*, 1896 and *Rodney Stone*, 1896. A fervent patriot, as was shown in his pamphlet 'The Great Boer War', 1900, he also wrote a one-act play, *Story of Waterloo*, which was enacted with Sir Henry Irving in the leading rôle.

Dryden, John (1631–1700)
Westminster Abbey, London, in the South Transept now known as 'Poets' Corner'.

Poet Laureate and dramatist. He was the acknowledged master of the heroic rhymed couplet. Educated at Westminster School under the famed Dr Busby, he was, in early life, an ardent admirer of Oliver Cromwell. After the Restoration he became an enthusiastic royalist and held several offices under the Crown. Soon after the accession of James II he became a Roman Catholic. His finest works, 'All for Love', 1678, and 'Absalom and Achitobel', 1681, probably the greatest English political satire, were published before his conversion, but his poem 'The Hind and the Panther', 1687, was written after. Following the Glorious Revolution Dryden refused to take the Oaths and therefore lost his laureateship as well as his office at the Customs which he had held since 1683. In consequence he died in poverty in Gerrard Street, Soho, but was buried with much ceremony near to Chaucer on 13 May 1700, and his monument was erected in 1720 by his friend, John Sheffield, Duke of Buckingham.

Grave of Sir Arthur Conan Doyle in All Saints' Churchyard, Minstead, Hampshire

Du Maurier, George Louis Palmella Busson (1834–1896)
St John's Churchyard, Church Row, Hampstead, London.

Novelist. He was born in Paris where he studied art. His three novels, *Peter Ibbetson*, 1891, *Trilby*, 1894, and *The Martian*, published posthumously, recall his life as an art student in Paris and Antwerp. He contributed occasional drawings to *Punch* from 1860, before joining the staff as a regular illustrator in succession to John Leech in 1864.

Dunsany, Edward John Morteon Drax Plunkett, 18th Baron (1878–1957)
St Peter and St Paul's Churchyard, Shoreham, Kent.

Best known for his plays and stories of fantasy and myth. His most famous stories include *The Gods of Pagana*, 1905, *Time and the Gods*, 1906 and *The Book of Wonder*, 1912. His first play, *The Glittering Gate*, 1909, was produced at the Abbey Theatre, and was followed by many others.

Eliot, George (Mary Ann Evans) (1819–1880)
Highgate 'new' Cemetery, Highgate, London.

Novelist. She broke away from her narrow religious upbringing when she met Charles Bray, a Coventry manufacturer. In 1850 she became a contributor to the *Westminster Review* and its assistant editor in 1851, a post she resigned two years later. In 1854 she published a translation of Feuerbach's *Essence of Christianity* and about that time went to live with George Henry Lewes the writer, and continued to live with him unmarried until his death in 1878. Under the influence of Lewes she began writing novels, *Amos Barton* appearing in *Blackwood's Magazine* in 1857. Of her novels, the most famous are *Middlemarch*, which was published in instalments during 1871 and 1872, *Daniel Deronda*, also published in instalments, from 1874 to 1876, *Adam Bede*, 1859, *The Mill on the Floss*, 1860, and *Silas Marner*, 1861. After the death of George Lewes she married J. W. Cross, but she never fully recovered from Lewes's death and died herself two years later in 1880.

Eliot, T.S. (Thomas Stearns) (1888–1965)
St Michael's Church, East Coker, Somerset. A stone commemorates him in Westminster Abbey, London, in the South Transept now known as 'Poets' Corner'.

Poet, dramatist and critic. Born in America he was educated at Harvard University, but later settled in London and took out British nationality. His principal poems are *The Waste Land*, dedicated to Ezra Pound, and published in the *Criterion* which he founded in 1922; and *The Four Quartets*, first published as a whole in New York in 1943. His *Sweeney Agonistes* in 1932 was an attempt to revive poetic drama and he continued with the celebrated *Murder in the Cathedral* in 1935. His other plays include *The Family Reunion*, 1939, and three 'comedies': *The Cocktail Party*, 1950, *The Confidential Clerk*, 1954, and *The Elder Statesman*, 1958. In 1948 he was awarded the Nobel Prize for Literature and received the Order of Merit.

Fleming, Ian Lancaster (1908–1964)
St Andrew's churchyard, Sevenhampton, Wiltshire.

Novelist, the name of whose fictional secret agent James Bond has become almost as evocative as Sherlock Holmes. He joined the staff of Reuters news agency as a reporter after failing to get a job in the Foreign Office. He had been educated at Eton, where he was a top athlete, and at Sandhurst. In 1933 he reported the trial of some British engineers in Moscow who had been accused of espionage, and during World War II he was a commander in the British naval intelligence division. His James Bond novels became widely read round the world, and it has been said that President Kennedy's mention of them triggered their mass readership. Fleming's brother Peter was also a writer (see entry in this section). Ian Fleming was married in Jamaica, where he had a house and wrote during the winter months, 'with a golden pen on a golden isle'. He had one son.

Fleming, (Robert) Peter (1907–1971)
Parish church churchyard, Nettlebed, Oxfordshire (distinctive blue slate headstone in family plot).

Travel author, eldest brother of Ian Fleming, q.v., he was educated at Eton and Oxford. After working in Wall Street during the financial crash he wrote his first travel book *Brazilian Adventure* (1933) which became widely popular as a Book of the Month Club edition. Other following books were *One's Company* (1934) and *News From Tartary* (1936), both being selected by the Book Society. At least five other books followed. As a Special Correspondent for *The Times*, of London, he covered activities in Manchuria, China, World War Two in Normandy, Greece and Burma. He contributed under the pen name Strix to the *Spectator*. His book *Operation Sea Lion* (1957) was an account of Hitler's projected invasion of England. He was awarded the O.B.E. and was High Sheriff of Oxfordshire. In 1935 he married the actress Celia Johnson; see p. 305.

Fletcher, John (1579–1625)
Southwark Cathedral, Southwark, London.
Dramatist. Son of the Bishop of London, he was educated at Benet College, Cambridge. From about 1606 to 1616 he collaborated with Francis Beaumont in the production of plays, but also worked with Massinger, Rowley and others on yet more dramas. He wrote not less than sixteen plays by himself, the principal being *The Faithful Shepherdess*, 1610, *The Island Princess*, 1621, *The Woman's Prize* or *The Tamer Tamed*, a comedy about the taming of Shakespeare's Petruchio, and *Rule a Wife and have a Wife*. He is believed to have collaborated with Shakespeare in *The Two Noble Kinsmen*, printed in 1634, and it is probable that he had a share in the composition of Shakespeare's *Henry VIII*.

Galsworthy, John (1867–1933)
Highgate 'new' Cemetery, Highgate, London, contains his memorial only, for his ashes were scattered over the Sussex Downs.
Educated at Harrow School and New College, Oxford. He is chiefly remembered for his series of novels about Soames Forsyte, a man with a passion for acquiring all things desirable, known as the *Forsyte Saga*. Of his plays the most notable are *The Silver Box*, 1909, *Strife*, 1909, about an industrial dispute, *Justice*, 1910, which criticized the existing prison system, *The Skin Game*, 1920 and *Loyalties*, 1922. Shortly before his death he won the Nobel Prize for Literature, but was too ill to go to Stockholm to receive it.

Gaskell, Elizabeth Cleghorn (1810–1865)
Brook Street Chapel, Knutsford, Cheshire.
Brought up by an aunt at Knutsford, Cheshire, which is the original of Cranford and of Hollingford in *Wives and Daughters*, she was married in 1832 to William Gaskell, the minister at the Cross Street Unitarian Chapel in Manchester. Her first novel, *Mary Barton*, based on the industrial strife during 1842 and 1843, was published in 1848. This brought her to the attention of Charles Dickens and thereafter she wrote much for his *Household Words* and *All the Year Round*. It was in *Household Words* that she first published the remarkable series of papers which were subsequently republished as *Cranford*, the work for which she is most famous. In 1857 she produced her great *Life of Charlotte*

Brontë, although some of her statements therein were criticized and withdrawn. Other novels include *North and South*, 1855, *Ruth*, 1853, *Lois the Witch*, 1859, and *Wives and Daughters* which was left uncompleted at her death in 1865.

Gay, John (1685–1732)

Westminster Abbey, London. His monument in the South Transept was moved to the triforium when a fine mediaeval fresco was discovered beneath it. The epitaph was written by himself:

> Life is a jest, and all things show it;
> I thought so once, and now I know it.

Poet and dramatist. Born at Barnstaple in Devon, he was apprenticed to a London mercer before becoming secretary to the Duchess of Monmouth from 1712 to 1714. He contributed to Steel's *Guardian*, and his first notable poem, 'Shepherd's Week', appeared in 1714. He wrote a number of plays but is principally remembered for his *Beggar's Opera*, 1728, which was extremely successful. He also wrote the libretto for Handel's *Acis and Galatea* which was performed in 1732.

Gibbons, Stella (1902–1989)

Highgate Cemetery (West), Highgate, London.

Author. A writer and a poet, Stella Gibbons is best known for her novel *Cold Comfort Farm*, which was a parody of the rural novel. It was written whilst she worked as an editorial assistant on the *Lady* magazine. Gibbons was born and raised in North London and was a school contemporary of the poet Stevie Smith. She studied journalism at University College, London, but was fired from her subsequent jobs at the British United Press news agency and the *London Evening Standard*. The success of *Cold Comfort Farm* prompted Gibbons to concentrate on her writing full time.

Gilbert, Sir William Schwenck (1836–1911)

St John the Evangelist Church, Great Stanmore, Greater London (ashes only).

Formerly an officer in the militia and a clerk in the Education Department, he became known as a writer of humorous verse through his contributions to *Fun*, chief of which were his *Bab Ballads*, later published in volume form. He wrote a number of dramatic comedies,

including *Pygmalion and Galatea* and *The Happy Land*, 1873, in collaboration with Gilbert Arthur à Beckett. He is principally remembered
for his work with Sir Arthur Sullivan in a long series of comic operas for
Richard D'Oyly Carte's opera company, he writing the libretti, Sullivan
composing the music. From 1882, after the production of *Iolanthe*, they
became known as the 'Savoy Operas', for from that date they were
produced at the Savoy Theatre.

Golding, Sir William (1911–1993)
Bowerchalke Village Churchyard, Bowerchalke, Wiltshire.

Nobel-prize winning author. William Golding was encouraged to
study science by his schoolteacher father, but changed his degree to
English literature whilst studying at Oxford University. In 1940 he took
up a post as a schoolmaster in the village of Bowerchalke and he
remained teaching there until 1962, excepting four years active service
during the Second World War.

Golding finished writing his first novel in 1953. It was rejected by
twenty-one different publishing houses until it was published by Faber
and Faber in 1954 as *Lord of the Flies*. It was a surprise success and was
made into a film directed by Peter Brook. In 1980, his eighth novel, *Rites
of Passage*, was published and won the Booker Prize. Three years later
Golding was awarded the Nobel Prize for Literature. He was knighted in
1988.

Goldsmith, Oliver (c.1730–1774)
The Temple Church, Temple, Fleet Street, London. His monument
was destroyed during the air-raid of 10 May 1941.

Son of an Irish clergyman who was himself rejected for ordination in
1751. He studied medicine at Edinburgh and Leyden, travelling in
Europe during 1755 and 1756, thereafter returning to London where for
a time he practised as a physician in Southwark and was a hack-writer on
Griffith's *Monthly Review*. Failing to qualify for a medical appointment
in India, he began writing and in 1758, under the name of James
Willington, published his translation of *The Memoirs of a Protestant
condemned to the Galleys of France for his Religion*. Subsequently he
contributed to various magazines. In 1761 he met Dr Johnson and
became a founder member of The Club. His novel, the *Vicar of
Wakefield*, though not published until 1766, saved him from arrest for
debt when Dr Johnson sold it on his behalf for £60. His first comedy,
The Good-natur'd Man, was moderately successful despite being rejected

by Garrick; his second, *She Stoops to Conquer*, produced at Covent Garden in 1773, was a huge success, and is the work for which he is chiefly remembered.

Gower, John (c.1325–1408)
Southwark Cathedral, Southwark, London, where there is a fine tomb towards the end of the north aisle.

Poet. A contemporary and friend of Chaucer who referred to him as 'moral Gower' because of the moral criticism contained in his poems. Of his chief works, the *Speculum Meditantis* or *Mirour de l'Omme* is written in French, the *Vox Clamantis* in Latin, and the *Confessio Amantis* in English. A Latin poem in leonine hexameters, *Cronica Tripertia*, relates the events of the last years of the reign of Richard II, including his deposition. Gower was a Kentish man of some wealth and is believed to have lived mostly in London and, during his later years, been well known at court. In 1400 he became blind and retired to the priory of St Mary Overies, Southwark, where he died.

Grahame, Kenneth (1859–1932)
St Cross's Churchyard, St Cross Road, Oxford.

Author of *The Wind in the Willows*, 1908, a children's book which brought its writer immense popularity and a fortune. He had previously written other works which had won him critical acclaim, notably *The Golden Age*, 1895, which was a study of childhood in the English countryside. This was followed by a sequel, *Dream Days*, in 1898.

Gray, Thomas (1716–1771)
St Giles's Churchyard, Stoke Poges, Buckinghamshire, where the Gray monument was erected in 1799 to the east of the church by John Penn to a design by James Wyatt. A monument stands in Westminster Abbey, London, in the South Transept, now known as 'Poets' Corner'.

Poet. Born in London and educated at Eton, with Horace Walpole, and at Peterhouse, Cambridge. He accompanied Walpole on a continental tour during 1739 to 1741, but they quarrelled and separated. They were reconciled in 1744 when Gray was living at Cambridge, at Peterhouse, removing to Pembroke College in 1756. He refused the Laureateship in 1757 but accepted the appointment of professor of history and modern languages at Cambridge in 1768. His first odes, 'On Spring', 'On a Distant Prospect of Eton College', and 'On Adversity' were published in 1742 together with the 'Sonnet on the Death of West',

Grave of Thomas Gray in St Giles's Churchyard, Stoke Poges, Buckinghamshire

Lines from Gray's 'Elegy in a Country Churchyard' engraved on a memorial to the poet in St Giles's Church, Stoke Poges, Buckinghamshire

his friend Richard West. In 1750 he completed his famous poem, 'Elegy in a Country Churchyard', the setting for which is believed to be that churchyard of St Giles in Stoke Poges in which he is buried. It was the popularity of the 'Elegy' which led to the offer of the Laureateship.

Hall, Marguerite Radclyffe (1886–1943)
Highgate 'old' Cemetery, Highgate, London.

Authoress of *The Well of Loneliness*, a novel dealing with lesbianism, a controversial theme when the book was published in the late 1920s. The novel was banned for some time. She also wrote a number of other novels but none brought her the notoriety of *The Well of Loneliness*.

Hardy, Thomas (1840–1928)
Westminster Abbey, London, ashes only in the South Transept, now known as 'Poets' Corner'; his heart is buried in the churchyard of St Michael's, Stinsford, Dorset.

Novelist and poet. His chief novels are *Far from the Madding Crowd*, 1874, *The Return of the Native*, 1878, *The Trumpet-Major*, 1880, *The Mayor of Casterbridge*, 1886, *Tess of the D'Urbervilles*, 1891, and *Jude the Obscure*, 1896. Of his poetry, the best known is that in the epic drama *The Dynasts*, 1904–1908, *Wessex Poems* and *Poems Past and Present*. He was born at Upper Bockhampton near Dorchester, the son of a builder, and started his working life as an architectural assistant in London, before returning to his native Dorset to write. The underlying theme of much of Hardy's writing, of many of the novels, is the struggle of man against the force, neutral and indifferent to his sufferings as Hardy conceives it, that rules the world; or, in another aspect, the ironies and disappointments of life and love. He was awarded the Order of Merit.

Harte, Francis Bret (1836–1902)
St Peter's Churchyard, Frimley, Surrey.

Short-story writer born at Albany in New York. At eighteen he went to California where he saw something of the mining life. Worked on various journals in San Francisco, submitting his short stories which made him famous: 'The Luck of Roaring Camp', 1868, 'Tennessee's Partner' and 'The Outcasts of Poker Flat' which appeared in *The Luck of Roaring Camp and Other Sketches* in 1870. From 1878–1880 he was the American consul at Crefeld in Germany, and from 1880 to 1885 at Glasgow. Thereafter he settled in England where he died.

The grave of Thomas Hardy, St Michael's Churchyard, Stinsford, Dorset, which is inscribed 'Here lies the heart of Thomas Hardy, O.M.'

Hazlitt, William (1778–1830)
St Anne's Churchyard, Dean Street, Soho, London.

Essayist and critic. His chief writings divide themselves into three categories: 1 – those of art and drama including the pleasant *Notes on a Journey through France and Italy*, 1826, and *A View of the English State*, 1818–1821; 2 – the essays on miscellaneous subjects which contain some of his best work, 'The Feeling of Immortality in Youth', 'Going on a Journey' and 'Going to a fight'; and 3 – the essays in literary criticism which many believe are his chief claim to fame, 'Characters of Shakespeare's Plays', 1817–1818, 'Lectures on the English Poets', 1818–1819, 'English Comic Writers', 1819, 'Dramatic Literature of the Age of Elizabeth', 1820, and 'Table Talk, or Original Essays on Men and Manners', 1821–1822. He was a quarrelsome and unamiable man.

Henty, George Alfred (1832–1902)
Brompton Cemetery, West Brompton, London.

Writer of boys' stories. After leaving Cambridge without a degree he volunteered for the Crimean War, and his letters describing the siege of

William Hazlitt, by William Bewick, 1825

Sebastopol were printed in the *Morning Advertiser*. He became a journalist for the *Standard*, volunteering as a war correspondent during the Austro-Italian war of 1866, and accompanied Garibaldi in his Tirolese Campaign. In middle life he edited the magazine for boys called the *Union Jack*, becoming its mainstay and contributing several serials in succession. They so pleased their public that they were subsequently published in book form. Altogether he wrote about eighty such works.

Hollis, Maurice Christopher (1902–1977)
St Andrew's Parish Church, Mells, Somerset, one of three low headstones with Sassoon and Knox (whom see).

Best known as an author, he was also a Conservative MP for Devizes, Wiltshire, who went against his party's views at the time as an abolitionist of capital punishment. He was a brother of Sir Roger Hollis (d.1973) who became a controversial figure as Director General of MI5, Britain's security service.

Hollis, Thomas (1720–1774)
A field in Corscombe, Dorset. On his own instructions he was buried 10 feet deep in his field, which was then to be ploughed over, in a completely unmarked location.

Born in London, his great-uncle having been the benefactor of Harvard College in America, Thomas also supported important causes and influential libraries throughout the world, including Harvard, Berne and Zurich. He was a member of Lincoln's Inn and an MP but regarded as an atheist by the church. He was a distinguished editor of Toland's *Life of Milton* (1761), Wallis's *English Grammar*, Locke's *Letters Concerning Toleration* (both in 1765) and seven other important works including not the least Algernon Sidney's works (1772), his last book. One of his eccentricities was that he named his farms and fields after famous patriots of history he felt should be honoured. A farm gate here can still be seen with 'Milton' on it.

Holtby, Winifred (1898–1935)
All Saints' Church, Rudston, East Yorkshire.

Novelist who is principally remembered for her novel, *South Riding*, which was not published until the year of her death. A close friend of the writer Vera Brittain for whom the latter wrote the celebrated *Testament of Friendship: The Story of Winifred Holtby*.

'Hope, Anthony' (Sir Anthony Hope Hawkins) (1863–1933)
St Mary and St Nicholas's Churchyard, Leatherhead, Surrey.
   Novelist. Wrote *The Prisoner of Zenda*, 1894, and *Rupert of Hentzau*, 1898, as well as *The Dolly Dialogues*, 1894, and other novels and plays. He was knighted in 1918 for his services to the Ministry of Information during the Great War.

Housman, A.E. (Alfred Edward) (1859–1936)
St Lawrence's Church, Ludlow, Shropshire where his ashes lie beneath the north wall.
   Poet. A distinguished classical scholar, he is remembered for his two volumes of lyrics, remarkable for their simplicity and economy of words: *A Shropshire Lad*, 1869, and *Last Poems*, 1922.

Hughes, Ted (1930–1998)
Ashes scattered on Dartmoor, close to the source of the River Taw. There is a large granite memorial stone nearby. The funeral service was held in St Peter's Church, North Tawton, Devon.
   Poet and author. Hughes grew up in Yorkshire before winning a scholarship to Pembroke College, Cambridge, where he met Sylvia Plath. They married just a few months later. In 1957 Hughes published his first volume of poetry, *The Hawk in the Rain*. His third volume, *Luperchal*, won the Somerset Maugham Award and in 1961 he won the Hawthornden Prize. Whilst Hughes was having success as a poet, Plath was not and her depressions led to accusations of infidelity and finally her suicide in London in 1963.
   Plath's death and his relationship with Assia Wevil, caused Hughes to be labelled a 'brute' by some members of the literary community. In 1969 tragedy struck again when Assia killed herself and their four-year-old daughter. His 1970 collection, *Crow,* is dedicated to them and is probably his most famous work. Hughes' study of Sylvia Plath's life, *Birthday Letters*, was published in 1998 and became a bestseller. He is also known as a children's writer - *The Iron Man*, published in 1968 was the inspiration for the animated movie *Iron Giant.*
   Hughes was awarded an OBE in 1977 and in 1984 he was appointed Poet Laureate.

Huxley, Aldous Leonard (1894–1963)
Compton Cemetery, Compton, Surrey.
   Novelist and essayist. He settled in California in the late 1930s where

he remained until his death. His best-known novels are *Crome Yellow*, 1921, *Antic Hay*, 1923, *Point Counterpoint*, 1928, *Brave New World*, 1932, and *Eyeless in Gaza*, 1936. His essays include 'The Olive Tree', 1936, and 'Ape and Essence', 1948.

Jefferies, John Richard (1848–1887)
Broadwater Cemetery, Worthing, Sussex.

Novelist and naturalist who, born at Coate Farm near Swindon, got his beginnings at the *North Wilts Herald*. At sixteen he ran away with a friend, intending to walk to Moscow, but they decided that language difficulties would debar that, so they elected to try America instead. When they ran out of money at Liverpool they returned to Swindon. Some of his first novels were *The Scarlet Shawl*, *Restless Human Hearts* and *The World's End*. His later novels of country life brought him enduring fame; *Greene Ferne Farm* and *Amaryllis at the Fair* (1888 and 1887 respectively) are full of his naturalist descriptions. One of his works, *After London* (1885), has a remarkably present-day theme: the inhabitants of London have fled, leaving a poisonous lake that is now the city, while wild beasts and a malign race of dwarfs occupy most of England.

Jerome, Jennie, Lady Randolph Churchill (d.1921)
St Martin's Church, Bladon, Oxfordshire.

Married to Lord Randolph Churchill, the High Tory politician, she was the mother of Sir Winston Churchill. An American by birth, she became a leader of London society at the turn of the century. In 1908 she published her *Reminiscences*, which was followed by two plays, *Borrowed Plumes* in 1909 and *The Bill* in 1912.

Jerome, Jerome K. (1859–1927)
St Mary's Churchyard, Ewelme, Oxfordshire.

Novelist and playwright. His most famous work was the celebrated *Three Men in a Boat* which appeared with *Idle Thoughts of an Idle Fellow* in 1889. His play *The Passing of the Third Floor Back* in 1908 brought him fame as a dramatist. In 1892 he founded, with others, *The Idler*, a successful monthly magazine.

Grave of Jerome K. Jerome, St Mary's Churchyard, Ewelme, Oxfordshire

Samuel Johnson, by Barry

Johnson, Samuel (1709–1784)
Westminster Abbey, London, in the South Transept, now known as 'Poets' Corner'.

Lexicographer and critic. Born at Lichfield and attended the local grammar school before going up to Pembroke College, Oxford. After an unsuccessful attempt at teaching, in 1737 he went to London accompanied by his pupil, David Garrick, in search of a career. His success was much slower than that of Garrick. His chief works are the great *Dictionary of the English Language*, 1756, and the *Lives of the Poets*, 1779–1781. In 1750 he started the *Rambler*, a periodical written almost entirely by himself, which for two years appeared twice weekly. In 1764, together with Goldsmith, Burke and Reynolds, he founded The Club, later known as the Literary Club.

Jonson, Ben (c. 1572–1637)
Westminster Abbey, London, in the north aisle of the Nave. His monument is in the South Transept, now known as 'Poets' Corner'. The tradition that he was buried upright was confirmed in the nineteenth century, in the course of digging a nearby grave. The inscription 'O rare

Gravestone of Ben Jonson in Westminster Abbey, London, in 'Poets' Corner'. His name was incorrectly spelled when the stone was renewed

Ben Jonson' was cut on his gravestone at the charge of Jack Young, who paid the mason eighteen pence for his work.

Dramatist and poet. He was educated at Westminster School under Camden, and was a friend of Shakespeare and Bacon. He was a tutor to the son of Sir Walter Raleigh and in 1619 became Poet Laureate. Of his many plays, the most celebrated are *Volpone*, *The Alchemist*, *Every Man in his Humour* which, when first performed at the Globe in 1598, had Shakespeare among the cast, and *Bartholomew Fair*.

Kingsley, Charles (1819–1875)
St Mary's Church, Eversley, Hampshire, where the north aisle, erected in 1876, was built as a memorial to Kingsley, who was vicar from 1844 to 1875.

Novelist. Born at Holne in Devon, he was educated at King's College, London and Magdalene College, Cambridge. He took holy orders and became the vicar of St Mary's in Eversley in 1844, holding the living there for the rest of his life. He was Professor of Modern History at Cambridge from 1860 to 1869 and thereafter held canonries at Chester and Westminster. He was an ardent social reformer, contributing, over the signature 'Parson Lot', to the *Politics of the People* in 1848 and to the *Christian Socialist* from 1850 to 1851. His principal novels were

Grave of Charles Kingsley, St Mary's Church, Eversley, Hampshire

Westward Ho!, 1855, *The Water Babies*, 1863, and *Hereward the Wake*, 1865. He also published numerous sermons, remarkable not only for their style but for the broad spirit of humanity they display.

Kipling, Rudyard (1865–1936)
Westminster Abbey, London, in the South Transept now known as 'Poets' Corner'.

Writer and poet. Born in Bombay, his voluminous output of short stories mainly concern the British Empire and India in particular. His novels include *The Jungle Books*, 1894 and 1895, *Kim*, 1901, *Just So Stories*, 1902, *Stalky & Co.*, 1899, *Puck of Pook's Hill*, 1906, and *Rewards and Fairies*, 1910. Of his poems, the best known are *Departmental Ditties*, 1886, and *Barrack-Room Ballads*, 1892. He was awarded the Nobel Prize for Literature in 1907.

Lewis, Cecil Day (1904–1972)
St Michael's Churchyard, Stinsford, Dorset.

Poet Laureate. Born in Ireland, he was educated at Wadham College, Oxford, where he became associated with a group of young Left-wing poets, which included W. H. Auden. He became a teacher and a member of the Communist Party, his early poems reflecting his political affiliation. Later, under the influence of Thomas Hardy, his poetry turned to more personal and pastoral themes. He also wrote several detective stories under the pseudonym of Nicholas Blake. From 1951 to 1956 he was Professor of Poetry at Oxford, and was appointed Poet Laureate in 1968.

Lewis, Clive Staples (1898–1963)
Heading Quarry churchyard, Oxford, Oxfordshire.

Writer who was much revered for his ability to bring an understanding of Christianity as he saw it to readers. He has also been described as a medievalist. His book *The Screwtape Letters* (1942) made his name familiar to a wide number of persons for its idealistic and gentle satire concerning Christian concerns. Belfast born he became Professor of Renaissance English at Cambridge. He was awarded the Hawthorne Prize for his *Allegory of Love* (1936) and one of his children's books *The Last Battle* earned him the Carnegie Prize in 1957. *The Problem of Pain* (1940), *Beyond Personality* (1944), *Out of the Silent Planet* (1938), *Perelandra* (1943), the last two science fiction, were some others of his books.

Grave of Cecil Day Lewis, St Michael's Churchyard, Stinsford, Dorset

Malory, Sir Thomas (d.1471)
Christ Church, Newgate Street, London. The original church was replaced by Sir Christopher Wren's between 1677 and 1691, but this was destroyed in an air-raid during 1940. Only the steeple of Wren's church now remains, the burial ground being laid out as a garden.

Identified by E. Vinaver with Sir Thomas Malory, Knight of Newbold Revel in Warwickshire and Winwick in Northamptonshire. A Member of Parliament in 1456, he is thought to have sided with Warwick the King-maker and joined the Lancastrians. Three 'prayers for deliverance' in his manuscript suggest that he wrote his celebrated *Le Morte d'Arthur* whilst in prison.

Marlowe, Christopher (1564–1593)
St Nicholas's Church, Deptford, London. The west wall records Marlowe's death in a tavern brawl nearby.

Poet and dramatist. Son of a Canterbury shoemaker, he was educated at King's School, Canterbury and Corpus Christi College, Cambridge. He joined the Earl of Nottingham's theatrical company, which produced most of his plays. His most famous dramas are *Tamburlaine*, c.1587, *Dr Faustus, The Jew of Malta*, after 1588, and *Edward II*, c.1593. He is believed to have collaborated with Shakespeare on *Titus Andronicus* and *Henry VI*. He translated Ovid's 'Amores' and paraphrased part of Musaeus's 'Hero and Leander'. He is thought to have been a government agent and that his death by the hand of Ingram Frisar had political complications.

Marryat, Frederick (1792–1848)
St Andrew and St Mary's Churchyard, Langham, Norfolk.

Novelist. A captain in the Royal Navy in which he served with distinction, he wrote a number of novels of sea-life of which the best-known are *Frank Mildmay*, 1829, *Peter Simple*, 1834, *Jacob Faithful*, 1834, *Mr Midshipman Easy*, 1836, *Masterman Ready*, 1841, and *The Children of the New Forest*, 1842. He spent the years 1837 to 1839 in Canada and the United States of America, publishing his *Diary in America* on his return, which contained an unflattering account of American manners.

Masefield, John (1878–1967)
Westminster Abbey, London, in the South Transept now known as 'Poets' Corner'.

Poet, novelist and dramatist. He ran away to sea and made his way to

America where he did various menial jobs to earn his living. When he returned to England he joined the staff of the *Manchester Guardian*. During the years 1900 to 1910 he wrote continuously, publishing the *Salt-Water Ballads* in 1902 which included the famous poem, 'I must go down to the sea again'; *Ballads and Poems*, 1910; collection of short stories, *A Mainsail Haul*, 1905, and *A Tarpaulin Muster*, 1907; plays, *The Tragedy of Pompey the Great*, 1910 and *The Tragedy of Nan*, 1909; and essays. His remarkable poem 'The Everlasting Mercy', about the conversion of the ruffianly Saul Kane, was published in 1911. His novels include *Captain Margaret*, 1908, *Odtaa*, 1926, and *The Bird of Dawning*, 1933. He was appointed Poet Laureate in 1930, and was also awarded the Order of Merit.

Maugham, William Somerset (1874–1965)
Ashes scattered near the Maugham Library, King's School, Canterbury, Kent.

Novelist, short-story writer and dramatist. His principal novels were *Of Human Bondage*, 1915, *The Moon and Sixpence*, 1919, *Cakes and Ale*, 1930, *The Razor's Edge*, 1944. Of his plays, *East of Suez*, 1922, *The Circle*, 1921, *The Constant Wife*, 1927 and *For Services Rendered*, 1932, are perhaps the best known. His short stories, several of which were dramatized, include 'Ashenden', 1928, 'The Trembling of a Leaf', 1921, and 'On a Chinese Screen', 1923. For many years he lived in the South of France, where he died.

Meredith, George (1828–1909)
Dorking Cemetery, Dorking, Surrey.

Novelist and poet. After being articled to a solicitor in London he turned to journalism, contributing to *Household Words* and *Chamber's Journal*. In 1849 he married the daughter of Thomas Love Peacock but the marriage was not a success for she left him in 1858. In 1864 he married Marie Vulliamy and they lived at Flint Cottage, facing Box Hill in Surrey. His most famous novel was perhaps *Diana of the Crossways* which appeared in 1885 and brought him a popularity that his previous novels, including *The Ordeal of Richard Feverel*, 1859, and *The Adventures of Harry Richmond*, 1871, had not. He was also a considerable poet, publishing many volumes of verse.

Milton, John (1608–1674)
St Giles' Church without Cripplegate, London Wall, London.

Poet. John Milton was educated at St Paul's School, London and Christ's College, Cambridge. Whilst at Cambridge he wrote the poems 'On the Death of a Fair Infant', 1625, and 'At a Vacation Exercise', 1627. After Cambridge he lived with his father at Horton in Buckinghamshire where he composed 'L'Allegro' and 'Il Penseroso' in 1632, 'Arcades', c.1633, and 'Comus', 1634. In 1637 he produced 'Lycidas' and thereafter wrote little poetry during the next twenty years until he began the composition of 'Paradise Lost'. In 1642 he married Mary Powell, the daughter of Royalist parents, and when she did not return to him after a visit to her parents he published his notorious pamphlets on the 'doctrine and discipline of divorce'. However, his wife returned in 1645. After the execution of the King, Charles I, in January 1649 he published the 'Tenure of Kings and Magistrates' and was appointed Latin Secretary to the new Council of State. Owing to his increasing blindness he was assisted in his duties by, among others, Andrew Marvell. His first wife died in 1652 and four years later he married Catharine Woodcock, who died two years later. After the Restoration he lost both his post and his freedom, for he was briefly arrested. He was fined but released. In 1662 he married his third wife, Elizabeth Minshull, and lived with her in Bunhill Row. Aubrey believed that 'Paradise Lost' was completed in 1663 but the agreement for the copyright was not signed until 1667. 'Paradise Regained' and 'Samson Agonistes' were published together in 1671. His most famous Latin poems are 'Epitaphium Damonis', 1639, on the death of his friend, Charles Diodati, and the address to 'Mansus'. He died from gout.

Mitford, The Hon Nancy Freeman (1907–1973)
St Mary's Churchyard, Swinbrook, Oxfordshire.

Novelist and biographer. Daughter of Lord Redesdale, she achieved great popularity with her satirical novels about aristocratic life and romance, *Love in a Cold Climate*, 1949, *The Pursuit of Love*, 1945, *The Blessing* and *Don't Tell Alfred*. She was a considerable biographer, writing *The Sun King* about Louis XIV of France, *Madame de Pompadour*, *Voltaire in Love*, *The Stanleys of Alderley* and *Frederick the Great*. She also wrote a most witty enquiry into the identifiable characteristics of the English aristocracy entitled *Noblesse Oblige*. For many years she lived just outside Paris at St Cloud.

Stone marking the burial site of John Milton, St Giles' Church without Cripplegate, London Wall, London

Moore, Thomas (1779–1852)
St Nicholas' Churchyard, Bromham, Wiltshire; under a large Celtic cross.

Irish poet, born in Dublin of a wine merchant, he became noted for his wit and literary abilities as a Trinity College, Dublin, student. In London his singing and playing ability brought him great popularity. He achieved fame and money with his *Irish Melodies*, for which over nearly thirty years he received more than £12,000. The story is told of him sitting with Byron on the banks of the Thames discussing fame. From the river came the voices of boaters singing Moore's popular songs, such as 'The Harp that once Through Tara's Halls' and 'She Wore a Wreath of Roses'; Byron said to Moore: 'That, is fame.' Moore now lived with his actress wife near Lord Lansdowne, his friend, whose Bowood House was near Bromham. Earlier, his success had induced Longman's to pay him £3,000 for a poem he had not even written at the time. It turned out to be *Lalla Rookh*, which was about the East, a subject made fashionable by Byron. Around 1815 Moore's *National Airs and Sacred Songs* were adapted to music and became as popular as his *Irish Melodies*. They included 'Oft in the Stilly Night' and 'Sound the Loud Timbrel'. After Byron died, Moore was asked to write his biography from the memoirs that Byron had given him, but Moore had burnt them. To get out of debt later, however, he wrote a life of Byron. Moore's last work, *The History of Ireland*, turned out to be such an exhausting and arduous task, needing four volumes to complete, that he could not even write a word of the preface and at times seemed to be reduced to a condition of 'little better than imbecility', aggravated no doubt by the deaths of five of his children. Moore was an 'amiable, generous, and affectionate' man who, rather than see his wife spurned by London society, for which she had neither the wit nor desire, had moved to Bromham to live in Sloperton Cottage. She died in 1865 and was buried in his grave.

Morris, William (1834–1896)
St George's churchyard, Cotswold-style gravestone, Kelmscott, Oxfordshire.

As a poet, author of prose romances, founder of both a publishing house and a firm of house decorators, his first intentions were to take holy orders. He was educated at Marlborough and Exeter College, Oxford. Through the poet Rossetti Morris turned to painting and handicrafts, which in turn gave him eventually an aversion to the growing technology, mass production and capitalism of the Victorian era. He became attracted to socialism. He was a typical Utopian, organising the Socialist League and also the Arts and Crafts Societies through which he was able to promote his socialism to the mostly manual workers of the Societies. *The Dream of John Ball* in 1888 was one of two romances he wrote as socialist propaganda. Other works of a more realistic nature followed, including *The House of Wolfings, The Roots of Mountains, The Story of the Glittering Plain*, all written between 1889 and 1891. His first volume of poetry *The Defence of Guinevere* had appeared in 1858. He established the Kelmscott Press at Hammersmith in 1890 where he published his own works and assorted reprints of classical works, including his own earlier translations of the Aeneid and the Odyssey. Margaret Grennan epitomized him as a 'Mediaevalist and Revolutionary' in her 1945 book.

Mulock, Dinah Maria (1826–1887)
Keston Churchyard, Keston, Kent, near hedge border and tall Celtic cross.

Novelist whose best-known work was *John Halifax, Gentleman*, 1857, which placed her in the front rank of the day's women novelists. Her other novels never commanded the great respect of the former but *A Life for a Life* brought her some financial success. She wrote many children's tales and some short stories as well as poems. In 1864 she married G. L. Craik, a partner in the firm of Macmillan & Co.

Orwell, George (Eric Blair) (1903–1950)
All Saints' Churchyard, Sutton Courtenay, Oxfordshire.

Satirical novelist. Born in Bengal, he was educated at Eton College. From 1922 to 1927 he served with the Indian Imperial Police in Burma, and his experiences are the basis for his first novel, *Burmese Days*, 1934. Later he returned to Europe, undertaking a series of ill-paid jobs in Paris and London which inspired *Down and Out in Paris and London*, 1933. He fought for the Republicans in the Spanish Civil War and his *Homage to Catalonia*, 1938, is a biographical record of that war. A democratic Socialist with a dislike for totalitarianism which brought a disillusion with the aims and methods of Communism, he wrote two satirical political novels, *Animal Farm*, 1945, and *Nineteen Eighty Four*, 1949, reflecting his views, which brought him great popularity. He wrote a number of essays and studies, such as *The Road to Wigan Pier*, 1937, about unemployment.

Palgrave, Francis Turner (1824–1897)
Barnes Cemetery, Barnes, Greater London.

Educated at Charterhouse and Balliol College, Oxford. A close friend of Tennyson, he is chiefly remembered for his anthology, *The Golden Treasury of Songs and Lyrics*, 1861. He was himself a poet, publishing *The Visions of England* which was perhaps his best sole work. From 1885 to 1895 he was Professor of Poetry at Oxford.

Pepys, Samuel (1633–1703)
St Olave's Church, Hart Street, City of London, beside the communion table alongside his wife Elizabeth. The bust he erected to his wife after her death in 1669 records that she bore no children because she could bear none worthy of herself.

Diarist. Educated at St Paul's School, London and at Trinity Hall and Magdalene College, Cambridge, he entered the household of his father's cousin, Sir Edward Montagu, later the Earl of Sandwich, under whose patronage he rose. He held many government appointments, though lost them briefly when he was committed to the Tower of London on suspicion of complicity in the 'Popish Plot' of 1679. He was soon released and regained his post of Secretary to the Admiralty in 1684. His famous *Diary* opens on 1 January 1660 and for nine years, until failing eyesight forced its closure on 31 May 1669, he kept a detailed record of his own life and times, not only revealing the author's own lovable nature but portraying a vivid picture of contemporary everyday life, of the administration of the navy, and of the ways of the court.

Plath, Sylvia (1932–1963)
St Thomas's Churchyard, Heptonstall, Hebden Bridge, West Yorkshire.

American-born poet, born in Boston, Massachusetts, who married Poet Laureate Ted Hughes in 1956 after graduating from college in America. Her poems and writings have been considered as reflecting a disturbed mind, for she seemed obsessed with disgust for the natural functions of the human body, including childbirth. She wrote an auto-biographical novel *The Bell Jar* (1963), and her collected poems, *The Colossus* (1960) and others which attracted a Pulitzer Prize in 1982, were more successful after her death. Her poems were popular with the feminist movement. Her poem *Daddy*, about her love – hate relationship with her father, was written just before her suicide.

Sylvia Plath's grave, Hebden Bridge

Pope, Alexander (1688–1744)

St Mary's Church, Twickenham, Greater London, where a monument was erected in 1761 bearing the inscription, 'To one who would not be buried in Westminster Abbey'. Pope is reputed to haunt the church following the exhumation of his skull which had been purchased for phrenological examination.

Poet and essayist. Largely self-taught, he showed precocious metrical skill in his 'Pastorals' written, he claimed, when he was sixteen. His 'Essay on Criticism', written when he was only twenty-three, was published in 1711, and contains the famous and oft-quoted lines, 'To err is human, to forgive, divine' (1.525) and 'A little learning is a dang'rous thing' (1.215). Its publication brought him into association with Addison's circle which led to the publication of his 'Messiah' in the *Spectator* in 1712. He became a member of the Scriblerus Club which included Swift, Gay and Arbuthnot among its members, and in 1715 issued the first volume of his translation in heroic couplets of Homer's *Iliad*. It was regarded as one of the great poems of the age and was completed in 1720. In 1719 he bought a lease of a house in Twickenham in Middlesex where he spent the remainder of his life. In 1733 he published the first of his miscellaneous satires, 'Imitations of Horace', entitled 'Satire 1', a paraphrase of the first satire of the second book of Horace, in the form of a dialogue between the poet and William Fortescue, the lawyer. This was followed by others.

Potter, Beatrix (1866–1943)

Ashes scattered on one of her fields at Near Sawrey, Cumbria, by her shepherd Tom Storey, who promised not to reveal the spot. He died in 1988 at ninety, having passed the secret on to his son, who suddenly dropped dead in 1989. No one knows now the exact spot, which is what she wanted (I am indebted to Mrs Irene Whalley of the Beatrix Potter Society for this information.-DG.)

An authoress, born in London, whose books became children's classics. She published her first two animal-story books *The Tale of Peter Rabbit* (1902) and *The Tailor of Gloucester* (1903), at her own expense. Later twenty-three of her animal stories were published. They were translated into many languages. She also illustrated her books with drawings and watercolours. Later she became a successful cattle breeder and landowner. Her first farmhouse, Hill Top, is owned by the National Trust, to whom she left her extensive farm properties. The small pub next to Hill Top is also a National Trust property.

Powys, John Cowper (1872–1964), Llewelyn (1884–1939),
Theodore Francis ('T.F.') (1875–1953)
Abbotsbury, Chesil Beach, ashes scattered (John Cowper); Swyre Head,
near Chaldon Herring, ashes under stone monument to him by Elizabeth
Muntz (Llewelyn); St Peter and Paul Church, Mappowder (Theodore
Francis), all in Dorset.

Three brother novelists who had virtually a cult following in the
USA. Between them they wrote scores of fiction and non-fiction books.
Their reputation probably rests largely on *Wolf Solent* (1929), set in
Bradford Abbas, Dorset, and *A Glastonbury Romance* (1932) by John
Cowper; *Dorset and Somerset Essays*, and *Skin for Skin* (1925) by Lle-
welyn; *Unclay* (1931) and *Mr Weston's Good Wine* (1927), set in Chaldon
Herring, Dorset, by Theodore Francis.

Priestley, J.B. (John Boynton) (1894–1983)
St Michael and All Angels Church, Hubberholme, Upper Wharfedale,
North Yorkshire.

Novelist and playwright who was born in Bradford, Yorkshire, from
which town and county he drew his characters in *The Good Companions*,
which became an immediate best-selling novel in 1929. Previously, after
being educated at Trinity College, Cambridge, he had produced several
critical books such as *The English Comic Character* (1925) and *English
Humour* (1928). His stage comedy *Laburnum Grove* (1933) was a West
End success, as were his more serious plays *Dangerous Corner* (1932) and
Time and the Conways (1937) with its theme of being able to foresee the
future by dreams. With his wife Jacquetta Hawkes (1910–1989), an
archaeologist, he wrote *Journey Down the Rainbow* (1955), a good-nat-
ured critique of American life. Four of his plays *Eden End* (1934),
Cornelius (1935), *Johnson Over Jordan* (1939) and *An Inspector Calls*
(1945) were graced by Sir Ralph Richardson (whom see) in their leading
roles.

'Q', Sir Arthur Thomas Quiller-Couch (1863–1944)
St Nicholas's Church, Fowey, Cornwall.

Poet, novelist and critic. He became Professor of English Literature at
Cambridge in 1912 and wrote many novels including *Dead Man's Rock*,
1887, *Troy Town*, 1888, and *The Splendid Spur*, 1889. He compiled *The
Oxford Book of English Verse*, 1900 and 1939, *The Oxford Book of Ballads*,
1910, *The Oxford Book of Victorian Verse*, 1912 and *The Oxford Book of
English Prose*, 1925. His books of criticism included *On the Art of*

Writing, 1916, and *On the Art of Reading*, 1920. He died after being hit by a jeep whilst walking near his home in Cornwall.

Rosenthal, Jack (1931–2004)
Golders Green Jewish Cemetery.

Scriptwriter and producer. The 1970s was the era of the TV play and Jack Rosenthal was one of Britain's finest TV dramatists. He won three BAFTA awards in succession with *Bar Mitzvah Boy*, *The Evacuees*, and *Spend, Spend, Spend*. In 1984 he co-wrote the film *Yentl*, which starred Barbara Streisand, and in 1986 his play *London's Burning* was first screened. This went on to become the long-running ITV series of the same name. In 1973 he married the actress Maureen Lipman and they remained together until his death in 2004.

Sassoon, Siegfried (1886–1967)
St Andrew's Parish Church, Mells, Somerset, one of three low head-stones with Knox and Hollis (whom see).

Poet, novelist and biographer. Educated at Marlborough and Clare College, Cambridge, he enlisted in the First World War and won the Military Cross. His bitter war poetry attacks the hypocrisy and romanticism of the war mood. His published poems include *The Old Huntsman*, 1917, *Counterattack*, 1918, *Satirical Poems*, 1926, *The Heart's Journey*, 1928, *Vigils*, 1935, and *Collected Poems*, 1947. He wrote a number of works of semi-autobiographical fiction including *Memoirs of a Fox-Hunting Man*, 1928, *Memoirs of an Infantry Officer*, 1930, and *Sherston's Progress*, 1936, as well as a biography of George Meredith in 1948.

Sayers, Dorothy Leigh (1893–1957)
St Anne's Church, Soho, London; ashes and memorial.

Novelist and playwright who appeared first in *Clouds of Witness* (1926). Born at Oxford, she was credited with being the 'most celebrated detective-story writer since Conan Doyle' in her earlier days. She set her scenes accurately and paraded her characters with taste and style. Among other titles of her mystery stories were *Murder Must Advertise* (1933), *The Nine Tailors* (1934) and *Busman's Honeymoon* (1937), the last of that genre. Later she used Christianity as a theme for two successful plays, *The Zeal of Thy House* (1937) and *The Devil to Pay* (1939) along with a broadcast series *The Man Born to be King* (1943). She was also an essayist on the same subject, for which she was no apologist but a sincere believer. A translator of Dante's *Inferno* (1949) and *Purgatorio* (1955), her *Paradiso* was unfinished at her death.

Sewell, Anna (1820–1878)
Old Quaker Meeting House Garden, Lamas, Norfolk.
Remembered solely for her great children's classic, *Black Beauty*, the 'autobiography' of a horse, which was published a year before she died.

Shakespeare, William (1564–1616)
Holy Trinity Church, Stratford-on-Avon, Warwickshire, by the north wall of the chancel. On his gravestone are the lines:

> Good friend, for Jesus' sake forebeare
> To digg the dust enclosed heare;
> Bleste be the man that spares thes stones,
> And curst be he that moves my bones.

Whilst his bust on the wall above bears the inscription:

IVDICIO PYLIVM GENIO SOCRATEM ARTE MARONEM
TERRA TEGIT POPVLVS MAERET OLYMPVS HABET
Stay Passenger, why goest thou by so fast,
Read if thou canst, whom envious death has plast,
Within this monument Shakespeare: with whome,
Quick nature dide: whose name does deck Y_s tombe,
Far more, then cost: Seih all, Y_t he hath Writt
Leaves living art, but page, to serve his Witt.

He was educated at the free grammar school in Stratford, and it is believed that before he went to London he may have been a schoolmaster. In 1582 he married Anne Hathaway and his first child, Susannah, was baptized in 1583. In 1585 he moved to London and secured Lord Southampton as his principal patron. It is established that by September 1592 Shakespeare was both an actor and playwright. He took part in the original performance of Ben Jonson's *Every Man in his Humour* in 1598 and *Sejanus*, 1603, after which he seems to have given up acting. He had a share in the establishment of the new Globe Theatre on the Bankside in 1599. His earliest work as a dramatist, the three parts of *Henry VI*, date from 1590 to 1591. Thereafter he wrote over thirty plays, all of which have been performed throughout the world. *Henry*

VIII was written during 1612 and 1613 and is believed to have been with the collaboration of John Fletcher.

Shaw, George Bernard (1856–1950)
Shaw's Corner, Ayot St Lawrence, Hertfordshire, his ashes being scattered in the garden of his home.

Irish playwright and critic. He began as a journalist, then turning to writing for the stage where his unorthodox turn of mind and distrust of conventions and accepted institutions soon revealed itself. *Man and Superman*, 1903, introduced Shaw's conception of the 'Life Force', a power that seeks to raise mankind, with their co-operation, to a higher and better existence, and he continued this doctrine in *Heartbreak House*, 1917, and *Back to Methuselah*, 1925, in which the causes of the failure of our civilisation, as demonstrated by the Great War, are examined. He became a founder member of the Fabian Society. He wrote numerous other plays including *St Joan*, 1924, *Candida, Mrs Warren's Profession* and the immensely popular *Pygmalion*.

Shelley, Mary Wollstonecraft (1797–1851)
St Peter's Churchyard, Bournemouth, Dorset.

Daughter of Mary Wollstonecraft and William Godwin, she became the second wife of Percy Bysshe Shelley. She was the author of *Frankenstein, or the Modern Prometheus*, 1818, *The Last Man*, 1826, about the destruction of the human race by an epidemic, *Valperga*, 1823, a mediaeval Italian romance, and the autobiographical *Lodore*, 1835.

Shelley, Percy Bysshe (1792–1822)
St Peter's Churchyard, Bournemouth, Dorset, where his heart was reinterred from its original resting place at the English Protestant Cemetery in Rome.

Poet. Educated at Eton College and University College, Oxford. He published his first poems whilst still at Eton, namely *Zastrozzi*, and in 1810, aged eighteen, published *St Irvyne*, romances in the style of 'Monk' Lewis. He was sent down from Oxford in 1811 for circulating a pamphlet on 'The Necessity of Atheism'. That year he married Harriet Westbrook, but his wandering life brought the marriage to an end and they separated three years later. During that time he wrote *Queen Mab*. In 1814 he left England with Mary Godwin, whom he later married when the unfortunate Harriet Westbrook drowned herself in the Serpentine in London in 1816. That year he formed his friendship with

George Bernard Shaw (International News Photos)

Byron and Shelley and Mary spent the summer with him in Switzerland. The next few years saw a large output of his work including the composition of his great lyrical drama *Prometheus Unbound*, 1820, *The Cenci*, 1819, and a translation of Plato's *Symposium*, *Adonais*, 1821 and *Epipsychidion*, also 1821. He was drowned while sailing near Spezia, and his body was burned on the beach. Trelawny at the last moment snatched his heart, which would not burn, from the flames and gave it to Mary Shelley.

Sheridan, Richard Brinsley (1751–1816)
Westminster Abbey, London, in the South Transept now known as 'Poets' Corner'.

Parliamentary orator and dramatist. Educated at Harrow School, and, when only twenty-three, wrote his great play, *The Rivals*, which was performed at Covent Garden in 1775. He acquired David Garrick's share in the Drury Lane Theatre in 1776 and the following year produced there *A Trip to Scarborough* and *The School for Scandal*. His famous farce, *The Critic*, was performed in 1779, but his play *Pizarro*, an adaptation of Kotzebue's *The Spaniards in Peru*, was performed in 1799 and showed a decline in style. In 1780 he entered Parliament as a supporter of Charles James Fox and became famous for the eloquence of his oratory, his speech of impeachment against Warren Hastings in 1788 being particularly memorable. His new theatre in Drury Lane was destroyed by fire in 1809 and he was ruined financially, being arrested for debt in 1813. He suffered from brain disease during the last years of his life. He received a great public funeral.

Sidney, Sir Philip (1554–1586)
'Old' St Paul's Cathedral, London.

Soldier and considerable poet, he is famous for his remark as he lay wounded at the Battle of Zutphen on 22 September 1586. He had received a bullet wound in the thigh and called for some water but, seeing a dying soldier nearby whom he felt to be in greater need than himself, he offered the water to him saying, 'Thy need is greater than mine'. He died at Arnhem on 17 October 1586. As a poet he is chiefly remembered for the series of sonnets addressed to Stella, known as *Astrophel and Stella* (Stella being the Lady Penelope Devereux, sister of Elizabeth's ill-fated Earl of Essex), and *Arcadia*.

Sitwell, Dame Edith (1887–1964)
St Mary's Churchyard extension, Weedon Lois, Northamptonshire. The monument is by Henry Moore and is a large tapering, upright slab, and attached to it is a square bronze plaque with two delicate hands in high relief, signifying Youth and Age.

Poet, novelist, biographer and essayist. She published a number of poems during the 1920s which exploited the musical qualities of the language. Some of them were set to music by William Walton and entitled *Façade*. Her biographical studies included that of *Alexander Pope*, 1930 and *The English Eccentrics*, 1933, and her historical novels included one on Elizabeth I and Mary, Queen of Scots entitled *The Queens and the Hive*. Her later poems developed a graver tone, in *Street Songs*, 1943, *Green Song*, 1944 and *Song of the Cold*, 1945. She was made a Dame of the British Empire in 1954.

Spenser, Edmund (c.1552–1599)
Westminster Abbey, London, in the South Transept now known as 'Poets' Corner'. The monument was erected by Ann Clifford, Countess of Dorset, Pembroke, and Montgomery, but, having fallen into decay it was replaced by an exact copy in 1778. The epitaph reads:

> Heare lyes (expecting the Second comminge of our Saviour Christ Jesus) the body of Edmond Spencer the Prince of Poets in his tyme whose Divine Spirit needs noe othir witnesse then the works which He left behinde him.

Poet. Educated at Merchant Taylors' School and Pembroke Hall, Cambridge. In his youth he wrote the 'Hymnes in honour of Love and Beautie', which reflect the Platonic influence. In 1578 he obtained a place in the household of the Earl of Leicester, Elizabeth's favourite, and there made the acquaintance of Sir Philip Sidney, with whom, and with Dyer and others, he formed a literary club called the Areopagus. He began his most famous poem, which he dedicated to Queen Elizabeth, 'The Faerie Queen'. In 1580 he was appointed secretary to Lord Grey de Wilton, Lord Deputy for Ireland. In 1586 he became one of the 'undertakers' for the settlement of Munster, and acquired Kilcolman Castle in County Cork where he reluctantly settled and occupied himself with literary work. In 1594 he married Elizabeth Boyle, celebrating the marriage in his 'Epithalamion'. In October 1598 his castle was burnt in an insurrection and he and his family – by then he had four children – fled to

Cork. He died in London in financial distress at a lodging in King Street, Westminster, and the expenses of his funeral were borne by the Earl of Essex.

Stacpoole, Henry de Vere (1863–1951)
St Boniface's Church, Bonchurch, Isle of Wight.
    Novelist. After qualifying as a doctor he sailed the world as a ship's physician. He was a prolific novelist, some fifty in all, but he achieved little financial success with them until his *The Blue Lagoon* (1908) which, with his novel of the previous year, *The Crimson Azaleas*, proved immediately popular because of their exotic and tropical setting. *The Blue Lagoon*, reprinted twenty-three times in the next twelve years, was made into a episodic play which was put on at the Prince of Wales Theatre in London in 1920, and also filmed. He was acquainted with many of the authors of the *Yellow Book* period, including Aubrey Beardsley.

Sterne, Laurence (1713–1768)
Originally buried in the St George's burial ground in the Bayswater Road, London, but a seemingly authentic rumour says his body was disinterred and sold for dissection. A monumental stone was later erected near the site. When the burial ground was built over his remains were removed to the churchyard of St Michael's, Coxwold, North Yorkshire, where he was vicar from 1760 to 1768.
    Novelist. After leaving Jesus College, Cambridge, he was ordained and became Vicar of Sutton-in-the-Forest in 1738, remaining there until 1759. He married Elizabeth Lumley in 1741 but his philanderings caused her much distress and she became insane in 1758. He began his famous novel, *Tristram Shandy*, in 1759, volumes i and ii being published the following year. He then came to London and published the first volumes of his *Sermons of Mr Yorick*. After the publication of four more volumes of *Tristram Shandy*, it was denounced by Dr Johnson, Richardson, Horace Walpole, Goldsmith and others on moral and literary grounds. In 1760 he was granted the perpetual curacy of Coxwold in North Yorkshire in the patronage of his friend Lord Fauconberg. He travelled abroad in France and Italy during 1765 and 1766, part of which journey is described in *A Sentimental Journey*, 1768. He died of pleurisy in lodgings in Old Bond Street.

Swinburne, Algernon Charles (1837–1909)
St Boniface's Church, Bonchurch, Isle of Wight.

Poet. Educated at Eton and Balliol College, Oxford, he became friendly with Rossetti and his circle. His first publication, *The Queen Mother. Rosamond. Two Plays*, 1861, attracted no attention but *Atalanta in Calydon*, 1865, a drama in the classical Greek form, did. Many regard his most perfect work as *Tristram of Lyonesse*, a romantic poem in rhymed couplets, which appeared in 1882. He suffered from illness but was supported by his friend and fellow critic, Theodore Watts-Dunton, who took him to live in his house in Putney from 1879 to his death, during those thirty years exercising a devoted and tactful control over the poet.

Tennyson, Alfred, 1st Baron Tennyson (1809–1892)
Westminster Abbey, London, in the South Transept now known as 'Poets' Corner'.

Poet. Educated at home by his father, who was Rector of Somersby, and at Trinity College, Cambridge, where he became the friend of Arthur Hallam, and where he also won the Chancellor's medal for English verse in 1829, with a poem 'Timbuctoo'. He is chiefly remembered for his 'In Memoriam', commemorating the death of his friend Arthur Hallam, and for the 'Ode on the Death of the Duke of Wellington', 1854, and the 'Idylls of the King'. He became Poet Laureate in 1850 in succession to William Wordsworth. In later life he published several historical plays, some of which were produced by Sir Henry Irving. His poem, 'Crossing the Bar', was set to music by Sir Frederick Bridge and was first sung at his own funeral in the Abbey. He was made a baron by Queen Victoria in 1884.

Thackeray, William Makepeace (1811–1863)
Kensal Green Cemetery, Kensal Green, London. A monument bust by Marochetti was erected in Westminster Abbey, London, in the South Transept now known as 'Poets' Corner'.

Novelist and essayist. He was born in Calcutta but was educated in England at Charterhouse and Trinity College, Cambridge, which he left without taking a degree. He attempted the law but also gave that up and in 1833 became the proprietor of *The National Standard*, for which he wrote and drew. It had a short existence and he then went to Paris to study drawing, where he married Isabella Shawe, whilst correspondent for *The Constitutional*, which, too, failed. He returned to London in 1837 and began writing for various journals. His wife's insanity brought about a breakdown in their marriage in 1840. In 1842 he began his contributions to *Punch* where the celebrated *Snobs of England* first appeared. His most memorable novels are *Vanity Fair*, portraying the appealing Becky Sharp, 1848, *Pendennis*, 1848, *Esmond*, 1852, and *The Virginians*, 1857–1858. He retired from *Punch* in 1854 and took up the editorship of the *Cornhill* in 1860.

Thomas, Brandon (1850–1914)
Brompton Cemetery, West Brompton, London.
   Actor-playwright who wrote one of the most famous comedies ever written for the English stage, *Charley's Aunt*, which was first produced in 1892. As an actor Thomas often appeared with the actress Marie Tempest.

Tolkien, J.R.R. (John Ronald Reuel) (1892–1973)
Wolvercote Cemetery, north Oxford, Oxfordshire, with his wife Edith.
   Author whose books *The Hobbit* (1937) and *The Lord of the Rings* (3 vols. 1945–55) enjoyed virtually a cult following that still exists to a somewhat lesser degree. Their allegorical connection to the present world, however, persists. Born in Bloemfontein, South Africa, he was educated at King Edward VI School, Birmingham and Oxford University. From 1925 to 1959 he taught Anglo-Saxon there as a professor of English language and literature. His great interest in philology led to the publication of several studies in that field. An edition of *Gawain and the Green Knight* (1925) was followed by studies of Chaucer and *Beowulf*. For *The Hobbit* he constructed an entire language and mythology. Its plot involved a perilous journey for his character Bilbo Baggins and other dwarfs. They had to recover treasure from a dragon, Smaug. Sequels had Bilbo's nephew Frodo on a mission in Mordor, the land of darkness and evil, out to destroy a powerfully dangerous ring of treacherous conspirators. It has been considered by some that there are indeed Biblical echoes in the allegory. Tolkien died as a widower while on holiday in Bournemouth. There is a picture of his grave on the internet along with widely linked information about him (http://users.ox.ac.uk/~talksoc/tolkiensOxford/grave.html).

Trollope, Anthony (1815–1882)
Kensal Green Cemetery, Kensal Green, London.
   Novelist. His early life was made miserable by his father's debts,

necessitating frequent changes of school and finally a refuge in Belgium where his mother supported the family by his writings. Trollope entered the Post Office as a clerk in 1834, and proved a valuable civil servant. His literary output was prolific and he is chiefly remembered for his Barsetshire novels, of which the first was *The Warden*, and the Palliser novels, sometimes called his political novels. Trollope regarded his presentation of Plantaganet Palliser, who became Prime Minister, and his wife Lady Glencora, as the best work of his life.

Wallace, Edgar (1875–1932)
Town Cemetery, Ferne Lane, Little Marlow, Buckinghamshire.

Mystery-story writer, journalist and playwright, he was called by his biographer Margaret Lane a 'phenomenon'. His life, from being found abandoned at nine days old and brought up by a Billingsgate, London, fish-porter to become one of England's best-known story writers, deserves such an appellation. After being a war correspondent for the *Daily Mail* during the Boer War in South Africa, in the twenties his output of, mostly, 'thrillers' involving Scotland Yard and various types of detectives was so great that 'this week's Edgar Wallace' novel became virtually an accurate description of his prolific production. His first success was *The Four Just Men* (1905); still in print. Two of his more serious works were *Sanders of the River* (1911) and *Bones* (1915), while his plays include *The Ringer* and *The Squeaker*. He died in Hollywood while working on *King Kong* of pneumonia aggravated by a long-standing diabetic condition.

Walpole, Sir Hugh Seymour (1884–1941)
St John's Churchyard, Keswick, Cumbria.

Novelist. His chief works are *Rogue Herries*, 1930, which was part of an historical sequence known as the Herries novels, *Judith Paris*, 1931, *The Fortress*, 1933, and *The Cathedral*, 1922.

Waugh, Evelyn Arthur St John (1903–1966)
St Peter and St Paul's Churchyard, Combe Florey, Somerset.

Novelist. Famous for his satirical, sophisticated and witty novels which include *Decline and Fall*, 1928, *Vile Bodies*, 1930, *Brideshead Revisited*, 1945, *Men at Arms*, 1952, *Officers and Gentlemen*, 1955, and *The Ordeal of Gilbert Pinfold*, 1957. He also wrote a life of Edmund Campion, 1935.

West, Dame Rebecca (Mrs H. M. Andrews) (1892–1983)
Brookwood Cemetery, Brookwood, Surrey.

Novelist and social critic, she was educated at Edinburgh and first attempted an acting career but soon turned to writing. She had a forthright style and soon became accepted as a notable novelist. Some of her books include *The Judge* (1922), *The Thinking Reed* (1936) and an outspoken work, *The Meaning of Treason* (1947), based on the Nuremberg Trials after the last war. She became a Dame of the British Empire in 1959 and in 1968 a Companion of Literature.

Wheatley, Dennis Yates (1897–1977)
Brookwood Cemetery, Brookwood, Surrey.

Novelist whose seventy-five books were remarkable for their wide-ranging subjects from modern and historical adventures to satanism. The son of a wine merchant, he carried on in his father's business until failing in the financial crash of 1930, after which he turned to writing. Among his early novels were *They Found Atlantis* and *The Forbidden Territory*, which was still selling forty years later and sold a million and a half copies. It had introduced his character the Duc de Richelieu, who appeared in ten later stories. Another of his characters, Gregory Sallust, was the hero in eleven other novels. His 'black magic' book, *The Devil Rides Out* (1935), gave him a reputation, with eight of the same genre, of being an expert on the subject but was merely a measure of his literary research into such lore. During the second world war he worked with an RAF commission to deceive the enemy. In his youth he had also been a naval cadet and a Royal Artillery Corps officer, being gassed in the trenches. His short biography of Charles II, *Old Rowley* (1933), is now virtually a classic.

Woolf, Virginia (1882–1941)
Monks House, Rodmell, Sussex, where her ashes were buried in the garden.

Novelist. The daughter of Sir Leslie Stephen, she made a positive contribution to the development of fiction in this century. She experimented with the form of the novel, minimizing the importance of fact, events, and character analysis in order to concentrate on the moment-by-moment experience of living. She elminated the author as narrator or commentator. Her principal novels were *Mrs Dalloway*, 1922, *To the Lighthouse*, 1927, *Orlando: A Biography*, 1928, *The Waves*, 1931, and *Between the Acts*, 1941. She also wrote a number of essays and other works which included *A Room of One's Own*, 1929, and *A Haunted House*, 1943. She suffered from mental illness and committed suicide by drowning. She was married to Leonard Woolf.

Wordsworth, William (1770–1850)
St Oswald's Churchyard, Grasmere, Cumbria. His monument is in Westminster Abbey, London, in the South Transept now known as 'Poets' Corner'.

Poet. Educated at the grammar school in Hawkshead and at St John's College, Cambridge. In 1790 he went on a walking tour in France, Italy and the Alps, during the height of the French Revolution which exercised a powerful influence on him. He met and fell in love with Annette Vallon, the daughter of a surgeon at Blois, and she bore him a daughter. The episode is reflected in 'Vaudracour and Julia', written in 1805. His enthusiasm for the Revolution gave way to pessimism which is also reflected in 'The Borderers' written during 1795 and 1796. In 1795 he received a legacy of £900 from his friend Raisley Calvert, and that same year saw his acquaintanceship with S. T. Coleridge which brought an enduring friendship. He married Mary Hutchinson of Penrith in 1802. He is chiefly remembered for 'The Prelude', completed in 1805 but not published until after his death, 'The White Doe of Rylstone', 1805, 'Lines written above Tintern Abbey', 1798, 'Ruth', 'Lucy Gray', 'Nutting' and 'Lucy', all written whilst at Goslar in Germany during the winter of 1798, and 'Michael', surely one of his most harmonious poems, which was written in 1800. He succeeded Southey as Poet Laureate in 1843. His prose works include the essay 'Concerning the Relations of Great Britain, Spain, and Portugal ... as affected by the Convention of Cintra', published in 1809 as an attack on the lack of vigour shown in English policy, and 'A Description of the Scenery of the Lakes in the North of England', written as an introduction to T. Wilkinson's *Select Views in Cumberland*.

Yonge, Charlotte Mary (1823–1901)
St Matthew's Churchyard, Otterbourne, Hampshire; beside Keble memorial cross.

Novelist whose story *Le Chateau de Melville* was sold when she was only fifteen years old. Her father, who had fought at the Battle of Waterloo, taught her classical languages and mathematics while tutors her French and Spanish. She was friendly with John Keble (*see* Hursley), whose parish included Otterbourne and who discovered her writing gifts and encouraged her. He also made her change some of her expressions that he and his wife thought 'coarse', such as when, in *Heartsease* (1854), she referred to the heart as a 'machine for pumping blood'. In Charlotte's first novel, *The Heir of Redclyffe* (1853), she had to substitute such words as 'jackanapes' for 'coxcomb', and no allusions to drukenness or insanity were allowed. Before its publication her family had also decided that it was not right for a woman to write commercially unless she devoted her earnings to some good cause. From her novel *The Daisy Chain* (1856) she gave £200 to a New Zealand missionary college. Her first works, which included *Abbey Church, or Self-control and Self-conceit* (1844); *Henrietta's Wish, or Domineering*: and *Kenneth, or the Rearguard of the Grand Army* (both in 1850) were brought out anonymousy under the stricture of her family's sensibilities about her writing. Other, later novels under her own name brought her wide fame. Such titles as *The Clever Woman of the Family* (1865) and *The Pillars of the House* (1873), and historical novels such as *The Pigeon Pie: a Tale of Roundhead Times* (1860) and *The Prince and the Page: a story of the Last Crusade* (1865) all appealed to the wide variety of her readers. Altogether she published 160 books, besides being the editor of *The Monthly Packet*, started in 1851 to imbue young women with the principles of the Oxford Movement, which she strongly supported along with its 'founder' John Keble. *The Heir of Redclyffe*, which appeared in 22 editions in about as many years, was eagerly read by officers in the Crimean War, and Charles Kingsley is said to have wept over *Heartsease*. She travelled only once out of her small village, when she visited Normandy, and, except for her writing, she devoted herself to the church and to teaching scripture at the village school. A year before she died she bought a new lychgate for St Matthew's Church with a present of £200 from subscribers to her magazine. In her last book, *Modern Broods* (1900), she contrasted the modern generation with the past one, with which she felt more in sympathy.

Chapter 9
Artists (including architects, painters and sculptors)

Beaton, Sir Cecil (1904–1980)
All Saints' Church, Broad Chalke, Wiltshire, blue slate headstone in churchyard.

Best remembered as a photographer, his brilliant talents included painting and writing. Better known as a portrayer of royalty and society personalities, he also photographed many film 'greats', including Marlene Dietrich and Gloria Swanson. In the theatre his skill as a costume designer was first seen in C. B. Cochran's *Streamline* review of 1934. The film *Gigi* (1959) won him his first Oscar for design, which was capped by another Oscar for the set design of the film version of *My Fair Lady*. He once proposed to Greta Garbo but, rejected, he died a bachelor.

Constable, John (1776–1837)
St John's Churchyard, Church Row, Hampstead, London.

Landscape painter. Born at East Bergholt, Suffolk, he was the son of a mill owner and, after schooling at Dedham Grammar School, he entered one of his father's mills. After initial attempts at painting he was allowed by his father to enter the Royal Academy as a student in 1799. He was strongly influenced by Benjamin West, the president of the Academy, as can be seen from the altarpiece painted by Constable for Brantham Church in 1804. However, Gainsborough, the Dutch masters and Girtin are the predominant influences in his landscapes. He took to portrait-painting around 1811, when trying to earn himself the money to marry Maria Bicknell, but this he was unable to do until after his father's death in 1816. He then settled in London, in Keppel Street, Russell Square, where a succession of his well-known paintings were completed: 'Flatford Mill', 1817, 'A Cottage in a Cornfield', and 'The White Horse', 1819. His famous 'Haywain', 1821, which was sold to a Frenchman, was exhibited at the Louvre and won him a gold medal. Other famous paintings include 'Salisbury Cathedral from the Bishop's Garden', 1823, 'Salisbury Cathedral from the Meadows', 1831, 'The Valley Farm', 1835, and 'Arundel Mill and Castle', 1837.

Sir Cecil Beaton, Broadchalk, Wiltshire

Cotman, John Sell (1782–1842)
St John's Wood Chapel, Wellington Road, St John's Wood, London.

Landscape painter and architectural draughtsman. He was born in Norwich, and after showing a talent for art was sent to London to study where he became friends with Turner, T. Girtin and other artists. He first exhibited at the Royal Academy in 1800. He returned to Norwich in 1807, joined the Norwich Society of Artists, and became its president in 1811. In 1825 he became an associate of the Society of Painters in Watercolours; in 1834 was made drawing-master at King's College, London, and in 1836 was elected a member of the Institute of British Architects. His work was not considered important in his lifetime but he now ranks as one of the great figures of the Norwich School, a fine draughtsman and a remarkable painter both in oil and watercolour. His architectural etchings, published in a series of volumes, the result of tours in Norfolk and Normandy, are valuable records of his interest in archaeology.

Crome, John 'Old Crome' (1769–1821)
St George's Church, Colegate, Norwich, Norfolk.

Landscape painter and chief representative of the Norwich School of painting. He was first apprenticed as a housepainter but through the influence of an art-loving patron he was able to exchange that trade for the position of drawing-master, remaining one for the remainder of his life. About 1790 he was introduced to Sir William Beechey, who encouraged and helped Crome in his art. In 1805 the Norwich Society of Artists was formed, with Crome as its president and the largest contributor to its exhibitions. He first exhibited at the Royal Academy in 1806, but throughout the next twelve years contributed only fourteen paintings. His important works include 'Mousehold Heath, near Norwich', 'Oak at Poringland', the 'Willow' and 'Slate Quarries'. He enjoyed only a limited reputation during his lifetime.

Epstein, Jacob (1880–1959)
Putney Vale Cemetery, West London, Section V. A large upright stone against the back wall.

Sculptor. Born in New York's Lower East Side, Jacob Epstein moved to Paris to study at the Academie Julian and under Augustine Rodin at the Ecole des Beaux-Arts in 1902. He moved to London in 1905 and later became a British citizen. Epstein was a pioneer of modern sculpture, often shocking the general public and challenging taboos,

Jacob Epstein, Putney Vale Cemetery, West London

particularly around sexuality. His first major commission of eighteen large nude sculptures was mutilated and his 'Rima' situated in London's Hyde Park was defiled by paint. Other famous works include a marble venus at the Yale Center for British Art in New Haven, Conneticut and 'Jacob and the Angel' at the Tate Britain, London. Epstein worked up until his death in 1959, completing 'Pan' in Hyde Park the same year.

Gainsborough, Thomas (1727–1788)
St Anne's Church, Kew Green, Kew, Surrey.

Portrait and landscape painter. Born at Sudbury in Suffolk where his father owned a woollen-carpet-making business. His mother excelled in flower painting and encouraged her son in the use of the pencil. He was sent to study in London at the academy in St Martin's Lane, where he spent three years before returning to the country. He fell in love with Margaret Burr, who was reputedly the daughter of either the Duke of Bedford or one of the exiled Stuarts. They married after he had painted her portrait and settled in Ipswich. He painted portraits to earn his living and used the surrounding countryside for his landscapes. In 1759, anxious to improve his reputation, he moved with his family to the more fashionable Bath where his skill as a portrait painter was much sought after. During this period he painted Sterne and Richardson, the authors, as well as Quinn, Henderson and Garrick, all actors. In 1774, his reputation fully established and his financial position assured, he moved to London and settled at Schomberg House in Pall Mall. Within a few months he was summoned to the palace and he shared with West the favour of the court, and with the Reynolds the favour of fashionable society. His most famous portraits are 'Lady Ligonier', 'Georgiana, Duchess of Devonshire', 'Master Buttall', known as 'The Blue Boy', 'Mrs Siddons', and 'The Hon Mrs Graham'. Of his other works the principals include 'the Cottage Door', 'the Return from the Harvest', 'Waggon and Horses passing a Brook' and 'the Market Cart'. His total output exceeded 300 paintings, of which 220 were portraits.

Greenaway, Kate (1846–1901)
Hampstead Cemetery, Fortune Green Road, London.

Artist and book illustrator. She was the daughter of John Greenaway, a well-known draughtsman and engraver on wood, and was born in London. She studied at South Kensington and at the Slade School, and began exhibiting her watercolours at the Dudley Gallery, London in 1868. Her illustrations for children, particularly *Little Folks*, 1873, attracted a great deal of attention. In 1879 she produced the work for which she is chiefly remembered, *Under the Window*, which is reputed to have sold 150,000 copies. She was elected a member of the Royal Institute of Painters in Watercolours in 1890.

Hepworth, Dame Barbara (1903–1975)
Carbis Bay Cemetery, Cornwall.

Britain's foremost female sculptor. Born in Wakefield, Yorkshire, Hepworth won a scholarship to Leeds School of Art, where she met Henry Moore. She then went to London to study at the Royal Academy of Art. Two years later, in 1928, she held her first solo exhibition at the Beaux Arts Gallery in London.

During the 1930s Barbara Hepworth developed her interest in abstract sculpture. She met the painter Ben Nicholson in 1931, who was to become her second husband, and became a member of several art groups, including the 'Seven and Five Society of Artists' and the 'Unit One Group'. In 1939 she moved to St Ives in Cornwall where she became an influential member of the artistic community and was to remain so until her death.

Hepworth was divorced from Nicholson in 1951 and moved into the Trewyn Studios where she produced some of her most famous works, including 'The Unknown Political Prisoner' and 'Three Monoliths'. She was created a Dame of the British Empire in 1965. Barbara Hepworth died in a fire in her studio on 20 May 1975. The studios are now open to the public as the Barbara Hepworth Museum.

Hogarth, William (1697–1764)
St Nicholas's Churchyard, Chiswick Mall, Chiswick, London.

Painter and engraver. He satirized the life of his day in numerous works chief of which were *Harlot's Progress*, 1732, followed by *Rake's Progress* in 1735, *Marriage à la Mode, Industry and Idleness*, and *The March to Finchley*.

Holbein, Hans 'The Younger' (1497–1543)
St Katherine Cree Church, Leadenhall Street, City of London. There is a brass tablet on the south wall of the church of St Andrew Undershaft, Leadenhall Street, commemorating the fact that Holbein lived within the parish. However, it is generally accepted that he was buried at St Katharine Cree nearby.

Painter. The favourite son of the painter, Hans Holbein the Elder, he was probably born at Augsburg. With his brother Ambrose, he sought employment as a book illustrator in Basel in the year 1515, and his first patron was believed to be Erasmus, for whom he illustrated, with a series of pen-and-ink sketches, an edition of the *Encomium Moriae*. He settled in London in 1532, residing in the parish of St Andrew Undershaft in

Grave of William Hogarth, St Nicholas's Churchyard, Chiswick Mall, Chiswick, London

the City, where he was rated as a 'stranger'. He enjoyed the patronage of the King, Henry VIII, for whom he executed a number of portraits, including those of members of the royal family: Jane Seymour, Prince Edward, later Edward VI, and Anne of Cleves whom Henry later married and divorced. He also painted many of the members of Henry's court, including the famous 'Duke of Norfolk'. He died of the plague in November 1543.

Hunt, William Holman (1827–1910)
St Paul's Cathedral, London.

Pre-Raphaelite painter. Born in London, he started work as a clerk in a city office but during his seventeenth year he entered the Royal Academy schools, where he met his lifelong friend, John Everett Millais. His first painting to be exhibited at the Royal Academy was 'Hark!' which appeared in 1846. In 1848, he, Millais, Dante Gabriel Rossetti and others formed the movement known as the Pre-Raphaelite Brotherhood, which was championed by Ruskin. His most famous painting, 'The Light of the World', was purchased and given to Keble College. Because he was dissatisfied with the way in which it was hung he executed a new painting, slightly altered from the original 'Light of the World'. This now hangs in St Paul's Cathedral. He spent two years in the Holy Land in order to revivify on canvas the facts of the Scriptures 'surrounded by the very people and circumstances of the life in Judaea of old days'. From his experiences there he produced 'The Scapegoat', exhibited at the Royal Academy in 1856, and this was followed by 'The Finding of our Saviour in the Temple', 1860. His other major work is 'The Triumph of the Innocents'.

John, Augustus Edwin (1878–1961)
Town Cemetery, Fordingbridge, Hampshire, beside the path from the second entrance. There is a statue of him by Ivor Robert-Jones in Fordingbridge Park.

Portrait painter whose Bohemian lifestyle made him unpopular with the art establishment. He was born, a solicitor's son, at Tenby, Dyfed, Wales, and entered the Slade School of Art in 1894 as a shy student. Swimming one day he dived into shallow water and cut his head on a rock. 'He hit his head whilst diving', wrote Virginia Shankland, 'and emerged from the water a genius!' He won a Royal Academy prize and produced a succession of masterly portraits until the later 1920s. His biographer Michael Holroyd said that his life was that of 'the great artist, the great lover, and great Bohemian.' He had eight children by his two wives, Ida Nettleship and Dorothy McNeill, and three illegitimate children. His second son Casper became First Sea Lord from 1960 to 1963.

Jones, Inigo (1573–1652)
St Benet's Church, Paul's Wharf, City of London, now the Metropolitan Welsh Church. A small tablet on the east wall records the inscription raised in the original church, which was destroyed in the Great Fire of 1666 and subsequently rebuilt by Sir Christopher Wren.

Architect who studied in Venice where he became addicted to the style of Palladio. In 1604 he had acquired such a reputation that he was invited by King Christian IV to Denmark where he is reputed to have designed the two royal palaces of Rosenborg and Frederiksborg. In 1605 he was appointed architect to Anne of Denmark, Queen of James I and VI, and Henry, Prince of Wales, being largely responsible for supplying the designs and decorations of the court masques. After a second visit to Italy in 1612 he was made Surveyor-General of royal buildings by James I. He built the Queen's House at Greenwich and the Royal Banqueting House, Whitehall; designed St Paul's Church, Covent Garden; and advised on the building of Wilton House, Wiltshire, for the Earl of Pembroke.

Landseer, Sir Edwin Henry (1802–1873)
St Paul's Cathedral, London.

Animal painter. Principally known for his 'Monarch of the Glen' and 'Stag at Bay' paintings, though his paintings of dogs, especially 'Suspense', which shows a dog watching at the closed door of his wounded master, and 'The Old Shepherd's Chief Mourner', are thought to be his finest achievements. He became a member of the Royal Academy in 1831, was knighted in 1850 and in 1867 unveiled the four lions which he had modelled for the base of Nelson's Column in Trafalgar Square.

Lawrence, Sir Thomas (1769–1830)
St Paul's Cathedral, London.

Portrait painter. He was encouraged by Sir Joshua Reynolds whom he later succeeded as Painter in Ordinary to King George III. He was made a Royal Academician in 1794 and painted most of the crowned heads of Europe, in 1818 going to Aix-la-Chapelle to paint the sovereigns and diplomats gathered there. Among his best-known works are those of

George IV, and of his wife Caroline of Brunswick. He was knighted in 1815 and became President of the Royal Academy in 1820, a post he held until his death ten years later. As a portrait painter he ranks highly, though not now so highly as he did in his lifetime; but his more ambitious works, in the classical style, such as his celebrated 'Satan', are practically forgotten.

Leighton, Frederick, 1st Baron Leighton of Stretton (1830–1896)
St Paul's Cathedral, London.

Painter and sculptor. Studied in Italy, Germany and Paris. His first painting to gain fame was his 'Cimabue's Madonna carried in Procession through the Streets of Florence', which appeared at the Royal Academy in 1855, in the same year as Holman Hunt's 'Light of the World' and at a time when the public's interest was absorbed by the Pre-Raphaelite school. It created a sensation and was purchased by Queen Victoria. Thereafter his works became famous: 'Dante in Exile', 1864, 'Venus Disrobing for the Bath', 1867, and 'Captive Andromache', 1888. He also painted a few portraits, including that of Sir Richard Burton, the explorer. Among his sculptures are the celebrated 'Athlete struggling with a Python', 1877, and 'The Sluggard', 1886. His drawings, sketches and landscapes were also much admired. He settled in London in 1860 and in 1886 moved to a house at 12 Holland Road, Kensington, which is now a museum to his memory and contains many of his finest works. He was knighted in 1878, on being elected President of the Royal Academy, made a baronet in 1886 and created a baron in 1896, just a few days before his death.

Lely, Sir Peter (1618–1680)
St Paul's Church, Covent Garden, London.

Painter. Born at Soest, Westphalia, the son of an army captain named van der Vacs; the son adopting his nickname of Le Lys or Lely as a surname later. After studying at Haarlem he moved to England in 1641 to avail himself of the advantage of Charles I's patronage of the arts. He soon gained a reputation for his landscapes and historical subjects and, shortly after the death of Van Dyck, Charles I requested Lely to paint his portrait. Later, he painted Cromwell. At the Restoration he won the favour of Charles II, who made him his State painter and gave him a knighthood. His most famous work is a collection of portraits of the ladies of the court of Charles II, known as the 'Beauties'. Of his few historical paintings the best is 'Susannah and the Elders'.

Lowry, L.S. (Laurence Stephen) (1887–1976)
Chorlton Southern Cemetery, next to his parents.

One of the most celebrated British artists. L. S. Lowry was born in Rusholme, Manchester in November 1887. He attended a local school and then found work as a rent collector with a Manchester firm. He was to stay with them for forty-two years.

He attended evening classes at the Manchester College of Art between 1905 and 1915. He then went to the Salford School of Art where he developed his interest in the urban landscape and his distinctive style of matchstick figures. In 1919 he exhibited for the first time at Manchester City Art Gallery and by the early 1930s he was exhibiting at the Royal Academy in London. He was elected to the Royal Academy in 1962 and given freedom of the City of Salford three years later.

Lowry is known to have produced over 10,000 works. The landscape of industrial Salford was his most frequent subject, which he characterised with great insight and humour, but without sentiment. Lowry had moved to Pendlebury in Salford with his parents in 1909. He remained there after his mother's death in 1939 and only left when the house was repossessed. Lowry never married and had no children. He left all his paintings to a girl named Lowry who had once written to him to ask his advice about becoming an artist. A major collection of his work is on display at the Lowry Centre in Salford Quays.

Millais, Sir John Everett (1829–1896)
St Paul's Cathedral, London.

Pre-Raphaelite painter. At the age of eleven he entered the Royal Academy schools where, at fifteen, he met and formed his lifelong friendship with Holman Hunt. In 1848, he and Hunt, with Dante Gabriel Rossetti and others, formed the Pre-Raphaelite Brotherhood which, according to Millais, had as its aim 'to present on canvas what they saw in Nature'. Ruskin espoused the movement's cause, showing his enthusiasm in letters to *The Times* and in a pamphlet entitled 'Pre-Raphaelism'. His most famous Pre-Raphaelite paintings are possibly. 'Orphelia', 1852 and 'The Huguenot', also 1852. Of his later paintings the most popular include 'The Boyhood of Raleigh' and 'Bubbles'. After the annulment of her marriage, Millais married Effie Ruskin. He was knighted in 1885 at Gladstone's suggestion and died of cancer of the throat in 1896, a few months after he had been made President of the Royal Academy on the death of Lord Leighton.

Moore, Henry (1898–1986)
Artist's Corner of the Crypt, St Paul's Cathedral, London.

Sculptor. Henry Moore was born in Castleford, Yorkshire, where his father was a coalminer. After the First World War he returned to Castleford and attended the Leeds School of Art as the first ever student of sculpture. In 1921 he won a scholarship to the Royal College of Art in London.

During the late 1920s Moore began to establish himself as a sculptor. He received his first public commission for the new London Transport Headquarters at St James Park Underground station, had his first solo exhibition at the Warren Gallery in London and finished 'Reclining Figure'. By the 1930s his work was becoming increasingly abstract and he became a member of the 'Seven and Five Society' and Paul Nash's 'Unit One Group'. In 1932 he was appointed Head of the Department of Sculpture at Chelsea School of Art. After a bomb damaged his Hampstead home during the Second World War, Moore and his wife, Irina, moved to Hogsland, a farmhouse in Perry Green, Hertfordshire. This was to be their home for the rest of their lives and is now home to the Henry Moore Foundation.

In 1941 Moore was appointed Official War Artist and then Director of the National Gallery. He won the International Prize for Sculpture in 1948. One of his most famous commissions, a monumental reclining figure, was for the UNESCO building in Paris. Another, the 'Knife Edge Two Piece' stands outside the Houses of Parliament in London. Many more of his sculptures can be seen at the Yorkshire Sculpture Park near Wakefield.

Henry Moore was awarded the Order of Merit in 1963.

Opie, John (1761–1807)
St Paul's Cathedral, London.

Historical and portrait painter. Born near Truro in Cornwall, by the age of twelve he had mastered Euclid and opened an evening school for arithmetic and writing. He showed an early talent for drawing and by 1780 he had gained a local reputation for painting portraits. He then went to London where he was introduced as 'the Cornish Wonder' and for a time enjoyed much fashionable patronage. When his popularity waned he once again began to study to correct the defects in his work, earning himself the praise of his rival, Northcote, who said of Opie, 'Other artists paint to live; Opie lives to paint'. In 1786 he exhibited his first important historical painting, the 'Assassination of James I', and in the following year the 'Murder of Rizzio', the merit of which earned him immediate election as an associate of the Royal Academy, of which he became a full member in 1788.

Orpen, Sir William (1878–1931)
Putney Cemetery, Putney, London. Grave is upright stone with flat top in section O or the cemetery.

Portrait painter whose work has been called the finest of the century for its accuracy, rendering of character and feeling. Born in Ireland, he studied art there and at the Slade School in London. An official peace-conference painter after the first world war, his sketches and paintings he did at the front during the war are displayed in the Imperial War Museum, London. In 1918 he was knighted, and he was elected an RA the following year.

Reynolds, Sir Joshua (1723–1792)
St Paul's Cathedral, London.

Portrait painter. Born at Plympton Earl in Devon, he was apprenticed at seventeen to the popular portrait painter, Thomas Hudson, in London. The first portrait to gain him any attention was that of Captain the Hon John Hamilton. He returned to Devon on the death of his father in 1746 and settled with his sisters at Plymouth Dock, where he came under the influence of the works of William Gandy of Exeter, who had died in 1730. Northcote said of Gandy that his painting came 'nearer to nature in the texture of flesh than that of any artist who ever lived'. The influence of Gandy's painting on Reynolds may be seen in the early self-portrait, being so rich in impasto and strong in light and shade, in which the artist is seen shading his eyes with his hand. Reynolds travelled abroad, visiting Spain, North Africa and Italy, which had been the object of his trip, during the 1750s, returning to London and settling in Leicester Square. His portraits became famous and when in December 1768 the Royal Academy was founded, Reynolds became its first president, receiving a knighthood from the King as well as a commission to paint his and the Queen's portraits. His most important portraits are 'Mrs Siddons as the Tragic Muse', 'Johnson', 'Sterne', 'Lord Heathfield', 'Gibbon', 'Burke', 'Fox', 'Garrick' and 'Goldsmith'. Mention must also be made of the 'Angels' Heads' and 'Nelly O'Brien'.

Sir William Orpen, Putney Vale Cemetery, West London

Romney, George (1734–1802)
St Mary's Church, Dalton-in-Furness, Cumbria.

Portrait painter. Born in Dalton-in-Furness, he was the son of a builder and cabinet-maker. Apprenticed at nineteen to an itinerant portrait painter named Steele, he made little progress because of his master's erratic habits. In 1756 he impulsively married a young woman who had nursed him through a serious illness and to earn enough money took to portrait painting on his own account. In 1761, having saved £100, part of which he gave to his wife and family, he left for London alone to seek his fortune. He soon became popular in London, his 'Death of General Wolfe' winning second prize at the Society of Arts in 1766. A period of study in their schools about 1769, brought him greater experience and he was soon prosperous. As a portrait painter he was soon seen as a rival to Reynolds, Lord Thurlow remarking that 'All the town is divided into two factions, the Reynolds and the Romneys, and I am of the Romney faction'. One of his most famous sitters was Emma Hart, the future Lady Hamilton and mistress of Nelson, whose bewitching face smiles from numerous canvases, Romney confessing that she was the inspiration for what was most beautiful in his art. Towards the end of his life he withdrew from portrait painting, turning to subjects such as Seven Ages and Visions of Adam with the Angel. In the summer of 1799 his health deteriorated and he returned to Kendal to his long-deserted wife, who nursed him through the last three years of his life.

Rossetti, Dante Gabriel (1828–1882)
All Saints' Churchyard, Birchington, Kent. By the south door there is a monument designed by Ford Madox Brown in the form of a Celtic Cross.

Painter and poet. The son of the Italian poet and liberal, Gabriele Rossetti, who had settled in London and married Frances Polidori, the sister of Byron's physician, Dr John Polidori. Their first son was christened Gabriel Charles Dante and from early childhood showed a marked aptitude for drawing and painting. He was impressed by some of Ford Madox Brown's early paintings and he went to study under him. He came into contact with Millais and Holman Hunt and with them and others formed the Pre-Raphaelite Brotherhood in the autumn of 1848. His first Pre-Raphaelite painting was 'The Girlhood of Mary, Virgin', which was exhibited in March 1849 at Hyde Park Corner, whilst his 'Ecce Ancilla Domini!' is regarded as the one perfect outcome of the motives of the Pre-Raphaelite Brotherhood. Rossetti married his model, Elizabeth Siddal, and when she died he was so grief-stricken that he buried his collected poems with her. Later, these were exhumed and published. His poetry is strongly influenced by the revival of the romantic spirit in English poetry. His 'Sister Helen', 'The Blessed Damozel', 'Eden Bower', and 'Troy Town' all reflect this trend.

Stubbs, George (1724–1806)
St Marylebone 'Old' Parish Church, Marylebone High Street, London.
The site of the old parish church and its graveyard is now marked by the
Garden of Rest in Marylebone High Street and contains a tablet com-
memorating some of the notable people buried there.

Animal painter and anatomist. Most famous for his paintings of
horses, one of his best being 'Phaeton and Pair', which hangs in the
National Gallery, Trafalgar Square, London. He was largely self-taught
and it was an interest in comparative anatomy which led him to study
horses, and eventually to the publishing of the *Anatomy of the Horse*,
1766, which still commands great respect. He also painted landscapes
and some portraits, chief of which were those of Lord Grosvenor and the
Duke of Richmond.

Sutherland, Graham Vivian (1903–1980)
The north side of St Peter and St Paul's Church, Tunbridge, Kent.

Artist. Graham Sutherland trained as an engineer, before changing his
career and studying at Goldsmith's College School of Art. He went on to
serve as an official war artist during the Second World War and in 1954
was commissioned by the Houses of Parliament to paint a portrait of Sir
Winston Churchill. His tapestry of Christ in Glory was unveiled in 1962
at the new Cathedral in Coventry.

Turner, Joseph Mallord William (1775–1851)
St Paul's Cathedral, London, in the crypt.

Painter who after studying under Sir Joshua Reynolds (whom see)
exhibited his first drawing, 'View of Lambeth Palace', in 1790 at the
Royal Academy. In his lifetime he is estimated to have produced over
1000 works, for which he visited Devonshire, the north of England,
Scotland, Italy, France, Venice and Switzerland. Some of his famous
paintings are 'The Battle of the Nile' (1799), 'The Fighting Temeraire'
(1839), Venetian scenes and such strangely mystical works as 'War – the
Exile' (1845) when he attempted to communicate vague thoughts by
colour language. The son of a barber, he was considered to have been
England's greatest painter of his time and style, which began to develop
after his early stage when the Old Masters had influenced his work. He
became a recluse toward the end of his life. There is a room in St Mary's
Church, Battersea, where he used to sit for hours gazing across the
Thames.

Van Dyck, Sir Anthony (1599–1641)
'Old' St Paul's Cathedral, London.

Painter. Born at Antwerp in Flanders, he studied under Rubens. He travelled extensively in Italy before settling in England where Charles I settled an annuity on him. He is principally known for his portraits of Charles I, his Queen, Henrietta Maria, their children and the court. He was knighted by Charles I. He died of the plague at Blackfriars.

Vanbrugh, Sir John (1664–1726)
St Stephen's Church, Walbrook, City of London, in the north aisle. There is an epitaph attributed to his fellow architect, Nicholas Hawksmoor:

Lie heavy on him, Earth! for he
Laid many heavy loads on thee.

Architect and dramatist. His most famous play, the *Provok'd Wife*, was written whilst under arrest in France as a spy during the period 1690 to 1692. But the first of his plays to be performed was *The Relapse* in 1696 and its success was followed by a performance of the *Provok'd Wife* at the theatre in Lincoln's Inn Fields in May 1697. This led to attacks on him for immorality, and it is thought that these attacks were partly responsible for his turning his attention to architecture. His many buildings include Blenheim Palace for the great Duke of Marlborough; Castle Howard in Yorkshire, and Seaton-Delaval. In 1716 he was appointed architect to the Greenwich Hospital.

Wheatley, Francis (1747–1801)
St Marylebone 'Old' Parish Church, Marylebone High Street, London. The site of the old parish church and its graveyard is now marked by the Garden of Rest in Marylebone High Street, and contains a tablet commemorating some of the notable people buried there.

Portrait and landscape painter. Born in Covent Garden, London, he studied at Shipley's drawing school and at the Royal Academy. He eloped to Ireland with the wife of the painter Gresse, and whilst in Dublin painted portraits as well as executing an interior of the Irish House of Commons. His scene of the 'Gordon riots in 1780' was admirably engraved by Heath, and is regarded as his best painting. He is well-known today for 'The London Cries', a series of London street scenes which lent themselves to engravings and are much valued by collectors.

Whistler, James Abbot McNeill (1834–1903)
St Nicholas's Churchyard, by the north wall of the new section, Chiswick Mall, Chiswick, London.

Painter. Born at Lowell in the United States, he studied in Paris before settling in England in 1859. His series of Thames etchings in 1859 disclosed a new vision of the great river. Of his oil paintings, the principals are 'Sarasate', 'Lady Archibald Campbell' and 'The Little Rose of Lyme Regis'. He was also a noted lithographer, his most popular being the 'nocturne' at Limehouse, and of the old Faubourg St Germain. He was a controversial figure and in 1878 he brought a libel action against Ruskin for the latter's remark that one of Whistler's nocturnes in the Grosvenor Gallery was 'a pot of paint flung in the public face'. After a long trial Whistler was awarded a farthing's damages.

Wren, Sir Christopher (1632–1723)
St Paul's Cathedral, London.

Architect who was born in Wiltshire. His plan for the rebuilding of the City of London after the Great Fire of 1666 was unsuccessful but he was asked to rebuild St Paul's Cathedral, which he began in 1675 and completed in 1710. He also built more than fifty other churches in the City of London including St Stephen's, Walbrook and St Mary-le-Bow, Cheapside. Other buildings designed by him include the Sheldonian Theatre and the Ashmolean at Oxford, and the Chelsea Hospital in London. A founder member of the Royal Society, he became its president in 1681. He was Professor of Astronomy at Gresham College, London and Savilian Professor of Astronomy at Oxford.

Wyatt, James (1746–1813)
Westminster Abbey, London, in the South Transept, now known as 'Poets' Corner'.

Architect of country houses and designer of London's Pantheon, which was demolished in 1937. His classical works were surpassed by his Gothic constructions: Fonthill Abbey, Wiltshire; Ashridge Park, Hertfordshire; and Lee Priory, Kent. He was Surveyor-General to the King, George III. He died in a coach accident near Marlborough on 4 September 1813.

Sir Christopher Wren, by Kneller

Zoffany, Johann (1733–1810)
St Anne's Church, Kew Green, Kew, Surrey.

Painter. Born in Frankfurt-on-Main, he studied in Italy before journeying to London in 1758 where he obtained, after some initial hardship, royal patronage. In 1769 he was a founder member of the Royal Academy. He was given an introduction to the Grand Duke of Tuscany by George III and whilst resident in Florence received a commission from the Empress Maria Theresa to paint the Tuscan royal family. She was so pleased with the result that she made Zoffany a baron of the empire. From 1783 to 1790 he lived in India, to which period belong some of his best-known paintings. For the last twenty years of his life he lived in England. His portrait groups of dramatic personalities are the most esteemed of his works.

Chapter 10
Musicians (including composers and singers)

Arne, Thomas Augustine (1710–1778)
St Paul's Church, Covent Garden, London.

Composer of 'Rule, Britannia!', which he wrote for the masque *Alfred* by Mallet and Thompson, performed in the gardens of the house of Frederick, Prince of Wales at Cliveden in August 1740. A prolific composer, he set to music such Shakespearean songs as 'Where the Bee sucks', as well as composing operas, *Artaserse*, oratorios, *Judith* and *Abel*, and a wealth of instrumental music.

Bach, Johann Christian (1735–1782)
St Pancras Old Churchyard, St Pancras Road, London.

Composer. The eleventh son of Johann Sebastian Bach, he studied music under his brother Emmanuel in Berlin after the death of his father in 1750. In 1754 he went to Italy to study under Padre Martini, and from 1760 to 1762 held the post of organist at Milan Cathedral, for which he wrote two Masses, a *Requiem*, a *Te Deum*, and other works. In 1762, having gained a reputation as the composer of opera, he was invited to England and became the most popular musician in England, his dramatic works being staged at the King's theatre, and his concerts, given in partnership with Abel at the Hanover Square rooms, being the most fashionable of London entertainments at the time. He was appointed music-master to Queen Charlotte and he has gone on record as the first composer to prefer the pianoforte to the older keyboard instruments.

Barbirolli, Sir John (1899–1970)
St Mary's Roman Catholic Cemetery, Kensal Green, London.

Conductor and cellist. He conducted many famous orchestras including that of the New York Philharmonic, which he took over from Toscanini, from 1937 to 1942, and that for which he is principally remembered, the Hallé Orchestra which he conducted from 1943 to 1970.

Baring-Gould, Sabine (1834–1924)
St Peter's Churchyard, Lew Trenchard, Devon.

Chiefly remembered for his famous hymn 'Onward Christian

Soldiers', which was but one of the hymns that he wrote. He was also a notable divine and author, publishing several theological works, including *The Origin and Development of Religious Belief*, 1869–1870, as well as folk-lore books and novels, the best known of which are *Mehalah*, 1880, which Swinburne likened to *Wuthering Heights*, and *The Brown Squire*, 1896. In all, from 1857 to 1920, he published 159 books. He was rector of the church in which he was buried, being a high churchman with a belief in the Catholicity of the Church of England.

Beecham, Sir Thomas (1879–1961)
Brookwood Cemetery, Brookwood, Surrey.

Conductor and impresario. He founded the London Philharmonic Orchestra in 1931, championed the music of Delius and introduced the operas of Richard Strauss and the Russian Ballet of Diaghilev to England.

Bolan, Marc (1947–1977)
Golders Green Crematorium. Plot located at the Keats Rosebed (no. 46087) and shared with his parents under the family name (Feld).

Singer. Marc Bolan formed T-Rex as an acoustic duo. However, in 1970 it expanded to an electronic quartet and became an important part of the emerging glam rock scene. The band had ten consecutive top ten hits, among them four number ones between 1970 and 1973. Memorable tracks of the era include 'Get It On', 'Children of the Revolution' and 'Twentieth Century Boy'. Bolan died in 1977 when his girlfriend, Gloria Jones, drove her purple mini home in the early hours of the morning and crashed into a tree. He was killed instantly. On the anniversary of his death fans still turn up at Golders Green Crematorium to honour his memory.

Bridgtower, George (1779–1860)
Kensal Green Cemetery, London.

Violinist. George Bridgtower was born in Poland in 1779 where his father, originally from Barbados, was the personal servant to a prince. George's first public performance was in Paris at the age of nine and there followed a series of concerts in London, Bath and Bristol. By 1791, the young Bridgtower was under the patronage of the Prince of Wales and at the age of twelve he was playing as a soloist and principal violinist and was a respected member of London's musical community. He was to be first violinist in the Prince's private band for fourteen years.

In 1802 Bridgtower met and made friends with Beethoven while touring in Germany. Beethoven dedicated the 'Kreutzer' sonata to him after his suggested amendments to the score had been warmly received by the composer.

Bridgtower died in poverty in Peckham, South London on 29 February 1860.

Britten, (Edward) Benjamin, 1st Baron Britten of Aldeburgh (1913–1976)
St Peter and St Paul's Church, Aldeburgh, Suffolk. Blue slate stone in churchyard.

Composer born at Lowestoft who founded the Aldeburgh Festival in 1948. He was an accomplished pianist and conductor whose more important compositions besides his numerous operas were the *Seven Sonnets of Michelangelo* (1940) and *War Requiem* (1962). *Variations on a Theme of Frank Bridge* won him his first world acclaim in 1937. Given the Aspen Award in 1964, in 1976 he became the first musician to become a life peer.

Butt, Dame Clara (1872–1936)
St Mary the Virgin Churchyard, North Stoke, Oxfordshire; near the fence stile behind the church.

Contralto concert singer, she was born at Southwick near Brighton, her father being a sea captain. Both he and her mother sang and played the piano. She was educated at Bristol, where her parents had gone, and she first sang in the Bristol Choir and achieved a scholarship to the Royal College of Music in 1890. Her debut at the Royal Albert Hall was in the part of Ursula in Sir Arthur Sullivan's *The Golden Legend*, after which she went on to achieve both popular and critical acclaim on the concert stage. Her six-foot-tall figure created an impressive presence. *Abide With Me* was set to music for her, while Sir Edward Elgar composed *Sea Pictures* and *The Dream of Gerontius* for her also. 'With her whole heart she sang songs, and loved him that made her' is inscribed on her gravestone.

Cherkassky, Shura (1909–1995)
Highgate Cemetery (East), London.

Concert pianist. Shura Cherkassky was one of the great Romantic pianists of the 1900s. Born in Odessa, Russia, he fled to the United States after the Russian Revolution. He came to public notice whilst still a boy, studied under Josef Hofmann and was an electrifying performer of an increasingly forgotten repertoire.

Coates, Eric (1886–1957)
Golders Green Crematorium, Golders Green, London; ashes dispersed in the Garden of Rest, section 1J.

As a conductor and composer Coates gained much of his experience as a leading viola player in London orchestras. He holds a special place among most English composers for his delightfully light, yet strangely stirring music such as *Knightsbridge March* (first chosen by the BBC for its *In Town Tonight* program in the early thirties, making Coates's composition famous), *London Calling March*, *The Three Bears Suite* and many others. He was born in Hucknall, Nottinghamshire, the younger son of a well-known surgeon. A musical prodigy, Coates received a scholarship to the Royal Academy of Music when he was twenty years old, studying composition and the viola. He composed a world-wide 'hit' called *By the Sleepy Lagoon* in 1930. Several of Coates's works were featured by Sir Henry Wood in his early Promenade Concerts, in which the composer had been lead viola.

Delius, Frederick (1862–1934)
St Peter's Churchyard, Limpsfield, Surrey, under an ancient elm tree.

Composer. Of German parentage, the idiosyncratic idiom of his music was more appreciated in Germany than in England, and it was not until Sir Thomas Beecham championed it that it became widely known in England. His most famous works are the atmospheric tone-poems for orchestra, such as *Brigg Fair*, the vocal and orchestral *A Mass of Life*, *Sea Drift* and *Appalachia*, and the opera *A Village Romeo and Juliet*. After temporary burial in the churchyard at Grez-sur-Loing, France, where he had lived since the 1880s, his body was brought to England and buried at Limpsfield, with Sir Thomas Beecham reading the funeral oration and conducting a picked orchestra in playing a selection of Delius pieces fitting for the occasion.

Donegan, Anthony James, 'Lonnie' (1931–2002)
Caversham Crematorium, Berkshire.

The first British pop star. Lonnie Donegan stormed on to the music scene in the 1950s with skiffle, a sound loosely based on American folk music. He had numerous chart hits on both sides of the Atlantic, including 'My Old Man's a Dustman' and 'Puttin' on the Style'.

Donegan enjoyed an international reputation and has been credited with instigating the 1960s British Blues revival. He received an MBE from Prince Charles in the late 1970s but never stopped touring. He died after collapsing mid-way through a UK tour on 3 November 2002.

Elgar, Sir Edward William (1857–1934)
St Wulstan's Churchyard, Wells Road, Little Malvern, Hereford and Worcester. A memorial stone lies in Westminster Abbey, London, in the floor of the north choir aisle of the Nave.

Composer. Generally considered the principal composer in the trio, comprising himself, Hubert Parry and Charles Stanford, that led to the revival of English music in the nineteenth century. Although influenced by Brahms they nonetheless established a new English tradition that has been carried on in the present time. His principal works include *The Dream of Gerontius*, an oratorio, over the score of which Elgar wrote 'This is the best of me', his symphonic study, *Falstaff*, his overtures, *Cockaigne*, a happy evocation of London, and *In the South*, written after a visit to Italy, his *Enigma Variations*, a series of sound portraits of his friends, and his *Pomp and Circumstance* marches which include the famous 'Land of Hope and Glory'. He was made Master of the King's Musick in 1924 and granted the Order of Merit in 1911, the first musician to receive the order, was knighted in 1904, and made a baronet in 1931.

Epstein, Brian (1934–1967)
Kirkdale Jewish Cemetery, Long Lane, Liverpool, Merseyside.

As The Beatles' first manager he was responsible for launching them on their phenomenal success. He was in charge of one of his father's music stores (NEMS: North End Road Music Stores) in Liverpool when he first heard them playing in The Cavern Club. This was only a few minutes walk from his shop. He managed others including Cilla Black, but became sole manager for The Beatles. Their overwhelming success, however, became too much for him. Unable to control their individual activities, he found he could not fit in with them.

Handel, George Frederick (1685–1759)
Westminster Abbey, London, in the South Transept, now known as 'Poets' Corner'. The statue is said to be an exact likeness, for the face was modelled from a death mask.

Composer. Born at Halle in Lower Saxony, the son of a surgeon-barber who disapproved of music. As an eight-year-old Handel contrived to be overheard by the Duke of Saxe-Weissenfels, to whom his half-brother was valet-de-chambre, when he was practising on the ducal organ. The Duke persuaded his father to exploit his son's talent and he was sent to become a pupil of Zachau, the cathedral organist at Halle. At twelve Zachau sent him to Berlin where he made an immediate and great impression and the Elector of Brandenburg, later Frederick I of Prussia, offered to send him to Italy for training. However, George's father declined and he returned to Halle to continue his education there. After his father's death he trained as a lawyer but in 1702 accepted the post of organist at Halle Cathedral. A year later, having completed his probation period at the cathedral, he suddenly left for Hamburg where the only German opera worthy of the name was flourishing, and there met Matheson, a prolific composer and writer on music. His first opera, *Almira*, was performed in Hamburg on 8 January 1705 and was followed a few weeks later by another work, now lost, *Nero*. The following year he travelled to Italy where he met many of the famous composers of the day including Domenico and Alessandro Scarlatti, and Domenico is reputed to have said on first hearing him play incognito that 'It is either the devil or the Saxon'; Handel being referred to in Italy as *Il Sassone*, the Saxon. In 1709 his fame led to an offer from the Elector of Hanover to become his Kapellmeister and Handel accepted on condition he should be allowed to travel to England for a visit. He arrived in London at the end of 1710 and earned his first success with his opera *Rinaldo* performed at the Haymarket Theatre on 24 February 1711. He returned to Hanover briefly then once more journeyed to England where he stayed, being in an awkward position when his deserted master arrived in London as George I. However, at the intercession of Baron Kielmansegge he was restored to favour when he composed his *Water Music*, and given a pension of £400 per annum. He composed over forty operas, chief of which are *Atlanta, Berenice*, and *Serse*; thirty-two oratorios, including *Saul, Samson, Messiah, Judas Maccabaeus* and *Jephtha*; and numerous other works. Eight years before his death he became blind and relied on the services of his friend, John Christopher Smith, to commit his music to paper.

Jones, Brian (1946–1969)
Priory Road Cemetery, Presbury, Gloucestershire.

Founder member and guitarist with The Rolling Stones. Brian Jones was influential in moulding the musical direction and bad boy image of

The Rolling Stones' early career. His talents as a multi-instrumentalist helped lift the band above any other at the time and gave them a distinct image and mass pop appeal. His reputation as a womanizer and substance abuser added to the Stones' bad boy image and ultimately led to the bad health and erratic behaviour which caused him to leave the band in 1969.

The same year Jones died in his own swimming pool on 3 July. The remaining Rolling Stones went ahead with a free concert in Hyde Park, London two days later as a tribute to their dead guitarist.

Lind, Johanna Maria, 'Jenny' (1820–1887)
The Cemetery, Great Malvern, Worcestershire, where her grave is covered by a plain slab of Swedish granite.

Singer. She was born in Sweden and was later known as 'the Swedish Nightingale' because of the remarkable range of her voice. Her professionalism distinguished her from her contemporaries but her immense popularity was due to the conviction she brought to her rôles, particularly when identifying with the favourite characters of Amina, Alice or Agathe. She sang throughout Europe and, from 1850 to 1852, in the United States, which she toured under the management of P. T. Barnum. She married Otto Goldschmidt and later settled in London where her husband conducted the Bach Choir, in which she also took an interest, and where she held the post of Professor of Singing at the Royal College of Music for some years.

Linley, Thomas (1732–1795)
Wells Cathedral, Wells, Somerset.

Musician. Born at Wells, he studied at Bath where he settled, becoming a singing master and conductor of concerts. From 1774 he was involved in the management of the Drury Lane Theatre where he composed many of the pieces of music produced there. He also wrote songs and madrigals and his work ranks high among English compositions. His children were also notable musicians: Thomas (1756–1778), a friend of Mozart, was a remarkable violinist and also a composer of songs and madrigals, later published in two volumes; William (1771–1835) held a writership at Madras but composed glees and songs; Elizabeth Anne (1754–1792) married Richard Brinsley Sheridan, but before her marriage was famous for the beauty of her voice, as well as her face. Her two sisters were also noted for their singing and their beauty.

Menuhin, Yehudi, Baron Menuhin of Stoke D'Abernon (1916–1999)
Yehudi Menuhin School, Stoke D'Abernon, Surrey, under a tree that he
planted himself two years before he died.

Violinist and conductor. Yehudi Menuhin was born in New York to
Russian-Jewish parents. He was a child prodigy and established himself
as a world-class violinist when he was only twelve with a performance of
the Beethoven concerto. Most of his performing career was spent in
Britain and in 1962 he established the Yehudi Menuhin School in
Surrey, where his pupils have included Nigel Kennedy and the Hun-
garian violist Csaba Erdelyi. During the 1980s he turned to conducting
and also explored jazz music, recording with Stephane Grappelli.

He received an honorary knighthood in 1965, which was upgraded in
1985 when he was awarded British citizenship. In 1993 he was made a
life peer.

Moon, Keith (1946–1978)
Golders Green Crematorium, ashes scattered on the crocus lawn, section
3-P. There is a wall tablet situated in West Memorial Court.

Drummer with 1970s rock band The Who. Keith Moon began his
career with The Beachcombers, moving to join The Who in the mid
1960s. Described as one of rock's most talented and exciting drummers
he was also one of the most hedonistic. His style and approach to
drumming was revolutionary and he was credited as being at the core of
The Who's rock'n'roll sound. He regularly trashed drum kits alongside
Pete Townsend's guitar smashing, contributing hugely to the band's
image. Moon possessed a wild abandon that he exhibited in his drumming style and his personal life and stories of excess and hedonistic
partying are as well documented as his musical achievements. His off
stage antics, fuelled by alcohol, drugs and elaborate practical jokes
earned him the affectionate name 'Moon the Loon' and contributed to
his death in a swimming pool on 8 September 1978.

Novello, Ivor (1893–1951)
Golders Green Crematorium, Golders Green, London; ashes under the
lilac tree in the Gardens, bust in the Cloisters.

Composer, actor and playwright, his mother being Clara Novello
Davies who was a well-known singer. After being educated at the
Magdalen College School at Oxford, at which he won a singing scholarship in its famous choir, he became a prodigy, composing and performing his own songs. Prior to obtaining a wartime commission in the

Royal Naval Air Service he composed the patriotic song *Keep the Home Fires Burning* (or officially *Till the Boys Come Home*), which became an overnight success and was widely popular in both Britain and the USA, giving him financial independence. He acted on stage and in films but eventually made his major contributions to the theatre as a composer and actor in his own musical plays. His romantic Ruritanian plays were generally tuneful and romantically escapist; not so sophisticated as many of those of Noel Coward, his friend, to whom he could be theatrically compared. *Glamorous Night* (1935), *Crest of the Wave* (1937), *The Dancing Years* (1939), *Perchance to Dream* (1945) and *King's Rhapsody* (1949) were among his well-known musical plays. His song *We'll Gather Lilacs*, the hit of the year, which he wrote for *Perchance to Dream*, is sadly reprised by the commemorative tree under which his ashes were placed.

Purcell, Henry (c.1658–1695)
Westminster Abbey, London, in the north choir aisle of the Nave, where the shield to his memory is inscribed with the following epitaph, which may have been written either by Dryden, his wife, Lady Elizabeth Dryden, or her sister-in-law, Dame Annabella Howard, who erected the monument:

Here Lyes
HENRY PVRCELL. Esqr.
Who left his life
And is gone to that Blessed Place
Where only his Harmony
can be exceeded.

Composer and organist. Born in Westminster where his father was a gentleman of the Chapel Royal. Henry Purcell was admitted to the Chapel Royal as a chorister and in 1676 was appointed copyist at Westminster Abbey. He composed the music for Dryden's *Aurenge-Zebe* that same year and in 1678 produced what was considered to be a masterpiece of musical composition in the overture and masque for Shadwell's new version of Shakespeare's *Timon of Athens*. In 1680, his master, Dr Blow, resigned as organist of Westminster Abbey in favour of his pupil, and at twenty-two Purcell gained one of the most important musical posts in the country. His opera *Dido and Aeneas* formed an important landmark in the history of English operatic music. His great

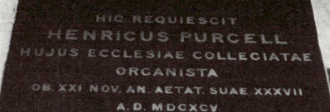

HIC REQUIESCIT
HENRICUS PURCELL
HUJUS ECCLESIAE COLLEGIATAE
ORGANISTA
OB. XXI NOV. AN. AETAT. SUAE. XXXVII
A. D. MDCXCV

PLAUDITE, FELICES SUPERI, TANTO HOSPITE; NOSTRIS
PRAEFUERAT, VESTRIS ADDITUR ILLE CHORIS:
INVIDA NEC VOBIS PURCELLUM TERRA REPOSCAT,
QUESTA DECUS SECLI DELICIASQUE BREVES
TAM CITO DECESSISSE, MODOS CUI SINGULA DEBET
MUSA PROPHANA SUOS, RELIGIOSA SUOS.
VIVIT, IO ET VIVAT, DUM VICINA ORGANA SPIRANT,
DUMQUE COLET NUMERIS TURBA CANORA DEUM.

FRANCISCA
HENRICI PURCELL UXOR
CUM CONJUCE SEPULTA EST
XIV FEB. MDCCVI

Gravestone of Henry Purcell, Westminster Abbey, London

anthems, 'I was glad' and 'My heart is inditing', were written for the coronation of James II. His greatest work is undoubtedly his *Te Deum and Jubilate* written for St Cecilia's Day 1694, the first English *Te Deum* ever composed with orchestral accompaniments.

Sargent, Sir Malcolm (1895–1967)
Stamford Cemetery, Stamford, Lincolnshire.

Conductor. He was born at Stamford and made his debut as a conductor at the old Queen's Hall. He succeeded Sir Adrian Boult in 1950 as conductor of the BBC Symphony Orchestra, a post he held until 1957. During his long career he conducted the American NBC Symphony Orchestra, the Royal Choral Society, and many others including the D'Oyly Carte Opera Company.

Scott, Ronnie (1927–1996)
Golders Green Crematorium. Half his ashes were removed and half were scattered on the crocus lawn, section 1-L. There is a wall tablet situated in West Memorial Court.

Jazz musician. Ronnie Scott was a tenor saxophonist and a prominent figure in London's post-war Jazz scene. He possessed a lyrical and harmonically complex style of playing that saw him become a household name in Britain via the numerous bands he toured and performed with. After co-founding 'Club Eleven', the first British club devoted to modern jazz, Scott opened the eponymous 'Ronnie Scott's' in 1959. Hosting numerous American jazz musicians, including Zoot Sims, Dexter Gordon, Stan Getz and Ella Fitzgerald, the club was an instant hit and become the epicentre of London's jazz community. Meanwhile, Scott continued to tour with pianist Stan Tracey and during the 1960s created some of the most idiosyncratic and experimental music of his career. He died on 23 December 1996.

Springfield, Dusty (1939–1999)
St Mary the Virgin Churchyard, Henley-on-Thames.

Singer. Born Mary O' Brien, she formed the folk trio The Springfields in 1960. The group became the UK's best-selling act of the time with hits like 'Breakaway' and 'Say I Won't Be There'. However, following a trip to Nashville in 1963 and exposure to Motown girl group sounds, Dusty Springfield went solo. Her first single reached the UK top five and became the first major record from a UK artist since the Beatles to reach the US top twenty. By the end of 1964 she was the biggest solo act at home and in 1966 she had her biggest international hit with 'You Don't Have to Say You Love Me'.

Springfield's subsequent career garnered critical acclaim but fell short of the commercial success she had enjoyed. It looked like her pop career might be over until collaboration with the Pet Shop Boys for the 1987 single 'What Have I Done to Deserve This?' resulted in a global hit and a whole new generation of fans. She enjoyed a renaissance in the late 1990s but was diagnosed with breast cancer in 1995 and died on 2 March 1999 aged fifty-nine.

Strummer, Joe (1952–2002)

The funeral service was at St Martin's Church, London. He was cremated and in 2003 a memorial stone was placed at Worthy Farm, Pilton, nr Glastonbury by Michael Eavis and his widow, Lucinda. Strummer had been a regular performer and visitor at Glastonbury festival.

Singer, songwriter and guitarist for legendary punk-rock band the Clash. Born John Graham Mellor, he earned the name Joe Strummer while playing guitar in the London Underground. Strummer formed the Clash in 1976 and became one of the figureheads of the punk scene. The band blended punk with reggae and world beat rhythms and used lyrics championing racial unity and combating political oppression. The Clash released six albums, including their self-titled debut in 1976 and the seminal *London Calling* in 1980.

Following the break-up of the band in 1985, Strummer went on to have a successful acting career in a number of films, including roles in *Straight to Hell* (1987) and *Mystery Train* (1989). He also continued song-writing for various film soundtracks as well as recording his own solo material and with Joe Strummer and the Mescaleros. Strummer died suddenly of a heart attack at his home in Somerset in December 2002, he was fifty years old.

Sullivan, Sir Arthur Seymour (1842–1900)

St Paul's Cathedral, London.

Composer. Born in London, he was the son of an Irish musician who was bandmaster at the Royal Military College, Sandhurst. He won the Mendelssohn Scholarship at the Royal Academy in 1856, and he did so well at the Academy that he was given a two-year extension of his scholarship. He is popularly remembered for the music he wrote for light operas, with W. S. Gilbert as the librettist, especially *The Pirates of Penzance, The Mikado, The Yeomen of the Guard* and *The Gondoliers*. He also wrote a great deal of religious music and, with a friend, discovered Schubert's lost *Rosamunde* music. He was knighted in 1883.

Tauber, Richard (1891–1948)
Brompton Cemetery, West Brompton, London.

Singer. He was born in Austria and became world famous for his singing rôles in operetta. His English success was made in Franz Lehar's *Land of Smiles*.

Vaughan Williams, Ralph (1872–1958)
Westminster Abbey, London, in the north choir aisle of the Nave.

Composer. Born in Gloucestershire, he was educated at Charterhouse and Cambridge. Thereafter he studied under Max Bruch in Berlin and later under Ravel, in Paris. He wrote nine symphonies, besides a large number of choral and orchestral works, operas – *Hugh the Drover, Riders to the Sea* – ballets, chamber music, and songs. He was awarded the Order of Merit.

Wood, Sir Henry Joseph (1869–1944)
Church of the Holy Sepulchre without Newgate, Holborn, London, in the Musicians' Chapel where his ashes lie under the central window to St Cecilia, the patron saint of music.

Conductor. Largely self-taught, as a child he deputised for the local organist. He is principally remembered as the founder of the Promenade Concerts at the Queen's Hall in 1895, which he conducted until his death, nearly fifty years later. He also conducted numerous orchestras both in England and abroad.

Chapter 11
Entertainers (including actors, directors, comedians and broadcasters)

Ashcroft, Dame Edith Margaret Emily, 'Peggy' (1907–1991)
After her cremation at Golders Green Crematorium, London, her ashes were scattered around the ancient Mulberry Tree at New Place, Stratford-upon-Avon, Warwickshire.

Actress. Peggy Ashcroft was one of Britain's most popular and highly acclaimed actresses. She was born in Croydon in December 1907 and studied acting at London's Central School of Dramatic Art. She made her stage debut in 1926 and in 1932 she began her work with the Old Vic Company, which established her reputation as a leading actress. She played the title role in George Bernard Shaw's *Cleopatra*, Rosalind in *As You Like It* and Juliet in John Gielgud's production of *Romeo and Juliet*.

She is best known on the screen for *The Thirty-nine Steps* (1935) and *A Passage to India* (1984), for which she won an Academy award for best actress in a supporting role. Perhaps her most notable television role was as Barbie Batchelor in *The Jewel in the Crown*, which appeared in the same year.

Peggy Ashcroft was awarded a CBE in 1951 and made a Dame in 1956. In 1962 a new London theatre was named in her honour.

Banks, Leslie James (1890–1952)
St Nicholas's Churchyard, Worth Matravers, Dorset; at the north-east side.

An actor, born at Derby, who, after winning a scholarship to Keble College, Oxford, and studying classics there, was attracted to the theatre. He played his first professional role in 1911 as old Gobbo in *The Merchant of Venice* at the Town Hall, Brechin, in Sir Frank Benson's company, later touring the United States and Canada. During the first world war he was wounded in the face but found that the resulting disfigurement did not handicap him in his acting.

He became a sought-after player whose name guaranteed success in any play he was in. He appeared in such plays as *The Circle, Goodbye, Mr Chips*, and *Life With Father* after the second world war, before which he had made his name in provincial repertory and in London. His many film appearances included Alfred Hitchcock's *The Man Who Knew Too Much* and *Jamaica Inn*. In private life his unassuming nature was praised by A. A. Milne as 'the man next door, a good neighbour and a good friend'. He was said, however, to have been brought to ruin by a 'streak of wild recklessness'. He was awarded the CBE in 1950. He lived in Worth Matravers during the summer but died in London.

Blondin, Charles (1824–1897)
Kensal Green Cemetery, Kensal Green, London.

Acrobat and tight-rope walker. Born in France, his real name was Jean François Gravelet. When he was nearly six he made his first appearance as an acrobat, being termed 'The Little Wonder'. In 1859 he first crossed the Niagara Falls, a feat he did again a number of times, but with different theatrical variations: blindfold, in a sack, trundling a wheel-barrow, on stilts, carrying a man on his back, sitting down midway while he made and ate an omelette. He first appeared in London at the Crystal Palace in 1861.

Cook, Peter (1937–1995)
St John's Churchyard, Hampstead, London, in an unmarked plot in the cemetery extension.

Actor and comedian. Peter Cook started writing sketches whilst studying at Cambridge University. These were performed in the West End and on graduating he decided not to follow his father into the diplomatic service. Instead he teamed up with Alan Bennett, Dudley Moore and Jonathan Miller for *Beyond the Fringe*. This lasted several years and was popular both in London and Broadway. At the same time he became a major shareholder in the satirical magazine *Private Eye*.

Peter Cook and Dudley Moore got together again in 1965 in a partnership that produced three series of *Not Only ... But Also*, several recordings as Pete and Dud and Derek and Clive, and five feature films. After touring with a stage show, *Behind the Fringe*, Moore refused to work with Pete again on account of his alcoholism. Peter Cook continued to make TV and film appearances until his death at the Royal Free Hospital.

Cooper, Dame Gladys (1888–1971)
Hampstead Cemetery, Fortune Green Road, London.

Actress. She began her career as Bluebell in *Bluebell in Fairyland* at the Theatre Royal, Colchester, when just seventeen. Thereafter she appeared in numerous roles both on the stage, in films and on television. She was made a Dame of the British Empire.

Dors, Diana (1931–1984)
Sunningdale Roman Catholic church, Sunningdale, Berkshire.

Actress who has been called 'the English Marilyn Monroe', perhaps mainly because of her blond hair and striking figure. She was also called 'The only sex symbol Britain has produced since Lady Godiva'. But, as in the case of Miss Monroe, her screen personality and ability gave her a universal appeal both on film and off. Not only that, after training at the Royal Academy of Dramatic Art she starred in over thirty-six films after appearing as young as fifteen in background 'sexy girl' bits. Some of her major films were *There's a Girl in My Soup* (1970) as an ex-wife of Peter Sellers, *Steptoe and Son Ride Again* (1973), in BBC Television Shakespeare *Timon of Athens* as Timandra (1981), *All Our Saturdays* (1973), a TV series; a hard-working actress in many substantial roles. Two of her three marriages ended in divorce; she had three sons. Born in Swindon she died at Windsor of meningitis. Before she died she devoted much of her time to religious and charity groups.

Fenton, Lavinia (Polly Peachum), later Duchess of Bolton (1708–1809)
St Alfege's Church, Greenwich, London.

Actress who took London by storm with the part of Polly Peachum in John Gay's (whom see) *The Beggar's Opera* (1728) and became the mistress of Charles Paulet, third Duke of Bolton (1685–1754) whom she married when his first wife died. Lady Mary Montagu pointed out that the Duchess of Bolton was 'crammed with virtue and good qualities ... despised by her husband and laughed at by the public', while 'Lavinia, bred in an alehouse and produced on the stage, found the way to be esteemed.'

Formby, George OBE (1904–1961)
Manchester Road Catholic Cemetery, Warrington, Cheshire.

Variety artist and film actor who was best known for his ukulele playing and comic singing. Born in Wigan, the son of a music-hall performer, George was warned by his father not to go on stage; its life, especially in those Edwardian days, was too hard, he believed. Formby senior died in 1921 and George did start to 'tread the boards' imitating his father's act, but poorly. Of his first appearance at the Hippodrome, Earlstown he said 'I died the death of a dog!' In 1923 he married Beryl

Ingham, of a clog-dancing team, who improved his act. After being signed up to make films at Ealing Studios by Basil Dean, their head, many successful films followed. The first film he made was *Off the Dole* in 1935. During the war he toured battlefronts in virtually every theatre of the war, including Normandy less than a week after D-day, where he was awarded the OBE. In 1951 he starred in his first West End musical, a new version of *Brewster's Millions*, which became a smash hit. While still in the show he suffered a major heart attack in 1952 while driving home after a performance. His wife nursed him back to health, however, and he eventually was able to appear about eighteen months later in Palladium and Palace Theatre shows such as *Fun and the Fair*, with Terry-Thomas and *Dick Whittington*. Shortly after his wife died in 1961, however, and an engagement to a younger woman he suffered another heart attack, which proved fatal. On his own request he was buried beside his father.

Garrick, David (1716–1779)
Westminster Abbey, London, in the South Transept, now known as 'Poets' Corner'.

Actor-manager. Son of an army officer, he was born in Lichfield. He was Dr Johnson's solitary scholar when Samuel Johnson set up a school near Lichfield, and he accompanied Johnson to London when the two set out to seek their fortunes, as Dr Johnson said, 'with twopence halfpenny in his pocket,' and Garrick 'with three halfpence in his'. Both Garrick's father and uncle shortly afterwards died and he was left £1,000. He and his brother decided to set up a wine business in Lichfield and London, David looking after the London office. It was not successful and he had soon spent half his capital. He was engrossed in the theatre and made an incognito appearance on the stage in *Harlequin Student, or The Fall of Pantomime with the Restoration of Drama*, March 1741. By October of that year he had gained popular applause for his role of Richard III at Goodman's Fields. He immediately gave up his wine business and took to the stage full-time. Within six months he had acted in eighteen roles and was immediately successful. His own farce, *The Lying Valet*, in which he played the part of Sharp, was so successful that his fortune was made. For the season of 1742 he was employed by Fleetwood for the Drury Lane Theatre, and he remained there until 1745 when he went to Dublin. He remained there as joint manager with Sheridan of the Theatre Royal in Smock Alley. In 1747 he took over the managership of the Drury Lane Theatre, opening in September of that year with a strong company of actors. He ceased to act in 1766 but continued with the managership of Drury Lane. He sold his share in the theatre in 1776 for £35,000 and took his leave by playing a round of his favourite characters: Hamlet, Lear and Richard III.

Glover, Brian (1934–1997)
Brompton Cemetery, West London.

Actor, writer and wrestler. Born in Barnsley, Brian Glover was a professional wrestler and a high school teacher before landing his first acting job in Ken Loach's film *Kes*. He went on to play many memorable TV roles in series such as *Porridge*, *Minder* and *Dr Who*. He also appeared in films such as *An American Werewolf in Paris*, *Alien 3* and *Leon the Pig Farmer*. Best known as a gruff, bald-headed character actor, he also wrote over twenty plays and short films, had a newspaper column and appeared on the BBC's political panel programme, *Question Time*.

Grimaldi, Joseph (1779–1837)
St James's Church (site of), Pentonville, London. Newly restored grave in iron-railed surround.

Clown, famous throughout the world in his time, who died penniless as a lifelong resident of Islington, London. A successful campaign by the Joseph Grimaldi Society, spearheaded by Lord Miles (actor Bernard Miles), saw the grave renovated and landscaped in 1987 on the 150th anniversary of the clown's death. A group of fourteen clowns attended the celebration, one of them wearing Grimaldi's original costume and wig. Grimaldi's career began as an infant dancer at Sadler's Wells. He later acted there and at Drury Lane for many years, as well as in the provinces and at Dublin. Covent Garden saw him in his most famous role as Squire Bugle in *Mother Goose*.

Guinness, Sir Alec (1914–2000)
St Lawrence's Roman Catholic Church, Petersfield, Hampshire.

Film actor, probably best known for his role as Obi-Wan Kenobi in the first three *Star Wars* films. Alec Guinness was born and brought up in London. He worked as an advertising copywriter whilst studying at the Fay Compton Studio of Dramatic Art and made his stage debut in 1936. After serving in the Royal Navy during World War II he made his mark on the film world with his portrayal of Herbert Pocket in *Great Expectations* (1946). There followed a string of films and in 1956 he was awarded a CBE. His work as 'Colonel Nicholson' in *The Bridge On the*

River Kwai in 1957 earned him a best actor Oscar. He continued to be an international star, having parts in *Lawrence of Arabia* (1962), *The Fall of the Roman Empire* (1964), *Doctor Zhivago* (1965) and *A Passage to India* (1984), as well as the *Star Wars* trilogy (1977-83). In 1980 the Academy presented him with an Honorary Award for the advancement of the art of screen acting.

Gwyn, Eleanor, 'Nell' (1650–1687)
St Martin-in-the-Fields, St Martin's Place, London.

Actress. Born in London, probably in an alley off Drury Lane. Her father was described as a broken-down soldier. She first sold oranges in the precincts of the Drury Lane Theatre and graduated to the stage around the age of fifteen, through the influence of the actor Charles Hart and a guards officer, Robert Duncan or Dungan, who had some influence with the management. Her first recorded appearance was in 1665 as Cydaria, Montezuma's daughter, in Dryden's *Indian Emperor*. Pepys in his diary entry for 25 March 1667 recorded that he was delighted with the acting of 'pretty, witty Nell,' and when he saw her playing Florimel in Dryden's *Secret Love, or the Maiden Queen*, he wrote 'so great a performance of a comical part was never, I believe, in the world before' and 'so done by Nell her merry part as cannot be better done by nature'. Her success brought her many leading roles and she stayed with the Drury Lane company until 1669. But it is as the mistress of Charles II that she is principally remembered. As his mistress she was popular with the public, probably to counter the public's distrust of Louise de Kéroualle, Duchess of Portsmouth, Charles's other mistress who was both Catholic and French, both characteristics likely to offend the English public. She bore Charles two sons, the future Duke of St Albans, and the young Lord Beauclerk who died in 1680. When Charles died he implored his brother, James II, 'Let not poor Nell starve', and the new King honoured his brother's dying wish. He settled an estate on the former mistress with reversion to her surviving son, the young Duke. Nell Gwyn did not long survive Charles II, dying in November 1687, her funeral sermon being preached by Thomas Tenison, Vicar of St Martin-in-the-Fields and afterwards Archbishop of Canterbury.

Hancock, Tony (1928–1968)
Ashes buried in St Dunstan's Churchyard, Cranford Park, Greater London. He was cremated in Sydney, Australia, and his ashes returned to England under the care of the comedian Willie Rushton.

Nell Gwyn, from the studio of Lely

Comedian. Tony Hancock is still a popular and influential comedian. Born in Birmingham, he first attempted stand-up comedy at the age of sixteen. He made his first radio broadcast in 1941 and by 1953 he was the resident comedian on *All-Star Bill*. He is best remembered for *Hancock's Half Hour*, which first appeared on radio in 1954 and later transferred to television. On the show he worked with Sid James, Kenneth Williams and Hatti Jacques, who where to become famous in their own right for the Carry On movies. Tony Hancock committed suicide in Australia as he feared his career was on the slide.

Hawthorne, Sir Nigel (1929–2001)
Parish Churchyard, Thunbridge, Ware, Hertfordshire.

Actor. Nigel Hawthorne's early career was difficult and produced limited success. He was largely ignored professionally until 1977 when he landed the television role of Sir Humphrey Appleby in the political sitcom *Yes, Minister*. The show was a huge success and earned Hawthorne four BAFTAs. Another BAFTA and an Oscar nomination followed for his title role in the film *The Madness of King George* (1994), he had already received an Olivier award for the stage version. His sixth BAFTA was awarded for the television mini-series *Fragile Heart* in 1996.

Three years later Hawthorne realised his ambition to appear at Stratford and took the title role in *Lear* to critical acclaim. He was awarded a knighthood in the same year.

Irving, Sir Henry (1838–1905)
Westminster Abbey, London, in the South Transept, now known as 'Poets' Corner'.

Actor-manager. He revolutionized the dramatic art of the nineteenth century by his revivals of Shakespeare, and other plays, at the old Lyceum Theatre from 1878 to 1899. His performances of Shylock and Malvolio were renowned. For many years he acted with Ellen Terry.

Jarman, Derek (1942–1994)
St Clement Graveyard, Old Romney, Kent.

Film director, artist and writer. Derek Jarman is best known as a filmmaker but graduated from the Slade School of Art and was a talented painter. He made ten full-length films during his lifetime and they all deliberately pushed the boundaries of cinema and imagination. His second film, *Jubilee* (1977), transported Queen Elizabeth I forward in time to a bleak twentieth century England ruled by her namesake. It was arguably the first UK punk movie. His last film, *Blue* (1993), was made as he was dying of AIDS related complications and he had lost his sight. A saturated blue colour fills the screen and Jarman describes his life and vision against an original soundtrack.

Johnson, Celia (1908–1982)
Parish Church churchyard, Nettlebed, Oxfordshire.

Actress who appeared in many popular films. Perhaps two of the best remembered are *Brief Encounter* (1945) by Noel Coward with Trevor Howard co-starring, and *The Captain's Paradise* (1953), with Alec Guinness. Two of her major films were *In Which We Serve* (1942), co-directed and produced by Noel Coward, who played Captain Kinross (she played his wife) and *This Happy Breed* (1944) based on the play by Noel Coward in which she played opposite Robert Newton. In 1969 the British Film Academy named her Best Supporting Actress in *The Prime of Miss Jean Brodie*. She was married to Peter Fleming, see in Section 6 here.

Karloff, Boris (1887–1969)
Mount Cemetery, in Garden of Remembrance, Guildford, Surrey.

Actor, born William Pratt, who is generally best known for his portrayal of Frankenstein's monster in the film of that name. He was, however, an accomplished stage actor and his return to the stage in *Arsenic and Old Lace* (1941) and as Captain Hook in 1951 brought him critical acclaim. Earlier, as the youngest child of a civil servant, he had been educated at Uppingham and the Merchant Taylor's School and had hoped for a diplomatic career after London University. After going to Canada and the United States at the age of twenty-one, though, he was for ten years in a repertory company, which culminated in his making several films in Hollywood before the one that brought him fame. As Frankenstein's monster and in other parts involving ghosts and resurrected mummies, to all of which he managed to bring a characterisation well above the otherwise crude pathos involved, he became a traditional role model. But a strong performance in a 1934 World War I film, *The Lost Patrol*, notably revealed his versatility. He also worked in television and remained active in his craft until his death.

Kean, Charles John (1811–1868)
All Saints' Church, Catherington, Hampshire.

Actor. Son of the actor Edmund Kean who, despite his father's wishes to the contrary, went on the stage. He played opposite his father during the latter's last appearance on the stage in *Othello*, his father playing the title role and he Iago. With his wife, Ellen Tree, he played in spectacular revivals at the Princess's Theatre, London, during the 1850s.

Kean, Edmund (1787–1833)
St Matthias's Churchyard, Friars' Stile Road, Richmond, Surrey.

Actor. He made his first appearance on the stage as Cupid in Noverre's ballet of *Cymon* when only four years old. As a child he became a cabin boy but so disliked it that he feigned deafness and lameness with such skill that he deceived the physicians. At fourteen he joined the York Theatre playing Shakespeare for twenty nights and thereafter joined a troupe of strolling players. He recited before George III at Windsor, and in 1807 was playing opposite Mrs Siddons in Dublin. In 1814 he opened at the Drury Lane Theatre as Shylock and the triumph was so great that he remarked 'I could not feel the stage under me'. He played twice in the United States, in 1820 and 1825, and last appeared on the English stage at Covent Garden on 25 March 1833 playing Othello to his son, Charles's Iago and his daughter-in-law, Ellen Tree's Desdemona. During the third act he became ill and, crying in a faltering voice, 'O God, I am dying. Speak to them, Charles,' he fell unconscious into his son's arms. He died a few weeks later at Richmond.

Kendall, Kay (1927–1959)
St John's Churchyard extension, Church Row, Hampstead, London.

Actress. A talented comedienne, she starred in many films, perhaps the most popular being *Genevieve*. She appeared also in Cole Porter's *Les Girls*. She was married to the actor, Rex Harrison. She died of leukaemia. She was of an acting family.

Kubrick, Stanley (1928–1999)
Childwickbury Manor, St Albans, Hertfordshire.

Film director. Born in the Bronx in New York, Stanley Kubrick was the son of a doctor who encouraged him in his interest in photography. This interest led to filmmaking in 1950 when he produced a sixteen-minute documentary about a boxer. This was sold to RKO-Pathe and encouraged the twenty-five-year-old Kubrick to make his first feature film funded from money borrowed from relatives and friends. He went on to make thirteen feature films, including *Lolita* (1962), *2001: A Space Odyssey* (1968), and *Full Metal Jacket* (1987). His movies were often controversial and provoked extreme reactions from audiences – he withdrew *Clockwork Orange* from British release in 1973 after it had been banned by several local authorities.

Kubrick was a perfectionist and often spent many years working on a film. At the time of his death he had been working on *Eyes Wide Shut*, staring Tom Cruise and Nicole Kidman, for nineteen months and had been given an unlimited timeframe by the studio, Warner Bros.

Kubrick had moved to England in 1961 in order to have greater independence from the American studios. Chidwickbury Manor was his Hertfordshire home.

Leigh, Vivien Mary (1913–1967)
Tickerage Mill, near Blackboys, Sussex, where her ashes are scattered on the lake.

Actress most famous for her role as Scarlett O'Hara in *Gone with the Wind*, for which she won an Academy award. Vivien Leigh was born in India to a British father and Irish mother and her fist taste of acting was in her convent school plays. When she was eighteen she went to study at the Royal Academy of Dramatic Art and a year later was married to barrister Herbert Leigh Homan. They had one daughter, Suzanne, but separated in 1937 when Vivian moved in with Laurence Olivier. It was her first movie with Olivier, *Fire over England*, that brought her to the attention of David O. Selznick, who was looking for someone to play Scarlett O'Hara. She married Olivier in 1940 and it was a marriage that lasted twenty years.

She was not a prolific actor and shunned the Hollywood lifestyle. However, in 1951 she played Blanche DuBois opposite Marlon Brando in *Streetcar Named Desire*, for which she was awarded her second Academy award. She was now suffering from severe bouts of manic depression and other health-related problems. She was found dead in her London home by the actor Jack Merivale on 7 July 1967.

Macready, William Charles (1793–1873)
Kensal Green Cemetery, Kensal Green, London.

Actor. Born at London and educated at Rugby. Instead of going to Oxford he helped his father in the running of his theatres and on 7 June 1810 made his first appearance as Romeo in Birmingham. His first

London appearance was as Orestes in *The Distressed Mother* at Covent Garden on 16 September 1816. Thereafter he played many roles, the most notable being his Richard III and Henry V. He managed both Covent Garden Theatre, 1837 to 1839, and the Drury Lane Theatre, 1841 to 1843. He travelled extensively in the United States but one of his visits to New York was marred by a riot at the Astor Opera House in 1849, inspired by a jealous actor, Edwin Forrest. He retired from the stage in a farewell performance of Macbeth at Drury Lane on 26 February 1851.

Matthews, Jessie (1907–1981)
St Martin's Church, Ruislip, Greater London, ashes in the Garden of Rest.

Stage and film actress born in Soho, London, who was one of the most popular performers of the 1930s, singing and dancing her way into the heart of cinema-goers as she had so appealed to theatre-goers in the twenties. She was a 'trim, musical star with a delicate face and a quivering, almost non-existent chin', Anthony Slide wrote of her. She was a dancer who should have but never did, partnered Fred Astaire, he believed. At age 12 she made her stage debut in *Bluebell in Fairyland*, going on to play in such plays and films as *This England* (1924), *The Good Companions* (1934), *Evergreen* (1935), Tom's mother in *Tom Thumb* (1958) and *The Hound of the Baskervilles* (1978). Her theme song was *Over My Shoulder*, which she sang to great applause in her solo concert at Los Angeles two years before she died of cancer. In 1970 she was awarded the OBE.

Milligan, 'Spike' (Terence Alan) (1918–2002)
Winchelsea Churchyard, Kent.

Comic entertainer and writer. Born in India in 1918, Spike did not return to England until he was sixteen. He took a job in a factory in South London, but joined his father's old regiment at the outbreak of the Second World War and served in North Africa, where he met Harry Secombe. He used his war experiences in his writings, such as *Adolf Hitler: My Part in his Downfall*, published in 1971.

Back in London after the war, he met up with Harry Secombe again. He also met Peter Sellers and Michael Bentine and in 1951 they started a radio sketch show that was to become the hugely successful *The Goon Show*. It lasted for nine years, with Milligan taking a major part in writing every show. By the time the show ended in 1960 his personal

Spike Milligan, the epitaph reads 'I told you I was ill' in Gaelic

demons were starting to dominate his life and he suffered numerous nervous breakdowns.

During the 1960s Milligan took to the stage, writing and performing in the bleakly comic *The Bed-sitting Room* and *Oblomov*, amongst others. In the 1970s he turned to cinema with, for example, *The Three Musketeers* (1973) and *Monty Python's Life of Brian* (1978).

He made frequent TV appearances, was a prolific writer and inspired a generations of comics. He was awarded an honorary knighthood in 2000.

Mills, Bertram Wagstaff (1873–1938)
St Giles's Church, Chalfont St Giles, Buckinghamshire.

Circus owner. He was the son of a Paddington coach builder and during the Great War of 1914–1918 he served in the Army Medical Corps. Bertram Mills' Circus became famous in Britain for its Christmas shows at Olympia in West London as well as for its provincial tours.

Mills, Sir John (1908–2005)
St Mary's Churchyard, Denham, Buckinghamshire.

Stage and screen actor. Born Lewis Ernest Watts Mills in February 1908, John Mills caught the acting bug as a schoolboy performing in amateur theatre groups. He moved to London to study at the Royal Academy of Dramatic Art and worked as a salesman to pay his way. On his professional stage debut, when he was just eighteen years, old he was spotted by Noel Coward and went on to become a prolific British character actor. Mills appeared in over a hundred films and won a best supporting Oscar for his role in *Ryan's Daughter*. He also received a Fellowship from the British Academy of Film and Television.

John Mills' career spanned over seventy-three years and he never retired. His only break was to serve as a Royal Engineer during the Second World War. His marriage to the playwright Mary Hayley Bell lasted over sixty years and, like his career, only came to an end on his death at the age of ninety-seven. They started a stage and screen dynasty with two actress daughters and a screen–writer/director son. Mills was awarded a CBE in 1960 and knighted in 1976.

Morecambe, Eric (1926–1984)
Church of St Nicholas, Harpenden, Herfordshire. His ashes were scattered in the Garden of Rememberance and there is a plaque bearing his real name, John Eric Bartholomes.

Comedian. He was born in the Lancashire seaside town of Morecambe, and became famous as one half of a comedy duo, along with Ernie Wise. The long-running Morecambe and Wise TV show was hugely popular and they attracted star guests, such as Laurence Olivier and The Beatles. The double act only came to an end when Eric died from a heart attack at the age of fifty-eight.

Neagle, (Dame) Anna (1904–1986)
Central London Cemetery, Manor Park (nearest station), London.

Actress who is perhaps best known for her role as Queen Victoria in the films *Victoria the Great* (1937) and *Sixty Glorious Years* (1938). She was also a great success in *Spring in Park Lane* (1948), for which she won the Picturegoer Medal. Born Majorie Robertson, she came to the stage via the chorus line and, married to the producer Herbert Wilcox, appeared in numerous films during the thirties, playing various heroines of history as in *Nell Gwyn* (1934), *Nurse Edith Cavell* (1939) and Amy Johnson in *They Flew Alone* (1942), plus many other highly acclaimed roles in *Goodnight Vienna* (1932), *Bitter Sweet* (1933), *Holiday Inn* (1936), *London Melody* (1937) and others. She cherished her role as the French resistance leader in *Odette* (1950) (Mrs Odette Hallowes, G.C.) whom she knew as a friend. It was considered one of her greatest portrayals. Another strong role a year later was her Florence Nightingale in *The Lady with the Lamp*. She was made a Dame of the British Empire in 1969 after her greatest stage success in *Charlie Girl* at the Adelphi. She was 'as much a part of Britain as Dover's white cliffs', Anthony Slide cited one critic as saying.

Olivier, Laurence Kerr, 1st Baron (1907–1989)
Westminster Abbey, London, ashes placed beneath plaque in 'Poets' Corner'.

An actor who was revered throughout the English-speaking world, he was also a director and producer. Born in Dorking, at seventeen he studied on a scholarship at the London School of Dramatic Art, played his first professional role in *Byron* (1924) and took part in a sketch that toured England the same year; his last performance was in Benjamin Britten's *War Requiem* in 1989. His Shakespearian debut was as Macbeth, as a member of the Birmingham Repertory Company (1926–28), and his first film part was in *Too Many Crooks* (1930). Since then his stage, film and television appearances varied widely from a role with Marilyn Monroe (*The Prince and the Showgirl*) to his towering portraits in Shakespeare.

He served for four years in the Fleet Air Arm, being released in 1944 to co-direct the Old Vic Theatre Company with Sir Ralph Richardson (whom see). Knighted in 1947, in recognition of his performances in the films *Henry V* and *Hamlet*, Olivier was either nominated for or received fifteen Best Actor awards. Married three times, his first marriage was to actress Jill Esmond, who bore him a son Tarquin. This marriage ended in divorce in 1940 when he married Vivien Leigh, from whom he was divorced in 1960. His third wife, actress Joan Plowright, bore him three children, Richard, Tamsin and Julie; he had married her in 1961 and his death widowed her.

Olivier's peerage came in 1981; he was the first actor ever to be so recognized. As Director of Chichester Festival, from 1962 he worked hard to raise money for a permanent home for the National Theatre, now on the South Bank of the Thames. Perhaps the only reservation made about his acting was that his remarkable virility and on-stage gusto were more physical than poetic; as John Gielgud said, 'I had the voice, but Larry had the legs'. Nevertheless theatre critic Eric Shorter wrote that as an actor Olivier 'conquered the world'.

Pavlova, Anna (1881–1931)
Golders Green Crematorium, Golders Green, London; urn in Ernest George Columbarium with a shrine there. Also in the Cloisters there is an Anna Pavlova standard rose and a rosebed in the Gardens.

Ballerina born in St Petersburg (Leningrad), Russia, who became world famous as a dancer, performing in her own company after being a prima ballerina in the Imperial Ballet Company of Moscow. She left Russia permanently in 1913 and toured the world both during and after the war. Her most famous performance was *The Dying Swan* which, with her small delicate figure and exquisitely graceful dancing, made her three-minute solo adored everywhere she performed.

Peel, John (1939–2004)
St Edmundsbury Cathedral, Saint Edmunds, Suffolk,

Radio DJ and broadcaster for over thirty-five years. He was born John Robert Parker Ravenscroft in Heswall near Liverpool in 1939. After completing national service in 1959 he went to America and landed his first DJ job for WRR radio in Dallas. Peel returned to England in 1967 and joined the pirate station Radio London before landing a job on the BBC's new national pop channel, Radio 1. His late night shows aimed to promote new talent and he was the first DJ to give exposure to punk, reggae and hip-hop. Acts that he championed included David Bowie, Joy Division, The Undertones and The Smiths, giving them studio time to record the legendary *Peel Sessions*.

In 1998 he started presenting *Home Truths* on Radio 4. Its eclectic nature and humorous reflections on family life made it a favourite with the audience and he was still presenting the show at the time of his death. He received an OBE in 1998 and in 2002 he was awarded a Sony Gold, the industry's highest accolade.

Richardson, Sir Ralph (1902–1983)
Highgate Cemetery (New), Swain's Lane, Highgate, London, near path.

An actor whose successful career lasted over fifty years from 1926 when he made his London debut at the Haymarket. He was an actor who could 'make an ordinary character seem extraordinary' and vice versa, it was said. His first stage appearance was at Brighton at the age of 20 in *The Emperor's Candlesticks* and he later played more important parts in various Shakespearean productions there. His versatility saw him play a gamut of roles in scores of plays and films from Bulldog Drummond to Macbeth and Cyrano de Bergerac. His lifelong association with Sir John Gielgud began in 1930, and with Sir Laurence Olivier in 1938 at the Old Vic. He served with the latter during World War II in the Fleet Air Arm. Sir Peter Hall said of him, 'He was one of the greatest actors who ever lived – I'm sure of that.' He worked right up to the end of his life, which ended with a brief illness. He had been knighted in 1947 while he was a co-director with Olivier at the 'New' Old Vic. 'The art of acting', he once said, 'lies in keeping people from coughing.'

Secombe, Sir Harry Donald (1921–2001)
Cranleigh Parish Hall, Guildford.

Comic entertainer, actor and singer. Harry Secombe met Spike Milligan while on duty in the Western desert during WWII. He was to work with Spike on the hugely successful *The Goon Show* after the war. By 1955 Secombe had his own TV show, *The Harry Secombe Show*. Two years later he starred in a film about a music hall performer but it was not a box office success. He was better known for his role as Mr Bumble in the 1968 musical version of *Oliver!* and for *The Magnificent Seven Deadly Sins* (1971). In later life, Harry Secombe was best known as the presenter of the long-running Christian praise programme, *Highway*. He was awarded a CBE in 1963 and was knighted in 1981 for services to entertainment and charity.

Sellers, Peter Richard Henry (1925–1980)
Golders Green Crematorium, Golders Green, London, his ashes being placed next to those of his parents beneath rose bushes.

Actor. He was born into a theatrical family: his mother was a pianist and actress, whilst his grandmother and eight of his uncles were on the stage. He made a name for himself in the radio series, *The Goon Show*, in the 1950s. Thereafter he appeared frequently in films, the most popular being his role of the German scientist in *Dr Strangelove*, Inspector Clouseau in the *Pink Panther* series, in *I'm All Right, Jack* and *The Mouse That Roared*.

Siddons, Sarah (1755–1831)

St Mary on Paddington Green Churchyard, Paddingon, London. There is a monument to her on the Green, which was unveiled by Sir Henry Irving in 1897.

Actress. Daughter of the manager Roger Kemble, she was accustomed to appearing on the stage from childhood. She fell in love with William Siddons, an actor in her father's company, but her parents opposed their marriage and he was dismissed. However, the couple eventually married in November 1773 and subsequently appeared in Cheltenham where Sarah attracted public notice. David Garrick sent his deputy to see her and she was engaged to appear at Drury Lane at a salary of £5 a week. Initially, she was not a great success and lost her position at Drury Lane, but, after touring and receiving much acclaim in Bath, she was engaged to appear at Drury Lane again in 1778. Thereafter her career was established and she played all the leading roles of her day. She was greatly respected by many of her contemporaries and Dr Johnson wrote his name on the hem of the garment which she wore for her Reynolds' painting saying, 'I would not lose the honour this opportunity afforded to me for my name going down to posterity on the hem of your garment'.

Terry, Dame Ellen Alice (1847–1928)

St Paul's Church, Covent Garden, London.

Actress. Born into a prominent theatrical family she made her first stage appearance at nine years old. Thereafter she played juvenile roles until her marriage to G. F. Watts, the artist, when she was sixteen. The marriage was a disaster and later he divorced her. She returned to acting and became famous for the roles she played opposite Sir Henry Irving at the Lyceum Theatre and during tours of the United States. She had two children, neither by her husband, Gordon Craig, the stage designer, and Edith Craig.

Tilley, Vesta (1864–1952)
Golders Green Crematorium, Golders Green, London; ashes under a lilac tree.

Male impersonator (born Matilda Alice Powles), she was a child prodigy who made her first stage appearance at the age of five in Nottingham. In London she became famous as 'principal boy' in pantomimes. Small of stature, she never approved of vulgarity, nor did she ever become touched with any scandalous rumours. She became as popular in the USA as she was in England; her perfectionism, her immaculate dress and petite figure combined with her unique voice and diction made her performances and her songs a memorable event for all who saw her. Her farewell performance on 5 June 1920 was a joyous and virtually hysterical landmark for the London stage. She was happily married to a member of parliament, becoming Lady de Frece.

Tree, Sir Herbert Beerbohm (1853–1917)
St John's Churchyard extension, Church Row, Hampstead, London.

Actor manager. He was the actor-manager of the Haymarket Theatre until 1897 when he built his own theatre, His Majesty's Theatre.

Walbrook, Anton (1900–1967)
St John's Churchyard extension, Church Row, Hampstead, London.

Actor. Born in Vienna, he first appeared on the English stage in Noel Coward's *Design for Living* at the Haymarket Theatre in 1939. Thereafter he starred in films and on the stage, becoming famous both in England and in the United States.

Chapter 12
Heroes and Heroines (including explorers, sportsmen, reformers and muses)

Blake, Sir Peter (1948–2001)
St Thomas a Becket Churchyard, Hampshire.

Champion yachtsman. During his thirty year sailing career, Peter Blake won the America's Cup, completed five Whitbread Round the World Races (winning the last one) and held the world record for the fastest non-stop circumnavigation of the world in 1994, with a time of just under seventy-five days. He received numerous accolades, including two Sportsmen of the Year awards and four Yachtsmen of the Year awards. He was named a MBE in 1983, awarded an OBE and was knighted in 1991. Blake had decided to devote his life to the preservation of the world's oceans but was tragically shot and killed on his yacht.

Booth, William, 'General' (1829–1912)
Abney Park Cemetery, Church Street, Stoke Newington, London.

Founder of the Salvation Army. He was born in Nottingham. In 1865, with the help of his wife, Catherine, he began mission work in the East End of London, which led in 1878 to the formation of the Salvation Army on military lines. It became an international organization, with members of his family organizing branches throughout the world.

Brandon, Richard (d.1649)
St Mary Matfelon Churchyard, Alder Street, Whitechapel, London.

Executioner of Charles I. He was the son of the common hangman Gregory Brandon, known as 'Old Gregory', whilst Richard was known as 'Young Gregory'. He was apparently reluctant to execute the King but was forced to do so, receiving 'thirty pounds for his pains, all paid in half-crowns, within an hour after the blow was given', as well as an orange 'stuck full of cloves' and a handkerchief out of the King's pocket. He sold the orange for ten shillings in Rosemary Lane, where he lived. He also executed many other prominent nobles, including the Earl of Strafford, Archbishop Laud, the Duke of Hamilton, the Earl of Holland and Lord Capel. Although he confessed to the execution of the King, William Hulet was condemned for having dispatched the monarch. Brandon is reputed to have died of remorse for killing Charles I.

Burton, Sir Richard Francis (1821–1890)
St Mary Magdalen's Churchyard, North Worple Way, Mortlake, London. His monument is a life-size tent with a crucifix above the place where the entrance seems to be.

Explorer, writer and linguist. He is famous for the pilgrimage he made to Mecca and Medina in 1853 disguised as a Moslem. He explored Central Africa and translated the *Arabian Nights*, which ran into sixteen volumes.

Carter, Howard (1874–1939)
Putney Vale Cemetery, South West London.

Archaeologist. Carter began his archaeological work in Egypt at the age of seventeen. He struggled to fund his excavations until 1907 when he met Lord Carnarvon, who was a wealthy and eager amateur. It was Lord Carnarvon who funded his search for the tomb of Tutankhamun, whose existence Carter had discovered. In November 1922 Carter found the tomb in the Valley of the Kings, near Luxor, Egypt. On 16 February the following year he opened the burial chamber. Carter died at the age of sixty-nine in 1939.

Cavell, Edith Louisa (1865–1915)
Norwich Cathedral, Norwich, Norfolk, outside the south-east transept wall.

Nurse. She was shot by the Germans for helping Allied fugitives to escape during the Great War. At her trial she admitted that she had received letters from the men she had aided, and this sealed her fate. Despite strenuous attempts from the American and Spanish ambassadors in Brussels, as well as worldwide condemnation, the Germans executed her by firing squad at 2 AM on 12 October 1915. After the war her body was brought to England and a memorial service held in Westminster Abbey.

Cornwell, John Travers, VC (1900–1916)
Manor Park Cemetery, City of London but memorial monument in Portland Naval Cemetery, Dorset.

The boy (1st class) hero of the Battle of Jutland 31 May 1916, who 'stood on the burning deck' of HMS *Chester* (reminding us of the poem by Mrs Felicia Hemans about an earlier boy hero, Giacomo Casabianca at the Battle of the Nile). Admiral Sir David Beatty said: '... Cornwell was mortally wounded early in the action. He nevertheless remained

Tomb of Sir Richard Burton, St Mary Magdalen's Churchyard, North Worple Way, Mortlake, London

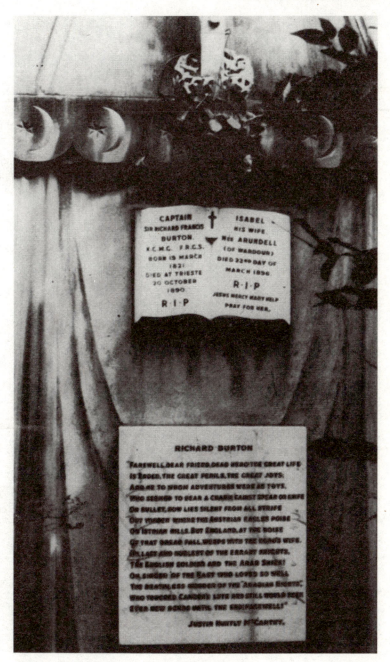

Inscription on the monument to Sir Richard Burton

Howard Carter, Putney Vale Cemetery, West London

Grave of Nurse Edith Cavell, Norwich Cathedral, Norfolk

standing alone at a most exposed post till the end of the action, with the gun crew dead and wounded all around him ... I recommend his case for special recognition in justice to his memory, and as an acknowledgment of the high example set by him.' Cornwell survived for twenty-four hours to die in Grimsby hospital just before his mother arrived from London. He knew she was coming, however; 'Give her my love,' were his last words.

Cribb, Tom (1781–1848)
St Mary's and St Andrew's Churchyard, Woolwich, London.

World champion bare-knuckle boxer. Tom Cribb first boxed at Wood Green in north London at the age of twenty-three. He won. He won again a month later and decided to become a professional. He trained under Captain Robert Barclay and five years later, in 1810, Cribb was awarded the British title. That same year he beat Tom Molineaux, a black American former slave, in order to become World Champion. And he beat him again in 1811.

Cribb retired from boxing the following year and went on to run a pub, the Union Arms, in Panton Street, London. He moved to Woolwich in 1839 and lived there until his death at the age of sixty-seven. There is a monument to his memory in the churchyard of St Mary's and St Andrew's.

Darling, Grace Horsely (1815–1842)
St Aidan's Churchyard, Bamburgh, Northumberland, where there is a Gothic shrine with metal colonettes and a recumbent effigy.

Heroine. Famous for the part she played in the rescue of passengers from the Forfarshire steamboat which was wrecked on the rocks off the Farne Islands on 7 September 1838. Her father was the lighthouse keeper on the Farne Island and espied some of the survivors of the boat huddled on a rock. With his daughter's help he launched and rowed a coble and managed to rescue four men and a woman, whom they returned to the lighthouse. Her father then returned to the rock and with the help of two men brought off four more survivors. Grace Darling received much public acclaim for her role in the rescue and was awarded a gold medal from the Humane Society. Subscriptions brought in money but throughout Miss Darling remained unspoiled by the publicity. She died of consumption.

Frobisher, St Martin (c.1535–1594)
St Giles' without Cripplegate, London Wall, City of London.

Explorer and navigator. He was the first British navigator to seek the north-west passage from the Atlantic to the Pacific through the Arctic seas. He is commemorated in Frobisher Bay on Baffin Island. He commanded the *Triumph*, the largest ship in the English fleet, during the battle with the Spanish Armada in 1588. Admiral Lord Howard had divided the fleet into four parts under himself, Drake, Hawkins and Frobisher, who was knighted for valour during the battle.

Fry, Elizabeth (1780–1845)
Friends' Burial Ground, Barking, Greater London.

Prison reformer. She was the daughter of John Gurney of Earlham Hall, Norfolk, a Quaker and banker. In August 1800 she married a London merchant, Joseph Fry. It was not until 1817 that the great work of her life began with the founding of the association for the Improvement of the Female Prisoners in Newgate prison. She soon, mostly through her own exertions, managed to bring about an amelioration in the conditions of the prisoners and her work was then extended throughout Britain. She toured the Continent, and received official permission to visit all the prisons in France.

Grace, W.G. (William Gilbert) (1848–1915)
Beckenham Cemetery, Elmers End Road, Beckenham, Kent (a cemetery plan is near the main gate). A traffic by-pass is planned that might eventually necessitate destruction of the burial ground.

A cricketer whose name came to be hallowed on the cricket pitches of England and wherever else the game is played. His record of scoring 1000s in season most times still stands along with at least two others. Born at Downend near Bristol, he came from a family that was also accomplished at cricket. His career lasted for forty-three years, during which time he scored 54,896 runs, made 126 centuries and took 2876 wickets, making him one of the top all-round players in first-class cricket to this day. He was a 6ft–6in. 'giant', black bearded and full of agility and stamina virtually to the end of his cricketing days. He practised as a surgeon in Bristol for 20 years, having been trained at St Bartholomew's and Westminster Hospitals. He twice played in Australia and also took a team of amateurs to the USA and Canada. Bowler J. C. Shaw of Nottinghamshire is cited as saying, 'I puts the ball where I likes, and Grace, he puts it where he likes'. A memorial gateway at Lords was erected to him in 1923 by the Marylebone Cricket Club, of which he became a member when he was twenty-one years old.

Hammett, James (1811–1891)
St John the Evangelist Church, Tolpuddle, Dorset.

He was the only one of the six Tolpuddle Martyrs to settle here when he returned from Australia after being transported to the penal settlement there. Six farm labourers had formed a local Friendly Society of Agricultural Labourers in an effort to get more pay, but were arrested and accused of administering unlawful oaths, contrary to an Act of 1797. Tried at Dorchester Assizes in 1834, they were all sentenced to penal transportation to Australia. Hammett's grave can represent the other five, who were all given seven-year sentences. They were George Loveless and his brother James, Thomas Standfield and his son John, and James Brine.

Herbert, George Edward Stanhope Molyneux, fifth Earl of Carnarvon (1866–1923)
Beacon Hill, Hampshire. Two miles west of Old Burghclere, just off the A343, the grave is on the top of the 853-ft hill; a stiff climb!

Discoverer of Tutankhamen's tomb, he had been born at Highclere Castle, the family seat of the Carnarvons. A serious automobile accident saw him recuperating in Egypt, where he became interested in archaeology. Financing and participating in the excavations of Howard Carter (1837–1939), antiquities chief at Luxor, they found some minor tombs after five years of digging. In 1922 when they were on the point of ending the search they discovered Tutankhamen's tomb in the Valley of Kings. In the antechamber they found a prodigious quantity of artifacts. The king had been a minor one of the 18th dynasty who died about 1352 BC. Later they found a huge gilded wooden shrine in which the king's mummy had been deposited. Carnarvon was bitten by a mosquito and within a month he had died from blood poisoning. At his wish he was buried on top of Beacon Hill.

Herbert, Mary, Countess of Pembroke (1561–1621)
Salisbury Cathedral, Salisbury, Wiltshire. All the Herberts, earls of Pembroke, were buried in the family vault in the front of the altar (except first- and second-creation first earls). Until the floor surface was renewed in recent years a slab marked the burial location. It was incised: 'Underneath this sable herse, Lies the subject of all verse, Sidney's

sister, Pembroke's mother ...', and it is now mounted on the south wall of the chancel.

Sister of Sir Philip Sidney, the poet and 'jewel in Elizabeth I's crown'. Mary and her brother were 'in perfect accord' and spent their time in literary studies, she being fluent in Latin, Greek and Hebrew. He wrote *The Arcadia* mostly in her presence, dedicating it to her: 'For you, only for you.' She was grief-stricken when he was killed in 1586; her father had also just died. She had married the second Earl of Pembroke in 1577 and, recovering from her grief, she became a generous patron of poets and men of letters, including Ben Jonson and Samuel Daniel, who tutored her son William at Wilton House. There was a theory, now thought unlikely, that Shakepeare addressed his sonnets to her eldest son William who became the third Earl. When her husband died, he left her 'as bare as he could'; there had been disagreement between them in their later married life, it was rumoured. James I, however, was generous to her and granted her Ampthill Park in Bedfordshire, where she built a magnificent mansion.

Hill, Graham (1929–1975)
St Botolph Churchyard, Shenleybury, Hertfordshire.

World Championship racing driver. Graham Hill was the only man to have won the Triple Crown – the World Championship, the Indianapolis 500 and the Le Mans 24 Hour race. In fact he won the World Championship twice and made a record 176 Grand Prix starts. Hill made his Grand Prix debut in 1958 and had only recently retired as a driver when his private plane crashed on to a golf course killing him and his fellow team members.

Hobbs, Sir John Berry, 'Jack' (1882–1963)
Hove Cemetery, Old Shoreham Road, Hove, Sussex.

Cricketer. He is considered to have been the most perfect batsman ever to take part in the English game. His career extended over thirty years, during which he played for the Surrey Cricket Club, and for his country. He was knighted for his services to the game.

Howard, John (1726–1790)
St Paul's Cathedral, London, monument only as he is buried in Russia.

Prison reformer. Having been imprisoned in France during the 1750s he experienced his first taste of prison life. In 1773 he was made Sheriff of Bedford and he began to enquire into the conditions of the prisons within his jurisdiction. This led him to enquire further afield and in 1774 he gave evidence before a House of Commons committee about conditions in the prisons, for which he received the committee's commendation and which led to an immediate act of Parliament to relieve conditions. He then travelled extensively abroad, particularly on the Continent, and died at Dophinovka, near Kherson, in southern Russia and there was buried.

Hoyle, Edmund (1672–1769)
St Marylebone 'Old' Parish Church, Marylebone High Street, London. The site of the old parish church and its graveyard is now marked by the Garden of Rest in Marylebone High Street, which contains a tablet commemorating some of the notable people buried there.

Codifier of the rules of whist. Whilst living in London he supported himself by giving instruction in the game of whist and for the use of his pupils drew up a *Short Treatise* on it, which was printed in November 1742. His authority is established by the phrase 'according to Hoyle', meaning 'on the highest authority'.

Hunt, Sir John, Baron of Llanvair Waterdine (1910–1998)
After cremation at Slough Crematorium, his ashes were scattered on the hills above Llanfair Waterdine (close to the Welsh border).

Explorer and British army officer. John Hunt is best remembered as the leader of the first successful expedition to the summit of Mount Everest. He had taken part in several expeditions to the Himalaya whilst serving with the King's Royal Rifle Corps in India. In 1940 he returned to England and became chief instructor of the Commando Mountain and Snow Warfare School. He was an obvious choice for leader of the 1953 Everest expedition and the summit was reached on 29 May 1953 by Edmund Hilary and Sherpa Tenzing Norgay. Hilary and Hunt were immediately knighted and Hunt was made a life peer in 1966. After retiring from the army, Hunt became the first director of the Duke of Edinburgh Award Scheme.

Jackson, 'Gentleman' John (1769–1845)
Brompton Cemetery, West Brompton, London, where his monument is surmounted by a recumbent lion.

Boxer. He was the English boxing champion from 1795 to 1803 and he opened a boxing academy in Bond Street, London, and numbered Lord Byron among his pupils.

Jones, Claudia Vera (1915–1964)
Highgate Cemetery, London, next to Karl Marx.

Political activist and rights campaigner. Trinidadian-born Claudia Jones emigrated to the slums of Harlem, New York, in 1922. She became active in the Communist Party at a young age and was an active campaigner for civil and women's rights. She became a target of the anti-communist witchhunts in the 1940s and, having been jailed three times, was eventually deported in 1955. Jones decided to travel to England rather than return to Trinidad and joined the Communist Party of Great Britain. She launched and edited the *West Indian Gazette* and was one of the founders of the Notting Hill Carnival after the Notting Hill race riots of 1958. She died on Christmas Eve, 1964.

Laker, James (1922–1986)
Cremated at Putney Vale Cemetery and his ashes were scattered at The Oval cricket ground in South London.

Cricketer. Known as one of the best off-spin bowlers in the game, Laker turned professional in 1947. He was part of the Surrey side that dominated the county cricket championships throughout the 1950s, winning the title in seven consecutive years. He was a *Wisden* Cricketer of the Year in 1952. He is best remembered for the fourth Test against Australia at Old Trafford in 1956 where he was the first cricketer to take all ten wickets in a single Test innings. During this remarkable Test performance he took nineteen wickets for ninety runs, a feat unequalled in the history of the game. At the time of his death, Laker was a BBC television cricket commentator as well as Chairman of Surrey's cricket committee.

Lawrence, Thomas Edward, 'Lawrence of Arabia' (1888–1935)
St Nicholas's Church, Moreton, Dorset.

He was educated at Jesus College, Oxford, became an archaeologist and travelled and excavated in Syria. During the Great War he was one of the British officers sent to help the Sheriff of Mecca in his rebellion against the Turkish Sultan. He gained great influence with the Arabs and entered Damascus with the leading Arab forces in 1918. He recalled his experiences in his celebrated *Seven Pillars of Wisdom*, which was privately printed for limited circulation in 1926, it not being commercially published until 1935. After the War he sought anonymity by joining the Royal Air Force as an aircraftman, taking the name of Ross, but his identity was discovered a few months later and he was forced to

'Lawrence of Arabia' grave, Moreton, Dorset

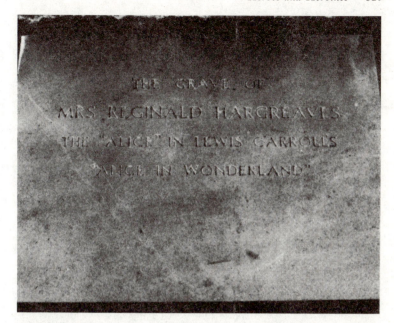

Grave of Alice Liddell, the 'Alice' of *Alice in Wonderland*, St Michael's Church, Lyndhurst, Hampshire

resign. He then joined the Tank Corps as Private T. E. Shaw, but he hated the army as much as he loved the air force and eventually was able to rejoin the Royal Air Force with the help of the Air Chief of Staff, Sir Hugh, later Lord, Trenchard. He was killed in a motor-cycle accident in Dorset.

Liddell, Alice (1852–1934)
St Michael's Church, Lyndhurst, Hampshire.

She was the original for Alice in Lewis Carroll's *Alice's Adventures in Wonderland*. Being the daughter of the Dean of Christchurch, Oxford, she met Charles Dodgson (Lewis Carroll) whilst he was lecturing in mathematics and he used to tell her the stories of Alice's adventures when they walked together.

Livingstone, Dr David (1813–1873)
Westminster Abbey, London, in the centre of the Nave.

Scottish explorer. He discovered the course of the Zambesi River, the Victoria Falls and Lake Nyasa, now Lake Malawi. He roused public opinion against the slave trade. Whilst exploring in Africa he was believed lost but was discovered by Sir Henry Morton Stanley, then a journalist on the *New York Herald*, at Ujiji on 13 October 1871. Together they explored Lake Tanganyika. Livingstone died in Africa and his body was borne to the coast by bearers, shipped to London, and buried in the Abbey eleven months after his death.

Lord, Thomas (1757–1832)
St John the Evangelist Churchyard, West Meon, Hampshire.

Sportsman. He is remembered as the founder of Lord's Cricket Ground, which took his name. He had, as ground-keeper for a London club, started a cricket ground on the site of the present-day Dorset Square, but in 1814 he moved to the present site of Lord's.

Matthews, Stanley (1915–2000)
Ashes interred under the pitch at the Britannia Stadium, Stoke-on-Trent.

Footballer, nicknamed 'the Wizard of Dribble'. Stanley Matthews began playing for his local club, Stoke City, as a winger in 1931. It would be the first and last club that he would play for professionally and he became its President in 1990. He won his first of 54 England caps in 1935. In 1937 he scored a hat trick for England against Czechoslovakia when his team were reduced to ten men. He also helped England to their 6–3 win against Germany in the Berlin Olympic Stadium – the team had been forced to give the Nazi salute.

During the Second World War, Matthews and his wife moved to Blackpool where he opened a small hotel. He played football for Blackpool as a guest during this time and was transferred to the club in 1947 for a fee of £11,500. The following year Blackpool made it to the FA Cup Final, where they lost to Manchester United but Matthews was voted Footballer of the Year. In 1951 he again played in the FA Cup Final where Blackpool lost to Newcastle United. In 1953 it was third time lucky as they beat Bolton Wanderers to the title.

Named as the first European Footballer of the Year in 1956 he stayed at Blackpool until 1961, when he returned to Stoke City at the age of forty-six. He helped Stoke win promotion to the First Division in 1963 and was again voted Footballer of the Year. Stanley Matthews was knighted in 1965.

Grave of Thomas Lord, St John the Evangelist Churchyard, West Meon, Hampshire

Moody, Richard Clement (1813–1887)
St Peter's Churchyard, Bournemouth, Dorset; up the south-east steps
and near to large white tomb of the Shelley-Godwins.

Founder of the town of New Westminster in British Columbia,
Canada and first governor of the Falkland Islands. He was born at
Barbados, became a colonel in the Royal Engineers and was sent to
British Columbia in 1887 as Lieutenant Governor under Sir Edward
Bulwer Lytton.

Moore, Robert Frederick Chelsea, 'Bobby' (1941–1993)
Garden of Remembrance under a large magnolia tree, City of London
Cemetery, Manor Park, London.

Footballer. He was born in Barking in 1941 and was discovered
playing football on an East London school playing field. He went on to
captain England a total of ninety times, most memorably to World Cup
victory in 1966. At the World Cup finals in Mexico four years later he
was famously accused of stealing a gold bracelet from a hotel jewellery
shop, was arrested and only declared innocent many weeks later.

In domestic football, Moore made his debut for West Ham United in
September 1958 and with them went on to win the FA Cup in 1964 and
The European Cup Winners' Cup the following year. He left West Ham
in 1973 to play his last three seasons for Fulham.

Nash, 'Beau' (Richard) (1674–1762)
Bath Abbey-church, Bath, Avon, under pew 33 in the nave; plaque on
wall in aisle.

Man of fashion who became known as 'the King of Bath', where as
Master of Ceremonies from 1704 he made the town a centre of attraction
for the society of his day from royalty to gamblers. He himself had
previously made a living by gambling. Born at Swansea, he was educated
at Jesus College, Oxford, and in 1693 entered the Middle Temple.

Nightingale, Florence (1820–1910)
St Margaret's Churchyard, East Wellow, Hampshire; only her initials,
'FN', appear on her tombstone.

Nurse and pioneer of nursing reform. During the Crimean War of
1854–1855, she organized a nursing service to relieve the suffering of the
war wounded. She earned herself the name of 'the lady with the lamp'
from her grateful soldiers. Despite a great deal of initial Establishment
opposition her nursing system was adopted and developed throughout

Florence Nightingale, photograph by H. Heving

the world. She was deemed to have 'raised the art of nursing from a menial employment to an honoured vocation'. In 1907 she received the Order of Merit, the first woman on whom it was bestowed. Her funeral service was held in St Paul's Cathedral.

Grave of Florence Nightingale, St Margaret's Churchyard, East Wellow, Hampshire

Pankhurst, Emmeline (1858–1928)
Brompton Cemetery, West Brompton, London.

Suffragette. She was the leader of the militant movement for women's suffrage. With her daughters Christabel and Sylvia she organized the Women's Social and Political Union. She was constantly arrested for civil disobedience but resorted to hunger strikes during internment. At the outbreak of the Great War the campaign of civil disobedience ended and she worked tirelessly recruiting women for munitions work. She travelled to the United States several times to gain support for her campaign. After the war she went to Canada but returned in 1926 and joined the Conservative Party. She died in London on 14 June 1928 shortly after the passing of the second Representation of the People Act which gave full and equal suffrage to men and women.

Parr, Thomas (c.1483–1635)
Westminster Abbey, London, in the South Transept now known as 'Poets' Corner'.

He was said to be 152 years old when he died and to have lived in the reigns of ten sovereigns, being reputedly born when Edward IV was still on the throne. His portrait was painted by Sir Anthony van Dyck. For most of his life he lived in Shropshire, where he was born, but in 1635 he was brought to London by the Earl of Arundel so that 'Old Parr', as he was known, could be presented to the King. The change of air affected him and he died shortly afterwards at Lord Arundel's house in London. The King ordered a post-mortem and Dr William Harvey found that his internal organs were in an unusually perfect state and his cartilages unossified.

Peel, John (1776–1854)
St Kentigern's Churchyard, Caldbeck, Cumbria.

Huntsman. His hunting prowess was enormous and his knowledge of the Cumbrian countryside faultless. As a young man he eloped with a Miss White and married her at Gretna Green. The marriage was extremely happy. The ballad, 'D'ye ken John Peel', was written by his friend, John Woodcock Graves, and happened by chance. One evening Graves and Peel were planning a hunting expedition when Graves's daughter asked whether they knew the words of an old Cumberland tune, 'Bonnie Annie'. Graves promptly wrote out the verses of 'D'ye ken John Peel', setting them to the tune of the traditional air.

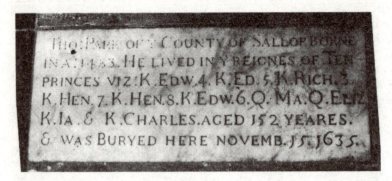

Gravestone of Thomas Parr, Westminster Abbey, London, in 'Poets' Corner'

Pocahontas (c.1595–1617)
St George's Church, Gravesend, Kent.

Daughter of Powhattan, over-king of the Indian tribe in Virginia. In 1607 she was credited with having interceded with her father to save the life of Captain John Smith, who had been captured by the Indians. Her plea was granted. In his initial account, Captain Smith made no mention of Pocahontas's intercession, first mention being made when he re-wrote his account in 1622. What is certain, however, is that from 1608 onwards Pocahontas was a frequent visitor to Jamestown, was fond of the local children, and acted as a kind of go-between for her father and the settlers. In 1612 she was herself held hostage for the return of some prisoners her father had taken. Shortly afterwards she became a Christian, taking the name of Rebecca, and married John Rolfe, a settler. In 1616 she visited London and became a great favourite at court, especially with the Queen, Anne of Denmark. She died at Gravesend as she was about to embark to return to America.

Raleigh, Sir Walter (c.1552–1618)
St Margaret's Church, Westminster, London. His decapitated body lies buried before the altar, his head being interred at West Horsley in Surrey. The west window contains a full-length figure of Sir Walter Raleigh spreading his cloak.

Explorer and writer. He rose to prominence at the court of Queen Elizabeth I, legend having it that he came to the Queen's notice by spreading his cloak over a muddy patch for her to walk upon. In 1580 he helped to put down the Irish rebellion, and in 1584 began his colonization of Virginia. He was responsible for the introduction of tobacco and potatoes to England. He did not find favour with James I on his accession and was sent to the Tower, where he languished for many years. During that time he wrote his *History of the World*. He was released in 1615 to lead an expedition to the Orinoco, using the lure of treasure in his bargaining with the King. The expedition was a dismal failure and also brought the death of Raleigh's son. On his return he was executed. His wife is believed to have had his head embalmed and to have carried it with her until her own death.

Ramsey, Sir Alfred Ernest, 'Alf' (1920–1999)
Old Ipswich Cemetery, Ipswich, Suffolk.

Football player and manager. Alf Ramsey was the manager of the 1966 World Cup winning English team. It was the greatest achievement in a remarkably successful career both on and off the pitch. Ramsey turned professional in 1944, playing for Southampton FC, and made his international debut for England in 1948. In 1949 he transferred to second division Tottenham Hotspur and the team won their league the following year and became champions of the first division the year after that. He also won the first division as a manager with Ipswich Town, a team he had taken over when they were only in the Third Division. He was manager of the England team 1963–1974 and was knighted in 1967 a year after their World Cup success.

Repton, Humphrey (1752–1818)
St Michael's Church, Aylsham, Norfolk.

Landscape gardener. After an unsuccessful attempt to be first a merchant, then involving himself in the postal service, as well as a brief spell as deputy-secretary to the Lord Lieutenant of Ireland, he decided to pursue landscape gardening to earn himself a living. He was guided by Lancelot Brown but gradually discarded Brown's formalism. His first major work was at Cobham in Kent in about 1790 and thereafter he laid out Russell Square and altered Kensington Gardens in London. He was the author of several works on gardening including *Sketches and Hints on Landscape Gardening*, 1794, as well as on local history and art.

Seacole, Mary (1805–1856)
St Mary's Catholic Cemetery, Harrow Road, London.

Nurse. For her services during the Crimean War, Mary Seacole became the first black woman to make her mark on British public life. Unlike Florence Nightingale, however, she has been almost forgotten until recently. She was born in Kingston, Jamaica, to a Scottish army officer and a practitioner of traditional medicine. Mary Seacole learnt her nursing skills from her mother and from trips to the Bahamas, Haiti, Cuba and Panama. She had encountered cholera epidemics in Jamaica and Panama, so when she heard that British soldiers were dying from cholera in Crimea she offered her services to the British Army. Her offers of help were rejected on three occasions but Seacole decided to fund herself. Whereas Nightingale's hospital was several miles from the front, Seacole established her British Hotel just a few miles from the battlefield and often treated her patients where they fell. Mary Seacole returned to England after the war in 1856. She hoped to work as a nurse in India but died in London on 14 May 1856.

Smith, Captain John (1580–1631)
Church of the Holy Sepulchre without Newgate, Holborn, London.

Adventurer and soldier who was saved from death by the Red Indian Princess Pocahontas after he was captured by the Powhatan Indians in December 1607 during an expedition to Virginia. On later expeditions he was captured by both the French and pirates, but escaped from each. A history of his adventures is recorded on a brass plate (a copy of the original which is no longer identifiable) on the south wall of the choir.

Stanley, Sir Henry Morton (1841–1904)
St Michael's Churchyard, Pirbright, Surrey, where a granite monolith above his grave bears the inscription, 'Henry Morton Stanley, 1841–1904,' with his African name 'Bula Matari' and, as an epitaph, one word, 'Africa'.

Born at Denbigh of English parents, he had a deprived childhood and went as a cabin boy to the United States where, in New Orleans, he took the name of the merchant for whom he worked, Henry Morton Stanley. He became a naturalized American citizen and fought in the Civil War on the Confederate side and was captured. He returned to England briefly, was rejected by his mother, and enlisted in the American navy in 1864. After that he became a journalist, eventually going to the *New York Herald* as a correspondent. He accompanied the British expedition to Abyssinia in 1867–1868 as a correspondent for the *Herald* and witnessed the fall of Magdala. He then received a roving commission from the newspaper and travelled extensively, until he was ordered to go and find Livingstone. They met at Ujiji on 10 November 1871, the young Stanley greeting the veteran Livingstone with the words, 'Dr

Livingstone, I presume'. With Livingstone he navigated the shores of Lake Tanganyika and thereafter, having completed lecture and other tours, he returned to Africa from 1874 to 1877. This expedition led to the founding of the Congo Free State in 1879 and to the partition of hitherto unappropriated regions of Africa between the western states of Europe. He became a close friend and associate of King Leopold II of The Belgians, and, after once more becoming a British subject, was knighted in 1899 in recognition of his services to Africa. For five years he was Liberal Member of Parliament for Lambeth, from 1895 to 1900.

Williams, Sir George (d. 1905)
The crypt at St Paul's Cathedral, London.

Founder of the YMCA. George Williams formed the first Young Men's Christian Association in St Paul's Churchyard, London, in 1844. Fifty years later this anniversary was marked by Williams receiving a knighthood from Queen Victoria and the Freedom of the City of London. The YMCA Movement has become one of the biggest Christian charities in the world, with over 30 million members in over 120 countries.

Younghusband, Sir Francis Edward (1863–1942)
Parish Churchyard (previously St Peter ad Vincula before its destruction by fire), Lytchett Minster, Dorset. There is a bas-relief of Lhasa on his headstone.

Soldier, explorer, diplomat and mystic who was born at Murree, India. After receiving a commission in the 1st (King's) Dragoon Guards at the age of nineteen – he had graduated from the Royal Military College at Sandhurst – he went on expeditions in the Himalayas, the Afghan border and Manchuria. From Peking he made an epic overland journey to India, becoming the first European to cross the Gobi desert. Appointed to the Indian foreign department in 1889, he was exploring in the northern part of India when he met a Russian patrol and was told to leave Russian territory. It was an area between that country, China and Afghanistan that had never been officially demarcated. Lord Salisbury, however, later received a Russian apology. As a man sensitive to the eastern religions he was able to penetrate into the then hostile territory of Tibet and sign a treaty in that country's mysterious capital of Lhasa. After retirement, Young-husband became the first chairman of the Mount Everest Committee and a founder of the Himalaya Club. He was awarded the Founder's Medal of the Royal Geographical Society and had been correspondent in Rhodesia and the Transvaal for *The Times*. He set down his religious philosophy in two books, *Life in the Stars* (1927) and *The Living Universe* (1933), and in 1936 he founded the World Congress of Faiths. Despite his beliefs in, and support of, mystic eastern religions, he chose to be buried in a Christian grave.

Chapter 13
Outlaws and Criminals (including highwaymen and killers)

Buckingham. Henry Stafford, 2nd Duke of (1st creation) (1454?–1483)
St Peter's Church, Britford, Wiltshire; in the chancel.

Is believed to have been the person who suggested the murder of the two Princes in the Tower to Richard, Duke of Gloucester. Buckingham married Catherine Woodville, sister of Edward IV's queen, but after Edward IV's death in 1483 he supported the claims of Edward's brother Richard to the throne and opposed those of Edward's son, the thirteen-year-old Edward VI. Edward and his brother were imprisoned in the Tower of London and put to death and Richard was crowned in Edward's place. Richard has been accused of the murder of the two Princes and Buckingham of putting the idea into Richard's mind. Buckingham very quickly turned against Richard. Soon after the new king's coronation he led a rising in the West Country in support of Henry, Earl of Richmond, later Henry VII. The rising failed abysmally and Buckingham, a hunted man, took refuge in a hut near Wem. What gave him away was the richness and unusual nature of the provisions that were seen being taken to the hut by Ralph Bannaster, his retainer who, when Buckingham was discovered, was quite ready to accept the reward. The Duke was tried at Salisbury on Saturday, 1 November 1483, and beheaded in the market place on the Sunday, his vast estates being confiscated. There is some doubt whether his head was buried with his remains or not.

Burgess, Guy Francis de Moncy (1910–1963)
St John the Evangelist Church, West Meon, Hampshire, ashes sprinkled on his mother's grave at night-time ceremony.

English traitor, a spy for Russia who was a member of the ring of four who met at Cambridge University (with Blunt, Philby and Maclean). He fled to Moscow with Maclean (whom see) in 1951 after Philby warned them of their impending arrest. Philby followed them twelve years later. They were all senior members of the British security service MI5, Burgess being also with the BBC during most of the war. The son of a naval officer, he had been educated at Eton.

Duval, Claude (1643–1670)
St Paul's Church, Covent Garden, London, in the centre aisle under a
stone with the epitaph:

> Here lies Du Vall: Reader if male thou art,
> Look to thy purse: if female to thy heart.

Highwayman. He came to England from Normandy after the
Restoration of Charles II in 1660, in attendance on the Duke of Richmond. He soon joined the ranks of highwaymen and became notorious
not only for his gallantry to ladies but for his daring exploits. He was
captured and tried at the Old Bailey and sentenced to be hanged at
Tyburn. Many ladies apparently interceded for his life but the King,
Charles II, refused. After his death his body lay in state at the Tangier
Tavern in St Giles's and so many people visited it amid much disorder
that the exhibition was stopped on a judge's order. It is also claimed that
he was buried in St Giles-in-the-Fields, Holborn.

Hood, Robin (c.12th and 13th centuries)
Kirklees Abbey, Mirfield, Yorkshire. The grave is available for viewing
only on Saturday afternoons, and even then it is uncertain. Permission
should be obtained from the Estate Office, Kirklees Estate, Mirfield,
Yorkshire. Proposed development might change this availability.

Legendary outlaw. Various attempts have been made to authenticate
his life but none has been successful. He was mentioned in *Piers
Plowman*, which says that the 'Rymes of Robyn Hood and Randolph erle
of Chestre' were popular with the English peasantry about 1377. He has
had many guises, both in myth and in drama and fiction, but one legend
has it that when ill, he went to Kirklees Abbey to have his blood let by
the Prioress, where he was allowed to bleed to death at the suggestion of
Sir Roger of Doncaster. He is said to have called for his bow as he lay
dying, shot an arrow through the window, and asked to be buried at the
spot where it landed.

Jack the Ripper? Druitt, John Montague, Prime suspect (1857–1888).
Wimborne Cemetery, Wimborne Minster, Dorset.

According to Sir Melville Macnaghten, Chief Constable of Scotland
Yard in 1889, Druitt was The Ripper. At least fourteen Scotland Yard
officials were involved. In the final version of Macnaghten's report not
released until 1966, he says: 'Personally and after much careful and

deliberate consideration' he exonerated other suspects and '(F)rom private information I have little doubt that his own family suspected this man of being the Whitechapel murderer, it was alleged that he was sexually insane.' Druitt, the son of a prosperous Wimborne surgeon, was a barrister and had been quite a brilliant student at Winchester College and New College, Oxford University. He was also a good cricketer; Winchester first eleven and a member of the Dorset County Cricket Club. He was found drowned as an apparent act of suicide in the Thames on 31 December 1888 by a Thames waterman. In 1973 a carefully correlated list appeared in *The Cricketer* of his cricketing activities and the murders, and although hard evidence against Druitt is less than for other suspects, there is the strongest of recognition that Scotland Yard both at the time and now believe Druitt was Jack the Ripper.

Jack the Ripper Victims:
Nichols, (née Walker) Mary Ann (Polly), the Ripper's first victim murdered 31 August, buried 6 September 1888. Age forty-two years, flat bronze marker in ground. City of London Cemetery, Manor Park.
Chapman, Annie, buried 14 September 1888, Manor Park cemetery 'in secret', grave number seventy-eight.
Stride, (née Gulafsdotter) Elizabeth, born Gothenburg, Sweden 1843, murdered 30 September 1888. East London Cemetery, West Ham, white marble 'frame grave', no headstone. Attendants can help locate if available.
Eddowes, Catherine, born Wolverhampton 1842, buried City of London Cemetery, Manor Park, 8 October 1888. Her grave is only a few yards away from that of Mary Ann Nichols.
Kelly, Mary Jane, born Limerick, Ireland, twenty-five years old, buried November 19, 1888, Leytonstone, St Patrick's Roman Catholic cemetery, row 67, grave 16 (marker stolen).
There were thirteen other alleged victims.

Little, John, 'Little John' (c.1230)
St Michael's Churchyard, Hathersage, Derbyshire.
One of Robin Hood's two lieutenants, the other being Will Scarlett. A grave of a John Little at Hathersage was opened in 1728 to reveal a thirty-two-inch thighbone, indicating he must have been about seven feet tall. A longbow, reputed to be that of Little John, is on display at the Cannon Hall Museum, near Barnsley, Yorkshire.

Grave of John Little, 'Little John', St Michael's Churchyard, Hathersage, Derbyshire

Maclean, Donald Duart (1913–1983)
Church of the Holy Trinity, Penn, Buckinghamshire, in family plot, ashes in urn decorated with hammer and sickle.

English traitor, a spy for Russia, who was recruited by Burgess (whom see) and Anthony Blunt (1907–1982; cremated in London), of the quartet of spies (including Harold Adrian Russell and 'Kim' Philby (1911–1988), buried in Moscow who were all Cambridge University students in the thirties. They became senior officers in MI5, the British security service. Maclean and Burgess escaped to Russia in 1951 after being warned of their pending arrest by Philby. Maclean was the son of a Liberal cabinet minister.

Scathelock, William, 'Will Scarlett' (*c.*12th and 13th centuries)
St Mary's Churchyard, Blidworth, Nottinghamshire.

One of Robin Hood's two lieutenants, the other being Little John. He was reputedly left behind, according to the manuscript of Bishop Percy, when Robin Hood and Little John went to Kirklees Abbey for Robin to be bled for 'the sickness that had come upon him'. In the village of

Blidworth there is a house which is rumoured to have been where Maid Marion lived before her marriage to Robin Hood. Scarlett's gravestone marker is thought to be from the pinnacle of the church tower.

Sheppard, John, 'Jack' (1702–1724)
St Martin-in-the-Fields, St Martin's Place, London.

Robber. Brought up in the Bishopsgate workhouse and later apprenticed as a carpenter. He fell in with Elizabeth Lyon, notorious as 'Edgeworth Bess' for her lack of morals. He lived with her and took to crime to gratify her tastes. He was arrested as a runaway apprentice and from then on he says 'I fell to robbing almost every one that stood in my way'. He twice escaped from jail and in mid-1724 was responsible for an almost daily robbery in or near London. He was captured and tried at the Old Bailey but with the help of Edgeworth Bess managed to escape the condemned cell. In September he was caught again and imprisoned in Newgate where he was chained to the floor. But he escaped up the chimney. Once more he was captured, hopelessly drunk, in the Clare Market tavern and was hanged at Tyburn on 16 November 1724. He was then not quite twenty-two. He was the hero of a novel by Harrison Ainsworth, entitled *Jack Sheppard*, 1839.

Turpin, Richard, 'Dick' (1706–1739)
St George's Churchyard, York, Yorkshire.

Highwayman. Born in Hempstead in Essex, he was apprenticed to a butcher in Whitechapel. He was caught stealing cattle and joined a gang of smugglers and deer-stealers who carried out some brutal robberies in Essex. He entered into partnership with the highwayman, Tom King, but inadvertently killed King when he tried to shoot the constable trying to arrest his friend. Before he died King must have given away some of Turpin's haunts, but he managed to evade arrest and got away to York, the journey presumably the basis for his 'famous ride to York' on his horse, Black Bess, of which much has been written. He was later apprehended in York and tried for horse-stealing, for which he was hanged at York on 7 April 1739, aged thirty-three. His body was rescued from the clutches of the surgeon by the mob and buried in St George's Churchyard.

Wilson, Charles (1932–1990)
Streatham Cemetery, Garratt Lane, Tooting, south London.

Train robber, one of the five members of the gang who stole

£5 million in the Great Train Robbery of 1963, a daring raid on the Glasgow to Euston train. Wilson was murdered in Spain because of suspected cheating in a drug-dealing activity. He had served about one-third of his prison sentence for his part in the robbery, being released in 1978, after which he lived in a luxury villa in Marbella where he was murdered.

Pinner Cemetery

PLACES OF EXECUTION

Historical places of execution exist all over England. Tyburn (the Tyburn Tree, named from the small river that flowed here; now underground) saw executions from 1196 to 1759. A small stone slab marking where the triangular gallows stood is on a traffic island at Marble Arch, London. There are no memorials here. Smithfield ('West' Smithfield), another execution place, where martyrs were burned, Wat Tyler (d. 1381) slain and Ann Askew (1521–1546) (Protestant martyr of Grimsby, turned out by her husband, tortured after attempting divorce and burned for heresy), saw numerous memorial plaques placed on the outside wall of St Bartholomew's Hospital.

Sir William Wallace, 'Braveheart' (c 1274–1305) was hanged, drawn, beheaded, quartered and his pieces sent to Newcastle, Berwick, Stirling and Perth with the intention that they discourage others from continuing the struggle for Scottish independence. After winning the Battle of Stirling Bridge (1297) he was elected governor of Scotland. After the Battle of Falkirk (1298) where he was beaten by Edward I Wallace went to France. Eventually caught, at first unrecognised, near Glasgow it is said, he was taken to London where he was tried in Westminster Hall and condemned to death.

A splendid memorial to him was placed on St Bartholomew's Hospital wall.

Geographical check-list by county

For speed of reference, this lists counties alphabetically rather than by geographical propinquity, as is sometimes done. But it is pointed out, especially for visitors from overseas, that three or four counties can often be visited within a relatively short distance, and convenient groupings can be made by using a map of England that clearly delineates county boundaries.

A few burial locations listed in the main entries are no longer physically marked. This applies mostly to London churches. St Martin-in-the-Fields, for example, was a burial place for thousands of people from all walks of life from the year 1222, burials being registered after 1525. When the old church was torn down in the sixteenth century, more than 3,000 coffins were cleared from the vaults. In 1853 the churchyard, which used to extend across to where the National Gallery now stands, and in other directions too, was also cleared of graves by an Act of Parliament. Some of the coffins were claimed by relatives and reinterred in St Martin's Cemetery, Camden Town. One of the coffins thus discovered was that of Dr John Hunter; it was transferred to an honoured position next to Ben Jonson's mortal remains in Westminster Abbey.

St Paul's Cathedral is another place where some famous burial sites are no longer marked; and at Glastonbury Abbey ruins, where several kings other than Arthur were buried, exact grave locations are no longer known. Even so, the knowledge that an honoured and famous historical person was buried there (in the case of Queen Boadicea, for instance, under an otherwise prosaic railway platform) imbues a particular area with a powerful attraction.

This check-list will help you to plan your route to such places. You will find the relevant page numbers of each location in the general Index on page 363. A query in brackets indicates a claimed, but not authenticated, burial place.

AVON
Bath, Abbey Church: Thomas Robert Malthus; Richard ('Beau') Nash. *Walcot Cemetery*: William Beckford; Fanny Burney, Mme d'Arblay.

BERKSHIRE
Caversham Crematorium: Lonnie Donegan. *Reading Abbey (ruins)*: Henry I. *Windsor Castle, St George's Chapel*: Charles I; Edward IV; Edward VII; Queen

Elizabeth the Queen Mother; George III; George IV; George V; George VI; Henry VI; Henry VIII; Princess Margaret; Queen Jane Seymour; William IV. *Windsor Home Park, Frogmore, Royal Cemetery*: Edward VIII; Duchess of Windsor. *Royal Mausoleum*: Prince Albert; Queen Victoria.

BUCKINGHAMSHIRE

Beaconsfield, Roman Catholic Cemetery: Gilbert Keith Chesterton. *St Mary and All Saints Church*: Edmund Burke; Edmund Waller. *Chalfont St Giles, St Giles' Church*: Bertram Mills. *Chalfont St Giles, Jordans, Quaker Meeting House*: William Penn. *Denham, St Mary's Churchyard*: Sir John Mills. *Great Missenden, Church of St Peter and St Paul*: Roald Dahl. *Hughenden, St Michael's Churchyard*: Benjamin Disraeli, 1st Earl of Beaconsfield. *Little Marlow, Town Cemetery*: Edgar Wallace. *Penn, Church of the Holy Trinity Churchyard*: Donald Duart Maclean (*ashes in urn*). *Stoke Poges, St Giles' Churchyard*: Thomas Gray. *Upton, Slough, St Laurence's Church*: Sir William Herschel.

CAMBRIDGESHIRE

Cambridge, Sidney Sussex College: Oliver Cromwell (head only). *Cambridge, Christ's College*: Alexander Todd (ashes scattered in the master's garden). *Cambridge, Parish of the Ascension Burial Ground*: G. E. Moore; Ludwig Wittgenstein. *Ely Cathedral*: St Ethelreda. *Little Gidding, St John's Churchyard*: Nicholas Ferrar. *Peterborough Cathedral*: Catherine of Aragon. *Wicken Fen, St Laurence's Church*: Henry Cromwell.

CHESHIRE

Chester Cathedral: Ranulf Higden. *Knutsford, Brook Street Chapel*: Elizabeth Gaskell. *Port Sunlight, Christ Church*: Lord Leverhulme, William Hesketh Lever.

CORNWALL

Carbis Bay Cemetery: Dame Barbara Hepworth. *Fowey, St Nicholas's Church*: Sir Arthur Quiller-Couch. *Trebetherick (north Cornwall), St Enodoc's Churchyard*: Sir John Betjeman.

CUMBRIA

Caldbeck, St Kentigern's Churchyard: John Peel. *Coniston, St Andrew's Churchyard*: John Ruskin. *Dalton-in-Furness, St Mary's Church*: George Romney. *Grasmere, St Oswald's Churchyard*: William Wordsworth. *Grasmere, Town Cemetery*: Dr William Archibald Spooner. *Keswick, St John's Churchyard*: Hugh Walpole. *Lanercost Priory*: Thomas Addison. *Nr Penrith, Dacre Parish Churchyard*: Willie Whitelaw.

DERBYSHIRE
Ault Hucknall, St John the Baptist Church: Thomas Hobbes. *Chatsworth Estate, Edensor village Churchyard*: 11th Duke of Devonshire. *Chesterfield, Trinity Church*: George Stephenson. *Cromford, St Mary's Church*: Sir Richard Arkwright. *Derby, Cathedral of All Saints*: Henry Cavendish. *Hathersage, St Michael's Churchyard*: John Little, ('Little John'). *Kedleston, All Saints' Church*: George Curzon, 1st Marquess of Kedleston. *Repton, St Wystan's Church*: Ethelbald I.

DEVONSHIRE
Exeter Cathedral: Bishop Leofric. *Hartland, St Nectan's Church*: John Lane. *Lew Trenchard, St Peter's Churchyard*: Sabine Baring-Gould. *North Tawton, St Peter's Church*: Ted Hughes (ashes scattered on Dartmoor). *Paignton Cemetery*: Oliver Heaviside. *St Budeaux, Plymouth, St Budiana's Church*: Sir Ferdinando Gorges.

DORSET
Bournemouth, St Peter's Churchyard: William Godwin; Mary Wollstonecraft Shelley; Percy Bysshe Shelley (heart); Mary Wollstonecraft (Mrs Godwin); Richard Clement Moody. *Bournemouth, Wimborne Road Cemetery*: Evelyn Baring, 1st Earl of Cromer; John Nelson Darby. *Broadstone, Town Cemetery*: Alfred Russel Wallace. *Corscombe, in private field*: Thomas Hollis. *Dorchester, Holy Trinity Church*: John White. *Kingston, Old Church graveyard*: John Scott, 1st Earl of Eldon. *Lytchett Minster, Parish Churchyard*: Sir Francis Edward Younghusband. *Mappowder, St Peter and Paul Churchyard*: Theodore Francis Powys. *Morton St Nicholas's Church*: T. E. Lawrence. *Shaftesbury Abbey (ruins)*: Edward the Martyr. *Sherborne, Abbey Church*: Ethelbald; Ethelbert; Sir Thomas Wyat. *Stinsford, St Michael's Churchyard*: Cecil Day-Lewis; Thomas Hardy (heart). *Swyre Head, near Chaldon Herring, St Mary's Church*: Llewelyn Powys (*ashes under monument*). *Tarrant Crawford, St Mary's Church*: Richard Poore, Bishop of Salisbury (body). *Tolpuddle, St John the Evangelist Churchyard*: James Hammett. *Wareham, Lady St Mary's Church*: Edward the Martyr(?). *Wimborne Minster, Minster Church*: John Beaufort, 1st Duke of Somerset; Ethelred I. *Wimborne St Giles, St Giles' Church*: Anthony Ashley Cooper, 7th Earl of Shaftesbury. *Winterborne Came, St Peter's Churchyard*: William Barnes. *Worth Matravers, St Nicholas Churchyard*: Leslie James Banks.

DURHAM, COUNTY
Durham Cathedral: The Venerable Bede; St Cuthbert; Ralph Neville, 1st Earl of Westmorland. *Houghton-le-Spring, St Michael and All Angel's Church*: Bernard Gilpin.

ESSEX
East Horndon, near Billericay, All Saints' Church: Anne Boleyn (heart?). *Hempstead, St Andrew's Church*: Sir Eliab Harvey; William Harvey. *Waltham Abbey*: Harold II.

GLOUCESTERSHIRE
Berkeley, St Mary's Church: Edward Jenner. *Daylesford, St Peter's Church*: Warren Hastings. *Gloucester Cathedral*: Edward II; Robert II, Duke of Normandy. *Presbury, Priory Road Cemetery*: Brian Jones. *Sudeley Castle, Winchcombe*: Queen Catherine Parr.

HAMPSHIRE
Beacon Hill, near Old Burghclere: George Edward Stanhope Molyneaux Herbert, 5th Earl of Carnarvon. *Binsted, Holy Cross Churchyard*: Field-Marshal Viscount Montgomery of Alamein. *Catherington, All Saint's Church*: Charles John Kean; Sir Charles Napier. *East Wellow St Margaret's Churchyard*: Florence Nightingale. *Eversley, St Mary's Church*: Charles Kingsley. *Exbury, St Catherine's Churchyard*: William Mitford. *Farnborough, Abbey Church of St Michael*: Napoleon III. *Fordingbridge, Town Cemetery*: Augustus Edwin John. *Hamble, St Andrew's Churchyard*: Sir Edwin Alliot Verdon-Roe. *Highcliffe, St Mark's Churchyard*: Harry Gordon Selfridge. *Hursley Church*: Richard Cromwell. *All Saint's Churchyard*: John Keble. *Little Somborne, Redundant Churchyard, near King's Somborne*: Sir Thomas Octave Murdoch Sopwith. *Lymington, Sir Thomas the Apostle Churchyard*: Caroline Ann Bowles (Mrs Robert Southey). *Lyndhurst, St Michael's Church*: Alice Liddell ('Alice in Wonderland'). *Micheldever, St Mary's Church*: Sir Francis Baring. *Minstead All Saint's Churchyard*: Sir Arthur Conan Doyle. *Old Alresford, St Mary's Church*: George Brydges Rodney, 1st Baron. *Otterbourne, St Matthew's Churchyard*: Charlotte Mary Yonge. *Petersfield, St Lawrence Roman Catholic Church*: Sir Alec Guinness. *Portsmouth, Royal Garrison Church*: Sir Charles James Napier. *Portsmouth, St Thomas' Cathedral*: Sir John Kempthorne. *Romsey, Romsey Abbey Church*: Earl Mountbatten of Burma. *Selborne, St Mary's Churchyard*: Gilbert White. *Southampton, Old Cemetery*: George Saintsbury. *Titchfield, St Peter's Church*: Henry Wriothesley, 3rd Earl of Southampton. *West Meon, St John the Evangelist Churchyard*: Guy Francis de Moncy Burgess (ashes); Thomas Lord. *Winchester Cathedral*: Jane Austen; Henry Beaufort; Canute; Egbert; Ethelwulf; Earl Godwin; St Swithin; William of Wykeham. *Whitchurch Churchyard*: Alfred Denning. *Winchester College Chapel, in the Garth*: Archibald Wavell, 1st Earl Wavell. *Winchester, St Bartholomew's Church: Hyde Street and Hyde Abbey ruins?*: Alfred the Great. *Winchester, 'New Minister'*: Edward the Elder; Hardicanute. *'Old Minister'*: Edred; Edwy.

HEREFORD AND WORCESTER
Evesham, Abbey Ruins: Simon of Montfort, Earl of Leicester. *Great Malvern Cemetery*: Johanna Maria ('Jenny') Lind. *Hereford Cathedral*: St Thomas de Cantelupe. *Little Malvern, St Wulstan's Churchyard*: Sir Edward Elgar. *Ridge, St Margaret's Church*: Field Marshall Earl Alexander of Tunis. *West Malvern, St James's Churchyard*: Peter Mark Roget. *Worcester Cathedral*: King John; Stanley Baldwin.

HERTFORDSHIRE
Ayot St Lawrence, Shaw's Corner: George Bernard Shaw. *Bushey Jewish Cemetery*: Frankie Vaughan. *Camfield Place (private residence)*: Dame Barbara Cartland. *Harpenden, Church of St Nicholas*: Eric Morecambe. *Hertingfordbury Church*: William Cowper, 1st Earl. *King's Langley, St Mary's Dominican Friary (ruins)*: Piers Gaveston, Earl of Cornwall. *St Albans Cathedral*: St Alban; Donald Coggan; Thomas De La Mare; Robert Runcie. *St Albans, St Michael's Church*: Francis Bacon. *Shenleybury, Former Churchyard of St Botolph*: Graham Hill. *Thunbridge Parish Churchyard*: Sir Nigel Hawthorne.

HUMBERSIDE
Little Driffield Church: Alfred the Great. *Rudston, All Saints' Church*: Winifred Holtby.

ISLE OF WIGHT
Bonchurch, St Boniface's Church: Henry de Vere Stacpoole; Algernon Charles Swinburne. *Newport St Thomas' Church*: Princess Elizabeth.

KENT
Beckenham, Town Cemetery: Hans Eysenck; William ('W. G.') Grace. *Birchington, All Saints' Churchyard*: Dante Gabriel Rossetti. *Boxley Abbey*: Sir Francis Wyatt. *Canterbury, Maugham Library, King's School*: Somerset Maugham (ashes scattered near). *Canterbury, Roman Catholic Cemetery*: Joseph Conrad. *Canterbury, St Dunstan's Church*: Sir Thomas More (head only). *Canterbury Cathedral*: St Anselm; St Thomas à Becket; St Dunstan; Edward, Prince of Wales, 'The Black Prince'; Henry IV; Joan of Navarre; Lanfranc; Cosmo Gordon, Baron Lang of Lambeth; John Morton; Archbishop Michael Ramsey; Frederick Temple; William Temple; Hubert Walter. *Cranbrook, Comforts Wood, Swattenden Lane*: Alexander Comfort. *Faversham Abbey*: King Stephen. *Gravesend, St George's Church*: Pocahontas (Mrs John Rolfe). *Keston Churchyard*: Dinah Maria Mulock, Mrs Craik. *Rochester Cathedral*: Walter de Merton. *Old Romney, St Clement Graveyard*: Derek Jarman. *Shipbourne, St Giles's Church*: Sir Henry Vane (the elder); Sir Henry Vane (the younger). *Shoreham, St Peter and St Paul's Churchyard*: Edward John Moreton Drax Plunkett Dunsany, 18th Baron.

LANCASHIRE
Manchester, Chorlton Southern Cemetery: L. S. Lowry. *Manchester, Old Jewish Cemetery*: Michael Marks.

LEICESTERSHIRE
Leicester Abbey: Richard III; Thomas Wolsey. *Lutterworth, St Mary's Church*: John Wycliffe.

LINCOLNSHIRE
Lincoln Cathedral: Robert Grossteste; Hugh of Avalon. *Stamford Cemetery*: Sir Malcolm Sargent. *Stamford, St Martin's Church*: Lord Burghley, William Cecil.

LONDON AND GREATER LONDON

Aldgate, St Andrew Undershaft Church: John Stow. *Barking, Friends' Burial Ground*: Elizabeth Fry. *Barnes Cemetery*: Francis Turner Palgrave. *Battersea, St Mary's Church*: Benedict Arnold; St John Henry Bolingbroke, 1st Viscount. *Bishopsgate, St Helen's Church*: Sir Thomas Gresham; Robert Hooke. *Canon Street, St Michael's Paternoster*: Richard ('Dick') Whittington. *Chelsea, St Mary's Church, Cadogan Street*: Madame Marie Tussaud. *Chiswick Mall, St Nicholas's Church*: Barbara Villiers, Duchess of Cleveland; Oliver Cromwell; William Hogarth; James Abbott McNeill Whistler. *City Road, John Wesley Chapel*: John Wesley. *Covent Garden, St Paul's Church*: Thomas Arne; Claude Duval; Sir Peter Lely; Dame Ellen Alicia Terry. *Cranford Park, St Dunstan's Church*: Tony Hancock. *Cripplegate, St Giles's Church*: Sir Martin Frobisher; John Milton. *Deptford, St Nicholas's Church*: Christopher Marlowe. *Finchley Cemetery*: Thomas Henry Huxley; Alfred Charles William Harmsworth, Viscount Northcliffe. *Finsbury, Bunhill Fields Burial Ground*: William Blake; John Bunyan; Daniel Defoe; Isaac Watts. *Finsbury, John Wesley Chapel, City Road*: see *City Road*. *Fleet Street, St Dunstan's in the West*: George Calvert, 1st Baron Baltimore; Lord Northcliffe (bust). *Fleet Street, Temple Church*: Oliver Goldsmith; William Marshal, Earl of Pembroke; John Seldon. *Fortune Green Road*: see *Hampstead Cemetery*. *Golders Green Crematorium, East Columbarium*: Sigmund Freud. *Ernest George Columbarium*: Anna Pavlova (*with shrine and rosebed in Gardens*). *Gardens and Cloisters*: Ivor Novello (Davies). *Garden of Rest*: Marc Bolan; Eric Coates; Keith Moon; Ronnie Scott; Peter Sellers; Sir Bernard Spilsbury (*Book of Remembrance in Chapel of Memory*); Vesta Tilley (*ashes under lilac tree*). *Golders Green Jewish Cemetery*: Rabbi Hugo Gryn; Jack Rosenthal. *Gower Street, University College, south cloister*: Jeremy Bentham. *Great Stanmore, St John the Evangelist Church*: Sir William Gilbert. *Greenwich, Naval Hospital Mausoleum*: Sir Thomas Masterman Hardy; six other Admirals as listed under Hardy. *St Alfege's Church*: Lavinia Fenton (Polly Peachum); James Wolfe. *Greenwich Royal Observatory*: Edmund Halley. *Hampstead, St John's Churchyard*: John Constable; George Palmella Burson Du Maurier; Sir Herbert Beerbohm Tree; Anton Walbrook. *Hampstead Cemetery, Fortune Green Road*: Gladys Cooper; Sebastian Ziani de Ferranti; Kate Greenaway; Joseph Lister. *Harrow Road, St Mary's Catholic Cemetery*: Mary Seacole. *Hart Street, St Olave's Church*: Samuel Pepys. *Hendon, St Mary's Church*: Sir Thomas Stamford Raffles. *Highgate Cemetery 'new'*: Shura Cherkassky; Yusuf Mohammed Dadoo; George Eliot (Mary Ann Cross); Stella Gibbons; William Friese-Green; John Galsworthy; Claudia Vera Jones; Karl Marx; Sir Ralph Richardson; Herbert Spencer. *Highgate Cemetery 'old'*: Sir Donald Alexander; Michael Faraday; William Alfred Foyle; Radclyffe Hall (Mabel Veronica Batten). *Highgate, St Michael's Church (adjoining cemetery)*: Samuel Taylor Coleridge. *Holborn, Church of the Holy Sepulchre without Newgate*: Roger Ascham; Captain John Smith; Sir Henry Wood. *Holborn, High Street, St Giles-in-the-fields*: Luke Hansard. *Islington, St Luke's Church, Old Street*: William Caslon. *Ivydale Road, Nunhead Cemetery*: Sir Frederick Abel. *Kensal Green Cemetery*: Charles Babbage; Charles Blondin; George Bridgtower; Isambard Kingdom Brunel; Sir Mark Isambard Brunel; John Cassell; Wilkie Collins; William Charles Macready; John Murray; Sir William Siemens; W. H.

Smith; William Makepeace Thackeray; Anthony Trollope. *Kensal Green, St Mary's Roman Catholic Cemetery*: Sir John Barbirolli. *King's Cross Railway Station, under platform 10*: Queen Boadicea. *Lambeth, Norwood Cemetery*: Mrs Beeton; Sir Henry Bessemer; Sir Hiram Stevens Maxim; Sir Henry Tate. *Lambeth, The Oval cricket ground*: James Laker (ashes scattered). *Lambeth, St Mary's Church*: Elias Ashmole; William Bligh; Thomas Tenison. *Leadenhall Street, St Andrew Undershaft*: John Stow. *Leadenhall Street, St Katherine Cree Church*: Hans Holbein (the younger); Sir Nicholas Throckmorton. *London Wall, St Giles's Church without Cripplegate*: See *Cripplegate*. *Manor Park, (nearest station), Central London Cemetery*: Bobby Moore; Dame Anna Neagle. *Mortlake, St Mary Magdalen's Churchyard*: Sir Richard Francis Burton. *Mortlake, St Mary's Church*: John Dee. *Newgate Street, Christ Church*: Isabella of France; Sir Thomas Malory. *Paddington Green, St Mary's Churchyard*: Sarah Siddons. *Paul's Wharf, St Benet's Church*: Inigo Jones. *Pentonville, St James' Church (site of)*: Joseph Grimaldi. *Putney Vale Cemetery*: Howard Carter; Jacob Epstein; Sir William Orpen. *Piccadilly, St James's Church*: John Arbuthnot. *Pinner Cemetery*: Screaming Lord Sutch. *St Giles High Street*: see *Holborn. St John's Wood Chapel, Wellington Road*: John Sell Cotman. *St Marylebone 'Old' Parish Church*: Edmund Hoyle; George Stubbs; Francis Wheatley. *St Pancras Old Churchyard*: Johann Christian Bach. *St Paul's Cathedral*: Sir Max Beerbohm; John Donne; General Charles Gordon (effigy); John Howard; William Holman Hunt; Sir Edwin Landseer; Sir Thomas Lawrence; Frederick Leighton; Sir John Everett Millais; John Opie; Sir Joshua Reynolds; Sir Arthur Sullivan; George Williams; Sir Christopher Wren. *St Paul's Cathedral Crypt*: David Beatty, 1st Earl; Cuthbert Collingwood, 1st Baron; Sir Alexander Fleming; Bernard Cyril Freyberg, 1st Baron; John Rushworth Jellicoe, Earl; Henry Moore; Horatio Nelson; Frederick Roberts, 1st Earl of Kandahar; Joseph Mallord William Turner; Arthur Wellesley, 1st Duke of Wellington; Sir Henry Hughes Wilson. *St Paul's 'Old Cathedral'*: Sir Nicholas Bacon; Ethelred the Unready; John of Gaunt; King Sebert; Sir Philip Sidney; Sir Francis Walsingham; Sir Anthony van Dyck. *Ruislip, St Martin's Churchyard*: Jessie Matthews (*ashes in Garden of Rest*). *Soho, St Anne's Churchyard, Dean Street*: William Hazlitt; Dorothy Leigh Sayers. *Southwark Cathedral*: John Fletcher; John Gower; Sam Wanamaker. *Stoke Newington, Abney Park Cemetery*: William Booth. *Strand, St Clement Danes*: Harold Harefoot. *Teddington Cemetery*: Richard Doddridge Blackmoore. *Tottenham Cemetery*: Bernie Grant. *Tower of London, St Peter ad Vincula*: Anne Boleyn; St John Fisher; Simon Fraser, Lord Lovat; Queen Catherine Howard; Lady Jane Grey; Duke of Monmouth; Sir Thomas More; Edward Seymour, Duke of Somerset; Thomas Seymour of Sudeley. *Trafalgar Square, St Martin-in-the-Fields*: Robert Boyle; Thomas Chippendale; Sir Winston Churchill (ancester of); Nell Gwyn; Jack Sheppard. *Twickenham, St Mary's Church*: Alexander Pope. *Walbrook, St Stephen's Church*: Sir John Vanbrugh. *Waltham Abbey (ruins)* see ESSEX. *West Brompton, Brompton Cemetery*: George Henty; 'Gentleman' John Jackson; Emmeline Pankhurst; John Snow; Richard Tauber; Brandon Thomas. *West Hampstead*: see *Hampstead Cemetery. Westminster, St Margaret's Church*: William Caxton; Sir Walter Raleigh. *Westminster Abbey, Edward the Confessor's Chapel*: Edward the Confessor; Edward I, Longshanks;

Edward III; Eleanor of Castile; Henry III; Henry V; Richard II. *Westminster Abbey, Henry VII's Chapel*: Queen Anne; Joseph Addison; George Villiers, 2nd Duke of Buckingham; John Sheffield, 1st Duke of Buckingham and Normandy; Caroline of Anspach; Charles II; Edward VI; Elizabeth I; George II; Henry VII; James I; Mary I; Mary II: Mary Queen of Scots; George Monck, 1st Duke of Albemarle; Prince Rupert; William III (see also *RAF Chapel*). *Westminster Abbey, Innocents' Corner*: Edward V; Richard, Duke of York. *Westminster Abbey, Nave, centre*: William Thomson Kelvin, 1st Baron; Andrew Bonar Law; Dr David Livingstone; Sir Isaac Newton; Ernest Rutherford. *Westminster Abbey, Nave, west end*: William Pitt the Younger (monument); The Unknown Warrior. *Westminster Abbey, Nave, north aisle*: Clement Attlee; Ernest Bevin; Sir John Herschel; John Hunter; Ben Jonson. *Westminster Abbey, Nave, north choir aisle*: Charles Darwin; Edward Elgar (memorial stone); Henry Purcell; Ralph Vaughan Williams; William Wilberforce (monument). *Westminster Abbey, Nave, south aisle*: John André; Neville Chamberlain; William Congreve. *Westminster Abbey, North Transept*: Charles James Fox; W.E. Gladstone; Henry John Temple Palmerston, Viscount; William Pitt the Elder; William Pitt the Younger; William Wilberforce. *Westminster Abbey, Poets' Corner*: Joseph Addison (monument); Francis Beaumont; Robert Browning; Geoffrey Chaucer; Charles Dickens; John Dryden; T. S. Eliot (memorial stone); David Garrick; George Frederick Handel; Thomas Hardy (ashes); Sir Henry Irving; Dr Samuel Johnson; Ben Jonson; Rudyard Kipling; Thomas Babington Macaulay; John Masefield; Laurence (Kerr) Olivier, 1st Baron Olivier; Thomas Parr; Richard Brinsley Sheridan; Edmund Spenser; Alfred, Lord Tennyson; William Makepeace Thackeray (bust); William Wordsworth (monument); James Wyatt. *Westminster Abbey, Presbytery, south side*: Anne of Cleves. *Westminster Abbey, RAF Chapel*: George Villiers, 1st Duke of Buckingham; Oliver Cromwell; Sir Hugh Caswell Dowding, 1st Baron; Hugh Trenchard, 1st Viscount. *Westminster Abbey, St George's Chapel*: Edmund Henry Hynman, Viscount Allenby. *Westminister Abbey, South Ambulatory*: King Sebert. *Westminster Abbey, Triforium*: John Gay. *Westminster Cathedral, St Gregory's Chapel*: Cardinal Basil Hume. *Whitechapel, Jewish Burial Ground*: Nathan Mayer Rothschild. *Whitechapel, St Mary Matfelon Churchyard*: Richard Brandon. *Willesden Jewish Cemetery*: Jack Cohen. *Woolwich, St Mary's Churchyard*: Henry Maudslay. *Woolwich, St Mary's and St Andrew's Churchyard*: Tom Cribb.

MERSEYSIDE
Liverpool, Cathedral of Christ the King: Cardinal Derek Worlock.

NORFOLK
Aylsham, St Michael's Church: Humphrey Repton. *East Dereham, St Nicholas's Church*: William Cowper. *Elvedon Park Church*: Anne Boleyn (heart?). *Houghton Hall, St Martin's Church*: Robert Walpole, 1st Earl of Orford. *Lamas, Old Quaker Meeting House Garden*: Anna Sewell. *Langham, St Andrew and St Mary's Churchyard*: Captain Frederick Marryat. *Norwich Cathedral*: Nurse Edith Cavell; Henry Despenser. *Norwich, St George's Church, Colegate*: John Crome. *Salle,*

Boleyn Church: Anne Boleyn (?). *Tittleshall, St Mary's Church*: Sir Edward Coke.
Upper Tasburgh, St Mary's Parish Church: Sir Malcolm Bradbury.

NORTHAMPTONSHIRE
Weedon Lois, St Mary's Churchyard extension: Dame Edith Sitwell.

NORTHUMBERLAND
Bamburgh, St Aidan's Churchyard: Grace Darling.

NOTTINGHAMSHIRE
Blidworth, St Mary's Churchyard: William Scathelock ('Will Scarlett').
Hucknall Torkard, St Mary Magdalen Church: George Gordon, Lord Byron.
Newark on Trent, Newark Cemetery: Wladyslaw Sikorski.

OXFORDSHIRE
Bladon, St Martin's Churchyard: Lord Randolph Churchill; Sir Winston
Churchill; Jenny Jerome (Lady Randolph Churchill). *Blenheim Palace Chapel*:
John Churchill, 1st Duke of Marlborough. *Cholsey, St Mary's Churchyard*: Dame
Agatha Christie. *Dorchester Abbey Church*: St Birinus. *East Hendred, St
Augustine's*: Roy Jenkins. *Elsfield, St Thomas of Canterbury Churchyard*: John
Buchan, 1st Baron Tweedsmuir. *Ewelme, St Mary's Churchyard*: Jerome K.
Jerome. *Henley-on-Thames, St Mary the Virgin Church*: Dusty Springfield.
Idbury, St Nicholas's Church: Sir Benjamin Baker. *North Stoke, St Mary the
Virgin Churchyard*: Dame Clara Butt. *Nuffield, Holy Trinity Church*: William
Richard Morris, 1st Viscount Nuffield. *Oxford, Broad Street, opposite Balliol
College*: The Three Martyrs. *Oxford, Merton College Chapel*: Sir Thomas Bodley.
Oxford, Oriel College Ante Chapel: Sir Henry Tizard. *Oxford, St Cross's
Churchyard*: Kenneth Grahame. *Oxford, St John's College Chapel*: William Laud.
Oriel College Antichapel: Sir Henry Tizard. *Stokenchurch, Getty Family Estate*
(private residence): Sir John Paul Getty. *Sutton Courtenay, All Saints'
Churchyard*: Henry Asquith, 1st Earl of Oxford; George Orwell. *Swinbrook, St
Mary's Churchyard*: Nancy Mitford. *Wolvercote Cemetery*: Sir Isaiah Berlin (in
Jewish section). *Wroxton, All Saints' Church*: Frederick North, Earl of Guildford.

SHROPSHIRE (SALOP)
Brosley, All Saints' Church: Abraham Darby. *Llanfair Waterdine* (scattered on the
fields above): Sir John Hunt. *Ludlow, St Lawrence Church*: A. E. Housman.
Moreton Say, St Margaret's Church: Robert Clive.

SOMERSET
Combe Florey, St Peter and St Paul's Churchyard: Evelyn Waugh. *East Coker, St
Michael's Church*: T. S. Eliot. *Glastonbury Abbey (ruins)*: King Arthur; Richard
Bere; Edmund I, the Magnificent; Edmund II, Ironside; Queen Guinevere.
Mells, St Andrew's Parish Church: Maurice Christopher Hollis; Ronald
Arbuthnot Knox; Siegfried Sassoon. *Wells Cathedral*: Thomas Linley.

STAFFORDSHIRE

Stoke-on-Trent, Britannia Stadium: Stanley Matthews. *Drayton Bassett, St Peter's Church*: Sir Robert Peel. *Whittingham, Litchfield, St Giles' Churchyard*: Thomas Spencer.

SUFFOLK

Aldeburgh, St Peter and St Paul's Churchyard: Benjamin Britten, 1st Lord Britten of Aldeburgh. *Bury St Edmunds, St Edmundsbury Cathedral*: John Peel. *Bury St Edmund's Abbey (ruins)*: St Edmund. *Garboldisham, Soldier's Hill*: Queen Boadicea (?). *Ipswich, The Old Cemetery*: Alf Ramsey. *Long Melford, Holy Trinity Church*: Edmund Blunden. *Playford, St Mary's Churchyard*: Sir George Airy. *Quidenham*: Queen Boadicea(?). *Sudbury, St Gregory's Church*: Simon of Sudbury. *Wingfield, St Andrew's Church*: William de la Pole, 1st Duke of Suffolk.

SURREY

Brookwood Cemetery: Sir Thomas Beecham; Dame Rebecca West; Dennis Yates Wheatley. *Burstow, St Bartholomew's Church*: John Flamsteed. *Compton Cemetery*: Aldous Huxley. *Dorking Cemetery*: George Meredith. *Farnham, St Andrew's Church*: William Cobbett. *Guildford, Carnleigh Parish Hall*: Sir Harry Secombe. *Guildford Cemetery*: Lewis Carroll (Charles Dodgson). *Kew, St Anne's Church*: Thomas Gainsborough; Johann Zoffany. *Leatherhead, St Mary and St Nicholas's Churchyard*: Anthony Hope. *Limpsfield, St Peter's Churchyard*: Frederick Delius. *Mickleham, St Michael's Churchyard*: Richard Bedford Bennett, 1st Viscount Bennett. *Pirbright, St Michael's Churchyard*: Sir Henry Stanley. *Richmond, St Matthias's Churchyard*: Edmund Kean. *Stoke D'Abernon* (under a tree in the grounds of the school): Yehudi Menuhin. *West Horsley*: Sir Walter Raleigh (head). *Wotton, St John's Church*: John Evelyn.

SUSSEX EAST AND WEST

Arundel, Arundel Castle, crypt of the Fitzalan Chapel: 17th Duke of Norfolk. *Blackboys, Tickere Mill*: Vivien Leigh. *Fletching, St Mary and St Andrew's Church*: Edward Gibbon. *Herstmonceaux, All Saint's Churchyard*: Quintin Hogg. *Horsted Keynes, St Giles' Churchyard*: Harold Macmillan, 1st Earl of Stockton. *Hove Cemetery*: Jack Hobbs. *Lewis, St John's Church*: Gundrada de Warenne. *Rodmell, Monks House*: Virginia Woolf. *Salehurst, St Mary's Churchyard*: Lord Alfred Milner, K. G. *West Grinstead, Church of Our Lady and St Francis*: Hilaire Belloc. *West Lavington, St Mary Magdalene Churchyard*: Richard Cobden. *Winchelsea Churchyard*: Spike Milligan. *Worthing, Broadwater Cemetery*: John Richard Jefferies.

WEST MIDLANDS/WARWICKSHIRE

Birmingham, Church of England Cemetery chapel vaults: John Baskerville. *Bourneville, Friends Meeting House*: George Cadbury. *Birmingham General Cemetery*: Joseph Chamberlain. *Handsworth, St Mary's Church*: James Watt. *Stratford-on-Avon Cemetery*: Marie Corelli (Mary MacKay). *Stratford-on-Avon, Holy Trinity Church*: William Shakespeare.

WILTSHIRE
Alvediston, St Mary's Churchyard: Sir Anthony Eden, 1st Earl of Avon. *Bemerton, St Andrew's Church*: George Herbert. *Britford, St Peter's Church*: Henry Stafford, 2nd Duke of Buckingham (2nd creation). *Broad Chalke, All Saints Church*: Sir Cecil Beaton. *Bromham, St Nicholas' Churchyard*: Thomas Moore. *Castle Combe, St Andrew's Churchyard*: Sir John Eldon Gorst. *Corsham, St Bartholomew's Churchyard*: Field Marshall Lord Methuen, Paul Sanford Methuen, 3rd Baron. *Farley, All Saints Church*: Sir Stephen Fox. *Hardenhuish, St Nicholas' Churchyard*: David Ricardo. *Lacock, Town Cemetery*: William Henry Fox Talbot. *Malmesbury, Abbey Church*: King Athelstan. *Salisbury Cathedral*: Mary Herbert, Countess of Pembroke; Edward Heath; William Herbert, 3rd Earl of Pembroke; St Osmund; Richard Poore (heart?). *Sevenhampton, St Andrew's Churchyard*: Ian Fleming. *Stourton, St Peter's Churchyard*: Sir Richard Colt Hoare. *Wilsford and Lake, St Michael's Churchyard*: Sir Oliver Lodge.

WORCESTER SEE HEREFORD AND WORCESTER

YORKSHIRE (EAST)
All Saints' Church, Rudston: Winifred Holtby

YORKSHIRE (NORTH)
Coxwold, St Michael's Churchyard: Laurence Sterne. *Hubberholme, Upper Wharfedale, St Michael and All Angels Church*: John Boynton Priestley. *Scarborough, St Mary's Churchyard*: Anne Brontë. *Whitby Abbey (ruins)*: King Oswy. *Whitby, St Mary's Churchyard*: Caedman. *York Minister*: Henry Bowett; Richard le Scrope. *York, Society of Friends burial ground*: Joseph Rowntree. *York, St George's Churchyard*: Richard ('Dick') Turpin.

YORKSHIRE (WEST)
Haworth Parish Church: Charlotte Bronte; Emily Bronte. *Heptanstall, Hebden Bridge, St Thomas' Churchyard*: Sylvia Plath. *Kirklees Abbey, Mirfield*: Robin Hood.

Index

Numbers in *italic* refer to illustrations